UNFOLDING BEAUTY

A California Legacy Book

Santa Clara University and Heyday Books are pleased to publish the California Legacy series, vibrant and relevant writings drawn from California's past and present.

Santa Clara University—founded in 1851 on the site of the eighth of California's original 21 missions—is the oldest institution of higher learning in the state. A Jesuit institution, it is particularly aware of its contribution to California's cultural heritage and its responsibility to preserve and celebrate that heritage.

Heyday Books, founded in 1974, specializes in critically acclaimed books on California literature, history, natural history, and ethnic studies.

Books in the California Legacy series will appear as anthologies, single author collections, reprints of important books, and original works. Taken together, these volumes will bring readers a new perspective on California's cultural life, a perspective that honors diversity and finds great pleasure in the eloquence of human expression.

Series editor: Terry Beers
Publisher: Malcolm Margolin
Advisory committee: William Deverell, Michael Duty, Peter Facione, Charles Faulhaben, David Fine, Steven Gilbar, Dana Gioia, Gerald Haslam, Ron Hanson, Robert Hass, Timothy Hodson, Maxine Hong Kingston, James Houston, Jeanne Wakatsuki Houston, Frank LaPena, Ursula LeGuin, Tillie Olsen, Ishmael Reed, Robert Senkewicz, Gary Snyder, Kevin Starr, Richard Walker, Alice Waters, Jennifer Watts, Al Young.

Thanks to the English Department at Santa Clara University and to Regis McKenna for their support of the California Legacy series.

UNFOLDING
BEAUTY

Celebrating California's Landscapes

Edited with an Introduction by Terry Beers

Santa Clara University ❧ Santa Clara
Heyday Books ❧ Berkeley

For my friend, Robert David.

Library of Congress Cataloging-in-Publication Data

Unfolding beauty : celebrating California's landscapes / edited with an introduction by Terry Beers.
    p. cm. — (A California legacy book)
  ISBN 1-890771-34-1 (pbk.)
  1. California—Description and travel. 2. Landscape—California. 3. California—History, Local. 4. California—In literature. I. Beers, Terry, 1955- II. Title. III. Series.
  F861.6 .U53 2000
  979.4—dc21
                        00-010757

Cover Art: Chiura Obata's "Point Lobos" (c. 1950)
Cover Design: Dave Bullen Design
Interior Design/Typesetting: Rebecca LeGates
Printing and Binding: Publishers Press, Salt Lake City, UT

Section title page illustrations by Paul Landacre, from *A Natural History of Western Trees*, by Donald Culross Peatie. New York: Bonanza Books, 1953.

Orders, inquiries, and correspondence should be addressed to:
Heyday Books
P. O. Box 9145, Berkeley, CA 94709
510/549-3564, Fax 510/549-1889
www.heydaybooks.com

Printed in the United States of America
10 9 8 7 6 5 4 3 2 1

Contents

Acknowledgments

For research assistance I am grateful to Reference Librarian/Humanities Liaison Leanna Goodwater and to Alice Whistler, Head of the Reference Services Division, both of the Orradre Library at Santa Clara University. I also owe thanks to Larry Schwartz, Collection Management Librarian at Minnesota State University, Moorhead.

I received valuable support from the English Department at Santa Clara University and from students Zachary Finley, Kara Thompson, and especially Shannon Nessier, all of whom helped with research and sorting through library materials. I am also grateful to the English Department's Canterbury Program for awarding the first California Legacy internship to Alistair Grant, who spent many hours on the preparation of this book.

Kevin Hearle supplied valuable advice on California Native American writers; Lillian Vallee helped with Central Valley writers; and my colleague Claudia McIssac offered insights on the Central Valley introduction. I am indebted to each of them.

I am especially grateful to Rebecca LeGates for working so hard on the production of this book and to Malcolm Margolin, publisher of Heyday Books, for his enthusiastic support of this project and for helping me find focus and balance in the initial selection of material. Rina Margolin took special care reading the book and suggesting improvements, and Jeannine Gendar brought a wonderful, fresh perspective. Finally, Carol Christensen gave the book polish and improved its coherence. She has been a wonderful reader and a fine critic.

Introduction

Every explorer names his island Formosa, beautiful. To him it is beautiful because, being first, he has access to it and can see it for what it is. But to no one else is it ever as beautiful—except the rare man who manages to recover it, who knows that it has to be recovered.
                    —Walker Percy, "The Loss of the Creature"

Before Juan Rodríguez Cabrillo became the first European to explore the California coast, novelist Garci Ordóñez de Montalvo had already described the place: "Know ye that on the right hand of the Indies there is an island called California...a land of great roughness, with a multitude of wild animals, including griffins the like of which are found nowhere else in the world." De Montalvo got a few things wrong, of course. California is not an island and there have not been any griffin sightings. But de Montalvo got the main things right: the roughness of the land, the multitude of wild animals, even the location, you might say, "near the Terrestrial Paradise." Pretty good for a writer who invented a name for a land he had never seen.

For many of the native people living in California before the coming of Europeans, this land—at least parts of it—was a paradise, as it was for many of the Spanish explorers, the Russian and American fur trappers, the gold-seeking forty-niners, the overland emigrants, and countless others seeking a better life. Today much of that paradise has disappeared under a seemingly endless tide of development, population explosion, environmental degradation, with some of the loveliest areas swamped by tourism. But other places—some remote regions like the High Sierra, the desert valleys, the northeastern volcanic plateaus, portions of California's over twelve hundred miles of coastline—are still relatively untouched. Maybe that is why so many people are still attracted to California's stunning natural landscapes.

This book is a celebration of that astonishing beauty as it unfolds in the writings of the men and women who have taken it for subject and setting. The book falls into seven parts, each devoted to a particular region of California and each prefaced with a bit of orienteering, a little background on natural and cultural history. The main selections within each part are roughly chronological to give readers a sense of how areas change—and resist change—as time passes and the human footprint presses ever deeper into California's soil. Shorter pieces provide additional perspectives, rounding out the main selections and enhancing the portrait of each area.

In a sense, this book is an attempt to recover and preserve for readers some of the paradise that California has lost. Never again will anyone enjoy the sight that greeted John Muir atop Pacheco Pass, the Central Valley spread out before him, its carpet of wildflowers "one furred, rich sheet of golden compositae"—delightful, like so many of these early accounts. But we cannot simply accept such secondhand perspectives, as Walker Percy has pointed out, asking how we can possibly *see* the Grand Canyon when it has been preformulated for us "by picture postcard, geography book, tourist folder, and the words 'Grand Canyon.'" Percy suggests one way to obtain a fresh perspective: cultivate a "dialectical movement," confront multiple viewpoints, compare them with your personal experience and imagination. You may want to read this book the same way: take in the different perspectives of the writers on the various regions, test them against your sensibilities, and discover *your* own beautiful island of California.

Terry Beers
August 2000

THE SAN FRANCISCO
BAY AREA

S an Francisco Bay is part of one of the largest estuaries on the West Coast. According to one estimate, three-quarters of all the shore-birds that migrate along the Pacific Flyway stop somewhere along its shoreline. That the area still attracts so much wildlife seems a minor miracle given the tremendous loss of tidal wetlands since the gold rush.

In only a hundred and fifty years, landfill and innumerable construc-tion projects—airports, marinas, manufacturing plants, private homes—have altered the ecology of the bay forever. The waters of Yerba Buena Cove once reached as far as present-day Montgomery Street in San Francisco's Financial District. The first landfill was timber from ships abandoned by gold seekers rushing inland after James Marshall found gold at Coloma on the south fork of the American River in 1848. Since then the usable shoreline has been pushed more than a half mile east. But the bay and the hills ringing it preserve their beauty, now an incomparable blend of the natural and artificial. Even an urban rat like Jack Kerouac found his eye drawn to its amazing view: "the blue passage of the Gate, the Alcatraz mad rock, the mouths of Tamalpais, San Pablo Bay, Sausalito sleepy hemming the rock and bush over yonder, and the sweet white ships cleanly cutting a path to Sasebo."

San Francisco Bay is actually a drowned river-mouth below the con-fluence of two major rivers, the Sacramento and the San Joaquin. Its southern arm is San Francisco Bay proper, which stretches along a hilly, wooded landmass, a peninsula separating the interior bay from the Pacific Ocean. The upper arm is San Pablo Bay, which extends north in a system of mudflats, sloughs, and rivers connecting to the wine country of the Napa and Sonoma valleys. Farther east, San Pablo Bay narrows to become the Carquinez Strait, which leads to Suisun Bay and then to the Sacramento Delta.

The bay itself was carved during the last ice age when fresh water from California's interior scoured a path to the ocean. Sea level was much lower at the time, but as global temperatures rose, so did the Pacific Ocean, which flooded the river-mouth, turning isolated hilltops into islands—Angel, Alcatraz, Yerba Buena, and Treasure. Most of the bay is relatively shallow, but some channels are over two hundred feet deep: Raccoon Straits, for example, between Tiburon and Angel Island, and the main channel through the Golden Gate, which is a mile-wide gap between the tip of the San Francisco Peninsula and the Marin Headlands. These channels allow deepwater vessels to take advantage of San Francisco Bay's natural protection, one of the features that makes it one of the world's best harbors.

Such a wonderful harbor waited a long time to be discovered by Europeans, probably because its entrance is so often cloaked in coastal fog. Portuguese explorer Juan Cabrillo missed the opening when he sailed up the coast in 1542. Sir Francis Drake also passed it in 1579, landing on a Marin beach, possibly at what is now known as Drakes Bay just south of Point Reyes, without realizing a better harbor lay close by. The first Europeans to see San Francisco Bay—while searching for Monterey Bay, where explorer Sebastián Vizcaíno had landed in 1602—were led by Gaspar de Portolá. Father Juan Crespí, chronicler of this 1769 expedition, saw the strategic and economic importance of this anchorage: "a very large and fine harbor, such that not only all the navy of our most Catholic Majesty but those of all Europe could take shelter in it."

More exploration—and development—followed. In 1772 Crespí returned in the company of Pedro Fages to scout the eastern shores of the bay, from which they sighted the Central Valley. In 1775 Juan Manuel Ayala made the first nautical survey of the bay. And in 1774 Captain Juan Bautista de Anza set out from northern Mexico with the second overland expedition to California, "to escort," in the words of Anza's chaplain, Father Pedro Font, "some families with whom to occupy and settle the port of San Francisco."

In 1776 Anza's expedition founded a presidio on a hilltop overlooking the Golden Gate and a mission dedicated to St. Francis of Assisi a mile south. Situated alongside a stream that de Anza named Arroyo de los Dolores—Stream of Our Lady of Sorrows—the mission soon became more familiarly known as Mission Dolores while the bay went by the name of San Francisco. With an eye to the defense of the Golden Gate, the Spanish had chosen to settle in one of the most desolate spots in the Bay Area, foggy, windy, and cold, even in the summer. The Native Americans already living in the Bay Area when the Spanish established that first settlement seem to have found warmer nearby areas more inviting. Over ten thousand of them lived in small, scattered settlements around the bay—Coast Miwok in the north, Ohlone in the east and south—the largest concentration of human beings in California.

The first Spanish settlers found Native Americans well established, enjoying a mild climate and an enviable variety of natural habitats—within a remarkably compact area—from marshlands at the shore to redwood forests in the coastal hills to oak savannas a few miles inland. Acorns were the staple of the native diet, but the region's ecological diversity made a variety of food available: antelope, deer, bear, and elk on the land; shellfish and salmon in the waters; waterfowl on the estuary's shores and islands. At one time, Alcatraz and Yerba Buena islands were guano-covered rookeries supporting thousands of geese, ducks, and gulls. Although no evidence of their permanent habitation has been found on Alcatraz, the Coast Miwoks and Ohlones must have visited the island often to gather seabird eggs. Legend (recounted by Darryl Babe Wilson) says that Alcatraz—which means "Rock Rainbow" or "Diamond Island" in some native languages —holds a treasure that can heal their troubles. Unfortunately, the Spanish missions brought them insurmountable troubles. Forced to work in the mission system, subject to new diseases, the Ohlones were unable to endure. More than half of them were eventually buried in unmarked graves at Mission Dolores.

Yerba Buena was already home to many Anglo settlers by the time U.S. Captain John Montgomery took possession in 1846, during the war with Mexico. When the settlement on the cove became U.S. territory, the little town was renamed San Francisco. Within a few years it was the port of choice for forty-niners heading to the goldfields. San Francisco's vitality and growing fame also attracted more than its share of speculators, gamblers, emigrants. The rest of the world was eager for news from the Gold Coast during "those strange, eventful days," and writers were quick to oblige. Among them were John C. Frémont and Eliza W. Farnham. Even English novelist Anthony Trollope visited San Francisco, reporting that "there is always a perfectly cloudless sky overhead unless when rain is falling in torrents, and perhaps nowhere in the world is there a more sudden change from heat to cold in the same day"—not as famous a quip as the one attributed to Mark Twain, during his brief stint as a journalist there, that the coldest winter he'd ever spent was a summer in San Francisco.

But San Francisco's justly deserved reputation as a mecca for writers derives more from those who stayed a while than from those who were just passing through. Notable among the city's early literary set were Bret Harte, Charles Warren Stoddard, and California's first poet laureate, Ina Coolbrith, the trio that wrote and edited the *Overland Monthly*.

The growing city was destroyed by fire in 1851 and again after the terrible 1906 earthquake—an 8.3 temblor on the Richter scale—but was quickly rebuilt, preserving some of its early character. Decades later, *San Francisco Chronicle* columnist Herb Caen dubbed the city "Baghdad-by-the-Bay," celebrating its enduring idiosyncrasies, its peculiar tolerance for the unconventional that continues to attract writers. In the 1950s it was the Beats, a generation of writers that included Allen Ginsberg, Jack Kerouac, and Lawrence Ferlinghetti. Their haunt was the North Beach neighborhood around Columbus Avenue, where Ferlinghetti established City Lights, America's first paperback bookstore, in 1953. Thirty-five years later, he petitioned San Francisco to rename several nearby streets for some of the city's famous writers; Jack Kerouac Street now runs next to the bookshop.

But the Bay Area is more than just San Francisco. While it was still Yerba Buena, the Spanish started moving into the valleys north of San Pablo Bay. In 1823 Franciscan monks established the northernmost of the California missions, Mission San Francisco Solano in Sonoma Valley, where they soon planted grapes for sacramental wine. Military commander Mariano Guadalupe Vallejo established even more vineyards when he arrived in 1833, sent by the Mexican government to keep an eye on the Russians at nearby Fort Ross. But it was Hungarian émigré Count Agoston Haraszthy who established Sonoma's reputation for fine wines when he founded the Buena Vista winery in 1856, introducing several European varieties of grapes.

Today the northern Bay Area is known for its food-and-wine writers, but it drew two very different authors in its early days. Robert Louis Stevenson set his 1883 book *The Silverado Squatters* in nearby Napa Valley, where he spent an unusual honeymoon. It was romance, too, that took Jack London to the Valley of the Moon, another name for Sonoma Valley and also the name of his 1913 novel: his love for his second wife and also for this rural setting.

Before forsaking urban living, London spent some time in Oakland, across the bay from San Francisco. Despite Gertrude Stein's famous comment about her hometown—"There's no there there"—Oakland was a transportation center; it was the last stop on the transcontinental railroad and a major seaport. London used the region as background for several works, including *Tales of the Fish Patrol*.

London also helped bring Santa Clara Valley to his many readers: it was the original home of Buck, canine hero of his popular *Call of the Wild*. Today Santa Clara is better known as Silicon Valley, the mythic home of American high tech, which makes it easy to forget the area's rural past. Pueblo de San José, established in 1777 like neighboring Mission Santa Clara, was still a small town when it was selected by the California Constitutional Convention of 1849 as the first state capital, a temporary distinction. The next city so honored was Vallejo, then San José again, then Sacramento, Vallejo again, then Benicia, before Sacramento became permanent capital in 1853. San José also housed California's first state college, established in 1857. But it was still a backwoods region when novelist and illustrator Mary Hallock Foote moved to a mining town nearby a few years later, proceeding to entertain East Coast readers of *Scribners* with rustic stories. At least the land was cultivated: agriculture remade the Valley of Heart's Delight, as the fertile Santa Clara Valley was known, dotting it with farms and orchards, in clear contrast to the mix of banks, hotels, and Barbary Coast watering holes that gave San Francisco much of its early character.

The tension between encroaching urbanization and established rural life is a theme taken up by Janet Lewis in *Against a Darkening Sky*, one of the best portraits of the landscape of Santa Clara Valley before it became Silicon. Peninsula settings have also inspired poet Dana Gioia, conservationist Wallace Stegner, and many others. San Francisco may be one of the most famous literary cities in the world, but the land beyond its city limits has inspired equally great writing.

The San Francisco Bay Area is ripe with the fruits of human progress. Where once only ferryboats traveled across the Golden Gate and between San Francisco and the East Bay, now the red towers of the Golden Gate Bridge and the metal cables of the Oakland Bay Bridge support spans that carry most of the traffic. The Bay Area Rapid Transit System connects San

Francisco and far-flung suburbs, with trains carrying eastbound riders through a tunnel beneath the bay. Multilane freeways—choked with automobiles during rush hour—provide north-south corridors along briny mudflats and marshes. These places, covered with salt grass and pickle weed, stand apart from the construction and landfill, the office parks and housing tracts—small reminders of the natural blessings that make the Bay Area one of the loveliest regions on the planet, and, thanks partly to the writers who have taken it as their subject, one of the best known.

John Charles Frémont

In 1842 John C. Frémont (1813–1890) set out on a Far West expedition: guided by Kit Carson, he mapped the Oregon Trail. The following year he and Carson made another expedition, this time crossing the Sierra at Carson Pass and descending to the Central Valley to Sutter's Fort, spending several weeks among U.S. settlers there. Frémont was actually a "pathmarker," says biographer Allan Nevins, since he mainly followed the trails of earlier explorers. But he and his wife, Jessie Benton Frémont, wrote reports of his expeditions that were an immediate sensation. The U.S. Congress and commercial houses here and abroad published several editions of both reports, which became guidebooks—complete with maps prepared by Frémont and Charles Preuss—for many emigrants going west.

Frémont's celebrity got him into trouble during his third trip to California. U.S. settlers involved him in the rowdy Bear Flag Revolt against the Mexican government. During the U.S. takeover that followed, he was caught in a dispute between Commodore Robert F. Stockton and Brigadier General Stephen Watts Kearney, and was later court-martialed for mutiny. He left the Army (although he was eventually pardoned) but remained influential. In 1851 he became a California senator; in 1856 he was an unsuccessful presidential candidate; and during the Civil War he was made a major general by Abraham Lincoln, a commission both Lincoln and Frémont regretted, since the "pathmarker" would show no talent for war. He is best known for his early reports but also made expeditions during the 1850s. The same precise —and sometimes loving—detail that he lavished on the Great Basin can be found in his Geographical Memoir *mapping Upper California. Here he describes the Golden Gate and the sweep of landscape enclosing it.* ❧

Naming the Golden Gate

The bay of San Francisco has been celebrated from the time of its first discovery as one of the finest in the world and is justly entitled to that character even under the seaman's view of a mere harbor. But when all the accessory advantages which belong to it—fertile and picturesque dependent country; mildness and salubrity of climate; connection with the great interior valley of the Sacramento and San Joaquín; its vast resources for ship—timber, grain, and cattle—when these advantages are taken into the account with its geographical position on the line of communication with Asia, it rises into an importance far above that of a mere harbor and deserves a particular notice in any account of maritime California. Its latitudinal position is that of Lisbon; its climate is that of southern Italy; settlements upon it for more than half a century attest its healthiness; bold shores and mountains give it grandeur; the extent and fertility of its dependent country give it great resources for agriculture, commerce, and population.

The bay of San Francisco is separated from the sea by low mountain ranges. Looking from the peaks of the Sierra Nevada, the coast mountains present an apparently continuous line, with only a single gap, resembling a mountain pass. This is the entrance to the great bay and is the only water communication from the coast to the interior country. Approaching from the sea, the coast presents a bold outline. On the south, the bordering mountains come down in a narrow ridge of broken hills, terminating in a precipitous point, against which the sea breaks heavily. On the northern side, the mountain presents a bold promontory, rising in a few miles to a height of two or three thousand feet. Between these points is the strait— about one mile broad in the narrowest part and five miles long from the sea

Tuesday, October 31, 1769. — The hills that prevented our passage along the shore, although easy of access for the ascent, had, on the other side, a very difficult and rough descent. The pioneers went out in the morning with the sergeant to make a road over [them], and afterwards, at eleven o'clock, we followed him with the pack animals.

From the summit we saw to the northwest a large bay formed by a point of land that extended a long distance into the sea and about which many had disputed on the preceding day as to whether or not it was an island; it was not possible at that time to see it as clearly as now on account of the mist that covered it. Farther out, about west-northwest from us, seven rocky, white islands could be seen; and, casting the eye back upon the bay, one could see farther to the north some perpendicular white cliffs. Looking to the northeast, one could see the mouth of an estuary that appeared to extend inland.

—Miguel Costansó, from *The Discovery of San Francisco Bay: The Portolá Expedition of 1769–1770* to the bay. Passing through this gate,[1] the bay opens to the right and left, extending in each direction about thirty-five miles, having a total length of more than seventy and a coast of about two hundred and seventy-five miles. It is divided by straits and projecting points into three separate bays, of which the northern two are called San Pablo and Suisún bays. Within, the view presented is of a mountainous country, the bay resembling an interior lake of deep water lying between parallel ranges of mountains. Islands, which have the bold character of the shores—some mere masses of rock and others grass covered, rising to the height of three and eight hundred feet—break its surface and add to its picturesque appearance. Directly fronting the entrance, mountains a few miles from the shore rise about two thousand feet above the water, crowned by a forest of the lofty cypress [redwood], which is visible from the sea and makes a conspicuous landmark for vessels entering the bay. Behind, the rugged peak of Mount Diavolo, nearly four thousand feet high, overlooks the surrounding country of the bay and San Joaquín. The immediate shore of the bay derives, from its proximate and opposite relation to the sea, the name of contra còsta, (counter-coast or opposite coast). It presents a varied character of rugged and broken hills, rolling and undulating land, and rich alluvial shores backed by fertile and wooded ranges, suitable for towns, villages, and farms, with which it is beginning to be dotted.

A low alluvial bottomland, several miles in breadth, with occasional open woods of oak, borders the foot of the mountains around the southern arm of the bay, terminating on a breadth of twenty miles in the fertile valley of St. Joseph, a narrow plain of rich soil, lying between ranges from two to three thousand feet high. The valley is openly wooded with groves of oak, free from underbrush, and, after the spring rains, covered with grass. Taken in connection with the valley of San Juan, with which it forms a continuous plain, it is fifty-five miles long and one to twenty broad, opening into smaller valleys among the hills. At the head of the bay it is twenty miles broad and about the same at the southern end, where the soil is beautifully

---

1. Called Chrysopylae (golden gate) on the map, on the same principle that the harbor of Byzantium (Constantinople afterwards) was called Chrysoceras (golden horn). The form of the harbor and its advantages for commerce (and that before it became an entrepôt of eastern commerce) suggested the name to the Greek founders of Byzantium. The form of the entrance into the bay of San Francisco and its advantages for commerce (Asiatic inclusive) suggest the name which is given to this entrance.

fertile, covered in summer with four or five varieties of wild clover several feet high. In many places it is overgrown with wild mustard, growing ten or twelve feet high, in almost impenetrable fields, through which roads are made like lanes. On both sides the mountains are fertile, wooded, or covered with grasses and scattered trees. On the west it is protected from the chilling influence of the northwest winds by the cuesta de los gatos, (wildcat ridge), which separates it from the coast. This is a grassy and timbered mountain, watered with small streams, and wooded on both sides with many varieties of trees and shrubbery, the heavier forests of pine and cypress occupying the western slope. Timber and shingles are now obtained from this mountain; and one of the recently discovered quicksilver mines is on the eastern side of the mountain, near the Pueblo de San José. This range terminates on the south in the Año Nuevo point of Monterey Bay and on the north declines into a ridge of broken hills about five miles wide, between the bay and the sea, and having the town of San Francisco on the bay shore near its northern extremity.

Sheltered from the cold winds and fogs of the sea and having a soil of remarkable fertility, the valley of St. Joseph (San José) is capable of producing in great perfection many fruits and grains which do not thrive on the coast in its immediate vicinity. Without taking into consideration the extraordinary yields which have sometimes occurred, the fair average product of wheat is estimated at fiftyfold, or fifty for one sown. The mission establishments of Santa Clara and San José in the north end of the valley were formerly, in the prosperous days of the missions, distinguished for the superiority of their wheat crops.

The slope of alluvial land continues entirely around the eastern shore of the bay, intersected by small streams and offering some points which good landing and deep water, with advantageous positions between the sea and interior country, indicate for future settlement.

Such is the bay and the proximate country and shores of the bay of San Francisco. It is not a mere indentation of the coast, but a little sea to itself, connected with the ocean by a defensible gate, opening out between seventy and eighty miles to the right and left, upon a breadth of ten to fifteen, deep enough for the largest ships, with bold shores suitable for towns and settlements, and fertile adjacent country for cultivation. The head of the bay is about forty miles from the sea and there commences its connection with the noble valleys of the San Joaquín and Sacramento.

Eliza W. Farnham

Eliza Farnham (1815–1864) was a formidable opponent of conventional thinking even before she came to California. Born near Albany, New York, Eliza Burhans was orphaned at four and lived with foster parents and an uncle before joining a married sister in Illinois, where she met her husband, Thomas Jefferson Farnham. While he was practicing law in Oregon and San Francisco, she worked in New York as matron of the women's division of Sing Sing prison, instituting reforms that earned her the enmity of conservative colleagues.

When Thomas died in 1848, Eliza went to California to settle his estate, bringing along a contingent of unmarried women to civilize the unruly frontier. She bought land near Santa Cruz and remarried, eventually divorcing and returning to the East. During the Civil War she nursed soldiers wounded at the Battle of Gettysburg before she succumbed to tuberculosis at the age of forty-nine. She argued female superiority in Woman and Her Era *and continued to help women move west, even after recording her own not entirely favorable impressions of the place in* California, In-doors and Out, *written shortly after her return east. Here she explains why life in San Francisco leads to a "state of physical wretchedness."* 🖎

That Wretched Place, San Francisco!

We had been but little more than a month settled before it became necessary for me to go to San Francisco, on which journey Mr. Anderson very obligingly undertook to be my escort. Miss S—— was to remain in charge of affairs at home, and especially to take care of Eddie, the great object of anxiety to us all, as his health seemed to have failed since we had been at Santa Cruz. The journey was to be made on horseback, and the road for the first day lies across the range of mountains that skirts the coast. We set out with formidable preparations of lunch, firearms, etc., Mr. A—— carrying two revolvers, and each of our horses having a satchel of provisions in addition to those of clothing. A habit-skirt, which I was assured I could not wear through the mountains, was packed conveniently, that it might be put on when we reached the inhabited regions on the other side. The road across these mountains is stern and solitary in the extreme. Portions of them are heavily wooded with the enormous redwood which abounds here. One tree especially is pointed out by the cicerone [guide], which is said to be 403 feet high. The valleys and many of the gentle slopes are fertile, and produce the wild oat and some varieties of clover in abundance, but immediately succeeding them we get precipitous cliffs of shale, in which the mule-path is so deep that rider and horse are swallowed up, and so narrow that there is only room to ride through without brushing the sides of the chasm. On either hand you have heather wastes intermingled with flowering shrubs, many of which, in their seasons, are very beautiful. At this time all the more productive regions were sparkling with the flowers common to the country, chief among them the eschcholtzia, purple and blue lupin, columbine, white and variegated convolvuli, fleur de lis, white lily, and innumerable smaller flowers of exquisite beauty, with whose names, being no botanist, I am unacquainted.

Something more than midway across, after all sorts of scramblings up and down rocky stairs, and through brush that has nearly torn your hat from your head, and certainly your spectacles from your face, you are quite surprised to find your horse treading a wagon-track, and riding further on, you find in a large valley shut in by high hills, partly wooded and partly covered with oats and grass, a house and sawmill. The proprietor of this valuable property is an emigrant from Ohio, who brought his family across the plains three or four years ago. He started with a company for Oregon, and says that when he reached the point where the California trail diverged, he let

One thing about the cove of Yerba Buena, or San Francisco, as it very soon came to be called, was the great number of good-sized fish that swam close in shore and were stranded by the out-going tide. These were the natural food of all sorts of predacious animals, which existed in enormous numbers and, being little interfered with by man, were for that reason indifferent to his presence. I often used to sit on the veranda of my father's house and watch bears, wolves and coyotes quarreling over their prey along what is now Montgomery street. These wild animals were perfectly harmless, only it was not wise to have too much fun with an old bear with cubs.

—Steve Richardson, "Bears, Wolves, and Coyotes"
in San Francisco Memoirs (c. 1850)

his oxen choose which they would take. They turned southward, and the consequence is that he is now the owner of one of the finest timber ranches in the country, whose wealth his children's children cannot exhaust. So inadequate and fantastical are sometimes the influences that produce to us the most grave results.

From the first summit eastward in this range, you get a magnificent view of the coast-table, the bay of Monterey, and the ocean; from the last you behold a portion of the bay of San Francisco, and the great valley of the Pueblo de San José, lying spread as it were at your very feet—one of the most beautiful views conceivable. And as the eye dwells upon the fertile plains, in some parts thickly dotted with the ancient and picturesque live oak, its branches laden with gray, trailing mosses, in others sparsely set with the same, and still others open and smooth as a shaven lawn, one readily imagines that the time is not long distant when from this mountaintop the famous pine-orchard view shall be rivaled. Cover the bay with sails and steamers, variegate the uniform green of the fertile plain with grainfields, orchards, gardens, farmyards, and houses; dot the sunny slopes with vineyards, and let the church spires be seen pointing heavenward from among occasional groups of dwellings, and I know not what would be wanting to complete the picture and make it one on which the heart and eye could dwell with equal delight. The valley itself, when you descend into it, though very pleasing by its smooth and open surface, is less beautiful to my taste than our own little rougher and brisker Santa Cruz. Advance a few miles from the foot of the mountain, and you have a monotonous level that lacks extent to give it grandeur—variety of any sort to give it everyday interest.

From the Pueblo to San Francisco, a distance of sixty miles, almost the entire road is over a surface so level that you see the broad bay, that puts up between you and El Contra Costa, only as a belt of water. An occasional sail seems to be gliding along in the grass over the top of which you look. Yet a ride through the valley is one of the most charming in the country, so fertile is it—so adorned with the orchardlike trees that take on new forms in their groupings from every point of view by which you approach or recede from them. It only begins to be disagreeable when you reach the hills some ten or twelve miles from San Francisco, and grows constantly more so till you reach the same point on your return. Here the San Francisco winds meet you face to face, and search you like an officer of the customs. They grow more unpleasant till you enter the city, by which time you are thoroughly chilled and dampened by the humidity with which they have been charged. Your eyes, ears, nostrils, and mouth are filled with the sand they have hurled at you, and you just begin to remember that out of Santa Cruz one must expect to encounter many disagreeable things that one has entirely forgotten the existence of in that delightful spot.

San Francisco, I believe, has the most disagreeable climate and locality of any city on the globe. If the winter be not unusually wet, there is some delightful weather to be enjoyed. If it be, you are flooded, and the rainy season closes to give place to what is miscalled summer—a season so cold that you require more clothing than you did in January; so damp with fogs and mists that you are penetrated to the very marrow; so windy that if you are abroad in the afternoon it is a continual struggle. Your eyes are blinded, your teeth set on edge, and your whole person made so uncomfortable by the sand that has insinuated itself through your clothing, that you could not conceive it possible to feel a sensation of comfort short of a warm bath and shower by way of preliminaries. These, as water is very scarce (and, for the most part, very bad), it is, as yet, impossible to have in dwelling-houses, consequently, you give yourself up to a state of physical wretchedness, your self-respect declines, and you go on from day to day, hoping more and more faintly, on each succeeding one, that your moral nature may withstand these trials of the material, but feeling, if you are possessed of ordinary sensibilities, lively apprehensions that your friends will have cause to deplore the issue.

Something like this has, at least, been my state when I have been compelled to sojourn for a season in that wretched place, and I believe it does not differ greatly from that of a majority of persons with whom I have compared notes. What sort of end the unfortunates, who spend their lives there, can expect under such circumstances, one does not easily foresee.

Ina Coolbrith

Ina Coolbrith (1841–1928) came from tough beginnings. Anti-Mormon gangs drove this niece of Mormon prophet Joseph Smith (who died before she was a year old) from her home in Nauvoo, which was to have been the new Zion. Determined to put their Mormon background behind them, her family crossed the Sierra to gold-rush California, with then ten-year-old Ina sharing the saddle of famous scout James P. Beckwourth. The family settled in Los Angeles where she began writing the poems that would eventually lead to an appointment as California's first poet laureate. Before leaving Southern California at twenty, Ina married, gave birth to a daughter (who soon died), and divorced a jealous husband.

She started a new life in San Francisco, working with Bret Harte and Charles Warren Stoddard on the Overland Monthly, *using her mother's maiden name. She also worked for the Oakland library, where she influenced the reading habits of Isadora Duncan and Jack London, among others. Another more than literary friend was Joaquin Miller, whose daughter she raised. Some of the poems she wrote for various periodicals during these years were eventually collected in* Songs from the Golden Gate *and the posthumously published* Wings of Sunset. *Bay Area settings sometimes inspired her finely wrought lyrics.* ❧

Evenfall at the Gate

A rose-shot purple on the sunset hills,
    And skies of golden fire;
Silence that like a benediction fills
    The hour, save where the lyre
Of ocean throbs, in strains that fall and rise,
    Against the harbor bar;
Then dusk, and on the brow of Tamalpais
    Trembles a single star.

Point Bonita

The wind blows cold and the wind blows keen,
  And the dreary wintry sleet is falling;
And ever the sand-dunes, white, between
  The Ocean voice is calling.

Calls with a sound that the sailor fears;
  And the gulls, low-flying, hasten in,
And the bent boughs shiver in fringe of tears
  While the long night hours begin.

But over the path thro' the Golden Door,
  Where the troubled billows foam and flee,
Bonita's Light from its rocky shore
  Shines out to the ships at sea.

Santa Clara Valley

Green pasture-slopes with dotting trees;
  Broad garden-stretches, far and fair;
White cloud on cloud of orchard-bloom;
  A balm, a fragrance, all the air!

Whistle of blackbird, song of lark,
  Carol of linnet!—where could be
A fairer land, a land as rare,
  Thou little vale of Arcady?

Mary Hallock Foote

Mary Hallock Foote (1847–1938) was a most reluctant westerner. Born in Milton, New York, she grew up in a Quaker household, where she met abolitionists such as Susan B. Anthony and Ernestine L. Rose. When she moved to New York City to attend the Cooper Union Institute's School of Design, her circle of influential acquaintances expanded to include writers like George Washington Cable. She soon earned recognition as an illustrator—she did some work for Harpers Weekly *and also for a prestigious edition of Longfellow's poems—becoming part of the East Coast literary establishment.*

And then she met Arthur De Wint Foote, a cousin of Henry Ward Beecher. Foote was a civil engineer visiting from California, where he had been working on Tehachapi Pass and the Sutro Tunnel. He soon went back but eventually convinced Mary Hallock to marry and join him. She later wrote, "No girl ever wanted less to 'go West' with any man, or paid a man a greater compliment by doing so." His professional opportunities (and disappointments) took their growing family all over the West, to Leadville, Colorado; Boise Canyon, Idaho; Grass Valley and Santa Cruz, California. Their travels gave Mary Hallock Foote material for illustrations plus twelve novels and numerous stories and sketches. Only a few of her works remain in print, but many readers know her from Wallace Stegner's 1971 novel Angle of Repose, *since one of its main characters, the narrator's grandmother Sarah Ward, is based on her life.*

One of Mary Hallock Foote's earliest sketches describes a stay in the South Bay, at the New Almaden mercury mine. She starts to get a feel for its arid late-summer mood by contrast with the pastoral East of her memories. ❧

from New Almaden

Toward the close of the dry season, when brown and dusty August burns into browner, dustier September, a keen remembrance of all cool, watery joys takes possession of one's thoughts. The lapping of ripples in pebbly coves, the steady thump of oars in row-locks, the smell of apple blossoms on damp spring evenings, old mill-races mossy and dripping, the bleating of frightened lambs at a sheep-washing and the hoarse, stifled complaint of their mothers mingled with the rushing of the stream—all these once common sounds and sights haunt the memory.

Every day the dust cloud grows thicker in the valley, the mountains fade almost out of sight against a sky which is all glare without color; a dry wind searches over the bare, brown hills for any lingering drop of moisture the sun may have left there; but morning and evening still keep a spell which makes one forget the burden of the day. At sunset the dust cloud in the valley becomes a bar of color stretching across the base of the mountains, deep rose and orange, shading by softest gradations into cool blue. I remember one sunset especially. The clouds of dust rolling up from the valley below were transformed by the light into level bars of color like a horizontal rainbow sweeping across the entire valley; above it the mountains rose; a wonderful variety of constantly changing hues made them look like something unreal. Then there came a sudden darkening of the lower part of the mountains so that the sunlit peaks seemed to float in the air above the bars of sun-colored dust, with a strip of cool shadow between. All is quiet; as in the morning, no birds chirp and twitter themselves to sleep; the stillness is only broken by the dull throbbing of the engine like a stifled breath in the distant shaft-house.

Every evening repeats this silent symphony of color, and every day it seems like something one has dreamed of. The rose and orange and blue have faded into the same dull, gray pall, which, to the valley stretched beneath, is never anything more; only those who see it from the hills know that sometimes this pall is a robe of glory.

We rode home one evening across the low, bare hills beyond the Mexican camp. It was during the "earth-shock weather" (as the miners call those last, dry, lurid weeks before the early rainfall), and one of the dull, red sunsets, peculiar to that season, had been flaming on the sky and mountains; its lingering glow colored the edge of the early moonlight. The soil here has a vermilion tinge, which is stronger after sundown; it was intensified that evening by the flush in the sky. There was no positive light or shadow, only a pink glow spreading over all the wide landscape, except where the cañon held its glooms, and above it a young moon slowly brightened in a sky of twilight blue. It was in sentiment like William Morris's poetry. I always think of it as the "land east of the sun, and west of the moon." While the moon is young and her light faint and pale, one can scarcely mark the time when the lingering twilight passes into the soft, dim radiance that spreads like a spell over the valley, across part of which lies the shadow of a

mountain. We cannot see the moon itself, only its light. The mountains opposite remain always shrouded in silence and mystery. But when nights
come for the full moon the place is a paradise: in the foreground the winding trails with black masses of shadow from the clumps of live oak crossing
them, the dark mountain lines rising grandly on every side, the mysterious
depths of the cañons, the lights of the Mexican camp scattered over the
hills, the closer clustered lights of the Cornish camp on the lower range, the
wide, dim valley below, and the far-off barrier of mountains.

Janet Lewis

Janet Lewis (1899–1998) was born in Chicago and raised in the suburb of Oak Park, Ernest Hemingway's home town. But unlike the flamboyant Hemingway, Lewis went on to lead a fairly quiet life. She attended the University of Chicago, began to publish poetry, and eventually married the poet and critic Yvor Winters. His career brought them to Stanford University in 1927, and they settled into a Los Altos cottage, planted a garden, and started a family. They raised goats, bred Airedales—and kept writing. Winters is more famous for his teaching and criticism—he is one of the pioneers of the New Criticism—than for his poetry. Lewis was selected to write and present a poem for the John Muir celebration at Yosemite in 1971, but her poetry is not as well known as her fiction: The Invasion, The Wife of Martin Guerre, Good-Bye, Son and Other Stories, *and* The Ghost of Monsieur Scarron.*

Lewis set many of her poems and short stories in California, but it was a novel that gave her the narrative space to evoke the semisettled landscapes of Santa Clara Valley in the Depression. The ominous title, Against a Darkening Sky, *derives from the disaster of the airship* Macon, *which crashed into the Pacific off the California coast in 1935. A short time before that event, the ship had seemed to convey the power of the human imagination: "It all lay in the design," observes one of the main characters. Its failure comes to symbolize the threat hanging over the world of the novel.*

In chapter one, two old friends, Mary Perrault and Agnes Hardy, take a leisurely tour of this endangered "vale of Arcady." ✍

from Against a Darkening Sky

Mary Perrault sat at the top of the short steep flight of steps which led to the small platform which was the front porch of her house, and looked down into the dusty tangle of her flower garden. From time to time she dabbed at the back of her neck with cotton soaked in an infusion of wormwood leaves in a white china cup. Behind her the small square house, a shell of redwood tongue and groove, sunned itself, concentrating in its four rooms the warmth of the September afternoon, and would have been as stifling as a brooder house had it not been for all the opened windows. As it was, Mary Perrault found it too warm to stay indoors now that her work was done.

It was a Friday afternoon. She felt something of the release which the children felt, the burden of the week being over, and the weekend to be dedicated more or less to friendliness and to enjoying her family. She smiled down at the black cat lying belly up on the hard black earth under the loquat tree, idly waving its forepaws above its face and slowly twitching its tail back and forth in a sweeping motion. Gradually the wormwood tea lessened the irritation on her neck.

Mary Perrault was Scottish. One had only to look at her to realize it, without waiting to hear her speak. She had the clear fresh ruddy skin which seems to have been scoured for generations by northern rain and mist. Twenty years of California drought and sun had been powerless to change it. Her eyes were a clear blue. Her long hair, once flaxen, now darkening to a soft brown, had grayed a little around the temples, but was still so fair that it showed no pronounced grizzle. It had on this afternoon been newly washed, and it waved a little in spite of the pressure of the hairnet which bound it to her head. Where it escaped from the net, at her temples and the nape of her neck, it curled loosely. Mary Perrault in her early fifties looked all of ten years younger. The blue eyes, the fair skin, the strong vigorous body, thickened with age, like a tree, all contributed to this look of youth, but it was chiefly the gaiety and repose about her eyes and forehead which made her seem, even when she had been working hard and was tired, as now, always ready and refreshed.

The platform on which she sat was no more than wide enough for the swing of the screen door as it opened; it was unpainted and without a railing, just as it had been seven years ago when Mr. Perrault had stopped working on the house. He meant still to build a wide verandah with a roof, large enough to be used as a sleeping porch, a room for one or two of the boys, but the matter was not urgent, and Mr. Perrault had always a number of other important things to do first. Mrs. Perrault had always considered the small porch a temporary matter, and so had never bothered to be dissatisfied with it. The eglantine and yellow honeysuckle, clambering up the wall of the house, flung out green sprays and tendrils on either side of the steps, veiling the ground and preventing the platform from seeming as high and as isolated as it actually was. Here she waited on this quiet afternoon in the sunshine of the northwestern end of the Santa Clara Valley, while all around her the gardens and small orchards exhaled their spicy autumnal fragrances. The dry uncultivated fields, also, spreading toward the foot of San Francisco Bay, steeped in uninterrupted sun, gave off an aromatic fragrance that was almost medicinal, compounded of tansy, tarweed, and wormwood, and when the breeze stirred from the bay, from time to time, there was added to these earthy odors, the freshness of salt water.

Mary Perrault was resting and not consciously expecting any visitor. She recognized, however, the rattle of a light car which presently came down the road, unseen, because of the hedge at the end of the garden, and stopped briefly at the Perrault driveway. A door slammed, the car went on its way, and Agnes Hardy came down the drive, stopping now and again to peer into the orchard across from the garden. Mrs. Perrault left the steps and went to meet her friend.

Agnes Hardy was only a little older than Mrs. Perrault, but of a frailer physique, and her years were all apparent in her figure and her face. She was wearing a black straw hat which she took off after greeting Mrs. Perrault and used as a fan, smiling slightly and complaining of the heat. Her hair, which was very gray, was plastered to her forehead. She pushed it back hastily with her free hand. She wore silver-rimmed spectacles before her dark eyes, and there was something unnaturally regular about her teeth which suggested that they might not be her own. It was a pleasant face, however, rather nervous, nevertheless patient, a little vague at times, and, as she looked at Mrs. Perrault, full of affection.

"I'm just back from town," she said. "It's hot as a nest of kittens, not a breath of air. On a day like this I'm glad we live on the flats. I asked Lem to drop me here—I just wanted to see you for a minute before I go home." She slipped her arm through that of Mrs. Perrault as they walked slowly along. "Lem is going for the little boys. They're to spend a week with Grandmama while their ma goes with their papa to Riverside."

"Well, that will make you blithe," said Mrs. Perrault. "You a grandma! I never get used to the idea with you so few years older than me. And my youngest only a bit older than your oldest grand."

"Ah, but you've four of your own, and I've only the one, and here she's married and walked out on me. Be watching out now—Melanie will be making a grandmother of you before you know it."

"At fifteen? Not if I can help it," answered Mrs. Perrault. "Come and sit down a minute and cool yourself. The warmth is not half bad if you don't stir around too much." She stooped, picking up a handful of cherry plums fallen to the dry earth under a small tree, and gave them to Mrs. Hardy. The two women went over to the porch and ate the plums, polishing the dust from them with their hands.

"Why would the folks be going to Riverside?" asked Mrs. Perrault, reverting to Mrs. Hardy's earlier remark.

"There's a ranch down there they think of buying. I don't wish they would, myself. It's so far away." She paused, and resumed, "I like these little yellow fellows. A bit tart, they are, and more refreshing than prunes, for instance, that are really too sweet. What I stopped by for was to ask if you'd care to drive with me to San Tomás tomorrow. I'm taking Bud to the clinic to have his hand dressed. His mother says he burnt it on the toaster. You know Buddy—he's that quick. He's out with his hand before you can stop him, wanting to have a finger on everything. Lem had meant to take the car apart tomorrow morning and grease it, but I guess it'll hold together for one more trip without lubrication." She laughed, a dry, quick laugh which resembled her voice. "Lem says it's only grease that holds the car together."

"I'd love to go," said Mrs. Perrault slowly, "but I don't see how I can. There's that program for the P.T.A. in the afternoon, and the men will never in the world leave the clubhouse ready for us. I'll likely spend the morning dusting and sweeping."

"Can't you get a few other mothers to do something sometimes?" asked Mrs. Hardy.

"The final responsibility always devolves upon the president," said Mrs. Perrault with mock formality. "They'll all be there to help, if I am."

"Well, if you can't..." said Mrs. Hardy. She tossed the plum pits into the vines, and, noticing the cup of wormwood, picked it up and sniffed it. "What in the world do you call this?" she asked.

"Wormwood," said Mrs. Perrault. "Didn't you ever see wormwood before? It's good to break a fever. But I'd a funny sort of rash on my neck and nothing I tried seemed to do any good. I happened to find some wormwood in the ditch, and remembered that my mother used it as a sort of lotion. So I thought I'd try it too. It seems to help." She pulled down the collar of her printed cotton housedress while Mrs. Hardy peered at her skin.

"It does seem to be a rash," said Mrs. Hardy. "Not spider bites or such. It couldn't be poison oak, could it?"

"Wrong time of year," said Mrs. Perrault. "It's about gone now, but how it did bother me, coming just where the edge of my dress rubbed and tickled it!"

They had been girls together, these two women, in a fishing and whiskey-manufacturing town in Argyleshire. Together they had emigrated, and had parted in New York, Agnes Wilkie going to Canada and Mary Knox to California. Agnes Wilkie had married, had borne a daughter, and lost her husband. Later she married again, this time a Canadian farmer by the name of Lemuel Hardy. She had gone west with him across the Canadian wheat-lands in a covered wagon, and had helped him homestead a bit of land in Alberta. But the life had been very hard, and when he could, Lem Hardy had brought his family to the coast where his brother lived, in Vancouver. There he had worked in the lumber business with his brother. Meanwhile Mary Knox had married in California a Swiss-French gardener by the name of Aristide Perrault, and, after living here and there about the region of the San Francisco Peninsula, had settled on these two acres of flat meadowland between the Coast Range and the southern end of the bay.

Here, two years later, trade being slack in the north, Lem Hardy came with his wife Agnes, and her daughter, and Agnes Wilkie and Mary Knox, to their great joy, found themselves neighbors again. The daughter had mar-ried almost immediately upon setting foot on California soil. Now she had two little boys, Billy, who was four years old, and Buddy, who was two and a half, the especial treasures of their grandmother.

Agnes Hardy was not pure Scottish, nor had she been born, like Mary Perrault, in Campbeltown. She had come there in her teens, and she liked to call her friend Mary of Argyle, "Because you are, you know," she would add, "and I am only a half and half, which maybe accounts for my never having enough thrift to do very well for myself." As a girl she had been dreamy, with a shrewd quick humor and sudden sallies of wit. Neither of these women would have cared to return to Campbeltown to stay, but they both remembered the town with affection, and were doubly dear to each other for having lived there. After so many years of strangers and strange places they were, each one, a sight of home for the other, and their talk was full of references to home, as now, when Mary Perrault, because her collar had rubbed her neck, said,

"Do you remember my mother had a little mole just here," touching her neck, "and do you remember the stiff little round white collars they used to wear, and how she always wore a soft lace one instead, because of that little mole that came just by the edge of her collar?"

Sitting there in the dry sweet sunlight with her hat on her knee, Mrs. Hardy looked into the garden, turning her head a little now and again to note a flower or a branch, and the lines of fatigue faded gradually from about her mouth and eyes. The skin of her face was much the same color as that of the hand laid over the rounded crown of her hat, a pale tan, a tan without much warmth of blood beneath it. A vague and dreamy expression came into her eyes, an expression which Mrs. Perrault remembered well from her girlhood, and which brought a quick tenderness into Mrs. Perrault's own face. She did not answer Mrs. Perrault's question, but said, after a long pause,

"I never knew your place to be so quiet of an afternoon. Where is all the shouting mob?"

"The shouting mob," said Mrs. Perrault, "is here and there. Jamie is with his father, helping to mend the leaks in the Company's pipes. Duncan and Andrew, I expect they're still at the schoolhouse for basketball practice. Unless Andrew is cutting a lawn somewhere for a bit of the needful."

"And Melanie?" prompted Mrs. Hardy.

"Melanie? Did you ever know Melanie to be at home when she could be some other place? Not since she was one year old and could go on her own legs. Look now, would you like some plums to take home with you? Wait till I get something to put them in."

She rose as she was speaking and went into the house, taking the cup of wormwood with her, and returned presently with a brown paper bag in her hand. Together the two women crossed the driveway into the orchard, the sun hot upon their heads and shoulders, and the warmth beating up from the dry earth. Their feet sank a little into the loose ground, for the orchard had been ploughed in order to kill the weeds, and no grass was growing under or between the small trees. It was a household orchard, not a commercial one—two fig trees, an early peach and a late-ripening one, long red plums, a quince tree loaded with heavy furred green fruit, and the tree with the little round yellow plums for which Mrs. Perrault was looking. The leaves and the fruit were dusty, the fruit was warm to the touch.

When she had filled the bag, Mrs. Perrault guided Mrs. Hardy by the elbow down past the chicken house, the barn and the garage and the long rows of rabbit hutches into the garden to the north of the house. Here, being free of the buildings, they felt more freshly the breeze from the bay, a faint, steady wind, the trade wind, that seemed to blow all summer. It hardly stirred the leaves today, but still, it cooled the air somewhat, and Agnes Hardy felt her fatigue slip from her finally. She drew a few deep breaths and looked about her more alertly. Mrs. Perrault was saying, "I want you to see my dahlias. I had such a fight with the gophers over them, and this year I won."

Chard, dahlias, artichokes, the flowers and the vegetables grew in long rows side by side, the artichokes with their long silvery jagged leaves falling in beautiful simple curves away from the thick central stalks, making a hedge along the raised edge of the ditch that was the north boundary of the Perrault land. It was late in the summer for artichokes. The big ones had tough and horny centers, and Mrs. Perrault had let many of them blossom, the bloom, like an enormous purple thistle, emerging from the cup of the great stylized bud. Mrs. Hardy, mounting the slight rise of ground, stood among the artichokes and looked down into the dusty ditch. Here, during the winter rains, a small torrent ran, discharging its muddy water into the bay; now there was dry grass, like faded hair, and weeds that not even the seasonal drought could kill.

"So there's your wormwood," remarked Mrs. Hardy. "It's no more nor less than yarrow."

"You needn't scoff," said Mrs. Perrault. "There's a deal of virtue in those old remedies. There's tansy now."

"Tansy tay," said Mrs. Hardy. "And what would that be good for?"

"They used to give it to young girls who were late in maturing. I wouldn't vouch for the goodness of that—but there's plenty there in the ditch."

"More than we need in this climate," said Mrs. Hardy.

"And yesterday at Mrs. Tremonti's, I saw her making for Joe's foot that was infected, the same kind of plaster my grandfather used to make. Soft soap—yellow soap, you know—brown sugar and a bit of olive oil. Except for the oil—and those Portuguese people, you know, use olive oil for everything from greasing babies, up—that's just the paste my grandfather used to make for us when we were kids. I can see him now, sitting by the kitchen fireplace and working the soap in the palm of his hand to get it soft. We were sewing nighties, Mrs. Tremonti and I, for the next little Munch."

"Another Munch?" interrupted Mrs. Hardy with some surprise.

"Another, next month."

"Well, I haven't seen her in some time," said Mrs. Hardy, "but she was even thin when I saw her."

"A slack before a pack, so Mrs. Tremonti says," said Mrs. Perrault.

She had put down the plums and was cutting dahlias as she spoke, admiring the rich autumnal colors and fluted petals, and holding them up for Mrs. Hardy's admiration. Mrs. Hardy, from the slight rise of ground, looked across the ditch and the uncultivated fields to a small house deserted now for several years and surrounded by bleached foxtail and wild oats which grew up against its walls like waves, and back to the dusty richness of her friend's trees and gardens. They continued to speak of trivial things, two women who knew each other so well that there was no need of their talk's being important, or even consecutive. They took a deep and quiet pleasure in each other's presence, and in the serenity of the day, and in the bounty of the small arid garden. It was a day so like a long procession of tranquil days that nothing could have warned them that it might be the last. And yet years afterward Mary Perrault was able to look back into that afternoon, as into a scene framed and set aside, and remember trivial words and gestures, trivial things observed, which assumed thereafter a dignity and a perma- nence beyond the words and gestures of any other afternoon.

"If you are picking those for me," said Mrs. Hardy, suddenly leaving the contemplation of the deserted house, "that's more than enough. I never did go home from this house with my hands empty, but I can't carry more'n so much."

"Last year I had none at all to give away," Mrs. Perrault reminded her. She took a match from her apron pocket and burnt each stem where it had been cut, sealing the long, open veins. "I'll walk home with you, Agnes," she said, "and help you carry your plunder."

The afternoon was perceptibly cooler as they moved down the road, crossing the bridge. The sun was dropping toward the western mountains that rose from gently rounded foothills, dun with faded grass, up to the wooded ridges, and so upward, still ridge by ridge, darkening with oak and evergreen to the last crest that shut the long valley from the sea, and inter- cepted the Pacific fog. The ridges were dim behind a silver haze of dust, not fog, but dust so fine that the air seemed perfectly pure and the haze itself but an excess of light. Beyond the bay, on the farther side of the valley, a line of lower hills, as pale as sand, was also veiled in the faint haze. The sun, penetrating them as it sank westward, emphasized their strange modeling, shapes as of sand under wind erosion, and filled the hollows with blue shad- ows. Delicate, unreal, floating there on the eastern horizon, they partook of the nature of a mirage, sometimes disappearing entirely, and sometimes, after a rain, distinct and beautiful with firm and lovely contours, but most- ly being, as this evening, half seen, half lost in air. Between the western mountains and these hills the valley seemed immensely spacious; the bay, unseen, left an emptiness before the eastern hills.

The two women walked forward on a clear straight road, running between bleached fields. Before them, the town of Encina lay under a mass of trees, but here, on the flats, there were no trees or shrubs which had not been recently planted, and the small ranches were widely spaced. These fields were for Mary Perrault in days to come remembered like fields before a storm, in which the sharp clear sunlight picks out familiar shapes in unfamiliar brightness against the dark piled clouds. The catastrophe is withheld, enhancing that which it is about to destroy.

She left Mrs. Hardy at the entrance to her driveway, declining an invitation to come in.

"I've supper to start," she said, handing the bag of plums to Mrs. Hardy, and watched a moment as the slight figure in the pale printed cotton, the black straw hat, the black cotton stockings and shoes, turned up the graveled way past the long plumes of a butterfly bush. She walked home, humming to herself. There was great peace in her heart, friendship, security, contentment. A train, going south, drew a long horizontal line of white smoke below the mounting ridges of the Coast Range.

Wallace Stegner

Wallace Stegner (1909–1993) is one of the most celebrated of contemporary American writers. Justly so—he produced critical essays, personal memoirs, a historical biography, many short stories, and at least two of the best novels ever written about the Far West, The Big Rock Candy Mountain *and* Angle of Repose. *The former is the tale of the Mason family, who move around the West in the early 1900s following Bo Mason's dream "to make a pile" and live in the fairy-tale land of the title. A similar dream inspires Sarah Ward and her engineer husband in* Angle of Repose—*they too pursue a success that is always just out of reach—but this story, based on the life of Arthur and Mary Hallock Foote, is set in the late 1800s. In these books Stegner has created compelling narratives—packed with incident and detail and set in a Western landscape that is vast, haunting, wild, often forbidding—and centered around truly sympathetic characters.*

Probably the sympathy that distinguishes Stegner's work derives from personal experience. Stegner, who was born in Iowa, spent the first twelve years of his life moving throughout the West, much the same territory depicted in The Big Rock Candy Mountain. *The family eventually settled in Salt Lake City, where Stegner attended college. He went back to Iowa to earn his Ph.D., married, and began a teaching career. From Harvard he moved to Stanford, where he headed the Creative Writing Program until his retirement in 1971. Stegner said of his adopted state: "I don't feel this country the way I would feel the short-grass plains or the Rocky Mountains." Yet in* All the Little Live Things, *the story of a retired literary agent living in the hills above San Francisco Bay, Stegner shows a keen feel for the natural world and its effect on its inhabitants. Narrator Joe Alston describes a landscape that is "very lively, very Californian."* ✍

from All the Little Live Things

Ordinarily this is not good walking country. In wet weather the adobe is like tar, and through the summer and early fall the open country is unpleasant with barbed and prickly seeds. In those seasons our walking is confined to roads and lanes. But when a rain or two has flattened the weeds and started the new grass without soaking the ground, then cross-country walking can be marvelous.

Last year, as this, the rains came early, and in October you would have seen us any afternoon, bald head following white head, country corduroy behind country tweed, me brandishing a blackthorn stick that an Irish poet once left at the apartment, starting through the Shieldses' pasture fence. We followed the path made by Julie LoPresti's black gelding, a path so uniformly double-grooved that it might have been made with skis. This ran into a trampled space under an oak where he used to sleep on his feet and switch flies, and then out again along the fence separating the pasture from Weld's apricot orchard.

Somewhere along there we always stopped to admire the view, with our backs to the orchard and our faces toward the pasture and woodland rolling steeply down and then more steeply up, ravine and ridge, to the dark forested mountainside and the crest. Across the mountain the pale air swept in from remote places—Hawaii, Midway, illimitable Japans. I have never anywhere else had so strong a feeling of the vast continuity of air in which we live. On a walk, we flew up into that gusty envelope like climbing kites.

The Shieldses, who own the pasture, have been abroad for a year. We pass their lane, turn left, turn right again past the LoPresti entrance. Almost any afternoon we could look down and see Julie working her horse in the ring or currying the dust out of his hide, and at the house, Lucio laying up adobes for another wing. (Ruth suggested that he unraveled each night what he had laid up during the day.) Fran would be chiseling or sanding languidly at one of her driftwood sculptures, sometimes crowding under the shade of the patio umbrella, sometimes quenched under a straw hat a yard across. She has had a couple of moles removed by needle, and fears actinic cancer.

From Lucio and Fran, a wave, perhaps a minute of shouted conversation. From their daughter, nothing. She was not nearsighted, she was just a girl who didn't know how to smile, and was not inclined to acknowledge the flappings and hoo-hooings of neighbors who meant no more to her than her horse's droppings. She had a certain cold ferocity of antagonism to her mother, a contemptuous toleration of her father, and a passion of attachment to her gelding. Those, I believe, constituted her total emotional life last October. By now, a year later, her capacity for feeling should be enlarged.

Ruth believes that boys are not found around stables because what they like is taking things apart and putting them together again, and for this

purpose horses are not so satisfactory as cars, motorcycles, and even bicycles, while girls adore horses because they are biological and have functions—just pat them and feel how warm! I wonder, on the contrary, if Julie
didn't spend all her time with her horse because she had no other friends
and because riding let her indulge her fantasies of having a bit in her father's
mouth and a Mexican spur in her mother's side. She was a dark-browed
girl, fifteen or sixteen, somewhat flat-chested, big in the behind. Off the
horse she was rawboned and awkward; mounted, she was almost beautiful.
She always rode bareback.

So there we went one day last fall. A wave from Lucio, a flutter of Fran's
uplifted glove across some sort of mosaic panel laid out on sawhorses. No
Julie—apparently not yet home from school—but the horse was hanging
his chin on the corral rail waiting. We turned into Ladera Lane under big
gum trees whose bark was starting to peel to reveal the delicate pastels
underneath and whose fallen buttons, crushed by passing cars, filled the air
with the smell I could never dissociate from the 1918 flu epidemic, during
which we went around in gauze masks soaked in that pungent oil. Past the
riding stable—more girls, no boys—and down a sudden gully smelling of
bay and sage, around the corner of a walnut orchard to Roble Road and
along it up a long hogback, the first crest visible from our house, until we
came out on a windy plateau with puckers of woods below us and hills
between us and the mountain.

It is a view that has the quality of bigness without actual size, and it used
to comfort me to know that these little mountains, like everything else
around, are very lively, very Californian. The range grows, they say, a half
inch or so a year, and in the same time moves about that distance northward.
It is a parable for the retired. Sit still and let the world do the moving.

The ridge was as far as we let our string out. Reeling in, we turned to
the right across the clods of a plowed orchard, climbed through a fence
beside a locked trail gate, and found ourselves in the pasture bought from
Tom Weld's father a long time ago by a school district looking to the future.
A walleyed white horse with a hanging lip and the black nose and black
feet he had got from wading around in tarweed watched us; he had a
decrepit Hooverville look like an old man dirty from picking through the
dump. Angus steers, three-dimensionally black against the dun hill, chewed
the cud under a dying grotesque of an oak.

Ahead and to the right the hills flowed into the valley. Roofs and trees
and streets receded toward the bay, and in the unsmogged breezy clarity we

could see the bridges—Dumbarton, San Mateo, even the Bay Bridge and far off on misty contracostal hillsides the white of continuous city.

Below or above the snuffling of the steers and the lazy rushes of wind through the oak I could hear the sough of traffic in the thousand streets of the valley, and I felt at once elated and besieged. A little more population pressure, that bigger water main that Tom Weld wanted, and our desert island would be quarter-acre lots and beatitude a memory.

A long slope led us down into the wood that thickened along the dry creek bed. There were dusty asters under the brush, an occasional scarlet gilia. Some trodden weed sent up a sudden minty smell. In the path I saw the scat of an animal, fox probably, all knotted up with fur and feathers, and I turned it over with the tip of the blackthorn. "Boy," I said, "that looks *painful*. How come a nice wild natural fox suffers from strangulated hemorrhoids?"

Holding her mouth as if she had been interrupted when just about to whistle, Ruth said in her mildest whisper, "I've got a Kleenex, if you want to take it home for your collection."

I made some suitably scatological remark and golfed the thing into the bushes. But there it was. I admire the natural, and I hate the miscalled improvements that spread like impetigo into the hills. But who can pretend that the natural and the idyllic are the same? The natural is often imperfect, and Homo fabricans, of whom I am one, is eager to perfect it. So I clean it up and grub out its poison oak and spray for its insect pests and plant things that bear blossoms instead of burrs, and make it all Arcadian and delightful, and all I do is help jar loose a tax increase, bring on roads and power lines, stir up the real-estate sharpies with their unearned increment, and get the hills cut up with roads and building lots. All our woe, with loss of Eden.

If I had three wishes—one would do—I would stop all development in its tracks and put the real-estate people to growing apricots again. Better a country fox with a hemorrhoid than a city fox with a pile. Aesop must have said it.

Through the brushy bottoms trail-riders had cut a ten-foot swath, but the summer's growth had half closed it in. Fronds of poison oak hung into the trail, dry cucumber vines and bindweed wove the walls of brush together. The ground, trodden by horses when wet, had dried again rough and hard as concrete. Passing under an oak, we got our faces full of late oak-moth caterpillars hanging on their threads, and Ruth was still pawing her face and shuddering when we came to the broken-down place in the bank where the riding trail crossed the creek between the Thomas cottage, then vacant and up for sale, and our south line. We slid down and clambered up, pulling ourselves by exposed roots.

And had a cold, visceral shock, a stoppage of the heart followed by a pounding pulse. For there, down in that quiet creek-bottom where nobody but an occasional horseman ever passed, and where the only wheeled tracks were those of the man who periodically serviced our well pump, was this motorcycle sitting quietly, and on its seat this person in orange helicopter coveralls bulging all over with zippered pockets. The suit was unzipped clear to his navel, and his hairy chest rose out of it and merged with a dark, dense beard.

Caliban.

Dana Gioia

Contemporary poet Dana Gioia (1950–) has had an unusual career. After earning B.A. and M.A. degrees at Stanford and Harvard, Gioia returned to his native California and got an M.B.A. from the Stanford Business School. Then he went to work for General Foods, where he rose to the position of vice president before quitting in 1992. Throughout those years he had continued to pursue his literary interests: he did translations, edited collections of Italian poetry, and wrote poems—published in the New Yorker, Hudson Review, *and* Poetry—*and essays. The title essay from his collection* Can Poetry Matter? Essays on Poetry and American Culture *argues that it is time for poets to "leave the well-ordered and stuffy classroom, time to restore a vulgar vitality to poetry and unleash the energy now trapped in the subculture." Naturally this essay, originally published in the* Atlantic, *generated strong partisan responses.*

Since he started writing full-time, Gioia has also been working with HarperCollins on a college literature series: he and coeditor X. J. Kennedy have been putting together introductions to fiction, poetry, and drama. With these textbooks Gioia may well exert more influence on the literary education of a generation of undergraduate students than many career academics. Gioia is "that rare thing, a contemporary American poet who lives wholly outside universities," notes reviewer Christopher Clausen, and this has enabled him to produce work in which "the range of experience and effects is impressively wide." This power is also evident in his poetic observations on landscapes and their meaning. ✺

California Hills in August

I can imagine someone who found
these fields unbearable, who climbed
the hillside in the heat, cursing the dust,
cracking the brittle weeds underfoot,
wishing a few more trees for shade.

An Easterner especially, who would scorn
the meagerness of summer, the dry
twisted shapes of black elm,
scrub oak, and chaparral, a landscape
August has already drained of green.

One who would hurry over the clinging
thistle, foxtail, golden poppy,
knowing everything was just a weed,
unable to conceive that these trees
and sparse brown bushes were alive.

And hate the bright stillness of the noon
without wind, without motion,
the only other living thing,
a hawk, hungry for prey, suspended
in the blinding, sunlit blue.

And yet how gentle it seems to someone
raised in a landscape short of rain—
the skyline of a hill broken by no more
trees than one can count, the grass,
the empty sky, the wish for water.

Becoming a Redwood

Stand in a field long enough, and the sounds
start up again. The crickets, the invisible
toad who claims that change is possible,

And all the other life too small to name.
First one, then another, until innumerable
they merge into the single voice of a summer hill

Yes, it's hard to stand still, hour after hour,
fixed as a fencepost, hearing the steers
snort in the dark pasture, smelling the manure.

And paralyzed by the mystery of how a stone
can bear to be a stone, the pain
the grass endures breaking through the earth's crust.

Unimaginable the redwoods on the far hill,
rooted for centuries, the living wood grown tall
and thickened with a hundred thousand days of light.

The old windmill creaks in perfect time
to the wind shaking the miles of pasture grass,
and the last farmhouse light goes off.

Something moves nearby. Coyotes hunt
these hills and packs of feral dogs.
But standing here at night accepts all that.

You are your own pale shadow in the quarter moon,
moving more slowly than the crippled stars,
part of the moonlight as the moonlight falls,

Part of the grass that answers the wind,
part of the midnight's watchfulness that knows
there is no silence but when danger comes.

Robert Louis Stevenson

Robert Louis Stevenson (1850–1894) visited California in 1880, staying only a year. He was engaged in his lifelong fight against tuberculosis, but this was a salutary period for him. He had met Fanny Van de Grift Osbourne in France and pursued her to the Bay Area, where they were married. They spent their honeymoon in Napa Valley, in the cabin of an abandoned silver mine on Mount St. Helena, the setting for his book Silverado Squatters. *Somewhat restored by this California sojourn, Stevenson took his new wife and stepson back to Scotland and then began a pilgrimage around Europe in search of a healthy climate. In 1888 the Stevensons made a brief stop in California while en route to Samoa, where they settled until his death in 1894. His determination had made him one of the most prolific writers of his time—and his talent, one of the most popular.*

Stevenson left a permanent impression on the cultural history of Northern California. A state park named for him (with a museum about his career) preserves some of the same landscape he described in The Silverado Squatters, *including 3,000 acres of the upper slopes of Mount St. Helena, from whose 4,343-foot summit the Sierra and Shasta-Cascade regions are visible. But Stevenson gives us a different view in "The Sea Fogs," looking down from the shoulders of his mountain retreat as fog rolls across the valley to create "a great level ocean."* ✍

from The Silverado Squatters

A change in the color of the light usually called me in the morning. By a certain hour, the long, vertical chinks in our western gable, where the boards had shrunk and separated, flashed suddenly into my eyes as stripes of dazzling blue, at once so dark and splendid that I used to marvel how the qualities could be combined. At an earlier hour, the heavens in that quarter were still quietly colored, but the shoulder of the mountain which shuts in the canyon already glowed with sunlight in a wonderful compound of gold and rose and green; and this too would kindle, although more mildly and with rainbow tints, the fissures of our crazy gable. If I were sleeping heavily, it was the bold blue that struck me awake; if more lightly, then I would come to myself in that earlier and fairier light.

One Sunday morning, about five, the first brightness called me. I rose and turned to the east, not for my devotions, but for air. The night had been very still. The little private gale that blew every evening in our canyon, for ten minutes or perhaps a quarter of an hour, had swiftly blown itself out; in the hours that followed not a sigh of wind had shaken the treetops; and our barrack, for all its breaches, was less fresh that morning than of wont. But I had no sooner reached the window than I forgot all else in the sight that met my eyes, and I made but two bounds into my clothes, and down the crazy plank to the platform.

The sun was still concealed below the opposite hilltops, though it was shining already, not twenty feet above my head, on our own mountain slope. But the scene, beyond a few near features, was entirely changed. Napa Valley was gone; gone were all the lower slopes and woody foothills of the range; and in their place, not a thousand feet below me, rolled a great level ocean. It was as though I had gone to bed the night before, safe in a nook of inland mountains, and had awakened in a bay upon the coast. I had seen these inundations from below; at Calistoga I had risen and gone abroad in the early morning, coughing and sneezing, under fathoms on fathoms of gray sea vapor, like a cloudy sky—a dull sight for the artist, and a painful experience for the invalid. But to sit aloft one's self in the pure air and under the unclouded dome of heaven, and thus look down on the submergence

Crude Poem Inspired by the Landscape

The ocean encircles a lone peak.
Rough terrain surrounds this prison.
There are few birds flying over the cold hills.
The wild goose messenger cannot find its way.
I have been detained and obstacles have been put my way for half a year.
Melancholy and hate gather on my face.
Now that I must return to my country,
I have toiled like the jingwei bird in vain."
—Anonymous, in *Poetry and History of Chinese Immigrants on Angel Island, 1910–1940*

of the valley, was strangely different and even delightful to the eyes. Far away were hilltops like little islands. Nearer, a smoky surf beat about the foot of precipices and poured into all the coves of these rough mountains. The color of that fog ocean was a thing never to be forgotten. For an instant, among the Hebrides and just about sundown, I have seen something like it on the sea itself. But the white was not so opaline; nor was there, what surprisingly increased the effect, that breathless, crystal stillness over all. Even in its gentlest moods the salt sea travails, moaning among the weeds or lisping on the sand; but that vast fog ocean lay in a trance of silence, nor did the sweet air of the morning tremble with a sound.

As I continued to sit upon the dump, I began to observe that this sea was not so level as at first sight it appeared to be. Away in the extreme south, a little hill of fog arose against the sky above the general surface, and as it had already caught the sun, it shone on the horizon like the topsails of some giant ship. There were huge waves, stationary, as it seemed, like waves in a frozen sea; and yet, as I looked again, I was not sure but they were moving after all, with a slow and august advance. And while I was yet doubting, a promontory of the hills some four or five miles away, conspicuous by a bouquet of tall pines, was in a single instant overtaken and swallowed up. It reappeared in a little, with its pines, but this time as an islet, and only to be swallowed up once more and then for good. This set me looking nearer, and I saw that in every cove along the line of mountains the fog was being piled in higher and higher, as though by some wind that was inaudible to me. I could trace its progress, one pine tree first growing hazy and then disappearing after another; although sometimes there was none of this fore-running haze, but the whole opaque white ocean gave a start and swallowed a piece of mountain at a gulp. It was to flee these poisonous fogs that I had left the seaboard, and climbed so high among the mountains. And now, behold, here came the fog to besiege me in my chosen altitudes, and yet came so beautifully that my first thought was of welcome.

The sun had now gotten much higher, and through all the gaps of the hills it cast long bars of gold across that white ocean. An eagle, or some other very great bird of the mountain, came wheeling over the nearer pine-tops, and hung, poised and something sideways, as if to look abroad on that unwonted desolation, spying, perhaps with terror, for the aeries of her comrades. Then, with a long cry, she disappeared again towards Lake County and the clearer air. At length it seemed to me as if the flood were beginning to subside. The old landmarks, by whose disappearance I had measured its advance, here a crag, there a brave pine tree, now began, in the inverse order, to make their reappearance into daylight. I judged all danger of the fog was over. This was not Noah's flood; it was but a morning spring, and would now drift out seaward whence it came. So, mightily relieved, and a good deal exhilarated by the light, I went into the house to light the fire.

I suppose it was nearly seven when I once more mounted the platform to look abroad. The fog ocean had swelled up enormously since last I saw it; and a few hundred feet below me, in the deep gap where the Toll House stands and the road runs through into Lake County, it had already topped the slope, and was pouring over and down the other side like driving smoke. The wind had climbed along with it; and though I was still in calm air, I could see the trees tossing below me, and their long, strident sighing mounted to me where I stood.

Half an hour later, the fog had surmounted all the ridge on the opposite side of the gap, though a shoulder of the mountain still warded it out of our canyon. Napa Valley and its bounding hills were now utterly blotted out. The fog, sunny white in the sunshine, was pouring over into Lake County in a huge, ragged cataract, tossing treetops appearing and disappearing in the spray. The air struck with a little chill, and set me coughing. It smelled strong of the fog, like the smell of a washing-house, but with a shrewd tang of the sea salt.

Had it not been for two things—the sheltering spur which answered as a dyke, and the great valley on the other side which rapidly engulfed whatever mounted—our own little platform in the canyon must have been already buried a hundred feet in salt and poisonous air. As it was, the interest of the scene entirely occupied our minds. We were set just out of the wind, and but just above the fog; we could listen to the voice of the one as to music on the stage; we could plunge our eyes down into the other, as into some flowing stream from over the parapet of a bridge; thus we looked on upon a strange, impetuous, silent, shifting exhibition of the powers of nature, and saw the familiar landscape changing from moment to moment like figures in a dream.

The imagination loves to trifle with what is not. Had this been indeed the deluge, I should have felt more strongly, but the emotion would have been similar in kind. I played with the idea, as the child flees in delighted terror from the creations of his fancy. The look of the thing helped me. And when at last I began to flee up the mountain, it was indeed partly to escape from the raw air that kept me coughing, but it was also part in play.

As I ascended the mountainside, I came once more to overlook the upper surface of the fog; but it wore a different appearance from what I had beheld at daybreak. For, first, the sun now fell on it from high overhead, and its surface shone and undulated like a great nor'land moor country, sheeted with untrodden morning snow. And next the new level must have been a thousand or fifteen hundred feet higher than the old, so that only five or six points of all the broken country below me still stood out. Napa Valley was now one with Sonoma on the west. On the hither side, only a thin scattered fringe of bluffs was unsubmerged; and through all the gaps the fog was pouring over, like an ocean, into the blue clear sunny country on the east. There it was soon lost; for it fell instantly into the bottom of the valleys, following the watershed; and the hilltops in that quarter were still clear-cut upon the eastern sky.

Through the Toll House gap and over the near ridges on the other side, the deluge was immense. A spray of thin vapor was thrown high above it, rising and falling, and blown into fantastic shapes. The speed of its course was like a mountain torrent. Here and there a few treetops were discovered and then whelmed again; and for one second, the bough of a dead pine beckoned out of the spray like the arm of a drowning man. But still the imagination was dissatisfied, still the ear waited for something more. Had this indeed been water (as it seemed so, to the eye), with what a plunge of reverberating thunder would it have rolled upon its course, disemboweling mountains and deracinating pines! And yet water it was, and seawater at that—true Pacific billows, only somewhat rarefied, rolling in midair among the hilltops.

I climbed still higher, among the red rattling gravel and dwarf underwood of Mount St. Helena, until I could look right down upon Silverado, and admire the favored nook in which it lay. The sunny plain of fog was several hundred feet higher; behind the protecting spur a gigantic accumulation of cottony vapor threatened, with every second, to blow over and submerge our homestead; but the vortex setting past the Toll House was too strong; and there lay our little platform, in the arms of the deluge, but still enjoying its unbroken sunshine. About eleven, however, thin spray came flying over the friendly buttress, and I began to think the fog had hunted out its Jonah after all. But it was the last effort. The wind veered while we were at dinner and began to blow squally from the mountain summit; and by half past one, all that world of sea fogs was utterly routed and flying here and there into the south in little rags of cloud. And instead of a lone sea-beach, we found ourselves once more inhabiting a high mountainside, with the clear green country far below us, and the smoke of Calistoga blowing in the air.

This was the great Russian campaign for that season. Now and then, in the early morning, a little white lakelet of fog would be seen far down in Napa Valley; but the heights were not again assailed, nor was the surrounding world again shut off from Silverado.

Jack London

Few American writers of his time could compete with the success enjoyed by Jack London (1876–1916), author of The Call of the Wild, White Fang, Martin Eden, *and scores of other works, both fiction and nonfiction. By 1913 London was at the height of his fame, writing for a growing audience, and receiving substantial advances. But it was also "the most disastrous year in his private life," says critic Arthur Calder-Marshall. The worst of a "long succession of misfortunes" was the fire that consumed Wolf House, his dream home, a few days before its completion. London was left deep in debt: the stone and timber mansion he was building on his Glen Ellen ranch was mortgaged against anticipated profits from his serialized novel,* The Valley of the Moon—*ironically, named for this area he loved.*

London first bought land in Sonoma Valley in 1905, and he continued to buy until he owned 1,350 acres. After years as an oyster pirate on San Francisco Bay, a prospector in the Klondike, and a sailor in the South Seas, London was drawn to this place. He would reject urban living and take root here. Grafting his back-to-the-land impulse onto the socialist perspective that informed his earlier books, London wrote The Valley of the Moon, *with main characters Saxon Brown and Billy Roberts based on the author and his second wife, Charmian. "This is our place," she says after they catch "their first sight of Sonoma Valley and the wild mountains that rimmed its eastern side." Unfortunately, the real-life Jack London lost his optimism about country living when he lost his home. His last years were marred by depression and ill health. He died in 1916 at the age of forty, probably due to stroke and heart failure. His widow gave their land to the state, and Beauty Ranch is now a historic park devoted to the author's memory.* 🖎

from The Valley of the Moon

South they held along the coast, hunting, fishing, swimming, and horse-buying. Billy shipped his purchases on the coasting steamers. Through Del Norte and Humboldt counties they went, and through Mendocino into Sonoma—counties larger than Eastern states—threading the giant woods, whipping innumerable trout streams, and crossing countless rich valleys.

Ever Saxon sought the valley of the moon. Sometimes, when all seemed fair, the lack was a railroad, sometimes madroño and manzanita trees, and, usually, there was too much fog.

"We do want a sun-cocktail once in a while," she told Billy.

"Yep," was his answer. "Too much fog might make us soggy. What we're after is betwixt an' between, an' we'll have to get back from the coast a ways to find it."

This was in the fall of the year, and they turned their backs on the Pacific at old Fort Ross and entered the Russian River Valley, far below Ukiah, by way of Cazadero and Guerneville. At Santa Rosa Billy was delayed with the shipping of several horses, so that it was not until afternoon that he drove south and east for Sonoma Valley.

"I guess we'll no more than make Sonoma Valley when it'll be time to camp," he said, measuring the sun with his eye. "This is called Bennett Valley. You cross a divide from it and come out at Glen Ellen. Now this is a mighty pretty valley, if anybody should ask you. An' that's some nifty mountain over there."

"The mountain is all right," Saxon adjudged. "But all the rest of the hills are too bare. And I don't see any big trees. It takes rich soil to make big trees."

"Oh, I ain't sayin' it's the valley of the moon by a long ways. All the same, Saxon, that's some mountain. Look at the timber on it. I bet they's deer there."

"I wonder where we'll spend this winter," Saxon remarked.

"D'ye know, I've just ben thinkin' the same thing. Let's winter at Carmel. Mark Hall's back, an' so is Jim Hazard. What d'ye say?"

Saxon nodded.

"Only you won't be the odd-job man this time."

"Nope. We can make trips in good weather horse-buyin'," Billy confirmed, his face beaming with self-satisfaction. "An' if that walkin' poet of the Marble House is around, I'll sure get the gloves on with 'm just in memory of the time he walked me off my legs—"

"Oh! Oh!" Saxon cried. "Look, Billy! Look!"

Around a bend in the road came a man in a sulky, driving a heavy stallion. The animal was a bright chestnut-sorrel, with cream-colored mane and tail. The tail almost swept the ground, while the mane was so thick that it crested out of the neck and flowed down, long and wavy. He scented the mares and stopped short, head flung up and armfuls of creamy mane tossing in the breeze. He bent his head until flaring nostrils brushed impatient knees, and between the fine-pointed ears could be seen a mighty and incredible curve of neck. Again he tossed his head, fretting against the bit as the driver turned widely aside for safety in passing. They could see the blue glaze like a sheen on the surface of the horse's bright, wild eyes, and Billy closed a wary thumb on his reins and himself turned widely. He held up his hand in signal, and the driver of the stallion stopped when well past, and over his shoulder talked draft horses with Billy.

Among other things, Billy learned that the stallion's name was Barbarossa, that the driver was the owner, and that Santa Rosa was his headquarters.

"There are two ways to Sonoma Valley from here," the man directed. "When you come to the crossroads the turn to the left will take you to Glen Ellen by Bennett Peak—that's it there."

Rising from rolling stubble fields, Bennett Peak towered hot in the sun, a row of bastion hills leaning against its base. But hills and mountains on that side showed bare and heated, though beautiful with the sunburnt tawniness of California.

"The turn to the right will take you to Glen Ellen, too, only it's longer and steeper grades. But your mares don't look as though it'd bother them."

"Which is the prettiest way?" Saxon asked.

"Oh, the right-hand road, by all means," said the man. "That's Sonoma Mountain there, and the road skirts it pretty well up, and goes through Cooper's Grove."

Billy did not start immediately after they had said good-bye, and he and Saxon, heads over shoulders, watched the roused Barbarossa plunging mutinously on toward Santa Rosa.

"Gee!" Billy said. "I'd like to be up here next spring."

At the crossroads Billy hesitated and looked at Saxon.

"What if it is longer?" she said. "Look how beautiful it is—all covered with green woods; and I just know those are redwoods in the canyons. You never can tell. The valley of the moon might be right up there somewhere. And it would never do to miss it just in order to save half an hour."

They took the turn to the right and began crossing a series of steep foothills. As they approached the mountain there were signs of a greater abundance of water. They drove beside a running stream, and, though the vineyards on the hills were summer-dry, the farmhouses in the hollows and on the levels were grouped about with splendid trees.

"Maybe it sounds funny," Saxon observed; "but I'm beginning to love that mountain already. It almost seems as if I'd seen it before, somehow, it's so all-around satisfying—oh!"

Crossing a bridge and rounding a sharp turn, they were suddenly enveloped in a mysterious coolness and gloom. All about them arose stately trunks of redwood. The forest floor was a rosy carpet of autumn fronds. Occasional shafts of sunlight, penetrating the deep shade, warmed the somberness of the grove. Alluring paths led off among the trees and into cozy nooks made by circles of red columns growing around the dust of vanished ancestors—witnessing the titanic dimensions of those ancestors by the girth of the circles in which they stood.

Out of the grove they pulled to the steep divide, which was no more than a buttress of Sonoma Mountain. The way led on through rolling upland and across small dips and canyons, all well wooded and a-drip with water. In places the road was muddy from wayside springs.

"The mountain's a sponge," said Billy. "Here it is, the tail end of dry summer, an' the ground's just leakin' everywhere."

I had been awestruck by the glories of the nights in the valley of the new settlement. One evening while sitting with my darling spouse, amid the night noises of crickets, tree frogs, and the occasional hoot of an owl, I became bewildered by the beauty, largeness and silvery color of the moon stealthily creeping across the valley of the settlers. As yet the settlement bore no name on our maps other than that of the mission. So beautiful beyond the language of poets to describe was this moon-drenched, peaceful settlement. Unable to curb my enthusiasm I cried aloud as if speaking to the Moon, "You fire my soul to its very depths with inspiration. Beneath us, in the valley below, all is so peaceful and beautiful, wrapped in your delicate mantle of gold, oh, eye from Heaven. I have it, my darling Francisca, what could be more appropriate? I shall name the lovely vision before our eyes, 'Sonoma (Valley of the Moon).'" [1]

—Harry D. Hubbard, from *Vallejo* (1941)

1. Sonoma is a Chocuyene Indian contraction for Valley of the Moon. The Chocuyene tribes inhabited the Marin and Sonoma Valley regions. They referred to the valley as Sonoma before Vallejo established his settlement.

"I know I've never been here before," Saxon communed aloud. "But it's all so familiar! So I must have dreamed it. And there's madroños!—a whole grove! And manzanita! Why, I feel just as if I was coming home [...] Oh, Billy, if it should turn out to be our valley."

"Plastered against the side of a mountain?" he queried, with a skeptical laugh.

"No; I don't mean that. I mean on the way to our valley. Because the way—all ways—to our valley must be beautiful. And this; I've seen it all before, dreamed it."

"It's great," he said sympathetically. "I wouldn't trade a square mile of this kind of country for the whole Sacramento Valley, with the river islands thrown in and Middle River for good measure. If they ain't deer up there, I miss my guess. An' where they's springs they's streams, an' streams means trout."

They passed a large and comfortable farmhouse, surrounded by wandering barns and cow-sheds, went on under forest arches, and emerged beside a field with which Saxon was instantly enchanted. It flowed in a gentle concave from the road up the mountain, its farther boundary an unbroken line of timber. The field glowed like rough gold in the approaching sunset, and near the middle of it stood a solitary great redwood, with blasted top suggesting a nesting aerie for eagles. The timber beyond clothed the mountain in solid green to what they took to be the top. But, as they drove on, Saxon, looking back upon what she called *her* field, saw the real summit of Sonoma towering beyond, the mountain behind her field a mere spur upon the side of the larger mass.

Ahead and toward the right, across sheer ridges of the mountains, separated by deep green canyons and broadening lower down into rolling orchards and vineyards, they caught their first sight of Sonoma Valley and the wild mountains that rimmed its eastern side. To the left they gazed across a golden land of small hills and valleys. Beyond, to the north, they glimpsed another portion of the valley, and, still beyond, the opposing wall of the valley—a range of mountains, the highest of which reared its red and battered ancient crater against a rosy and mellowing sky. From north to southeast, the mountain rim curved in the brightness of the sun, while Saxon and Billy were already in the shadow of evening. He looked at Saxon, noted the ravished ecstasy of her face, and stopped the horses. All the eastern sky was blushing to rose, which descended upon the mountains, touching them with wine and ruby. Sonoma Valley began to fill with a purple flood, laving the mountain bases, rising, inundating, drowning them in its purple. Saxon pointed in silence, indicating that the purple flood was the sunset shadow of Sonoma Mountain. Billy nodded, then chirruped to the mares, and the descent began through a warm and colorful twilight.

On the elevated sections of the road they felt the cool, delicious breeze from the Pacific forty miles away; while from each little dip and hollow came warm breaths of autumn earth, spicy with sunburnt grass and fallen leaves and passing flowers.

They came to the rim of a deep canyon that seemed to penetrate to the heart of Sonoma Mountain. Again, with no word spoken, merely from watching Saxon, Billy stopped the wagon. The canyon was wildly beautiful. Tall redwoods lined its entire length. On its farther rim stood three rugged knolls covered with dense woods of spruce and oak. From between the knolls, a feeder to the main canyon and likewise fringed with redwoods, emerged a smaller canyon. Billy pointed to a stubble field that lay at the feet of the knolls.

"It's in fields like that I've seen my mares a-pasturing," he said.

They dropped down into the canyon, the road following a stream that sang under maples and alders. The sunset fires, refracted from the cloud-driftage of the autumn sky, bathed the canyon with crimson, in which ruddy-limbed madroños and wine-wooded manzanitas burnt and smoldered. The air was aromatic with laurel. Wild grapevines bridged the stream from tree to tree. Oaks of many sorts were veiled in lacy Spanish moss. Ferns and brakes grew lush beside the stream. From somewhere came the plaint of a mourning dove. Fifty feet above the ground, almost over their heads, a Douglas squirrel crossed the road—a flash of gray between two trees; and they marked the continuance of its aerial passage by the bending of the boughs.

"I've got a hunch," said Billy.

"Let me say it first," Saxon begged.

He waited, his eyes on her face as she gazed about her in rapture.

"We've found our valley," she whispered. "Was that it?"

He nodded, but checked speech at sight of a small boy driving a cow up the road, a preposterously big shotgun in one hand, in the other as preposterously big a jackrabbit.

"How far to Glen Ellen?" Billy asked.

"Mile an' a half," was the answer.

"What creek is this?" inquired Saxon.

"Wild Water. It empties into Sonoma Creek half a mile down."

"Trout?"—this from Billy.

"If you know how to catch 'em," grinned the boy.

"Deer up the mountain?"

"It ain't open season," the boy evaded.

"I guess you never shot a deer," Billy slyly baited, and was rewarded with:

"I got the horns to show."

"Deer shed their horns," Billy teased on. "Anybody can find 'em."

"I got the meat on mine. It ain't dry yet—"

The boy broke off, gazing with shocked eyes into the pit Billy had dug for him.

"It's all right, sonny," Billy laughed, as he drove on. "I ain't the game warden. I'm buyin' horses."

More leaping tree squirrels, more ruddy madroños and majestic oaks, more fairy circles of redwoods, and, still beside the singing stream, they passed a gate by the roadside. Before it stood a rural mailbox, on which was lettered "Edmund Hale." Standing under the rustic arch, leaning upon the gate, a man and woman composed a picture so arresting and beautiful that Saxon caught her breath. They were side by side, the delicate hand of the woman curled in the hand of the man, which looked as if made to confer benedictions. His face bore out this impression—a beautiful-browed countenance, with large, benevolent gray eyes under a wealth of white hair that shone like spun glass. He was fair and large; the little woman beside him was daintily wrought. She was saffron-brown, as a woman of the white race can well be, with smiling eyes of bluest blue. In quaint sage-green draperies, she seemed a flower, with her small vivid face irresistibly reminding Saxon of a springtime wake-robin.

Perhaps the picture made by Saxon and Billy was equally arresting and beautiful, as they drove down through the golden end of day. The two couples had eyes only for each other. The little woman beamed joyously. The man's face glowed into the benediction that had trembled there. To Saxon, like the field up the mountain, like the mountain itself, it seemed that she had always known this adorable pair. She knew that she loved them.

"How d'ye do," said Billy.

"You blessed children," said the man. "I wonder if you know how dear you look sitting there."

That was all. The wagon had passed by, rustling down the road, which was carpeted with fallen leaves of maple, oak, and alder. Then they came to the meeting of the two creeks.

"Oh, what a place for a home," Saxon cried, pointing across Wild Water. "See, Billy; on that bench there above the meadow."

"It's a rich bottom, Saxon; and so is the bench rich. Look at the big trees on it. An' they's sure to be springs."

"Drive over," she said.

Forsaking the main road, they crossed Wild Water on a narrow bridge and continued along an ancient, rutted road that ran beside an equally ancient worm-fence of split redwood rails. They came to a gate, open and off its hinges, through which the road led out on the bench.

"This is it—I know it," Saxon said with conviction. "Drive in, Billy."

A small, whitewashed farmhouse with broken windows showed through the trees.

"Talk about your madroños—"

Billy pointed to the father of all madroños, six feet in diameter at its base, sturdy and sound, which stood before the house.

They spoke in low tones as they passed around the house under great oak trees and came to a stop before a small barn. They did not wait to unharness. Tying the horses, they started to explore. The pitch from the bench to the meadow was steep yet thickly wooded with oaks and manzanita. As they crashed through the underbrush they startled a score of quail into flight.

"How about game?" Saxon queried.

Billy grinned, and fell to examining a spring which bubbled a clear stream into the meadow. Here the ground was sunbaked and wide open in a multitude of cracks.

Disappointment leaped into Saxon's face, but Billy, crumbling a clod between his fingers, had not made up his mind.

"It's rich," he pronounced; "—the cream of the soil that's ben washin' down from the hills for ten thousan' years. But—"

He broke off, stared all about, studying the configuration of the meadow, crossed it to the redwood trees beyond, then came back.

"It's no good as it is," he said. "But it's the best ever if it's handled right. All it needs is a little common sense an' a lot of drainage. This meadow's a natural basin not yet filled level. They's a sharp slope through the redwoods to the creek. Come on, I'll show you."

They went through the redwoods and came out on Sonoma Creek. At this spot was no singing. The stream poured into a quiet pool. The willows on their side brushed the water. The opposite side was a steep bank. Billy measured the height of the bank with his eye, the depth of the water with a driftwood pole.

"Fifteen feet," he announced. "That allows all kinds of high-divin' from the bank. An' it's a hundred yards of a swim up an' down."

They followed down the pool. It emptied in a riffle, across exposed bedrock, into another pool. As they looked, a trout flashed into the air and back, leaving a widening ripple on the quiet surface.

"I guess we won't winter in Carmel," Billy said. "This place was specially manufactured for us. In the morning I'll find out who owns it."

Half an hour later, feeding the horses, he called Saxon's attention to a locomotive whistle.

"You've got your railroad," he said. "That's a train pulling into Glen Ellen, an' it's only a mile from here."

Saxon was dozing off to sleep under the blankets when Billy aroused her.

"Suppose the guy that owns it won't sell?"

"There isn't the slightest doubt," Saxon answered with unruffled certainty. "This is our place. I know it."

Jack Kerouac

It is always good to be skeptical of claims on the covers of paperbacks. Otherwise, when you pick up an aging copy of The Dharma Bums *you might believe that Jack Kerouac (1922–1969) was "the man who launched the hippie world, the daddy of the swinging psychedelic generation." While it is certainly true that Kerouac became a counterculture icon—thanks partly to his willingness to ignore middle-class conventions regarding sexuality and drugs—it is also true that he declined the title of "intellectual forebear" to the "deluge of alienated radicals, war protesters, dropouts, hippies and even 'Beats.'" Even so, he was one of the best known—and most widely read—of those Beats when he died of too much drink at the age of forty-seven.*

Born in 1922 to French-Canadian parents, Jean-Louis Kerouac grew up in Lowell, Massachusetts, reading Saroyan and Hemingway and playing high school football—well enough to win a scholarship to Columbia in 1939. Depressed by the impending war, he left school in 1941 and shipped out as a merchant seaman. He tried the Navy in 1943, but was quickly discharged for "indifferent character," an honorable escape. He hung about New York with friends Allen Ginsberg and William S. Burroughs and with a young man from Denver, Neal Cassady, whose wild energy fascinated Kerouac. They caromed across the continent, hopping freights, hitching rides, with Kerouac recording the sheer joy of movement, trying to be "always honest ('ludicrous'), spontaneous, 'confessional,' interesting, because not 'crafted.'" These are the qualities he aimed for in his most famous works, On the Road, The Subterraneans, *and* The Dharma Bums, *in which Kerouac—in the guise of Ray—and Japhy Ryder (modeled after the poet Gary Snyder) light briefly in California. Here he is in his element, on the trail, talking and tramping his way 'round the mountain.* ✎

from The Dharma Bums

Japhy was in high spirits. "Goddammit it feels good to get away from dissipation and go in the woods. When I get back from Japan, Ray, when the weather gets really cold we'll put on our long underwear and hitchhike through the land. Think if you can of ocean to mountain Alaska to Klamath a solid forest of fir to bhikku in, a lake of a million wild geese. Woo! You know what woo means in Chinese?"

"What?"

"Fog. These woods are great here in Marin, I'll show you Muir Woods today, but up north is all that real old Pacific Coast mountain and ocean land, the future home of the Dharma-body. Know what I'm gonna do? I'll do a new long poem called 'Rivers and Mountains Without End' and just write it on and on on a scroll and unfold on and on with new surprises and always what went before forgotten, see, like a river, or like one of them real long Chinese silk paintings that show two little men hiking in an endless landscape of gnarled old trees and mountains so high they merge with the fog in the upper silk void. I'll spend three thousand years writing it, it'll be packed full of information on soil conservation, the Tennessee Valley Authority, astronomy, geology, Hsuan Tsung's travels, Chinese painting theory, reforestation, Oceanic ecology and food chains."

And at night! If one is weary of crowds and bustle and the constant talk of money, money, money, let him go to the "Top of the Mark" cocktail lounge, order a drink whether he wants it or not (he would be invited to leave if he did not), and from that lofty eminence on the summit of Nob Hill revel in one of the loveliest pictures this world has to offer.

The lounge is almost dark. The walls are of glass. On every side one may see San Francisco and the cities across the Bay in a perfect beauty that only night can give them. Not a hint of commerce, business big and little, crime, hatreds, despair, greed, magnificence, or poverty. From Twin Peaks to Mount Diablo, from North Beach to the southernmost rim of the city, broken only by the Bay, one looks down upon a multiplicity of glittering lights—no, not quite unbroken, for that sea of glorified fireflies is diversified by a skyscraper here and there that looks like a huge Christmas tree illuminated from base to crown, and the Bay Bridge, the Golden Gate Bridge are two necklaces of lights as round and as brilliant as the lamps of Aladdin. And there are scattered lights on [Mount] Tamalpais, among the redwoods at its base, on the islands of the Bay.

—Gertrude Atherton, from *My San Francisco: A Wayward Biography* (1946)

"Go to it, boy." As ever I strode on behind him and when we began to climb, with our packs feeling good on our backs as though we were pack animals and didn't feel right without a burden, it was that same old lonesome old good old thwap thwap up the trail, slowly, a mile an hour. We came to the end of the steep road where we had to go through a few houses built near steep bushy cliffs with waterfalls trickling down, then up to a high steep meadow, full of butterflies and hay and a little seven a.m. dew, and down to a dirt road, then to the end of the dirt road, which rose higher and higher till we could see vistas of Corte Madera and Mill Valley far away and even the red top of Golden Gate Bridge.

"Tomorrow afternoon on our run to Stinson Beach," said Japhy, "you'll see the whole white city of San Francisco miles away in the blue bay. Ray, by God, later on in our future life we can have a fine free-wheeling tribe in these California hills, get girls and have dozens of radiant enlightened brats, live like Indians in hogans and eat berries and buds."

"No beans?"

"We'll write poems, we'll get a printing press and print our own poems, the Dharma Press, we'll poetize the lot and make a fat book of icy bombs for the booby public."

"Ah the public ain't so bad, they suffer too. You always read about some tarpaper shack burning somewhere in the Middlewest with three little children perishing and you see a picture of the parents crying. Even the kitty was burnt. Japhy, do you think God made the world to amuse himself because he was bored? Because if so he would have to be mean."

"Ho, who would you mean by God?"

"Just Tathagata, if you will."...

"What are you thinking about?"

"Just makin' up poems in my head as I climb toward Mount Tamalpais. See up there ahead, as beautiful a mountain as you'll see anywhere in the world, a beautiful shape to it, I really love Tamalpais. We'll sleep tonight way around the back of it. Take us till late afternoon to get there."

The Marin country was much more rustic and kindly than the rough Sierra country we'd climbed last fall: it was all flowers, flowers, trees, bushes, but also a great deal of poison oak by the side of the trail. When we got to the end of the high dirt road we suddenly plunged into the dense redwood forest and went along following a pipeline through glades that were so deep the fresh morning sun barely penetrated and it was cold and damp. But the odor was pure deep rich pine and wet logs. Japhy was all talk this morning. He was like a little kid again now that he was out on the trail. "The only thing wrong with that monastery shot in Japan for me, is, though for all their intelligence and good intentions, the Americans out there, they have so little real sense of America and who the people are who really dig Buddhism here, and they don't have any use for poetry."

"Who?"

"Well, the people who are sending me out there and finance things. They spend their good money fixing elegant scenes of gardens and books and Japanese architecture and all that crap which nobody will like or be able to use anyway but rich American divorcees on Japanese cruises and all they really should do is just build or buy an old Jap house and vegetable garden and have a place there for cats to hang out in and be Buddhists, I mean have a real flower of something and not just the usual American middleclass fuggup with appearances. Anyway I'm looking forward to it, oh boy I can just see myself in the morning sitting on the mats with a low table at my side, typing on my portable, and my hibachi nearby with a pot of hot water on it keeping hot and all my papers and maps and pipe and flashlight neatly packed away and outside plum trees and pines with snow on the boughs and up on Mount Hieizan the snow getting deep and sugi and hinoki all around, them's redwoods, boy, and cedars. Little tucked-away temples down the rocky trails, cold mossy ancient places where frogs croak, and inside small statues and hanging buttery lamps and gold lotuses and paintings and ancient incense-soaked smells and lacquer chests with statues." His boat was leaving in two days. "But I'm sad too about leaving California [...] s'why I wanted to take one last long look at it today with ya, Ray."

We came up out of the glady redwood forest onto a road, where there was a mountain lodge, then crossed the road and dipped down again through bushes to a trail that probably nobody even knew was there except a few hikers, and we were in Muir Woods. It extended, a vast valley, for miles before us. An old logger road led us for two miles then Japhy got off and scrambled up the slope and got onto another trail nobody dreamed was there. We hiked on this one, up and down along a tumbling creek, with fallen logs again where you crossed the creek, and sometimes bridges that had been built Japhy said by the Boy Scouts, trees sawed in half the flat surface for walking. Then we climbed up a steep pine slope and came out to the highway and went up the side of a hill of grass and came out in some outdoor theater, done up Greek style with stone seats all around a bare stone arrangement for four-dimensional presentations of Aeschylus and Sophocles. We drank water and sat down and took our shoes off and watched the silent play from the upper stone seats. Far away you could see the Golden Gate Bridge and the whiteness of San Francisco.

Japhy began to shriek and hoot and whistle and sing, full of pure gladness....What hope, what human energy, what truly American optimism was packed in that neat little frame of his! There he was clomping along in front of me on the trail and shouting back "Try the meditation of the trail, just walk along looking at the trail at your feet and don't look about and just fall into a trance as the ground zips by."

We arrived at Laurel Dell camp at about ten, it was also supplied with stone fireplaces with grates, and picnic tables, but the surroundings were infinitely more beautiful than Potrero Meadows. Here were the real meadows: dreamy beauties with soft grass sloping all around, fringed by heavy deep green timber, the whole scene of waving grass and brooks and nothing in sight....

At noon we started for the beach. It was a tremendously grinding trip. We climbed way up high on meadows, where again we could see San Francisco far away, then dipped down into a steep trail that seemed to fall directly down to sea level; you had sometimes to run down the trail or slide on your back, one. A torrent of water fell down at the side of the trail. I went ahead of Japhy and began swinging down the trail so fast, singing happily, I left him behind about a mile and had to wait for him at the bottom. He was taking his time enjoying the ferns and flowers. We stashed our rucksacks in the fallen leaves under bushes and hiked freely down the sea meadows and past seaside farmhouses with cows browsing, to the beach community, where we bought wine in a grocery store and stomped on out into the sand and the waves. It was a chill day with only occasional flashes of sun. But we were making it. We jumped into the ocean in our shorts and swam swiftly around then came out and spread some of our salami and Ry-Krisp and cheese on a piece of paper in the sand and drank wine and talked....

THE NORTHWEST
AND SHASTA COUNTRY

T hink of the Northwest and Shasta country as forming a broad upside-down fishhook, stretching hundreds of miles through the coastal range north of the Bay Area, curving inland through the southern Cascades, and ending in a short prong of volcanic land just past Lassen Peak (also known as Mount Lassen) on the Modoc Plateau. These diverse terrains include some of the most rugged and inaccessible landscapes in the West.

For many, the mystical center of this region is Mount Shasta, a 14,162-foot volcano at the southern end of the Cascade Range. Though not as tall as the highest Sierra Nevada peaks, the snow-capped, almost-perfect pyramid rises "grand and solitary above a vast volcanic plain, dominating the landscape for a hundred miles," in the words of Charis Weston. Naturally this mountain has inspired legends (more than any other natural landmark, according to Philip Fradkin). One story tells how Coyote's salmon was stolen by yellow jackets and hidden inside it: the volcano smoked the fish and scattered it to the four winds, demonstrating the earth's life-sustaining power.

Northwest of Mount Shasta lie Shasta Valley and then the Klamath Mountains, which are cut by three rivers—the still-wild Smith, draining the Siskiyou Mountains in the north; the Klamath in the Salmon and Marble Mountains; and the Trinity in the southern Trinity Alps. South of these mountains the northern section of the Coast Range parallels the Pacific Ocean down to the Bay Area. The western slopes of these mountains catch heavy fogs rolling in from the sea. Coastal redwoods thrive in this atmosphere, growing over three hundred feet tall and creating an ethereal canopy above streams and rivers marked by deep, clear pools, with luxuriant ferns clinging to their banks and spilling onto trails. State and national parks now protect some old-growth redwoods and the wildlife they shelter. But these northern forests have been logged for over a century: Eureka and Arcata on Humboldt Bay became important lumber centers almost as soon as they were founded in 1850.

The Coast Range below the Klamath Mountains—also cut by three rivers, the Mad, the Eel, and the Russian—is separated from Mount Shasta by the upper reaches of yet another river, the Sacramento. Adjacent, however, is the perfect place to view Shasta's still-steaming cone: Castle Crags, a devil's playground of ominous gray spires rising above the surrounding forest. Until 1852, a convoluted granite crag now called Castle Rock was known as Devil's Castle. The name, which reflected the white settlers' feelings and echoed more ancient sentiments, was a rare instance of accord between natives and white settlers.

Northeast of Shasta is another unique feature: an ancient lava flow, bounded in the east by the lofty Warner Range. The Modoc Plateau, as the volcanic uplands are known, remains almost uninhabited: fewer than ten thousand people live in all of Modoc County, over four thousand square miles, comprising most of California's northeast corner. The grassland and sagebrush covering much of the region make it look arid, but many fresh and hot springs percolate through its porous lava. Some of this water flows into the Pit River and gets carried along with rain and snowmelt to artificial Shasta Lake, which supplies the Central Valley. Underground reservoirs also surface in the rivulets feeding Burney Falls, near the western edge of the plateau. Burney Creek provides the main flow for this 129-foot cascade, but numerous smaller streams also pour through the fern-covered cliff face, rendering an effect so spectacular that Teddy Roosevelt called it the "eighth wonder of the world." The falls are flanked by firs, oaks, cedars, and pines, creating one of the area's few scattered forests.

Northern California includes territories originally inhabited by many native groups. In the west lived the Shasta, Karuk, Wintu, Yurok, Pomo, and Coast Miwok; in the east, the Northern Paiute, the Maidu, the Achumawi, the Atsugewi, and the fierce Modoc. Early European exploration barely touched their lands. Much of the region remained under native stewardship while Mexico controlled California. Under native care, the land provided abundantly: there were salmon and steelhead in the northern rivers; small game and oaks in the Eel and Russian river valleys; mussels, fish, and sea lions along the coast. Some of the native people built boats—dug out from redwood logs or woven from tule—for gathering food, but they were careful to ensure that life remained in balance.

Things changed drastically soon after U.S. settlers began to move through and into the region. In 1828 explorer Jedediah Smith, on his second foray into California, led his men through the northern redwoods into Oregon. Commodore Charles Wilkes, commander of a major U.S. scientific expedition, sent a party to explore the upper Sacramento River in 1841. And in 1849 gold miners arrived to search for riches in the northwest's many streams, bringing none of the native's regard for natural resources. Transplanted Oregonian Joaquin Miller, so-called poet of the Sierra, wrote of miners along Soda Creek who turned the world "upside down. The rivers ran dark and sullen with sand and slime. The fishes turned on their sides and died." Starving Native Americans soon clashed with miners. Their skirmishes culminated in the Modoc War of 1872 when Kientepoos, also called Captain Jack, defied the U.S. Army by refusing to live on reservation lands. He and a small band of followers holed up on the lava beds south of Tule Lake, inflicting heavy casualties on pursuing soldiers until he was captured, tried, and hanged.

As hostilities waned, ranchers joined miners in the area, and cattle began foraging in the flooded alluvial meadows of the northeast. Judging from at least one anonymous ballad, life for northern cowboys could be grim:

> Used to be a ranch hand, I could rope or ride;
> Here in Modoc County I'm just froze or fried.

Cowboys or not, the writers of this rugged and isolated region have been an independent lot, making for an eclectic assortment of literary advocates. Native American Darryl Babe Wilson gives old Pit River tales a contemporary tone. An unlikely pair of writers, Mary Ellicot Arnold and Mabel Reed—"Field Matrons in the U.S. Indian Service"—describe life with the Karuks along the Klamath and Salmon rivers. Abandoning the literary circles of San Francisco, Charles Warren Stoddard visits the Russian River to savor the solitary timelessness of life among the redwoods. Nonconformist Richard Brautigan has a fresh take on the rivers of Northern California, while naturalist David Rains Wallace spins an unusual story about the web of life in its interior.

As for descriptions of Mount Shasta, sacred to many of the Native Americans living nearby, one of its first celebrations was penned by a non-Californian, a Cherokee drawn to California by the gold rush—

especially ironic given the usual enmity between natives and forty-niners. Yellow Bird, also known as John Rollin Ridge, included his poem about Mount Shasta in his *Life and Adventures of Joaquín Murietta,* the first Native American novel. Ridge's 1852 poem declared of Mount Shasta that "no human foot hath stained its snowy side." But only two years later the first recorded ascent took place, and soon after a description of an 1855 climb—attributed to Israel S. Diehl—appeared in *Scenes of Wonder and Curiosity in California,* the booster's tract by James M. Hutchings. Until geologist Clarence King surveyed Mount Shasta's flanks, however, the mountain's glaciated landscape had not been fully recognized. King's detailed portrayal sets the stage for Joaquin Miller's 1900 dramatic depiction of a wilderness in flames.

Mount Shasta is still amazing. Maybe this is because it draws its own weather, as Philip Fradkin tells us; maybe because it really is a spiritual center. Whatever your beliefs, the mountain and the country around it stand out among California's natural treasures, and will undoubtedly continue to attract and inspire.

Darryl Babe Wilson

Born in Pit River country (in Fall River Mills, where the Fall meets the Pit), son of an Achumawi mother and an Atsugewi father, Darryl Babe Wilson (1939–) feels a special connection to his native land, "from Ako-Yet (Mount Shasta) and Wai-ko-qu (Mount Lassen) east to Watak-josi (the Warner Mountains stretching between California and Oregon)." More interested in nature than in school, Wilson spent much of his childhood hunting and fishing with his father. When his mother and a younger brother were killed in a collision with a logging truck, the family fell apart and Wilson found himself in foster care. In high school, Wilson's English teacher helped convince him to become a writer, an idea that inspired him to "study harder and with more conviction." Despite further heartbreak—the mother of Wilson's young twin sons was also killed in an auto accident—Wilson went on to earn a B.A. from the University of California, Davis, and a Ph.D. from the University of Arizona, Tucson.

Author of essays, reviews, and short stories, Wilson has been widely published in academic and literary journals. He has also edited two books: Dear Christopher, *a collection of letters addressed to Columbus, and* Voices from the Earth, *an anthology of interviews with Native Americans. His recent memoir,* The Morning the Sun Went Down, *tells of his life growing up in northeastern California.* Gedin Ch-Lum-Nu *(Let It Be This Way) is Wilson's retelling of a traditional tale.* ✍

Gedin Ch-Lum-Nu

In the teachings of my elders, such as Craven Gibson (he is from the Big Valley, which is in the heart of the Pit River country, and claimed that he was born on Alcatraz island in about 1855), there is the story of the time when the Hawaiian people were visiting the coast of California.

Their huge lumja-wi (canoe) broke apart on the rocks, and they struggled to the shore. For many, many years they wandered the Coast Range and the huge Sacramento–San Joaquin valley. Eventually their wandering brought them inland, and they somehow found their way over the Sierra Nevada range and into the land of my people, the A-juma-wi. The land of my people lies in the northeastern corner of California. It is just south of the Modoc. The Warner Range separates us from the Paiutes, Eagle Lake and Mount Lassen comprise the southern boundary, and Mount Lassen and Mount Shasta are our western "cornerstones."

Upon viewing Bo-ma-rhee (the Fall River Valley), they immediately fell in love with the earth and the people because both reminded them so much of their homeland in Hawaii. They settled and mingled with my people. Ako-Yet (Mount Shasta) stood guard over them at night, A-juma (the big river) sang to them as they dreamed and upon waking greeted them with a fresh song. The winds moved softly through their spirits. Fall brought many shades of rainbow colors to the earth. There was the distinct call of the traveling goose, magic migrations of fleeting deer, and splashing rivers of salmon.

Winter, something of a miracle to them, made the land clean and cold, carpeted as if with powdered diamonds. Trees were fat and white with heaps of snow that tumbled to earth in clouds of cold dust when a branch was touched. Stars were frozen in the silent cold. Warm fire was most welcome. Long nights were filled with songs and lessons and legends and dreams.

Spring was a solid carpet of chartreuse, and the forest was an orchestra of blossom-flavored bird songs. The people prepared to live. They readied

Place names; the significance of a particular area; the favorite or customary hunting, fishing, and gathering and harvesting places; permanent and temporary living sites; the tiny villages; the caves; the hidden trails; the exact locale of a bear fight, a massacre, a close escape—all these became as real to the white men as they already were to Ishi. Here you swung down on a rope to the creek far below and returned to the bank above without risk of being seen; here were the ashes from a funeral pyre; in this cave were buried the bones of the ancestral dead, this a place no living Yahi in Ishi's time had ever disturbed. The memories crowded one on another—here and here and here—the ordinary day-to-day comings and goings, the route of the last retreat, and the agony and chaos of the dispersal.

—Theodora Kroeber, from *Ishi in Two Worlds: A Biography of the Last Wild Indian in North America* (1961)

to hunt dok (jackrabbits) and do-se (deer) and to work the big river for allis (salmon) and sal (mussels). It was an exciting time of ceremonies greeting another season and a preparation for the approaching phases of all of the seasons of their lives. In this manner the people prepared to live forever.

In summer they lounged in the dark shade of the tall forests or swam in the churning, sometimes whispering river. They gathered apas (sweet roots the size of your little finger, growing just below the ground) in the meadow and nuts from the pines. When they gathered sal and ali wakqa (freshwater clams), the Hawaiians remembered the shellfish of their homeland. Often they sang their songs of the sea when pearls were beneath the ripples, rolling with the sands.

Happiness seemed to be everywhere.

Children laughed, dogs barked, elders dreamed, council gathered, lessons were remembered and taught by the fire. Life was good. But to the Hawaiians this was not home. It was very similar, except for the powdery winter snows. It was a good land. It was a good time of their life. They should have been happy.

But they were not dancing upon their own land. They were feasting, but not upon their own food. They were dreaming, but not dreaming the same dreams as they did in their homeland. Their children laughed and ran and played, but they were not doing all of these things upon their own earth.

There was something missing. They knew that they must return to their homeland or their songs and dances, their traditions and their customs, their language and their lessons would perish. Should these things disappear, they would have no purpose upon the earth—they would vanish, too!

This was a serious decision because some Hawaiians of A-juma-wi blood would have to go, and some A-juma-wis of Hawaiian blood would have to stay. Families were to be divided. Earth ceased breathing.

There was a thick quiet over the land. The smoke from the fire climbed into the sky, then spread across the blue, making a cloud canopy. Fire was worried. Ako-Yet leaned over the council and listened. The winds of the forest were silent, and the forest leaned and listened also. Birds and butterflies no longer fluttered in the brush but listened quietly. The hawk and the eagle hovered high over the council, suspended in time and space, and listened. The deer always listen, but on this day their listening was intense. You could touch their listening with the finger of your hand. Bear looked with small eyes upon the gathered people and Bear, too, listened. Earth was silent. Then, from the west, like a distant drum singing, a decision approached.

At the great council, as the A-juma-wi watched, the Hawaiians danced their dance of loneliness for their home. As they danced, they sang a song of the winds and of the pearls resting in the heart of the sea. They sang of swaying trees and of the bright and wholesome sun that bathed and warmed the earth. They sang of the moon rising over the vast ocean and of the silver trail that leads to the center of its heart. They sang of the vast panorama of stars that had no mountains to interfere with their vision. They sang of the earth, the people—and the children with flowers in their hair. They sang of the sterling laughter that can be heard from nations dwelling only upon their very precious land as children run with excited life beating in their hearts.

With one huge heart, the people of Hawaii and my people wept.

The decision was made. Gathered in council were the elders of the Hawaiians and the elders of the A-juma-wi. Their decision was painful but swift—like an arrow to the heart of your spirit.

In the silence, our silver-haired grandfather stood strong in the presence of all the world and in the face of the sun. His hair rippled in the soft winds, his cloudy eyes peered into an unknown time. With a trembling in his husky voice, he said loudly so everything could hear, "The Hawaiian people must return to their island home."

He hesitated for a moment. A tear came from his heart and watered the earth with a splash that the world still remembers. Softly he said, "Now is the proper time for the council to gather for the last time to make decisions."

It was decided that A-poni-ha (Cocoonman, one of the earth makers) would travel to the top of Ako-Yet and gather power so he could help the Hawaiians and those of mixed blood return to their warm islands of sand and sunshine. Cocoonman said, "Dupt-da!" which means, in our language, "We are going!"

He led the departing people to the land of the Kashaya Pomo. After explaining his purpose there and asking permission, he constructed a small fire. The Hawaiians, not knowing of the power within Cocoonman or the power within Ako-Yet, wondered how they were to return to their island, which was very far away. There was a vast ocean between them and their island. Their lumja-wi was smashed by the waves long ago, and it had washed away. They had no lumja-wi to replace it. Neither, it seemed, was

Cocoonman concerned with a lumja-wi! How was a small fire and a song going to get them back to their homeland, as the council had instructed?

The A-juma-wi and some mixed-blood people stayed in our land with sad hearts. But animals and birds were permitted to follow the departing people as Cocoonman led them across the mountains, across the wide valley and over the ocean range to the land of the Kashaya Pomo. One animal and one bird, one of everything, was there to witness this event. They were the messengers back to their own "people" so that all of life would know this story.

Cocoonman sang a little song to the spirits of the universe and to the spirits that dwell far, far beyond the farthest stars. He sprinkled into the fire the blossoms of the sage and the pollen of the pine, the flowers of the valley and the perfume of the plum, the dust of the grasses and the lichen from the highest rock of the great mountain Ako-Yet.

From that little fire there arched a beautiful, intense rainbow. It reached from the land of the Kashaya Pomo to the heart of the islands known as Hawaii. It was powerful. It was beautiful. The Hawaiians were frightened, as they had not yet fully understood the power of the song, the power of the mountain and the land, the power of Cocoonman, or the power of the final decision of the council.

Cocoonman invited the Hawaiians to walk across the rainbow and return to their homeland. They dared not! Cocoonman then walked upon the rainbow to show them it was solid and firm. They refused!

His duty, decided by the council, was to assist the Hawaiian people back to their homeland—safely, not full of fright. He sang a song and dreamed a dream, and in a brilliant flash his dream gave him instructions.

Cocoonman positioned himself and extended his left hand toward Hawaii—to where the end of the rainbow touched the earth. Then he extended his right hand back across the land of the Kashaya Pomo and said, "Gedin ch-lum-nu." In the language of my precious people this means, "Let it be this way."

Instantly a land the width of two grown men removed itself from the earth and lay across the waters, a bridge breathing upon the ocean to the end of the rainbow. Cocoonman then walked upon this bridge to show the gathered people that it was sturdy. They could walk upon earth, but they dared not walk upon the rainbow for the fear of falling through. Still, they were not certain about the end of the bridge, whether it reached their islands.

Cocoonman then instructed Yas (Weasel) to walk with them to their home. Yas fashioned a flute from a reed that he found in the nearby stream, tuned it to his satisfaction, and began playing soft music. Cocoonman tended the fire and continued singing the song to all of the powers of all of the universe.

As Yas played, he danced, and his dance led him to the rainbow bridge, and he floated upon it like a hawk landing upon a pine limb. He then walked across that beautiful bridge high in the sky. As he walked the rainbow path, he played the flute. As he walked the rainbow path, the Hawaiians walked the land bridge far below, without fear. And the music that came from the flute was so beautiful that it was heard all around the world.

As Yas moved into the distance, the music dimmed. Soon the music could be heard growing louder. Yas returned. He stepped off the rainbow and placed the reed back in the stream so it would continue to grow beautiful music forever.

The Hawaiians were safely home. The land bridge returned to the mainland. The rainbow returned to the fire. The Kashaya Pomo returned to their homes. The birds and animals returned to their domains, and the songs and the music returned to silence and peace.

Alone, Cocoonman glided like the thick shadow of a great eagle. He floated across the snowcapped mountains and over the valleys, observing everything. He remembered again and again the departure of the people. Something soft caught in his throat.

He settled at the base of Ako-Yet, folded up there, knelt before Mis Misa[1] and, because he had, for the second time in his existence, accomplished the impossible, trembled.[2]

A very old Grandfather of the Pit River Nation, Craven Gibson, told me this story in 1971 under an immeasurable vastness of frozen stars in the

---

1. Mis Misa is the small power that dwells deep within Ako-Yet. It balances the earth with the universe and the universe with the earth. Like a pendulum, it shifts each time Great Wonder stirs the vastness with that immense yet invisible ja-pilo-o (canoe paddle). As is its assigned purpose, Mis Misa keeps us in balance with all that there is.

2. The first time Cocoonman "accomplished the impossible" was when he helped make the world. At this point he realized that he had received, as a gift upon his birth, an amazing power to create

heart of winter (this has also been told by Ramsey Bone Blake and Wes Cline). He had always wanted to go to wade in the warm waters of Hawaii and look for pearls, especially when the winter winds whipped through the cracks of his little home and howled during the winter night like a pack of desperate wolves. He said that we are all related, the Hawaiians and the A-juma-wi, and to prove it there is a way:

Take a handful of earth from Hawaii
and rub it on the A-juma-wi
and the dirt and the skin will remain the same hue.

Take a handful of earth from A-juma-wi
and rub it on the Hawaiian
and the dirt and the skin will remain the same hue..

Mary Ellicott Arnold
and Mabel Reed

In the year 1908 Mary Ellicott Arnold (1876–1968) and Mabel Reed (18_–19_) stood on the deck of the SS Pomona *as it sailed through the Golden Gate bound for Eureka, where they planned to take up appointments as "Field Matrons in the U.S. Indian Service, Department of the Interior." They knew next to nothing about the country, even less about the people who lived there, and still less about their official duties. "I think," said the local Indian agent upon their arrival, "the government's idea of appointing field matrons is that women will have a civilizing influence." In the two years they spent among the Karuk Indians near the Klamath and Salmon rivers, they did not observe much need for this: "An Indian characteristic that impressed us very much," they commented later, "was what we would call good breeding, a code of manners and feeling that stood out in sharp contrast to the lower social level of the average pioneer white man."*

At the end of every day, they each wrote down a record of events and compared the two accounts so that they could arrive "at a true statement of what our friends had said and done in the Indian country in the year 1909, in what was called the roughest place in the United States." In the Land of the Grasshopper Song *is Arnold and Reed's memoir of their life "on the rivers," where in the sixty miles between Happy Camp and Orleans, they were "the only white women, and most of the time quite scared enough to satisfy anybody." Their clear, forceful prose conveys a vivid impression of this rugged, unspoiled landscape. The following selection is from the chapter entitled "We Cross Marble Mountain and Find the Indian Ain't Got No Chance in White Men's Country."* 🪶

from In the Land of the Grasshopper Song

At long last we are to see Marble Mountain. Ever since we came to the Rivers, they have told us of Marble Mountain. It lies in a jumble of mountains somewhere between the Klamath and Scott's Valley, and famous packers like Mr. Hilding pass over it as they cross the mountains with supplies, instead of taking the long way around, by the Forks of Salmon and Sawyer's Bar. Now Mr. Mortsoff has written us from Hoopa that an Indian in Scott's Valley is in some trouble with the whites. He thinks it is in regard to land, and he asks us, when it is convenient, please to look into the matter.

Of course, we could go the long way around, but it would be both cheaper and pleasanter to take Steve and Annie as guides and cross the mountains. Steve's interest in the trip mounted when he learned that we planned to go to Etna. "We might get to ride in a buggy," he said hopefully.

We think he must mean a spring wagon. Few of the older Indians on the Rivers have ever ridden in a wagon. I do not think Steve has ever been in one. We had hoped to get off the day after the Fourth but for two days Steve has been off hunting for the mules. Steve found them in Orleans. Now they are back; and we are off for Marble Mountain the first thing in the morning. Everything is ready and all is smooth sailing except White Puppy.

We do not know why the Hickoxes called him White Puppy. He is not white and he most certainly is not a puppy. He is a large, rangy dog, with long hair and pointer blood, and we don't know how many different ancestors. He belongs to Luther Hickox. On the days when we have been in Ossi-puk, White Puppy got in the habit of dropping in for breakfast. We would find him lying outside the front door when we opened it in the morning. Still, we looked on him as only a casual acquaintance.

But the last school day in Ossi-puk, when we saddled the mules to ride upriver, White Puppy fell in behind us. That would never do. That would never, never do. Our relations with Luther have been of the pleasantest, but we were doubtful whether he would think well of us as dog stealers. We yelled at White Puppy and told him to go home. We continued to yell until we saw White Puppy trotting up the trail toward the Hickoxes. Then we settled back in our saddles and thumped along upriver. We stopped a minute at Mark-faced Steve's. We were just out of sight of his cabin when we saw something move in the bushes behind us. It came out of the bushes and wagged its tail. It was White Puppy.

This was serious. We got off the mules and threw rocks at White Puppy. Big ones. Mark-faced Steve came up and joined us and also threw rocks. White Puppy disappeared. We rode on. As we drew into Ronell's Creek, there, lying on the trail waiting for us, was White Puppy. We got off our mules and beat White Puppy. Old-Woman-from-Ronell's-Creek came out and helped us throw rocks. She also told White Puppy just what we thought of him in Indian. It was plain from White Puppy's expression that his feelings were hurt. He put his tail between his legs and drew back out of sight. Then he footed up the situation. He took up a position about a quarter of a mile behind the mules. When we looked ahead, he would creep up closer to the mules. When we looked behind, he would disappear from sight. He was on the trail, waiting for us, when we turned down toward the corral at I-ees-i-rum. He is now on the porch with a loaf of stale bread inside him and a benign expression. We plan to send him back to Luther by the mail-rider. He is to be securely tied up tonight and handed over to Mr. Wright in the morning. For the big day has come, and we are off for Marble Mountain a little before daylight.

All last evening we spent planning the trip with Steve. What we should pack. Where we should camp. Then I thought of something Sandy Bar Tom had told us.

"Plenty of panther up on Marble Mountain?" I asked Steve.

"*Ha,*" said Steve abstractedly.

"Going to pack your gun?" I asked a few minutes later.

Steve shook his head.

"Maybe good to have a gun, Steve, if there are so many panthers?" I said encouragingly.

Steve made no answer. After a while he said, "I guess I ain't take no gun."

I sat up. "Steve, why won't you take your gun?" I asked urgently.

Steve sat for a few minutes, looking thoughtful. "Cost too much money," he said finally.

"What do you mean, cost too much money?" said Mabel, coming into the conversation.

"Well," said Steve sadly, "last time I pack my gun, I got to pay four hundred dollars."

Dear, dear. Four dead men. No wonder Steve has a reputation on the Rivers. Maybe, after all, it is better that we should not press the question.

We were up a little before light, breakfasting on coffee and corn pones, when Steve came over to ask if we were ready. The river was so low that he was going to ford the animals, and Jetty had come over to help him. Pete was going to put us across and then take the dugout back to the I-ees-i-rum side. But as the dugout swung into the current, there was something swimming strongly beside it. It couldn't be. Yes, it was White Puppy.

"Pete," we cried, "you promised us to have that dog securely tied up."

"I tie him," said Pete serenely. "I think maybe he get loose."

We struck at White Puppy with the paddle. From the bank, Steve threw rocks at him. Like ourselves, Steve did not care to put too much strain on Luther's good nature. White Puppy dodged the paddle and swam the river a little farther downstream. He evaded Pete's efforts to catch him and was waiting for us when the mules commenced the climb.

It was a climb of nine miles to the top of the first ridge. The trail was obscure. In some places it was no trail at all. It was lucky we had not tried to make it alone. The ground was covered with fallen tree trunks, and across these the mules had to pick their way. You jumped what you could, and when you could not jump you painfully made your way around them. All traces of a trail disappeared. We saw Steve glance around thoughtfully and then look up at the mountain to get his bearings. He chose the easiest lie of ground and we made our own trail.

Every now and then we caught glimpses of the valley and saw the Klamath, now far below us. Then the Klamath and the river valley were gone, and we came out into a great stretch of manzanita and snowbush. There was no sign of any trail, and the bush was so high I could only follow Pet and Daisy and Mr. Darcy, who were ahead of me, by the movements of the top branches of the bush. Sometimes I would catch a glimpse of a head bobbing along, but when it disappeared beneath the bush I would have to follow as best I could. Later, we passed the famous Hay Press Meadows, where five hundred head of cattle can pasture, and then we began to climb again.

We were now following along a ridge upon which some indications of trail appeared. This ridge grew narrower and narrower, until there were only a few high peaks above us. Annie was the first up, then Mabel, and I followed her. On every side were mountains. We were on the top of the world. To our right, lay something that looked like a white cloud.

"Salmon summit," said Steve. "Plenty snow."

Farther on, there was the unmistakable white cone of Shasta, first misty and obscure and then shining out, white and glorious, against a clear blue sky. The trail lay directly along the top of the ridge. The mountains changed as different ridges were lost or came into sight. But hour after hour there was the seemingly limitless expanse. As the shape of the ridges changed or came into view, every mountain we had seen on the Rivers also came into view and then was lost again. Sheldon's Butte, which we see from Orleans. Then the white peak that we tried to photograph at Happy Camp appeared in faint outline on our left. Then Bald Mountain, just below Hoopa.

"That one," said Steve pointing, "he last one before ocean."

As we rode in single file, Mabel pointed to some white rock below the trail.

"Is that marble?" she asked Steve.

"No," said Steve disgustedly. "He snow."

It was snow. At I-ees-i-rum, now far below us, it would be one hundred degrees in the shade. I scrambled down the cliff, wanting to hold some of the snow in my hand. I need not have taken the trouble, for soon it lay on every side of us. At one place the snow was so deep on the trail that we had to get off the mules and walk across it with considerable care, for if anyone slipped on that trail there was no telling where he would end up.

We thought of Ossi-puk and Orleans baking in the heat. We scuffed our feet in the snow and gazed out over the snowcapped peaks on all sides of us.

Annie, on Pet, was well ahead of us, but Steve was some distance behind. Evidently Steve did not intend to stop for lunch. We took a few crackers out of our saddlebags and munched as we rode. Steve called out that Cuddihy's, one of the few camping places in the mountains, lay right ahead of us. As he spoke, there was a hail from just below us, and George McCash and his sister joined us. They had started the night before and had camped in the Hay Press Meadows.

Steadily at the heels of the mules trotted White Puppy. When the entire party rode close together, White Puppy would take the lead. But when the party separated, and Mabel and I rode by ourselves, White Puppy would take up his station at Mr. Darcy's tail, between Mabel and myself. He was polite to the Indians, but that was all. White Puppy was our dog, and he wanted to be sure that everything was as it should be.

Annie had fallen behind with Steve, and George McCash now rode in the lead. George had no illusions in regard to panthers on Marble Mountain, and he packed a gun. On his last trip across, George had a sharp brush with a panther. He told us how scared he had been and all the things he did that he should not have done, and we laughed so hard we quite forgot to notice that George had not only killed the panther, but that he had held a badly frightened horse and a lantern with his other hand and had shot the panther in the eye, in the shifting light. No mean feat for any man. As we thought about the panther, we were very glad to have George with us. And especially glad that he had his gun. But I did look a little doubtfully at the way George carried his gun. Its muzzle was trained on me. Not exactly on my eye, but right smack on my abdomen. As George jolted along and the gun jolted along, I could see quite clearly down the muzzle. I did not want to bother George with such a small detail, but if George's horse were to stumble, and the gun were to go off, aimed, as it was, right at me, I couldn't help feeling it would be a pity.

The country was changing. We passed beautiful, clear, green lakes, far, far below us. They might easily have been a couple of miles down. Green grass grew on their shores. Then we sighted a jagged twin peak, standing out from the jumble of mountains. It was white, and flashed in the sun.

"Marble Mountain," said Steve briefly.

Marble Mountain is not really marble. As we came closer to it, we could see that it was light granite color. But it stood away clear from everything else, and flashed more brilliantly in the sun with every mile that lessened the distance to it. We would lose sight of it, and then the trail would wind around and there it would be again, directly ahead of us, white and glistening, the side next to us one great formidable precipice as far down as the eye could see. Later, we rounded this precipice and began to edge our way carefully toward the top. At one place, George made us get off our mules and crawl to the edge, so we could look down. I have never seen such a breathtaking drop. We were not sorry to crawl back again to safety. After that, we drew a little away from the ridge and began winding down a beautiful grassy slope, with the tumbled mountains on every side. They were just beginning to color with the most wonderful pinks and purples when we dropped suddenly into a little dell. There were tall pines around us, and we could hear a trickle of water. This was Cold Springs, where Steve planned to spend the night. We had come fifty miles and had been thirteen hours in the saddle.

Charles Warren Stoddard

Charles Warren Stoddard (1843–1909) came west from New York at twelve and moved right into the best California literary circles. He became a pupil of Louise Amelia Knapp Smith Clappe, also known as Dame Shirley. He knew Mark Twain, Ina Coolbrith, and Bret Harte (who edited a selection of his poems in 1867), and he even met Robert Louis Stevenson. Despite such stellar companions, the restless Stoddard was not satisfied to remain in California. He made many trips elsewhere, which gave him abundant material for his books: South Sea Idyls *about his visit to Tahiti, and* The Lepers of Molokai, *about his two visits to Father Damien's leper colony in Hawaii.*

Stoddard also toured Europe and the Middle East, and he taught at the University of Notre Dame and the Catholic University of America. Back in California, he wrote about his local wanderings. In the Footprints of the Padres *collects some of Stoddard's essays and shows its author to be "a sensitive, observant, slightly mystical, knowledgeable bookworm, curiously transplanted to the California coast in the 1850s," according to Robert L. Gale. In "Primeval California," the bookworm finds himself "at liberty for an indefinite period" and heads for the Russian River.* ✎

from In the Footprints of the Padres

"Primeval California" was inscribed on the knapsack of the Artist, on the portmanteau of Foster, the Artist's chum, and on the flyleaf of the notebook of the Scribe. The luggage of the boisterous trio was checked through to the heart of the Red Woods, where a vacation camp was pitched. The expected "last man" leaped the chasm that was rapidly widening between the city front of San Francisco and the steamer bound for San Rafael, and approached us—the trio above referred to—with a slip of paper in his hand. It was not a subpoena; it was not a dun; it was a round-robin of farewells from a select circle of admirers, wishing us joy, Godspeed, success in art and literature, and a safe return at last.

The wind blew fair; we were at liberty for an indefinite period. In forty minutes we struck another shore and another clime. San Francisco is original in its affectation of ugliness—it narrowly escaped being a beautiful city—and its humble acceptation of a climate which is as invigorating as it is unscrupulous, having a peculiar charm which is seldom discovered until one is beyond its spell. Sailing into the adjacent summer—summer is intermittent in the green city of the West—we passed into the shadow of Mount Tamalpais, the great landmark of the coast. The admirable outline of the mountain, however, was partially obscured by the fog, already massing along its slopes.

The narrow gauge of the N.P.C.R.R. crawls like a snake from the ferry on the bay to the roundhouse over and beyond the hills, but seven miles from the sea-mouth of the Russian River. It turns very sharp corners, and turns them every few minutes; it doubles in its own trail, runs over fragile trestle-work, darts into holes and reappears on the other side of the mountains, roars through strips of redwoods like a rushing wind, skirts the shore of bleak Tomales Bay, cuts across the potato district and strikes the redwoods again, away up among the sawmills at the logging camps, where it ends abruptly on a flat under a hill. And what a flat it is!—enlivened with a first-class hotel, some questionable hostelries, a country store, a post office and livery-stable, and a great mill buzzing in an artificial desert of worn brown sawdust.

Here, after a five hours' ride, we alighted at Duncan's Mills, hard by the river, and with a girdle of hills all about us—high, round hills, as yellow as brass when they are not drenched with fog. In the twilight we watched the fog roll in, trailing its lacelike skirts among the highland forests. How still the river was! Not a ripple disturbed it; there was no perceptible current, for after the winter floods subside, the sea throws up a wall of sand that chokes the stream, and the waters slowly gather until there is volume enough to clear it. Then come the rains and the floods, in which rafts of driftwood and even great logs are carried twenty feet up the shore, and permanently lodged in inextricable confusion.

I remember the day when we had made a pilgrimage to the coast, when from the rocky jaws of the river we looked up the still waters, and saw them slowly gathering strength and volume. The sea was breaking upon the bar without; Indian canoes swung on the tideless stream, filled with industrious occupants taking the fish that await their first plunge into salt water. Every morning we bathed in the unpolluted waters of the river. How fresh and sweet they are—the filtered moisture of the hills, mingled with the distillations from cedar boughs drenched with fogs and dew!

Lounging upon the hotel verandah, turning our backs upon the last vestiges of civilization in the shape of a few guests who dressed for dinner as if it were imperative, we were greeted with mellow heartiness by a hale old backwoodsman, a genuine representative of the primeval. It was Ingram, of Ingram House, Austin Creek, Red Woods, Sonoma County, Primeval California. It was he, with ranch wagon and stalwart steeds. The Artist, who was captain-general of the forces, at once held a consultation with Ingram, whom we will henceforth call the Doctor, for he is a doctor—minus the degrees—of divinity, medicine, and laws, and master of all work; a deer-stalker, rancher, and general utility man; the father of a clever family, and the head of a primeval house.

In half an hour we were jolting, bag and baggage, body and soul, over roads wherein the ruts were filled with dust as fine as flour, fording trout streams, and winding through wood and brake. We passed the old logging camp, with the hills about it blackened and disfigured for life; and the new logging camp, with its stumps still smoldering, its steep slides smoking with the friction of swift-descending logs, the ring of the ax and the vicious buzz of the saw mingled with the shouts of the woodsmen. How industry is devastating that home of the primeval!

Soon the road led us into the very heart of the redwoods, where superb columns stood in groups, towering a hundred and even two hundred feet above our heads! A dense undergrowth of light green foliage caught and held the sunlight like so much spray; the air was charged with the fragrance of wild honeysuckle and resiniferous trees; the jaybird darted through the boughs like a phosphorous flame, screaming his joy to the skies; squirrels fled before us; quails beat a muffled tattoo in the brush; snakes slid out of the road in season to escape destruction.

We soon dropped into the bed of the stream, Austin Creek, and rattled over the broad, strong highway of the winter rains. We bent our heads under

Gripped by the spirit of the forest, I dropped to my knees and began to sob. I sank my fingers into the layer of duff, which smelled so sweet and so rich and so full of layers of life, then lay face down and breathed it in....[Two weeks later, I found out that]...these majestic ancient places which are the holiest of temples, housing more spirituality than any church, were being turned into clear-cuts and mud slides.

—Julia Butterfly Hill, from *Legacy of Luna* (2000)

low-banging boughs, drove into patches of twilight, and out on the other side into the waning afternoon; we came upon a deserted cottage with a great javelin driven through the roof to the cellar; it had been torn from one of the gigantic redwoods and hurled by a last winter's gale into that solitary home. Fortunately no one had been injured, but the inmates had fled in terror, lashed by the driving storm.

We came to Ingram House in the dusk, out of the solitude of the forest into a pine-and-oak opening, the monotony of which was enlivened with a fair display of the primitive necessities of life—a vegetable garden on the right, a rustic barn on the left, a house of "shakes" in the distance, and nine deerhounds braying a deep-mouthed welcome at our approach.

In the rises of the house on the hill-slope is a three-roomed bachelors' hall; here, on the next day, we were cozily domiciled. There were a few guests in the homestead. The boys slept in the granary. The deerhounds held high carnival under our cottage charging at intervals during the night upon imaginary intruders. We woke to the blustering music of the beasts, and thought on the possible approach of bear, panther, California lion, wildcat, 'coon, and polecat; but thought on it with composure, for the hounds were famous hunters, and there was a whole arsenal within reach.

We were waked at 6:30, and come down to the front "stoop" of the homestead. The structure was homemade, with rafters on the outside or inside according to the fancy of the builder; sunshine and storm had stained it grayish brown, and no tint could better harmonize with the background and surroundings. In one corner of the stoop a tin washbasin stood under a waterspout in the sink; there swung the family towels; the public comb, hanging by its teeth to a nail, had seen much service; a piece of brown soap lay in an abalone shell tacked to the wall; a small mirror reflected kaleido-scopical sections of the face, and made up for its want of compass by mul-tiplying one or another feature. We never before ate at the hour of seven as we ate then; then a pipe on the front steps and a frolic with the boys or the dogs would follow, and digestion was well under way before the day's work began. Then the Artist shouldered his knapsack and departed; the lads trudged through the road to school; the women went about the house with untiring energy; the male hands were already making the anvil musical in the rustic smithy, or dragging stock to the slaughter, or busy with the thou-sand and one affairs that comprise the sum and substance of life in a self-sustaining community. We were assured that were war to be declared between the outer world and Ingram House, lying in ambush in the heart of our black forest, we might withstand the siege indefinitely. All that was needful lay at our hands, and yet, a stone's throw away from our shake-built citadel, one loses himself in a trackless wood, whose glades are still untrodden by men, though one sometimes hears the light step of the bronco when Charlie rides forth in search of a strong bull. All work was like play there, because of a picturesque element which predominated over the practical. Woodcutting under the window of the best room, trying out fat in a cauldron or an earth-oven against our cottage, dragging sunburnt straw in a rude sledge down the hillside road, shoeing a neighbor's horse in a circle of homely gossips, hunting to supply the domestic board at the distant market—is this all that Adam and the children of Adam suffer in his fall?

At noon a clarion voice resounded from the kitchen door and sent the echoes up and down the creek. It was the hostess, who, having prepared the dinner, was bidding the guests to the feast. The Artist came in with his sketch, the Chum with his novel, the Scribe with his notebook, followed by the horny-handed sons of toil, whose shoulders were a little rounded and whose minds were seldom, if ever, occupied with any life beyond the hills that walled us in. We sat down at a camp board and ate with relish. The land was flowing with milk and honey; no sooner was the pitcher drained or the plate emptied than each was replenished by the willing hands of our hostess or her boys.

Another smoke under the stoop followed, and then, perhaps, a doze at the cottage, or in one of the dozen rocking chairs about the house, or on the rustic throne hewn from a stump in the grove between the house and the barn. The sun flooded the cañon with hot and dazzling light; the air was spiced with the pungent odor of shrubs; it was time to rest a little before beginning the laborious sports of the afternoon. Later, we all wandered on the banks of the creek and were sure to meet at the swimming pool about four o'clock. Meanwhile the Artist has laid in another study. Foster has finished his tale, and is rocking in a hammock of green boughs; the Scribe has booked a half-dozen fragmentary sentences that will by and by grow into an article, and the boys have come home from school.

By and by we wanted change; the monotony of town life is always more or less interesting; the monotony of country life palls after a season. Change comes over us in a most unexpected guise. Our cañon was decked with the flaming scarlet of the poison oak; these brilliant bits of foliage are the highlights in almost every California landscape, and must satisfy our love of color, in the absence of the Eastern autumnal leaf. The gorgeous shrubs stand out like burning bushes by the roadside, on the hill-slope, in the forest recesses, and almost everywhere. The Artist's chum gave evidence of a special susceptibility to the poison by a severe attack that prostrated him utterly for a while. Yet he stood by us until his vacation came to an end, and, to the last, there was no complaint heard from this martyr to circumstances.

Richard Brautigan

In the 1960s Richard Brautigan (1935–1984) helped to create the New Fiction, penning self-conscious, protean, playful works that explore the limits of traditional storytelling and question the relationship between language and the world. Small press editions of his early work included Trout Fishing in America, *which was already one of the most popular books on college campuses by the time Brautigan found a major publisher (thanks to Kurt Vonnegut, Delacorte Press reprinted three of his novels). Brautigan's vision of industrial society under attack from "Trout Fishing in America Terrorists" appealed to a growing body of readers sensitive to the threat that rampant materialism posed to nature.*

Brautigan died of an apparently self-inflicted gunshot wound in 1984. But during his short lifetime, he published short stories, several collections of poetry, and a number of offbeat, idiosyncratic novels, including A Confederate General from Big Sur *and* In Watermelon Sugar. *But the quirky* Trout Fishing in America *is still his best known and best loved work. This episodic tour-de-force often filters the landscape through unusual, even surreal perspectives—here, a plumber's and a phone-user's.* 🖎

from Trout Fishing in America

Tom Martin Creek

I walked down one morning from Steelhead, following the Klamath River that was high and murky and had the intelligence of a dinosaur. Tom Martin Creek was a small creek with cold, clear water and poured out of a canyon and through a culvert under the highway and then into the Klamath.

I dropped a fly in a small pool just below where the creek flowed out of the culvert and took a nine-inch trout. It was a good-looking fish and fought all over the top of the pool.

Even though the creek was very small and poured out of a steep brushy canyon filled with poison oak, I decided to follow the creek up a ways because I liked the feel and motion of the creek.

I liked the name, too.

Tom Martin Creek.

It's good to name creeks after people and then later to follow them for a while seeing what they have to offer, what they know and have made of themselves.

But that creek turned out to be a real son-of-a-bitch. I had to fight it all the God-damn way: brush, poison oak and hardly any good places to fish, and sometimes the canyon was so narrow the creek poured out like water from a faucet. Sometimes it was so bad that it just left me standing there, not knowing which way to jump.

You had to be a plumber to fish that creek.

After that first trout I was alone in there. But I didn't know it until later....

THE HUNCHBACK TROUT

The creek was made narrow by little green trees that grew too close together. The creek was like 12,845 telephone booths in a row with high Victorian ceilings and all the doors taken off and all the backs of the booths knocked out.

Sometimes when I went fishing in there, I felt just like a telephone repairman, even though I did not look like one. I was only a kid covered with fishing tackle, but in some strange way by going in there and catching a few trout, I kept the telephones in service. I was an asset to society.

It was pleasant work, but at times it made me uneasy. It could grow dark in there instantly when there were some clouds in the sky and they worked their way onto the sun. Then you almost needed candles to fish by, and foxfire in your reflexes.

Once I was in there when it started raining. It was dark and hot and steamy. I was of course on overtime. I had that going in my favor. I caught seven trout in fifteen minutes.

The trout in those telephone booths were good fellows. There were a lot of young cutthroat trout six to nine inches long, perfect pan size for local calls. Sometimes there were a few fellows, eleven inches or so—for the long distance calls.

I've always liked cutthroat trout. They put up a good fight, running against the bottom and then broad jumping. Under their throats they fly the orange banner of Jack the Ripper.

Also in the creek were a few stubborn rainbow trout, seldom heard from, but there all the same, like certified public accountants. I'd catch one every once in a while. They were fat and chunky, almost as wide as they were long. I've heard those trout called "squire" trout.

It used to take me about an hour to hitchhike to that creek. There was a river nearby. The river wasn't much. The creek was where I punched in. Leaving my card above the clock, I'd punch out again when it was time to go home.

I remember the afternoon I caught the hunchback trout.

A farmer gave me a ride in a truck. He picked me up at a traffic signal beside a bean field and he never said a word to me.

His stopping and picking me up and driving me down the road was as automatic a thing to him as closing the barn door, nothing need be said about it, but still I was in motion traveling thirty-five miles an hour down the road, watching houses and groves of trees go by, watching chickens and mailboxes enter and pass through my vision.

Then I did not see any houses for a while. "This is where I get out," I said.

The farmer nodded his head. The truck stopped.

"Thanks a lot," I said.

The farmer did not ruin his audition for the Metropolitan Opera by making a sound. He just nodded his head again. The truck started up. He was the original silent old farmer.

A little while later I was punching in at the creek. I put my card above the clock and went into that long tunnel of telephone booths.

I waded about seventy-three telephone booths in. I caught two trout in a little hole that was like a wagon wheel. It was one of my favorite holes, and always good for a trout or two.

I always like to think of that hole as a kind of pencil sharpener. I put my reflexes in and they came back out with a good point on them. Over a period of a couple of years, I must have caught fifty trout in that hole, though it was only as big as a wagon wheel.

I was fishing with salmon eggs and using a size 14 single egg hook on a pound and a quarter test tippet. The two trout lay in my creel covered entirely by green ferns, ferns made gentle and fragile by the damp walls of telephone booths.

The next good place was forty-five telephone booths in. The place was at the end of a run of gravel, brown and slippery with algae. The run of gravel dropped off and disappeared at a little shelf where there were some white rocks.

One of the rocks was kind of strange. It was a flat white rock. Off by itself from the other rocks, it reminded me of a white cat I had seen in my childhood.

The cat had fallen or been thrown off a high wooden sidewalk that went along the side of a hill in Tacoma, Washington. The cat was lying in a parking lot below.

The fall had not appreciably helped the thickness of the cat, and then a few people had parked their cars on the cat. Of course, that was a long time ago and the cars looked different from the way they look now.

You hardly see those cars any more. They are the old cars. They have to get off the highway because they can't keep up.

That flat white rock off by itself from the other rocks reminded me of that dead cat come to lie there in the creek, among 12,845 telephone booths.

I threw out a salmon egg and let it drift down over that rock and WHAM! a good hit! and I had the fish on and it ran hard downstream, cutting at an angle and staying deep and really coming on hard, solid and uncompromising, and then the fish jumped and for a second I thought it was a frog. I'd never seen a fish like that before.

God-damn! What the hell!

The fish ran deep again and I could feel its life energy screaming back up the line to my hand. The line felt like sound. It was like an ambulance siren coming straight at me, red light flashing, and then going away again and then taking to the air and becoming an air-raid siren.

The fish jumped a few more times and it still looked like a frog, but it didn't have any legs. Then the fish grew tired and sloppy, and I swung and splashed it up the surface of the creek and into my net.

The fish was a twelve-inch rainbow trout with a huge hump on its back. A hunchback trout. The first I'd ever seen. The hump was probably due to an injury that occurred when the trout was young. Maybe a horse stepped on it or a tree fell over in a storm or its mother spawned where they were building a bridge.

There was a fine thing about that trout. I only wish I could have made a death mask of him. Not of his body though, but of his energy. I don't know if anyone would have understood his body. I put it in my creel.

Later in the afternoon when the telephone booths began to grow dark at the edges, I punched out of the creek and went home. I had that hunch-back trout for dinner. Wrapped in cornmeal and fried in butter, its hump tasted sweet as the kisses of Esmeralda.

David Rains Wallace

David Rains Wallace (1945–) wants to "awaken readers to the fact that we remain a part of the biosphere, that we cannot destroy it without destroying ourselves." He takes them into the thick of a detailed landscape to prove his point. His observations have grown into many books: Idle Weeds: The Life of Sandstone Ridge; The Wilder Shore; The Turquoise Dragon; The Quetzal and the Macaw: The Story of Costa Rica's National Parks; *and* The Monkey's Bridge: The Mystery of Evolution in Central America. *His balanced and evocative prose has garnered many awards, including the John Burroughs Medal for Nature Writing for* The Klamath Knot: Explorations of Myth and Evolution, *placing him "among the first rank of science writers."*

Wallace was born in Charlottesville, Virginia, and attended Wesleyan University before graduate study at Columbia and Mills College, where he earned an M.A. in 1974 with a thesis that became his first book, The Dark Range: A Naturalist's Night Notebook. *In it he blends actual encounters with events "from conversations with other observers, from natural history literature, or from conjecture, speculation, and other euphemisms for storytelling." Here he follows a young bear (and others) through the Yolla Bollies, interior mountains forming part of the northern Coast Range.* ❦

from The Dark Range

The Sugar Pine

> For trees, you see, rather conceal themselves in daylight.
> They reveal themselves only after sunset.
> > —Algernon Blackwood, *The Man the Trees Loved*

On a July afternoon the chaparral-covered ridges are even hotter than the foothills. They lack even the dubious shade of the small oaks, and the streambeds are inaccessible at the bottom of steep, brush-covered canyon walls. The brushy slopes are like an endless inferno, but there is an end. Running along the ridgetop is a rim of green, darker than the olive drab of the brush, where the chaparral belt ends as it began—in patches—indicating

89

a change in soil patterns. As the thin clay of the ridge gives way to the deeper, yellowish loam of the Klamath plateau, the chaparral plants are shaded out by the dark rim: the forest of the Transition zone.

It is a dry, spare forest. Ponderosa pines and incense cedars grow in open stands on a mat of needles that is bare and dusty in July. Only in shaded gullies and hollows do denser stands of white fir, big-leaf maple, golden-cup oak, and California black oak grow. Even so, it is a great change to move from the chaparral into the shade of the pines. Under the dustiest, most sun-blasted trees at the edge of the forest there is a breeze and a faint tinge of ice in the air that is entirely absent under the blue oaks of the foothills.

A few hours before the red-tailed hawk frightened the ground squirrels in the foothill pasture, a peculiar black bear sat against one of the trees at the forest's edge idly eating carpenter ants and looking with a certain degree of amazement at the shade. He was about half bear-size and thin enough to be a dog. He was small because he was half grown and thin because his mother had recently disowned him, and he wasn't yet adept at getting food. The peculiar thing about this bear was his fur. On his head and legs it was typically black and glossy, but it grew from his back and sides in long mottled patches of reddish blonde, as if he had been doused with a mixture of peroxide and hair grower. The tendency toward color mutations in black bears is well known; cinnamon-furred black bears are common in California, and striped and spotted individuals have been reported. But this bear seemed to have reached for the limits of aberrance.

He looked at the cool forest shade with surprise because he hadn't known before that morning there was anything else. Since his mother had driven him off, he had wandered around more or less at random. Nobody had told him that black bears stay in the forest. The previous night he had followed a canyon so far that, looking up from the ground on which he had been tracing an intriguing sequence of smells, he noticed that there were no trees at all on the slopes above. He had been in open places before this, but the shaggy shapes of pine or fir had always been nearby.

He had sniffed at this new arrangement of things suspiciously, but the intriguing new odors in the air made him linger despite his uneasiness. Then events had distracted him. A porcupine appeared, another straggler from the woods whose greeting—raised quills and a taciturn grunt—had been familiar enough. He had found ripe manzanita berries and had spent a long time stripping the branches of them, savoring their sweet sourness at the back of his tongue. But after the sun had come up, the place had begun to lose its fascination. Neither the digger pines nor the chaparral plants afforded enough shade for an animal as large and black as a bear, and the ground, so interestingly bare and dusty in the dark, had begun to scorch even his tough paws. He had retreated back upstream along the canyon until he saw dark silhouettes topping its walls; then he pulled himself up the steep slopes of scrub oak until he reached them. His slimness was deceptive; he was already stronger than a man.

He was thirsty, so when some Steller's jays—the crested, indigo jays of conifer forests—found him and began to scold, he left the glare of the forest's edge and moved deeper into the trees. He walked the length of the ridge, sniffing around the gullies for a spring and listening for the trickle of water under the hissing of wind through pine needles. But it was only a spur ridge. He would have to move farther into the mountains along the maze of logging roads that covered the ridgetops to find water.

THE SWEET PLACE

Deep in the forest, a spring burst from under a ridgetop and made a steep little meadow on a pocket of black, marshy soil, then rushed away down a gully. This soil oozed and bubbled with the icy water from under the mountains and was covered with blossoming hosackia—a native relative of clover with violet-yellow flowers—and studded with clumps of leopard lily, corn lily, and bleeding heart. The bright green of these plants could be seen for a long way through the dusty woods.

Being nearsighted and at least partly colorblind, the bear didn't see the green, but he smelled the spring even before it was visible through the trees. The scent of wet earth and vegetation—pollen, nectar, and the transpiration of water-rich leaves—was easy to distinguish from that of pine resin. He quickened his pace along the road he'd been following and started to run when he reached an abandoned track that cut across the top of the meadow. At the spring he paused to enjoy the coolness of the mud on his paws and took a long drink at a puddle.

Then he sidled over to a warm spot and sat on his multicolored rump. The conversation of a pair of ravens flying along the canyon below drifted to his ears, carried on a gentle breeze. It was just the right kind of breeze for smelling—warm and moist—and the bear opened his nostrils wide to get all the nuances. The lazy buzzing of flies and bumblebees called up pleasant associations of grubs and honey. A few inches from his hind paws a red, white, and gray *Phidippus* jumping spider, a daytime spider, ambled contentedly through the dust and twigs.

These raptures were interrupted by a mountain quail, as young and disheveled as the bear, who trotted out from behind a manzanita bush at the edge of the trees and appeared to succumb to an attack of hiccups. He jumped and squawked in evident distress, the clownish bobbing of his long head plume contributing to his drunken aspect. He was actually trying to scare the bear away from the clearing, but his performance only served to remind the intruder of a breakfast of quail eggs his mother had once provided. After listening to several minutes of denunciation, the bear rose and walked toward the manzanita bush. The quail shut up and scuttled into the woods, driving before him a whole tribe of variously aged relatives, all chattering at once in the voluble way of their species.

Not finding quail eggs, the bear wandered over to a pine stump on a knoll beside the meadow where carpenter ants with reddish fuzz on their black abdomens toiled around the entrance to their nest. The bear thought perhaps he might raid this nest. A little gray fence lizard rushed around the stump out of his way as he thrust his snout down to sniff at the hole. He smelled the tender white grubs in their larval chambers at the bottom of the hole and began to rake away the earth between the roots of the stump. But the nest was protected by a large root, and after a while he grew tired of clawing and chewing at it, contenting himself instead with licking up the aroused hordes of soldiers and workers that swarmed out among the bits of yellow green wolf lichen and orange cedar mistletoe littering the ground.

Like the creekbeds of the foothills, the spring meadow was a locus of activity in an otherwise dry landscape. Now that the day was about to end, that activity increased. A golden-mantled ground squirrel, resembling an oversized chipmunk, ran out of the hosackia and began to forage on the small herbs of the knoll, biting off fuzzy seed capsules and stuffing them into her cheek pouches. A Douglas squirrel scolded from the treetops, and the sound of falling pinecone scales from the other side of the clearing indicated where another was at work. The colors in the clearing became brighter for a little while before the sun set. A dead pine on the middle of the knoll turned orange as the reddening light touched its brown needles. Three birds resting on its top—a junco and two creepers—turned orange with it.

Another junco, a purple finch, two western bluebirds, and a chipping sparrow converged on the puddle to drink, but all except the sparrow were nervous at the bear's presence and soon flew away. The sparrow took a leisurely drink, bathed, and then flew to the knoll, where he proceeded to pick at the herbs the ground squirrel had just left. A few Steller's jays called in the woods, but none appeared in the clearing. As the sun dropped below the treetops, isolated rays of light streaked across the hosackia and glittered on spiderwebs. A black-and-white bird—an Audubon's warbler—was fluttering through one of these shafts of fading light, chasing gnats.

After fading from the meadow, the sunlight colored the treetops briefly, then disappeared—the birds with it. The air cooled quickly as the damp which had been dissipated all day by the sun's heat rose from the meadow. Remnants of sun-warmed air stirred the trees, but the clearing was still. A chipmunk popped out of his burrow and rushed boldly to the top of the dead pine. Like the ground squirrels in the foothills, he wanted to find out what was going on before darkness fell. He saw the last sunlight touch the peaks to the southwest and gleam on the breast of a Cooper's hawk that flew past. The chipmunk flattened himself against the tree until the hawk was out of sight, then slipped back to the ground.

The increasing coolness stupefied the bees and flies; they dropped to the stems and leaves of the meadow plants and clung there, bowing them slightly with their weight. But the carpenter ants remained active, hurrying to repair the damage that the bear had done to their tunnel. Long lines of them ran back and forth from the succulent corn lilies, which provided a food supply in the form of honeydew exuded from the abdomens of green aphids that sucked the juices of the lilies. Many moths also fluttered around the lilies, attracted by the sweet smell of the white flower spikes.

A robin sang a few notes in the already dark forest as if to signal the end of the daytime sounds. A long-jawed orb weaver—an attenuated spider with a zebra-striped abdomen and carrot-colored jaws—sidled to the center of her web, which was nearly two feet wide and was built horizontally over the main channel of springwater. She crouched upside-down underneath the web, waiting for insects, who come to lay their eggs in the water, to land on top of it. She would catch them from below. A crane fly, looking like a giant mosquito, blundered into the web and out again before she could grab it. In the channel, the golden-bodied, black-headed scavenger beetles that had spent the daylight burrowing in the mud gyrated erratically. Water boatmen and striders that had been active throughout the day seemed indifferent to the darkness and kept on rowing about. Down on the mud bottom, hundreds of tiny, red, wormlike creatures stood on their tails, waving in the current like a bed of eelgrass and filtering nourishment from the water with microscopic gills. These were the larvae of the gnats that the warbler had been chasing. Another larva, that of the caddis fly, crawled along a submerged pine needle. In the cylindrical case that it had made for itself out of rotten bark, it looked like an animated twig.

The stars began to come out, sparkling above the pine tops with a quiet authority they had lacked when seen through the denser air of the foothills. As if in deference to this authority, the clearing was hushed. There were no tree crickets in the pines and manzanita, and the ground crickets sang in scattered bursts that grew more and more infrequent as the temperature dropped. The only sustained sound was the whisper and chuckle of the spring.

Other species were indifferent to the higher altitude. A *Calosoma* ground beetle identical to the wood rat's visitor in the foothills loomed up out of a mouse hole and stalked off in search of a caterpillar. Wolf spiders patrolled the shores of the puddle on which floated, like petals, the white wings of pine looper moths that had fallen in and been eaten by the scavenger beetles. Multitudes of the pale moths clustered around the blossoms of western pennyroyal—drab violet flowers by day but strangely bright in the moonlight—or blundered into the traps set for them by gray cobweb-weaver spiders. A western toad, his black eyes lustrous and his skin the same color and texture as the ground, walked across the knoll.

John Rollin Ridge

*John Rollin Ridge (1827–1867) came to the California goldfields already
scarred by violence. His father and grandfather—both Cherokee leaders—
had been murdered when Ridge was only twelve. His family later settled in
Arkansas and sent Ridge to school in New England. Four years later illness
brought Ridge home, where he too shot a man who had apparently provoked
the incident. It may have been self-defense, but Ridge fled Arkansas for
Missouri. After failing to raise funds to pay for a fair trial, he joined up with
a company of gold seekers going west. In California Ridge had less success
as a miner than a writer. He contributed poems and articles to San Francisco
serials like* Golden Era, Hesperian, *and* Pioneer, *signing his pieces
"Yellow Bird," a translation of his Cherokee name, Cheesquatalawny.*

With the publication of The Life and Adventures of Joaquín
Murietta *in 1854, Ridge created a cottage industry for mythmakers. "This
fictionalized biography," says scholar A. LaVonne Brown Ruoff, "established
Murietta's image as a folk hero and precipitated the flood of stories, dramas,
and films that have kept him such a popular figure in the folklore of
California and Mexico." There is probably very little truth to the story of
this Mexican Robin Hood, but two things do ring true in Ridge's telling:
the prejudice of the gold miners, "lawless and desperate men, who bore the
name of Americans but failed to support the honor and dignity of that title,"
and the evocation of majesty in this poem set within the novel.* ✌

Mount Shasta,
Seen from a Distance

Behold the dread Mount Shasta, where it stands,
Imperial midst the lesser height, and like
Some mighty, unimpassioned mind, companionless
And cold. The storms of Heaven may beat in wrath
Against it, but it stands in unpolluted
Grandeur still; and from the rolling mists up-heaves
Its tower of pride e' en purer than before.
Each wintry shower, and white-winged tempest leave

Their frozen tributes on its brow, and it
Doth make of thorn an everlasting crown.
Thus doth it day by day, and age by age,
Defy each stroke of time—still rising higher
Into Heaven!

Aspiring to the eagle's cloudless height,
No human foot hath stained its snowy side,
Nor human breath has dimmed the icy mirror
Which it holds unto the moon, and stars, and sov'reign
Sun. We may not grow familiar with the secrets
Of its hoary top, whereon the Genius
Of that mountain builds his glorious throne!
Far-lifted in the boundless blue, he doth
Encircle, with his gaze supreme, the broad
Dominions of the West, that lie beneath
His feet, in pictures of sublime repose,
No artist ever drew. He sees the tall,
Gigantic hills arise in silentness
And peace, and in the long review of distance
Range themselves in order grand. He sees the sun-light
Play upon the golden streams that through the valleys
Glide. He hears the music of the great and solemn
Sea, and over-looks the huge old western wall,
To view the birth-place of undying Melody!

Itself all light, save when some loftiest cloud
Doth for a while embrace its cold forbidding
Form—that monarch-mountain casts its mighty
Shadows down upon the crownless peaks below,
That, like inferior minds to some great
Spirit, stand in strong contrasted littleness!
All through the long and summery months of our
Most tranquil year, it points its icy shaft
On high, to catch the dazzling beams that fall
In showers of splendor round that crystal cone,
And roll, in floods of far magnificence,
Away from that lone vast Reflector in
The dome of Heaven.

Still watchful of the fertile
Vale, and undulating plains below, the grass
Grows greener in its shade, and sweeter bloom
The flowers. Strong Purifier! From its snowy
Side the breezes cool are wafted to "the peaceful
Homes of men," who shelter at its feet, and love
To gaze upon its honored form; aye, standing
There, the guarantee of health and happiness!
Well might it win communities so blest
To loftier feelings, and to nobler thoughts—
The great material symbol of eternal
Things! And well, I ween, in after years, how,
In the middle of his furrowed track, the plowman,
In some sultry hour, will pause, and, wiping
From his brow the dusty sweat, with reverence
Gaze upon the hoary peak. The herdsman
Oft will rein his charger in the plain, and drink
Into his inmost soul the calm sublimity;
And little children, playing on the green, shall
Cease their sport, and, turning to that mountain
Old, shall, of their mother ask, "Who made it?"
And she shall answer, "God!"
And well this Golden State shall thrive, if, like
Its own Mount Shasta, sovereign law shall lift
Itself in purer atmosphere—so high
That human feeling, human passion, at its base
Shall lie subdued; e'en pity's tears shall on
Its summit freeze; to warm it, e'en the sunlight
Of deep sympathy shall fail—
Its pure administration shall be like
The snow, immaculate upon that mountain's brow!

Clarence King

In 1871 Clarence King (1842–1901) thought he was the first European to reach the summit of Mount Whitney, the tallest peak in the continental United States, named for his former chief in the Geological Survey of California. Unfortunately for King, he had climbed the wrong peak, a mistake he discovered two years later, when it was pointed out during a meeting of the California Academy of Sciences. In the East when he got the news, King returned to the Sierra Nevada to try again. This time he climbed the right mountain, but as historian Francis P. Farquhar observes, "alas for him, he was too late for the first ascent. On the summit he found a monument and the records of two preceding parties." His chagrin must have been acute—he had written so vividly of the now-discredited triumph in his book Mountaineering in the Sierra Nevada.

Such disappointment, however, would have been a rare experience for King. With a Yale degree in hand, he had come to California in 1863 to join Josiah Whitney's team of geologists. He had spent three years on the survey and then held a number of other government appointments, including director of the U.S. Geological Exploration of the Fortieth Parallel. He was head of the U.S. Geological Survey between 1878 and 1881 and then established himself as a private mining engineer. His intellect, wit, and—in the words of Henry Adams—his "aesthetic faculty" impressed his companions. This last quality is amply apparent in King's account of his survey team exploring the perilous terrain of Mount Shasta. ✍

from Mountaineering in the Sierra Nevada

The California haze had again enveloped Shasta, this time nearly obscuring it. In [a] forest along the southeast base, we came upon the stream flowing from McCloud glacier, its cold waters milky white with fine sandy sediment. Such dense, impenetrable fields of chaparral cover the south foothills that we were only able to fight our way through limited parts, getting, however, a clear idea of lava flows and topography. Farther east, the plains rise to seven thousand feet, and fine wooded ridges sweep down from Shasta, inviting approach.

While Munger and Watkins camped to make studies and negatives of the peak, Fred Clark and I packed one mule with a week's provisions, and mounting our saddle-animals, struck off into dark, silent forest.

It was a steep climb of eight or ten miles up tree-covered ridges and among outcrops of gray trachyte; nearly every foot showing more or less evidence of glacial action; long trains of morainal rocks upon which large forest trees seemed satisfied to grow; great rough regions of terminal rubbish, with enclosed patches of level earth commonly grass-grown and picturesque. It was sunset before we came upon water, and then it flowed a thousand feet below us in the bottom of a sharp, narrow cañon, cut abruptly down in what seemed glacial débris. I thought it unwise to take our mules down its steep wall if there were any camp-spot high up in the opener head of the cañon, and went off on foot to climb the wooded moraines still farther, hoping to come upon a bit of alpine sward with icy pool, or even upon a spring. When up between two and three hundred feet, the trees became less and less frequent, rugged trains of stone and glacier-scored rock in places covering the spurs. I could now overlook the snow amphitheatre which opened vast and shadowy above. Not a sign of vegetation enlivened its stony bed. The icy brook flowed between slopes of débris. At my feet, a trachyte ridge narrowed the stream with a tortuous bed, and led it to the edge of a five-hundred-foot cliff, over which poured a graceful cascade. Finding no camp-spot there, I turned northward and made a detour through deep woods, by-and-by coming back to Clark. We faced the necessity, and by dark were snugly camped in the wild cañon bottom. It was one of the loneliest bivouacs of my life. Shut in by high, dark walls, a few clustered trees growing here and there, others which floods had undermined lying prostrate, rough boulders thrown about, an icy stream hurrying by, and chilly winds coming down from the height, against which our blankets only half defended us.

Our excursion next day was south and west, across high, scantily wooded moraines, till we came to the deep cañon of the McCloud glacier.

I describe this gorge as it is one of several similar, all peculiar to Shasta. We had climbed to a point about ten thousand feet above the sea, and were upon the eastern edge of a cañon of eleven or twelve hundred feet depth. From the very crest of the Shasta, with here and there a few patches of snow, a long and remarkably even débris slope swept down. It seemed as if these small pieces of trachyte formed a great part of the region, for to the very bottom our cañon walls were worked out of it. A half mile below us the left bank was curiously eroded by side streams, resulting in a family of pillars from one to seven hundred feet high, each capped with some hard lava boulder which had protected the soft débris beneath from weathering. From its lofty névé the McCloud glacier descended over rugged slopes in one long cascade to a little above our station, where it impinged against a great rock buttress and turned sharply from the south wall towards us, rounding over in a great solid ice-dome eight or nine hundred feet high. For a mile farther, a huge accumulation, looking like a river of débris, cumbered the bottom. Here and there, on close scrutiny, we found it to be pierced with caverns whose ice-walls showed that the glacier underlaid all this vast amount of stone. Boulders rattled continually from the upper glacier and down both cañon walls, increasing the already great burden. Along both sides were evidences of motion in the lateral moraine embankments, and a very perceptible rounding up of terminal ramparts, from which in white torrent poured the subglacial brook.

It is instructive to consider what an amount of freighting labor this shrunken ice-stream has to perform besides dragging its own vast weight along. In descending Shasta we had found glacial ice which evidently for a mile or more deeply underlaid a mass of rock similar to this. It is one of the curiosities of Mount Shasta that such great bulk of ice should be buried, and in large part preserved, by loads of rock fragments. Fine contrasts of color were afforded high up among the sérac by a combination of blue ice and red lavas. We hammered and surveyed here for half the day, then descended to our mules, who bore us eagerly back to their home, our weird little cañon camp.

A pleasant day's march, altogether in woods and over glacial ridges, during which not a half hour passed without opening views of the cone, brought us high on the northern slope, at the upper forest limit, in a region of barren avalanche tracks and immense moraines.

Between those great straight ridges which jut almost parallel from the volcano's base, are wide, shelving valleys, the pathways of extinct glaciers; and here the forest, although it must once have obtained foothold, has been uprooted and swept away before powerful avalanches, crushed and up-piled trunks in sad wreck marking spots where the snow-rush stopped.

Two brooks, separated by a wide, gently rounding zone of drift, flowed down through the glacier valley which opened directly in front of our camp.

Early next morning Clark and I made up a bag of lunch, shouldered our instruments, and set out for a day on the glacier. Our slow, laborious ascent of the valley was not altogether uninteresting. Constant views obtained of moraines on either side gave us much pleasure and study. It was instructive to observe that the bases of their structure were solid floors of lava, upon which, in rude though secure masonry, were piled embankments not less than half a mile wide and four hundred feet high. Among the huge rocks which formed the upper structure, the tree forms were peculiar. Apparently every tree had made an effort to fill some gap and round out the smooth general surface. No matter how deeply twisted between high boulders, the branches spread themselves out in a continuous, dense mat, stretching from stone to stone. It was only rarely, and in the less elevated parts of the moraine, that we could see a trunk. The whole effect was of a causeway of rock overgrown by some dense green vine.

Similar patches of stunted trees grew here and there over the bottom of our broad amphitheater. Oftentimes we threaded our way among dense thickets of pines, never over six or eight feet in height, having trunks often two and three feet in diameter, and more than once we walked over their tops, our feet sinking but two or three inches into the dense mat of foliage. Here and there, half buried in the drift, we came across the tall, noble trunks of avalanche-killed trees. In comparing their straight, symmetrical growth with the singularly matted condition of the living dwarfed trees, I find the indication of a great climatic change. Not only are the present avalanches too great to permit their growth, but the violent cold winds which drift over this region bend down the young trees to such an extent that there are no longer tall, normal specimens. Around the upper limits of arborescent vegetation we passed some most enchanting spots; groves, not over eight feet in height, of large trees whose white trunks and interwoven boughs formed a colonnade, over which stretched thick living thatch. Under these strange galleries we walked upon soft, velvety turf and an elastic cushion of pine needles; nor could we resist the temptation of lying down here to rest beneath the dense roof. As we looked back, charming little vistas opened between the old and dwarfed stems. In one direction we could see the moraine with its long, graded slope and variegated green and brown surface; in another, the open pathway of the old glacier worn deeper and deeper between lofty forest-clad spurs; and up to the great snow mass above us, with its slender peak in the heavens looking down upon magnificent sweep of névé.

Only the strong desire for glaciers led us away from these delightful groves. A short tramp over sand and boulders brought us to the foot of a broad, irregular, terminal moraine. Two or three milky cascades poured out from under the great boulder region and united to form two important streams. We followed one of these in our climb up the moraine, and after an hour's hard work, found ourselves upon an immense pile of lava blocks, from which we could overlook the whole.

In irregular curve it continues not less than three miles around the end of the glacier, and in no place that I saw was less than a half mile in width. Where we had attacked it the width cannot be less than a mile, and the portion over which we had climbed must reach a thickness of five or six hundred feet.

About a half mile above us, though but little lifted from our level, undulating hillocks of ice marked the division between glacier and moraine; above that, it stretched in uninterrupted white fields. The moraine in every direction extended in singularly abrupt hills, separated by deep, irregular pits and basins of a hundred and more feet deep.

As we climbed on, the footing became more and more insecure, piles of rock giving way under our weight. Before long we came to a region of circular, funnel-shaped craters, where evidently the underlying glacier had melted out and a whole freight of boulders fallen in with a rush. Around the edges of these horrible traps we threaded our way with extreme caution, now and then a boulder, dislodging under our feet, rolled down into these pits, and many tons would settle out of sight. Altogether it was the most dangerous kind of climbing I have ever seen. You were never sure of your foothold. More than once, when crossing a comparatively smooth, level boulder field, they began to sink under us, and we sprang on from stone to stone while the great mass caved and sank slowly behind us. At times, while making our way over solid-seeming stretches, the sound of a deep, subglacial stream flowing far beneath us came up faint and muffled through the chinks of the rock. This sort of music is not encouraging to the nerves. To the siren babble of mountain brook is added all the tragic nearness of death.

We looked far and wide in hope of some solid region which should lead us up to the ice, but it was all alike, and we hurried on, the rocks settling and sinking beneath our tread, until we made our way to its edge, and climbed with relief upon its hard, white surface. After we had gained the height of a hundred feet, climbing up a comparatively smooth slope between brooks which flowed over it, a look back gave a more correct idea of the general billowy character of our moraine; and here and there in its deeper indentations we could detect the underlying ice.

It is, then, here as upon the McCloud glacier. For at least a mile's width the whole lower zone is buried under accumulation of morainal matter. Instead of ending like most Swiss glaciers, this ice wastes chiefly in contact with the ground, and, when considerable caverns are formed, the overlying moraine crushes its way through the rotten roof, making the funnels we had seen.

Thankful that we had not assisted at one of these engulfments, we scrambled on up the smooth, rooflike slope, steadying our ascent by the tripod legs

One late spring, I slid down through the manzanita to visit Petey. He was sitting in shade, working his rocker, a pipe in his teeth. A cluster of tents was along the bank, and here and there an old car; it was quite a camp, with a dozen people in it, at least, and easygoing Petey was its hierarch. Dragonflies were darting about him; the air was scented with mint and juniper; catbirds were filling a toyon bush with their screams....

"You're finding color, Petey?"

"A show. More'n that some days. I c'n tell you something. If I find pay dirt I stay and dig. There's some that lift a shovelful of dirt, then on up or down the crick. I tell these youngsters here if they see a man with a stake, he's stayed in one place. He's dug to grass roots, then up to his pants buttons, then over his head. He's got bacon, he's got terbaccy, he's got sense."

He pointed to the boulders in the creek. "There's not a boulder around here that hasn't been turned over twenty times since Andrew Jackson was President. The whole country from Oregon down was gone over with a fine-tooth comb. But we get along, and have a fine time at it, and next week you won't know what you'll find."

The name of Whiskey Creek commemorates a tragedy still a legend in these hills, and Petey indicated the site where it befell Amos Grimes, who came here from Shasta in 1852 with a string of pack burros, on the staunchest of which he had roped a keg of whiskey. It was a confidence misplaced, for on the high trail this animal grew unruly and fell into the creek.

"The burro swam in, but the keg was lost. That keg," added Petey, somberly, "was worth fifty burros."

—Idwal Jones, from "Farm, Rock, and Vine Folk" (1946)

used as alpenstock. When we had climbed perhaps a thousand feet, the surface angle became somewhat gentler and we were able to overlook before us the whole broad incline up to the very peak. For a mile or a mile and a half, the sharp blue edges of crevasses were apparent here and there, yawning widely for the length of a thousand feet, and at other places intersecting each other confusedly, resulting in piled-up masses of shattered ice.

We were charmed to enter this wild region, and hurried to the edge of an immense chasm. It could hardly have been less than a thousand or twelve hundred feet in length. The solid white wall of the opposite side—sixty feet over—fell smooth and vertical for a hundred feet or more, where rough wedged blocks and bridges of clear blue ice stretched from wall to wall. From these and from numerous overhanging shelves hung the long crystal threads of icicles, and beyond, dark and impenetrable, opened ice-caverns of unknown limit. We cautiously walked along this brink, examining with deep interest all the lines of stratification and veining and the strange succession of views down into the fractured regions below.

I had the greatest desire to be let down with a rope and make my way among these pillars and bridges of ice, but our little twenty feet of slender rope forbade the attempt. Farther up, the crevasses walled us about more and more. At last we got into a region where they cut into one another, breaking the whole glacier body into a confused pile of ice blocks. Here we had great difficulty in seeing our way for more than a very few feet, and were constantly obliged to climb to the top of some dangerous block to get an outlook, and before long, instead of a plain with here and there a crevasse, we were in a mass of crevasses separated only by thin and dangerous blades of ice.

We still pushed on, tied together with our short line, jumping over pits and chasms, holding our breath over slender snow ridges, and beginning to think the work serious. We climbed an ice-crag together; all around rose strange, sharp forms; below, in every direction, yawned narrow cuts, caves trimmed with long stalactites of ice, walls ornamented with crystal pilasters, and dark blue grottoes opening down into deeper and more gloomy chambers, as silent and cold as graves.

Far above the summit rose white and symmetrical, its skyline sweeping down sharp against the blue. Below, over ice-wreck and frozen waves, opened the deep valley of camp, leading our vision down to distant forest slopes.

We were in the middle of a vast convex glacier surface which embraced the curve of Shasta for four miles around, and at least five on the slope line, ice stretching in every direction and actually bounding the view on all sides except where we looked down.

The idea of a mountain glacier, formed from Swiss or Indian views, is always of a stream of ice walled in by more or less lofty ridges. Here a great curved cover of ice flows down the conical surface of a volcano without lateral walls, a few lava pinnacles and inconspicuous piles of débris separating it from the next glacier, but they were unseen from our point. Sharp white profiles met the sky. It became evident we could go no farther in the old direction, and we at once set about retracing our steps, but in the labyrinth soon lost the barely discernible tracks and never refound then. Whichever way we turned impassable gulfs opened before us, but just a little way to the right or left it seemed safe and traversable. At last I got provoked at the ill luck, and suggested to Clark that we might with advantage take a brief intermission for lunch, feeling that a lately quieted stomach is the best defense for nerves. So when we got into a pleasant, open spot where the glacier became for a little way smooth and level, we sat down, leisurely enjoying our repast. We saw a possible way out of our difficulty, and sat some time chatting pleasantly. When there was no more lunch we started again, and only three steps away came upon a narrow crack edged by sharp ice-jaws. There was something noticeable in the hollow, bottomless darkness seen through it which arrested us, and when we had jumped across to the other side, both knelt and looked into its depths. We saw a large domed grotto walled in with shattered ice and arched over by a roof of frozen snow so thin that the light came through quite easily. The middle of this dome overhung a terrible abyss. A block of ice thrown in fell from ledge to ledge, echoing back its stroke fainter and fainter. We had unconsciously sat for twenty minutes lunching and laughing on the thin roof, with only a few inches of frozen snow to hold us up over that still, deep grave. A noonday sun rapidly melting its surface, the warmth of our persons slowly thawing it, and both of us playfully drumming the frail crest with our tripod legs. We looked at one another, and agreed that we lost confidence in glaciers.

Splendid rifts now opened to north of us, with slant sunshine lighting up one side in vivid contrast with the cold, shadowed wall. We greatly enjoyed a tall precipice with a gaping crevasse at its base, and found real pleasure in the north edge of the great ice-field, whither we now turned. A low moraine, with here and there a mass of rock which might be solid, flanked the glacier, but was separated from it by a deeply melted crevasse, opening irregular caverns along the wall down under the very glacier body. We were some time searching a point where this gulf might be safely crossed. A thin tongue of ice, sharpened by melting to a mere blade, jutted from the solid glacier over to the moraine, offering us a passage of some danger and much interest. We edged our way along astride its crest, until a good spring carried us over a final crevasse and up upon the moraine, which we found to be dangerously built up of honeycombed ice and boulders. The same perilous sinks and holes surrounded us, and alternated with hollow archways over subterranean streams. It was a relief, after an hour's labor, to find ourselves on solid lava, although the ridge, which proved to be a chain of old craters, was one of the most dreary reaches I have ever seen.

In the evidence of glacier motion there had seemed a form of life, but here among silent, rigid crater rims and stark fields of volcanic sand, we walked upon ground lifeless and lonely beyond description: a frozen desert at nine thousand feet altitude. Among the huge rude forms of lava we tramped along, happy when the tracks of mountain sheep suggested former explorers, and pleased if a snowbank under rock shadow gave birth to spring or pool. But the severe impression of arctic dreariness passed off when, reaching a rim, we looked over and down upon the volcano's north foot, a superb sweep of forest country waved with ridgy flow of lava and gracefully curved moraines.

Afar off, the wide sunny Shasta Valley, dotted with miniature volcanoes, and checked with the yellow and green of grain and garden, spread pleasantly away to the north, bounded by Klamath hills and horizoned by the blue rank of Siskiyou Mountains. To our left the cone slope stretched away to Sisson's, the sharp form of the Black Cone rising in the gap between Shasta and Scott Mountain.

Here again the tremendous contrast between lava and ice about us, and that lowly expanse of ranches and verdure impressed anew its peculiar force.

Joaquin Miller

His real name was Cincinnatus Hiner Miller (1837–1913), but somehow that impressive mouthful didn't seem romantic enough for the writer who was to become "poet of the Sierra." At the behest of poet Ina Coolbrith, Miller took the name of one of the West's legendary outlaws, Joaquín Murietta. Perhaps Miller's lifelong identification with underdogs and outcasts prompted the choice, or perhaps it was a hope that the bandit's notoriety would rub off on him. Whatever the motivation, Joaquín is a fitting name for this flamboyant literary personality.

Miller spent his early years in Indiana, moving to Oregon with his family in 1852. There young Miller met "Mountain Joe" DeBloney, who had been a scout for Frémont before establishing a trading post at Soda Springs, near the upper Sacramento River just south of Castle Crags. Miller joined up with DeBloney and began his astonishing—some say unbelievable—career as an Indian fighter, outlaw, and frontiersman. He also created a literary character that played especially well in 1870s' London, where his long beard, Mexican sombrero, flannel shirts, and Western boots matched English fantasies of a desperado. Local critics proclaimed him "America's most important writer"— high praise considering that his contemporaries included Mark Twain, Emily Dickinson, and Walt Whitman. Miller's work no longer earns such comparisons, but it does include some memorable poems and prose. His 1874 autobiographical novel, Unwritten History: Life Among the Modocs *may be a tall tale of his exploits, but it is also a pioneering work of social protest, in which he describes the mistreatment of Northern California Indians while creating a clear portrait of their homeland. Here is his deft portrayal of a devastating fire in the Shasta-Cascade region.* ✒

A Bear on Fire

It is now more than a quarter of a century since I saw the woods of Mount Shasta in flames, and beasts of all sorts, even serpents, crowded together; but I can never forget, never!

It looked as if we would have a cloudburst that fearful morning. We three were making our way by slow marches from Soda Springs across the south base of Mount Shasta to the Modoc lava beds—two English artists and myself. We had saddle horses, or, rather, two saddle horses and a mule, for our own use. Six Indians, with broad leather or elk-skin straps across their foreheads, had been chartered to carry the kits and traps. They were men of means and leisure, these artists, and were making the trip for the fish, game, scenery and excitement, and everything, in fact, that was in the adventure. I was merely their hired guide.

This second morning out, the Indians—poor slaves, perhaps, from the first, certainly not warriors with any spirit in them—began to sulk. They had risen early and kept hovering together and talking, or, rather, making signs in the gloomiest sort of fashion. We had hard work to get them to do anything at all, and even after breakfast was ready they packed up without tasting food.

The air was ugly, for that region—hot, heavy, and without light or life. It was what in some parts of South America they call "earthquake weather." Even the horses sulked as we mounted; but their mule shot ahead through the brush at once, and this induced the ponies to follow.

The Englishmen thought the Indians and horses were only tired from the day before, but we soon found the whole force plowing ahead through the dense brush and over fallen timber on a double quick.

Then we heard low, heavy thunder in the heavens. Were they running away from a thunderstorm? The English artists, who had been doing India and had come to love the indolent patience and obedience of the black people, tried to call a halt. No use. I shouted to the Indians in their own tongue. "Tokau! Kisa! Kiu!" (Hasten! Quick! Quick!) was all the answer I could get from the red, hot face that was thrown for a moment back over the load and shoulder. So we shot forward. In fact, the horses now refused all regard for the bit, and made their own way through the brush with wondrous skill and speed.

We were flying from fire, not flood! Pitiful what a few years of neglect will do toward destroying a forest! When a lad, I had galloped my horse in security and comfort all through this region. It was like a park then. Now it was a dense tangle of undergrowth and a mass of fallen timber. What a feast for flames! In one of the very old books on America in the British Museum—possibly the very oldest on the subject—the author tells of the parklike appearance of the American forests. He tells his English friends back at home that it is most comfortable to ride to the hounds, "since the Indian squats (squaws) do set fire to the brush and leaves every spring," etc.

But the "squats" had long since disappeared from the forests of Mount Shasta; and here we were tumbling over and tearing through ten years' or more of accumulation of logs, brush, leaves, weeds, and grass that lay waiting for a sea of fire to roll over all like a mass of lava.

And now the wind blew past and over us. Bits of white ashes sifted down like snow. Surely the sea of fire was coming, coming right on after us! Still there was no sign, save this little sift of ashes, no sound; nothing at all except the trained sense of the Indians and the terror of the "cattle" (this is what the Englishmen called our horses) to give us warning.

In a short time we struck an arroyo, or canyon, that was nearly free from brush and led steeply down to the cool, deep waters of the McCloud River. Here we found the Indians had thrown their loads and themselves on the ground.

They got up in sulky silence, and, stripping our horses, turned them loose; and then, taking our saddles, they led us hastily up out of the narrow mouth of the arroyo under a little steep stone bluff.

They did not say a word or make any sign, and we were all too breathless and bewildered to either question or protest. The sky was black, and thunder made the woods tremble. We were hardly done wiping the blood and perspiration from our torn hands and faces where we sat when the mule jerked up his head, sniffed, snorted, and then plunged headlong into the river and struck out for the deep forest on the farther bank, followed by the ponies.

The mule is the most traduced of all animals. A single mule has more sense than a whole stableful of horses. You can handle a mule easily if the barn is burning; he keeps his head; but a horse becomes insane. He will rush right into the fire if allowed to, and you can only handle him, and that with difficulty if he sniffs the fire, by blindfolding him. Trust a mule in case of peril or a panic long before a horse. The brother of Solomon and willful son of David surely had some of the great temple-builder's wisdom and discernment, for we read that he rode a mule. True, he lost his head and got hung up by the hair, but that is nothing against the mule.

As we turned our eyes from seeing the animals safely over, right there by us and a little behind us, through the willows of the canyon and over the edge of the water, we saw peering and pointing toward the other side dozens of long black and brown outreaching noses. Elk!

They had come noiselessly, they stood motionless. They did not look back or aside, only straight ahead. We could almost have touched the nearest one.

They were large and fat, almost as fat as cows; certainly larger than the ordinary Jersey. The peculiar thing about them was the way, the level way, in which they held their small, long heads—straight out; the huge horns of the males lying far back on their shoulders. And then for the first time I could make out what these horns are for—to part the brush with as they lead through the thicket, and thus save their coarse coats of hair, which is very rotten, and could be torn off in a little time if not thus protected. They are never used to fight with, never; the elk uses only his feet. If on the defense, however, the male elk will throw his nose close to the ground and receive the enemy on his horns.

Suddenly and all together, and perhaps they had only paused a second, they moved on into the water, led by a bull with a head of horns like a rocking chair. And his rocking chair rocked his head under water much of the time. The cold, swift water soon broke the line, only the leader making the bank directly before us, while the others drifted far down and out of sight.

Our artists, meantime, had dug up pencil and pad and begun work. But an Indian jerked the saddles, on which the Englishmen sat, aside, and the work was stopped. Everything was now packed up close under the steep little ledge of rocks. An avalanche of smaller wild animals, mostly deer, was upon us. Many of these had their tongues hanging from their half-opened mouths. They did not attempt to drink, as you would suppose, but slid into the water silently almost as soon as they came. Surely they must have seen us, but certainly they took no notice of us. And such order! No crushing or crowding, as you see cattle in corrals, aye, as you see people sometimes in the cars.

And now came a torrent of little creeping things: rabbits, rats, squirrels! None of these smaller creatures attempted to cross, but crept along in the willows and brush close to the water.

They loaded down the willows till they bent into the water, and the terrified little creatures floated away without the least bit of noise or confusion. And still the black skies were filled with the solemn boom of thunder. In fact, we had not yet heard any noise of any sort except thunder, not even our own voices. There was something more eloquent in the air now, something more terrible than man or beast, and all things were awed into silence—a profound silence.

And all this time countless creatures, little creatures and big, were crowding the bank on our side or swimming across or floating down, down, down the swift, wood-hung waters. Suddenly the stolid leader of the Indians threw his two naked arms in the air and let them fall, limp and helpless at his side; then he pointed out into the stream, for there embers and living and dead beasts began to drift and sweep down the swift waters from above. The Indians now gathered up the packs and saddles and made a barricade above, for it was clear that many a living thing would now be borne down upon us.

The two Englishmen looked one another in the face long and thoughtfully, pulling their feet under them to keep from being trodden on. Then, after another avalanche of creatures of all sorts and sizes, a sort of Noah's ark this time, one of them said to the other:

"Beastly, you know!"

"Awful beastly, don't you know!"

As they were talking entirely to themselves and in their own language, I did not trouble myself to call their attention to an enormous yellow rattlesnake which had suddenly and noiselessly slid down, over the steep little bluff of rocks behind us, into our midst.

But now note this fact—every man there, red or white, saw or felt that huge and noiseless monster the very second she slid among us. For as I looked, even as I first looked, and then turned to see what the others would say or do, they were all looking at the glittering eyes set in that coffinlike head.

The Indians did not move back or seem nearly so much frightened as when they saw the drift of embers and dead beasts in the river before them. But the florid Englishmen turned white! They resolutely arose, thrust their hands in their pockets and stood leaning their backs hard against the steep bluff. Then another snake, long, black, and beautiful, swept his supple neck down between them and thrust his red tongue forth as if a bit of the flames had already reached us.

Fortunately, this particular "wisest of all the beasts of the field," was not disposed to tarry. In another second he had swung to the ground and was making a thousand graceful curves in the swift water for the further bank.

The world, even the world of books, seems to know nothing at all about the wonderful snakes that live in the woods. The woods rattlesnake is as large as at least twenty ordinary rattlesnakes; and Indians say it is entirely harmless. The enormous black snake, I know, is entirely without venom. In all my life, spent mostly in the camp, I have seen only three of those monstrous yellow woods rattlesnakes; one in Indiana, one in Oregon and the other on this occasion here on the banks of the McCloud. Such bright eyes! It was hard to stop looking at them.

Meantime a good many bears had come and gone. The bear is a good swimmer, and takes to the water without fear. He is, in truth, quite a fisherman; so much of a fisherman, in fact, that in salmon season here his flesh is unfit for food. The pitiful part of it all was to see such little creatures as could not swim clinging all up and down and not daring to take to the water.

Unlike his domesticated brother, we saw several wildcats take to the water promptly. The wildcat, as you must know, has no tail to speak of. But the panther and California lion are well equipped in this respect and abhor the water.

I constantly kept an eye over my shoulder at the ledge or little bluff of rocks, expecting to see a whole row of lions and panthers sitting there, almost "cheek by jowl" with my English friends, at any moment. But strangely enough, we saw neither panther nor lion; nor did we see a single grizzly among all the bears that came that way.

We now noticed that one of the Indians had become fascinated or charmed by looking too intently at the enormous serpent in our midst. The snake's huge, coffin-shaped head, as big as your open palm, was slowly swaying from side to side. The Indian's head was doing the same, and their eyes were drawing closer and closer together. Whatever there may be in the Bible story of Eve and the serpent, whether a figure or a fact, who shall say?—but it is certainly, in some sense, true.

An Indian will not kill a rattlesnake. But to break the charm, in this case, they caught their companion by the shoulders and forced him back flat on the ground. And there he lay, crying like a child, the first and only Indian I ever saw cry. And then suddenly boom! boom! boom! as if heaven burst. It began to rain in torrents.

And just then, as we began to breathe freely and feel safe, there came a crash and bump and bang above our heads, and high over our heads from off the ledge behind us! Over our heads like a rocket, in an instant and clear into the water, leaped a huge black bear, a ball of fire! his fat sides in flame. He sank out of sight but soon came up, spun around like a top, dived again, then again spun around. But he got across, I am glad to say. And this always pleases my little girl, Juanita. He sat there on the bank looking back at us quite a time. Finally he washed his face, like a cat, then quietly went away. The rattlesnake was the last to cross.

The beautiful yellow beast was not at all disconcerted, but with the serenest dignity lifted her yellow folds, coiled and uncoiled slowly, curved high in the air, arched her glittering neck of gold, widened her body till broad as your two hands, and so slid away over the water to the other side through the wild white rain. The cloudburst put out the fire instantly, showing that, though animals have superhuman foresight, they don't know everything before the time.

"Beastly! I didn't get a blawsted sketch, you know."

"Awful beastly! Neither did I, don't you know."

And that was all my English friends said. The Indians made their moaning and whimpering friend who had been overcome by the snake pull himself together and they swam across and gathered up the "cattle."

Some men say a bear cannot leap; but I say there are times when a bear can leap like a tiger. This was one of the times.

Philip Fradkin

Philip Fradkin (1945–) has enjoyed a remarkable career as a writer. As a reporter for the Los Angeles Times *during the sixties, he shared a Pulitzer Prize for coverage of the Watts riots and covered Vietnam during the height of the war. He has been Western editor of* Audubon *and also taught at Stanford University's Mass Media Institute. He has authored five books on the American West, including* A River No More: The Colorado River and the West, *which describes the escalating demands for water made upon a large but limited watershed. Wallace Stegner called the work "the most comprehensive book there is about the Colorado River."*

Fradkin's Western writing combines the journalist's analytical eye with the naturalist's feel for the rhythms of the world. In The Seven States of California, *he gives the natural and human history of each geographic region, creating an elegant exposition accompanied by evocative descriptions. The third region he treats is the northeast "Land of Fire," dominated by Mount Shasta, "looking down on California like some unblinking, protuberant third eye."*

from The Seven States of California

Mount Shasta attracts its own distinctive weather pattern. Dark masses of towering cumulus clouds issued from its heights on a summer afternoon, much like an ash cloud from a volcanic eruption.

I watched Shasta from the summit of Little Mount Hoffman, some thirty-five miles distant, for a number of days. I am mesmerized by the latent power of volcanoes. I have traveled to Hawaii to watch the lava, blinking red in the night, creep down the side of Kilauea on the Big Island and devour everything within its reach before meeting the ocean in a steaming froth. As a young man, I climbed a perfect Mount St. Helens; in middle age, I returned to wander through the dead trees, felled like so many victims of a nuclear blast.

There was an unobstructed view of Mount Shasta from the cinder cone that sits on the lip of the Medicine Lake Caldera. Medicine Lake, a low shield volcano of greater volume than any other volcano in the Cascade Range, is attached to Shasta by a series of vents in the form of bare hillocks, pine forests, and ropy extrusions of lava that constitute a ridge. The Medicine Lake Volcano merges with the undulating Modoc Plateau to the north and east. The descent from Mount Shasta to the plateau is steep at first, then gradual.

The plateau, a tableland varying from four to five thousand feet in elevation, was formed by a series of lava flows. It is cut off from the remainder of California by the southern extension of the Cascade Range. The Medicine Lake Volcano is a long, dark presence that sits atop the tableland like an inverted saucer. It has erupted seventeen times in the last eleven thousand years.

Five neighboring tribes, including the Modocs and the Shastas, shared Medicine Lake in the summer months when the highland was free of snow. The Modocs camped near Mount Hoffman on the [south] side of the volcano, which was closest to their territory. Here among the sugar pines and firs, away from the hot valleys, there was game to hunt. There was also a plentiful supply of obsidian on Glass Mountain—a valuable trade item that could be fashioned into sharp blades for weapons or tools. They held their religious ceremonies around the lake that lies within the caldera and whose water is always clear, although there is no outlet. Here they fasted, conducted puberty rites, and experienced their power dreams....

At daybreak there was not a cloud in the sky, and Shasta was reborn in the shape of a broad arrowhead unattached to any shaft. It rose well without any visible means of support and floated above the horizon on a sea of gray blue vapor. The mountain was backlit by a light pink sky. The first touch of sun upon the summit was like a match to a candle, and California came alive for another day. I drove down the dirt track and into geo-history.

The geology of war goes back to the late Pleistocene, perhaps ten thousand years ago, when a six-mile chain of vents along the northeast side of the Medicine Lake Volcano erupted within a one-hundred-year time span and spewed out basaltic lava via long, sinuous tubes over two-thirds of the present-day Lava Beds National Monument. Most likely the lava that formed the stronghold where the Modoc Indians held the U. S. Army at bay for five months (December 1872 to April 1873) came from Modoc Crater, although there are some who believe that nearby Mammoth Crater was the source.

As the molten lava emerged from the vents and spilled down the volcano, the sides and tops of the tubes congealed. Fresh lava extended the tubes. Some eventually reached fifteen miles in length. Where the roofs of the tubes later collapsed, there were entrances to caves; some of the underground cavities were a few miles in length, while others were just large enough for an Indian family to find shelter.

In the last stages of the eruption, the Modoc stronghold was formed. As flow followed flow through the tubes, a low plateau emerged at the edge of Tule Lake, a shallow body of water bordering the stronghold on the north and serving as a source of drinking water for the Indians and the troops. At the edge of the flow the fingerlike tongues of crust turned down and cracks and fissures formed in the flaps of lava, the natural trenches utilized by the Modocs. These interlocking trenches were continuous along three sides of the Modoc stronghold. Outside this inner perimeter, detached portions of the plateau—also laced with fissures—served as outposts.

I waken with the poet's small book on my lap, the reading light still on. It is first dawn, and the northbound all-night bus out of San Francisco is now swaying to the familiar curves of rivers. Out the white-line window I can just make out the silhouette of madrone and fir on the ridges above the Eel. Down below, silvery willow on the banks, behind them dark and ancient columns of redwood. Strands of fog hang suspended in the trees and above the swift current. A faint, rippled reflection of sky, the river sweeps along with us, full of having been somewhere, almost home. An hour more will bring us out at the Pacific.

I return to home as I left it, trying to hold together the pieces. To the casual traveler's eye, we are following a thread of serpentine water through the groves of an emerald forest. But behind this green curtain, the land is in a state of exhaustion, the forest at the bottom of a third cycle of depletion and recovery, the human community wondering what it's going to do for money. Each time, less comes back—because too much has been taken, and too little *given* back. The long-term balance of accounts is visible beneath the river's reflection, in the silted water and the erosion-choked riverbed. It is not as easily seen, however, where it touches our human business most closely—in the web of living things that has been broken and scattered and spent. It was this inquiry that set me on the present quest: How can we redeem such enormous loss? For all that land and life, with what shall we make return?

—Jerry Martien, from *Shell Game* (1996)

The result, after a veneer of vegetation was acquired, was almost total camouflage. The stronghold was a complex terrain that appeared from a short distance away to be a smooth, easily accessible rise in the landscape. Actually the plateau was a tortuous labyrinth whose congealed lava had sharp edges that could easily pierce the skin of defender and attacker alike.

Water mixed with fire to form a shallow lake that covered 1,096 square miles in the Klamath River Basin during the late Pleistocene. Lava flows burst through the lake's water, ash from eruptions at nearby Crater Lake and elsewhere blanketed its surface, and a lava flow that snaked its way down the eastern flank of Medicine Lake Volcano blocked the outlet to the south. The level of the lake rose and fell, and the early Indians adjusted to the varying heights by moving their villages accordingly. With the coming of a drier climate, the water level dropped one hundred feet and the large lake split into three parts: Upper and Lower Klamath lakes and Tule Lake in the southeastern portion of the basin.

THE SIERRA NEVADA

The highest peak in the contiguous United States, Mount Whitney rises 14,495 feet. From its summit, you can see the Owens Valley to the east, a distant floor of high-country desert. Turn to the west and northwest, and you can see the stern, gray faces of the peaks of the Kaweah group and the Great Western Divide. Mount Whitney provides the perfect symbol of John Muir's "Range of Light," lofty, indifferent, aloof. Yet each spring and summer this range attracts so many hikers and mountaineers that the Forest Service has to regulate their numbers. It's hard to believe that the range remained virtually untouched, at least by Europeans, until relatively late in California's recorded history.

This four-hundred-mile mountain range runs from Lassen Peak south to Tehachapi Pass. Its eastern slope presents a steep and rugged face, especially in its Mammoth Mountains. The western slope is gentler, falling away gradually through foothills toward the Great Central Valley. The range's formation explains this difference: the mountains were created when a portion of the earth's crust lifted—as much as eleven thousand feet above the Owens Valley—and tilted east to west. Most of the range is granite, much of it fissured with cracks, the signature of relentless geological forces. The additional pressure exerted by snow, ice, tree roots, and the constant tug of gravity has flaked away huge pieces of rock, leaving behind massive round domes and sheer cliffs, some of them thousands of feet high. Even when its granite peaks are mantled in snow, the range presents a jagged silhouette, a feature marked by its Spanish name, Sierra Nevada.

Pedro Fages and Juan Crespí were the first Europeans to see these mountains, but it was Pedro Font who coined their name, describing them as "una gran sierra nevada"—literally, a snowy sawtooth range.

Though other Spanish explorers would touch the foothills, none would have the opportunity to explore its summits. Not until 1827, with Jedediah Smith's eastbound crossing of the High Sierra near what is now called Ebbetts Pass, did the high country begin to give up its secrets to Europeans. Fur trappers soon began trying to find better routes to California. Among the U.S. explorers was Joseph Reddeford Walker, who led the first west-bound expedition across the Sierra crest in 1833, sighting Yosemite Valley on the way. Zenas Leonard, a member of the party, kept a journal in which he described "many small streams which would shoot out from under...high snowbanks, and after running a short distance in deep chasms, which they have through the ages cut in the rocks, precipitate themselves from one lofty precipice to another, until they are exhausted in rain below."

Leonard's diary also records his first sighting of giant redwood trees, *Sequoiadendron gigantea,* among the largest living things in the world. Sequoia National Park contains the biggest tree, "General Sherman," which is 273 feet tall and close to 37 feet thick at the base. Interestingly, the same tree was named "Karl Marx" by a cooperative colony of Communists living there in the late nineteenth century, before the land became a national park.

But long before that—and long before the births of Sherman and Marx—native people lived in the valleys and foothills of the Sierra: the Yokuts, the Maidu, and the Miwok on the western side; the Washo, the Paiute, and others on the east. And long before Smith, Walker, and Leonard, these native people were crossing the Sierra for purposes of trade, according to Francis P. Farquhar's *History of the Sierra Nevada.* For example, the Yokuts regularly exchanged deer, antelope, and elk hides for the pinyon nuts the Paiutes gathered and for the sinew-backed bows they made. Many valley and foothill groups also traveled to higher elevations every summer to escape the valley heat.

While the Spanish and Mexican conquest had little impact on the Sierra region and its natives, the U.S. takeover and gold rush, with their huge influx of people, had dramatic impact. Competition for resources, cultural misunderstandings, and the white man's typical disregard for Native American concerns inevitably led to conflict.

One of the most significant of these conflicts occurred when a small group of Ahwahneechee—natives of Yosemite—raided a trading post near Mariposa and were pursued by a volunteer militia, the Mariposa

Battalion, into what they later called Yosemite Valley. While the militia members may not have been the first outsiders to enter this valley, they were among the first to publicize its grandeur. One member of this militia was L. H. Bunnel, who wrote later of the "religious emotions or thoughts. . . aroused by the mysterious power of the surrounding scenery." Bunnel and the Mariposa Battalion bestowed names upon many of the spectacular features in and around the valley. Maps still mark Tenaya Lake, for the leader of the Ahwahneechee, and Three Brothers Rocks, for Tenaya's captured sons. The Ahwahneechee, of course, had their own names for these landmarks. Three Brothers Rocks was Kompo-pai-ses or Leaping Frog Rocks, since it looked like three frogs sitting on their haunches. Tenaya reacted to the supposed honor of having a lake named for him by saying, "It already has a name," a small but significant act of resistance.

Meanwhile, the gold rush lured all kinds of fortune seekers to California, not all of them miners. Dr. Fayette Clappe hoped to improve his own health while tending to the medical needs of the forty-niners. His wife Louise joined him in a mining camp where she wrote some of the richest descriptions of life in the California's "glorious hills"—rivaling even the sparkling facsimile of gold-camp doings that Bret Harte created out of his placer-mine experience in the Sierra. Sarah Royce and her husband traveled overland to California, and her memoir of the gold rush era—written years later at the request of her son, Harvard philosopher and California historian Josiah Royce—records their muleback trip through Carson Pass, whose rocky walls "towered nearly perpendicular, hundreds of feet."

Though the gold rush eventually played out, the Sierra's astonishing valleys, towering sequoias, and jagged peaks continued to exert a powerful attraction, especially upon artists, writers, and scientists, but also upon entrepreneurs. James Hutchings built the first hotel in Yosemite Valley and published *Scenes of Wonder and Curiosity in California,* in part to bring in tourists. Artists like Thomas A. Ayers and Albert Bierstadt took the Sierra landscape for subject, as did artists in succeeding generations, notably photographer Ansel Adams. Even Mark Twain was so captivated by the region that he dropped his usual sardonic tone to observe that Lake Tahoe's water was so clear that his "boat seemed floating in the air!"

John Muir arrived in Yosemite in 1868 and stayed on to write many transporting descriptions of his beloved "Range of Light." Muir, an amateur scientist, was followed to the Sierra summits by a number of professionals, geologists like Clarence King, William Brewer, and Joseph LeConte. Another contributor to the growing body of Sierra literature was Englishman J. Smeaton Chase, who traveled on horseback through the Sierra early in the twentieth century, recording his detailed descriptions of the landscape in *Yosemite Trails*. Like Muir, he helped to convey the absolute value of the relative solitude to be found in the wild Sierra landscape.

Chase and Muir both loved Hetch Hetchy, a valley whose beauty is said to have rivaled Yosemite's. It was dammed in 1931 and now provides water to San Francisco. Other dams have strangled mountain rivers to provide power and water for Californians; many of the old mining towns have grown into vacation spots; and ski resorts—especially near Lake Tahoe—have altered the slopes in the name of recreation and tourism. Even so, the relationship between human beings and pristine nature continues to appear as theme in more recent Sierra literature, especially in the works of two of California's most gifted poets, Kenneth Rexroth and Gary Snyder.

Well-known destinations in the Sierras—Mount Whitney, Yosemite Valley, Lake Tahoe, among others—draw so many visitors now that it is almost impossible to find a solitary moment to enjoy the landscape. Yet many other places in the range almost never feel the footprints of human beings. And even some of the more accessible spots can be deserted—or almost so—in the winter. At that time of year, the small lakes and rivers, Muir once told us, are "obliterated from the winter landscape," sealed by ice and snow. Then, places like Mount Whitney once more become what they used to be: untouched, lofty, aloof, indifferent. Magnificent beyond human measure.

Louise Amelia Knapp Smith Clappe

Soon after Louise Amelia Knapp Smith (1819–1906) married Dr. Fayette Clappe, the self-described nomad found herself aboard ship, bound for gold-rush San Francisco. She and her new husband lived there over a year, although the Golden Gate weather did not agree with him. Louise recorded Dr. Clappe's symptoms with a remarkable combination of gruesome detail and sardonic wit: "an entire year, with fever and ague; bilious, remittent, and intermittent fevers—this delightful list, varied by an occasional attack of jaundice." This was in the first of the twenty-three letters that Louise—in the humorous guise of "Dame Shirley"—later wrote to her sister Molly. A friend suggested a cure: move to the mountains to set up practice in the mining camp of Rich Bar, where the "purity of the atmosphere" would be no less important than the dearth of medical competition. Dr. Clappe left for the mining camp, and even if the competition wasn't as scarce as he'd hoped—more than a couple of dozen other physicians showed up in Rich Bar within weeks of his arrival—his health improved, encouraging him to send for Louise.

Clappe, who had had a sound education in languages and literature, was already a published writer by the time she arrived in Rich Bar. Encouraged by Alexander Everett, U.S. diplomat and author, she had published several poems and sketches in California, but none as fine as her sisterly dispatches from the gold country. She addressed these as personal letters, but may always have meant them for publication. After she returned to San Francisco and her marriage ended, she provided copies to Ferdinand Ewer, who ran them in the Pioneer, where they reached a wider audience. In an act of artistic claim-jumping, Bret Harte mined Dame Shirley's letters for literary gold, walking away with incidents he used in "The Luck of Roaring Camp" and "The Outcasts of Poker Flat." Dame Shirley is known for her sharp observation of the grimy side of life in a mining camp. But just as acute are her descriptions of the natural world of the gold country. ❧

from The Shirley Letters

LETTER FIRST

About eleven o'clock we went back into the woods and camped for the night. Our bed was quite comfortable, and my saddle made an excellent pillow. Being so much higher in the mountains, we were a little chilly; and I was disturbed two or three times by a distant noise, which I have since been told was the growling of grizzly bears that abounded in that vicinity. On the whole, we passed a comfortable night, and rose at sunrise, feeling perfectly refreshed and well. In less than an hour, we were eating breakfast at Pleasant Valley Ranch, which we easily discovered by daylight.

Here they informed us that "we had escaped a great marcy"—as old Jim used to say in relating his successful run from a wolf—inasmuch as the "grizzlies" had not devoured us during the night! But seriously, dear M——, my heart thrills with gratitude to the Father, for his tender care of us during that journey, which, view it as lightly as we may, was certainly attended with *some* danger.

Notwithstanding we had endured so much fatigue, I felt as well as ever I did, and after breakfast insisted upon pursuing our journey, although F—— anxiously advised me to defer it until next day. But imagine the horror, the crème de la crème of borosity, of remaining for twelve mortal hours of wakefulness in a filthy, uncomfortable, flea-haunted shanty, without books or papers, when Rich Bar—easily attainable before night, through the loveliest scenery, shining in the yellow splendor of an autumnal morning— lay before us! *I* had no idea of any such absurd self-immolation. So we again started on our strange, eventful journey.

I wish I could give you some faint idea of the majestic solitudes through which we passed; where the pine trees rise so grandly in their awful height, that they seem looking into Heaven itself. Hardly a living thing disturbed this solemnly beautiful wilderness. Now and then a tiny lizard glanced in and out among the mossy roots of the old trees, or a golden butterfly flitted languidly from blossom to blossom. Sometimes a saucy little squirrel would gleam along the somber trunk of some ancient oak, or a bevy of quails, with their pretty, tufted heads and short, quick tread, would trip athwart our path. Two or three times, in the radiant distance, we descried a stately deer, which, framed in by embowering leaves, and motionless as a tableau, gazed at us for a moment with its large, limpid eyes, then bounded away with the speed of light into the evergreen depths of those glorious old woods.

Sometimes we were compelled to cross broad plains, acres in extent, called chaparrals, covered with low shrubs which, leafless and barkless, stand like vegetable skeletons along the dreary waste. You cannot imagine what a weird effect these eldritch bushes had upon my mind. Of a ghastly whiteness, they at first reminded me of a plantation of antlers, and I amused myself by fancying them a herd of crouching deer; but they grew so wan and ghastly, that I began to look forward to the creeping across a chaparral (it is no easy task for the mules to wind through them) with almost a feeling of dread.

But what a lovely sight greeted our enchanted eyes, as we stopped for a few moments on the summit of the hill leading into Rich Bar. Deep in the shadowy nooks of the far down valleys, like wasted jewels dropped from the radiant sky above, lay half a dozen blue-bosomed lagoons, glittering and gleaming and sparkling in the sunlight, as though each tiny wavelet were formed of rifted diamonds. It was worth the whole wearisome journey, danger from Indians, grizzly bears, sleeping under the stars, and all, to behold this beautiful vision. While I stood breathless with admiration, a singular sound and an exclamation of "A rattlesnake!" from F—— startled me into common sense again. I gave one look at the reptile, horribly beautiful, like a chain of living opals, as it corkscrewed itself into that peculiar spiral which it is compelled to assume in order to make an attack, and then, fear overcoming curiosity—although I had never seen one of them before—I galloped out of its vicinity as fast as my little mule could carry me.

The hill leading into Rich Bar is five miles long, and as steep as you can imagine. Fancy yourself riding for this distance, along the edge of a frightful precipice, where, should your mule make a misstep, you would be dashed hundreds of feet into the awful ravine below. Everyone we met tried to discourage us, and said that it would be impossible for me to ride down it. They would take F—— aside, much to my amusement, and tell him that he was assuming a great responsibility in allowing me to undertake such a journey. I, however, insisted upon going on. About halfway down, we came to a level spot a few feet in extent, covered with sharp slate-stones. Here, the girth of my saddle—which we afterward found to be fastened only by four *tacks*—gave way, and I fell over the right side, striking on my left elbow. Strange to say, I was not in the least hurt, and again my heart wept tearful thanks to God; for had the accident happened at any

other part of the hill, I must have been dashed, a piece of shapeless noth-
ingness, into the dim valleys beneath.

F—— soon mended the saddle-girth, I mounted my darling little mule,
and rode triumphantly into Rich Bar, at five o'clock in the evening. The
Rich Barians are astonished at my courage in daring to ride down the hill.
Many of the miners have told me that they dismounted several times while
descending it. I of course feel very vain of my exploit, and glorify myself
accordingly; being particularly careful all the time not to inform my admirers that my courage was the result of the know nothing, fear nothing principle; for I was certainly ignorant, until I had passed them, of the dangers
of the passage. Another thing that prevented my dismounting was the
apparently utter impossibility, on such a steep and narrow path, of mounting again. Then, I had much more confidence in my mule's power of picking the way and keeping his footing than in my own. It is the prettiest sight
in the world to see these cunning creatures, stepping so daintily and cautiously among the rocks. Their pretty little feet, which absolutely do not
look larger than a silver dollar, seem made on purpose for the task. They are
often perfect little vixens with their masters, but an old mountaineer who
has ridden them for twenty years told me that he never knew one to be
skittish with a woman. The intelligent darlings seem to know what a bun-
dle of helplessness they are carrying, and scorn to take advantage of it.

We are boarding at present at the "Empire"—a huge shingle palace in
the center of Rich Bar—which I will describe in my next letter. Pardon,
dear M——, the excessive egotism of this letter; but you have often
flattered me by saying that my epistles were only interesting when profusely illuminated by that manuscriptal decoration represented by a great I. A
most intense love of the ornament myself makes it easy for me to believe
you, and doubt not that my future communications will be as profusely
stained with it as even you could desire....

LETTER SEVENTH
From our log cabin, Indian Bar
October 7, 1851

You will perchance be surprised, dear M——, to receive a letter from me
dated Indian instead of Rich Bar; but as many of F——'s most intimate
friends reside at this settlement, he concluded to build his log cabin here.

Solemn council was held upon the ways and means of getting "Dame Shirley" to her new home. The general opinion was that she had better mount her fat mule and ride over the hill, as all agreed that it was very doubtful whether she would be able to cross the logs and jump the rocks, which would bar her way by the water-passage. But that obstinate little personage, who has always been haunted with a passionate desire to do everything which people said she could *not* do, made up her willful mind immediately to go by the river. Behold then, the "Dame" on her winding way, escorted by a deputation of Indian Barians, which had come up for that important purpose.

It is impossible, my sister, for any power of language over which *I* have command, to convey to you an idea of the wild grandeur and the awful magnificence of the scenery in this vicinity. This fork of the Feather River comes down very much "as the water does at Lodore," now gliding along with a liquid measure, like a river in a dream, and anon bursting into a thousand glittering foam-beads over the huge rocks, which rise dark, solemn, and weirdlike, in its midst. The crossings are formed of logs, often moss-grown. Only think how charmingly picturesque, to eyes wearied with the costly masonry or carpentry of the bridges at home. At every step gold diggers or their operations greet your vision. Sometimes in the form of a dam, sometimes in that of a river, turned slightly from its channel, to aid the indefatigable gold hunters in their mining projects. Now, on the side of a hill you will see a long-tom—a huge machine invented to facilitate the separation of the ore from its native element—or a man busily engaged in working a rocker, a much smaller and simpler machine used for the same object, or more primitive still, some solitary prospector, with a pan of dirt in his hands, which he is carefully washing at the water's edge, to see if he can "get the color," as it is technically phrased, which means literally the smallest particle of gold.

As we approached Indian Bar, the path led several times fearfully near deep holes, from which the laborers were gathering their yellow harvest, and "Dame Shirley's" small head swam dizzily as she crept shudderingly by.

The first thing which attracted my attention, as my new home came in view, was the blended blue, red, and white of the American banner, undulating like a many-colored snake amid the lofty verdure of the cedars which garland the brown brow of the hill behind our cabin. This flag was suspended on the Fourth of July last, by a patriotic sailor who climbed to the top of the tree to which he attached it, cutting away the branches as he descended, until it stood among its stately brethren, a beautiful moss-wreathed Liberty pole, flinging to the face of Heaven the glad colors of the Free.

When I attempt, dear M——, to describe one of these spots to you, I regret more than ever the ill health of my childhood, which prevented my obtaining any degree of excellence in sketching from Nature. Had it not been for that interruption to my artistic education, I might, with a few touches of the pencil or the brush, give you the place and its surroundings.

Not all the earth contains gold. Often there is a superincumbent layer of fifty or more feet which is worthless before they reach the immense gravel deposit which marks the course of the ancient river; and from this gravel, waterworn, and showing all the marks of having formed once the bed of a rushing torrent, the gold is taken. Under great pressure this gravel—which contains, you must understand, rocks of large size, and is not gravel in our sense of the word at all—has been cemented together, so that even the powerful streams of water directed against it make but a feeble impression; and to hasten and cheapen the operation, a blast of from twelve to fifteen hundred kegs of powder is inserted in a hillside, and exploded in such a way as to shatter and loosen a vast bulk of earth and stones, whereupon the water is brought into play against it.

If you want to know how a part of the surface of our planet looked some thousands of years ago, here is a good opportunity; for what two or three men with torrents of water wash away into the Yuba River in a few weeks must have taken many centuries to accumulate; and below, you see a mass of water-washed stone, rounded boulders, and large gravel, twenty or fifty or even a hundred feet deep, which was so plainly the bed of a torrent or rapidly rushing river once that even children recognize it.

Of course the acres washed away must go somewhere, and they are filling up the Yuba River. This was once, I am told by old residents, a swift and clear mountain torrent; it is now a turbid and not rapid stream, whose bed has been raised by the washings of the miners not less than fifty feet above its level in 1849. It once contained trout, but now I imagine a catfish would die in it.

—Charles Nordhoff, from *California for Health, Pleasure and Residence* (1872)

But alas! my feeble pen will convey to you a very faint idea of its savage beauty.

This bar is so small, that it seems impossible that the tents and cabins scattered over it can amount to a dozen; there are, however, twenty in all, including those formed of calico shirts and pine boughs. With the exception of the paths leading to the different tenements, the entire level is covered with mining holes, on the edges of which lie the immense piles of dirt and stones which have been removed from the excavations. There is a deep pit in front of our cabin and another at the side of it; though they are not worked, as when "prospected," they did not "yield the color."

Not a spot of verdure is to be seen on this place; but the glorious hills rising on every side vested in foliage of living green, make ample amends for the sterility of the tiny level upon which we camp. The surrounding scenery is infinitely more charming than that of Rich Bar. The river, in hue of a vivid emerald—as if it reflected the hue of the fir trees above—bordered with a band of dark red, caused by the streams flowing into it from the different sluices, ditches, long-toms, etc., which meander from the hill just back of the bar, wanders musically along. Across the river and in front of us, rises nearly perpendicularly a group of mountains, the summits of which are broken into many beautifully cut conical and pyramidal peaks. At the foot and left of these eminences, and a little below our bar, lies Missouri Bar, which is reached from this spot by a log bridge. Around the latter, the river curves in the shape of a crescent, and singularly enough, the mountain rising behind this bend in the stream outlines itself against the lustrous Heaven, in a shape as exact and perfect as the moon herself in her first quarter. Within one horn of this crescent the water is a mass of foam sparkles, and it plays upon the rocks which line its bed an everlasting dirge suggestive of the "grand forever" of the ocean.

At present the sun does not condescend to shine upon Indian Bar at all, and the old settlers tell me that he will not smile upon us for the next three months; but he nestles lovingly in patches of golden glory all along the brows of the different hills around us, and now and then stoops to kiss the topmost wave on the opposite shore of the Rio de las Plumas.

The first artificial elegance which attracts your vision is a large rag shanty, roofed, however, with a rude kind of shingle, over the entrance of which is painted in red capitals ("to what base uses do we come at last") the name of the great Humboldt spelled without the *d*. This is the only hotel in this vicinity, and as there is a really excellent bowling alley attached to it, and the barroom has a floor upon which the miners can dance, and, above all, a cook who can play the violin, it is very popular. But the clinking of glasses, and the swaggering air of some of the drinkers, reminds us that it is no place for a lady, so we will pass through the dining room and emerging at the kitchen, in a step or two reach our log cabin. Enter my dear; you are perfectly welcome; besides, we could not keep you out if we would, as there is not even a latch on the canvas door, though we really intend in a day or two to have a hook put on to it.

The room into which we have just entered is about twenty feet square. It is lined over the top with white cotton cloth, the breadths of which being sewed together only in spots, stretch gracefully apart in many places, giving one a bird's-eye view of the shingles above. The sides are hung with a gaudy chintz, which I consider a perfect marvel of calico printing. The artist seems to have exhausted himself on *roses;* from the largest cabbage, down to the tiniest Burgundy, he has arranged them in every possible variety of wreath, garland, bouquet, and single flower; they are of all stages of growth, from earliest budhood up to the ravishing beauty of the "last rose of summer." Nor has he confined himself to the colors usually worn by this lovely plant; but, with the daring of a great genius soaring above nature, worshiping the ideal rather than the real, he has painted them brown, purple, green, black, and blue. It would need a floral catalogue to give you the names of *all* the varieties which bloom upon the calico; but, judging by the shapes—which really are much like the originals—I can swear to moss roses, Burgundies, York and Lancaster, tea roses, and multifloras.

A curtain of the above-described chintz (I shall hem it at the first opportunity) divides off a portion of the room, behind which stands a bedstead that in ponderosity leaves the Empire couches far behind. But before I attempt the furniture, let me finish describing the cabin itself.

The fireplace is built of stones and mud, the chimney finished off with alternate layers of rough sticks and this same rude mortar; contrary to the usual custom, it is built inside, as it was thought that arrangement would make the room more comfortable; and you may imagine the queer appearance of this unfinished pile of stones, mud, and sticks. The mantelpiece— remember that on this portion of a great building, some artists, by their exquisite workmanship, have become world renowned—is formed of a beam of wood covered with strips of tin procured from cans, upon which still remain in black hieroglyphics the names of the different eatables which they formerly contained. Two smooth stones—how delightfully primitive—do duty as fire-dogs. I suppose that it would be no more than civil to call a hole two feet square in one side of the room a window, although it is as yet guiltless of glass. F—— tried to coax the proprietor of the Empire to let him have a window from that pine and canvas palace; but he of course declined, as to part with it would really inconvenience himself; so F—— has sent to Marysville for some glass, though it is the general opinion that the snow will render the trail impassible for mules before we can get it. In this case, we shall tack up a piece of cotton cloth, and should it chance at any time to be very cold, hang a blanket before the opening. At present the weather is so mild that it is pleasanter as it is, though we have a fire in the mornings and evenings, more, however, for luxury than because we really need it. For my part, I almost hope that we shall not be able to get any glass, for you will perhaps remember that it was a pet habit of mine, in my own room, to sit by a great fire in the depth of winter, with my window open.

One of our friends had nailed up an immense quantity of unhemmed cotton cloth—very coarse—in front of this opening, and as he evidently prided himself upon the elegant style in which he had arranged the drapery, it went to my heart to take it down, and suspend in its place some pretty blue linen curtains which I had brought from the valley. My toilet table is formed of a trunk elevated upon two claret cases, and by draping it with some more of the blue linen, neatly fringed, it really will look quite handsome, and when I have placed upon it my rosewood workbox, a large cushion of crimson brocade, some Chinese ornaments of exquisitely carved ivory, and two or three Bohemian glass cologne stands, it would not disgrace a lady's chamber at home.

The looking glass is one of those which come in paper cases for dolls' houses; how different from the full-length Psyches so almost indispensible to a dressing room in the States.

The washstand is another trunk covered with a towel, upon which you will see for bowl, a large vegetable dish, for ewer, a common-sized dining pitcher; near this, upon a small cask, is placed a pail, which is daily filled with water from the river. I brought with me from Marysville a handsome carpet, a hair mattress, pillows, a profusion of bed linen, quilts, blankets, towels, etc., so that in spite of the oddity of most of my furniture, I am in reality as thoroughly comfortable here as I could be in the most elegant palace.

We have four chairs which were brought from the Empire. I seriously proposed having three-legged stools; with my usual desire for symmetry I thought that they would be more in keeping; but as I was told that it would be a great deal of trouble to get them made, I was fain to put up with mere chairs; so you see that even in the land of gold itself, one cannot have everything that she desires. An ingenious individual in the neighborhood, blessed with a large bump for mechanics and good nature, made me a sort of wide bench, which covered with a neat plaid, looks quite sofalike. A little pine table with oilcloth tacked over the top of it stands in one corner of the room, upon which are arranged the chess and cribbage boards. There is a larger one for dining purposes, and as unpainted pine has always a most dreary look, F——— went everywhere in search of oilcloth for it, but there was none on any of the bars; at last "Ned," the Humboldt Paganini, remembered two old monte table covers which had been thrown aside as useless. I received them thankfully, and with my planning and Ned's mechanical genius, we patched up quite a respectable covering; to be sure, the ragged condition of the primitive material compelled us to have at one end an extra border, but that only agreeably relieved the monotony. I must mention that the floor is so uneven that no article of furniture gifted with four legs pretends to stand upon but three at once, so that the chairs, tables, etc., remind you constantly of a dog with a sore foot.

At each end of the mantelpiece is arranged a candlestick, not, much to my regret, a block of wood with a hole in the center of it, but a real Britannia-ware candlestick; the space between is gaily ornamented with F———'s meerschaum—several styles of clay pipes, cigars, cigaritos, and every procurable variety of tobacco—for you know the aforesaid individual is a perfect devotee of the Indian weed. If I should give you a month of Sundays you would never guess what we use in lieu of a bookcase, so I will put you out of your misery by informing you instantly that it is nothing more nor less than a candle-box, which contains the library, consisting of a Bible and prayer book, Shakespeare, Spenser, Coleridge, Shelley, Keats, Lowell's *Fable for Critics,* Walton's *Compleat Angler,* and some Spanish books—spiritual instead of material lights, you see.

There, my dainty Lady Molly, I have given you, I fear, a wearisomely minute description of my new home. How would you like to winter in such an abode? In a place where there are no newspapers, no churches, lectures, concerts, or theaters; no fresh books, no shopping, calling, nor gossiping little tea-drinkings; no parties, no balls, no picnics, no tableaux, no charades, no latest fashions, no daily mail (we have an express once a month), no promenades, no rides, nor drives; no vegetables but potatoes and onions, no milk, no eggs, no *nothing?* Now I expect to be very happy here. This strange, odd life fascinates me. As for churches, "the groves were God's first temples," "and for the strength of the hills, the Swiss mountains bless him;" and as to books, I read Shakespeare, David, Spenser, Paul, Coleridge, Burns, and Shelley, which are never old. In good sooth I fancy that nature intended me for an Arab or some other Nomadic barbarian, and by mistake my soul got packed up in a Christianized set of bones and muscles. How I shall ever be able to content myself to live in a decent, proper, well-behaved house, where toilet tables are toilet tables, and not an ingenious combination of trunk and claret cases, where lanterns are not broken bottles, book cases not candle-boxes, and trunks not washstands, but every article of furniture, instead of being a makeshift, is its own useful and elegantly finished self, I am sure I do not know. However, when too much appalled at the humdrumish prospect, I console myself with the beautiful promises, "that sufficient unto the day is the evil thereof," and "as thy day is, so shall thy strength be," and trust that when it is again my lot to live amid the refinements and luxuries of civilization, I shall endure them with becoming philosophy and fortitude.

Sarah Royce

*Born at Stratford-upon-Avon, Sarah Eleanor Bayliss (1819–1891) came
to the United States as an infant, graduated from Phipps Union Female
Seminary in New York state, and became a schoolteacher in Rochester. In
1849 she went West with her husband, Josiah Royce, and their two-year-
old-daughter, Mary. Bound for California like thousands of others, they got a
late April start, making the trip more dangerous. Sarah Royce "dearly prized
the benefits of civilization," wrote her daughter-in-law, "the churches, the
libraries, the schools, and the companionship of an enlightened society. She
was indeed giving up much." Despite the "hardships and rude conditions of
living," Sarah's energy and cheerfulness were remarkable. After the family settled in Grass Valley, Sarah opened a "School for Young Ladies and Misses."*

*Despite its name this school was coeducational, and the boys Sarah
taught included her own son Josiah, who went on to become a distinguished
professor of philosophy at Harvard. When he began work on a history of
California (its subtitle, tellingly, was* A Study in American Character*),
he asked his mother to turn her diary into a story of the overland journey
west. Though more than three decades had elapsed, she built a compelling
narrative from her forthright entries, vividly detailing the rough terrain and
its effect upon travelers. Here she tells of one last daunting obstacle between
her family and their future home.* ❧

from A Frontier Lady

But the great Sierra Nevada Mountains were still all before us, and we had
many miles to make, up [the Carson] River, before their ascent was fairly
begun. If this sand continued many miles as looked probable, when should
we ever even begin the real climbing? The men began to talk among themselves about how much easier they could get on if they left the wagon; and
it was not unlikely they would try starting out without us, if we had to travel too slowly. But they could not do this to any real advantage unless they
took with them their pack-mule to carry some provisions. All they had was
the bacon they found on the desert, and some parched cornmeal; but they
felt sanguine that they could go so much faster than the cattle with the

wagon, they could easily make this last them through. But the bargain had been, when we agreed to supply them with flour, that the pack-mule, and the old horse if he could be of any use, should be at our service to aid in any pinch that might occur, to the end of the journey. Having shared the perils of the way thus far, it certainly seemed unwise to divide the strength of so small a party when the mountains were to be scaled.

I wished most heartily there was some more rapid way for Mary and me to ride. But it was out of the question; for only a thoroughly trained mountain animal would do for me to ride carrying her. Besides this, all the clothing and personal conveniences we had in the world were in our wagon, and we had neither a sufficient number of sound animals nor those of the right kind, to pack them across the mountains. So the only way was to try to keep on. But it looked like rather a hopeless case when, for this whole day, we advanced but a few miles.

The next morning, Friday the twelfth of October, we set out once more, hoping the sand would become lighter and the road easier to travel. But, instead of this, the wheels sank deeper than yesterday, there was more of ascent to overcome, the sun shone out decidedly hot, and, towards noon, we saw that we were approaching some pretty steep hills up which our road evidently led. It did not look as though we could ascend them but we would at least try to reach their foot. As we neared them we saw dust rising from the road at one of the turns we could distinguish high up in the hills a few miles off. Probably it was some party ahead of us. There was no hope of our overtaking anybody, so when we lost sight of the dust we did not expect to see it again. But soon another section of the road was in sight, and again the dust appeared; this time nearer, and plainly moving toward us. Conjecture now became very lively. It was probably Indians; but they could not be of the same tribes we had seen. Were they foes? How many were there? Repeatedly we saw the dust at different points, but could make out no distinct figures.

We were now so near the foot of the hills that we could distinctly see a stretch of road leading down a very steep incline to where we were moving so laboriously along. Presently at the head of this steep incline appeared two horsemen, clad in loose, flying garments that flapped, like wings on each side of them, while their broad-brimmed hats blown up from their foreheads, revealed hair and faces that belonged to no Indians. Their rapidity of motion and the steepness of the descent gave a strong impression of coming down from above, and the thought flashed into my mind, "They look heaven-sent." As they came nearer we saw that each of them led by a halter a fine mule, and the perfect ease with which all the animals cantered down that steep, was a marvel in our eyes. My husband and myself were at the heads of the lead cattle, and our little Mary was up in the front of the wagon, looking with wonder at the approaching forms.

As they came near they smiled and the forward one said "Well sir, you are the man we are after!" "How can that be?" said my husband, with surprise. "Yes, sir," continued the stranger, "you and your wife, and that little girl, are what brought us as far as this. You see, we belong to the Relief Company sent out by order of the United States government to help the

---

I sit in my van at the end of the plowed section of the Ebbetts Pass road—Highway 4. The storm began last night, and just now the snow topped the running board: two feet. I think it might let up soon, but I may be surprised. Late winter storms in mid-March surprised even Snowshoe Thompson, the intrepid mailman who skied across the Sierra and back for twenty years beginning in 1856.

One hundred feet beyond my rusty-colored van, the world disappears in an atmosphere of solid white, but for most Californians, this storm is merely rain. I imagine it: soaking wet and stacked for hundreds of miles out across the sea, the clouds transfer water from ocean to land, blowing in and spattering their soggy load on the beaches. Above the oak-veneered hills of the Coast Ranges, green with the juicy grass of March, the clouds climb and the rain pounds harder, greasing the bare dirt. East of the hills in the seventy-mile-wide Central Valley, the rain eases to a steady gray curtain....

Where I sit, the storm realizes its greatest potential. Two more inches in an hour. The snow loads the needles of the lodgepole pine and bends young trees to the ground. Some will never recover and will grow with bizarre U-shaped contortions in their trunks. Animals take refuge in the air pockets made by the doubled-over lodgepoles. At high elevations, the hemlock are weighted until lower branches sag and touch the ground; upper branches shed their load by drooping to dump clumps of snow, making tiny craters under the trees. Juniper cope with the snow differently: they support the weight on muscular limbs that tremble not at all. Fir trees are pointed and shed snow like steep roofs.

—Tim Palmer, from *The Sierra Nevada: A Mountain Journey* (1988)

late emigrants over the mountains. We were ordered only as far as Truckee Pass. When we got there we met a little company that had just got in. They'd been in a snowstorm at the summit; 'most got froze to death themselves, lost some of their cattle, and just managed to get to where some of our men had fixed a relief camp. There was a woman and some children with them; and that woman set right to work at us fellows to go on over the mountains after a family she said they'd met on the desert going back for grass and water 'cause they'd missed their way. She said there was only one wagon, and there was a woman and child in it; and she knew they could never get through them cañons and over them ridges without help. We told her we had no orders to go any farther then. She said she didn't care for orders. She didn't believe anybody would blame us for doing what we were sent out to do, if we did have to go farther than ordered. And she kept at me so, I couldn't get rid of her. You see I've got a wife and little girl of my own; so I felt just how it was; and I got this man to come with me and here we are, to give you more to eat, if you want it, let you have these two mules, and tell you how to get right over the mountains the best and quickest way."

While he thus rapidly, in cheery though blunt fashion, explained their sudden presence with us, the thought of their being heaven-sent—that had so lightly flashed into my mind as I at first watched their rapid descent of the hill, with flying garments—grew into a sweetly solemn conviction; and I stood in mute adoration, breathing, in my inmost heart, thanksgiving to that Providential Hand which had taken hold of the conflicting movements, the provoking blunders, the contradictory plans, of our lives and those of a dozen other people, who a few days before were utterly unknown to each other, and many miles apart, and had from those rough, broken materials wrought out for us so unlooked-for a deliverance.

Having made their hasty explanation, our new friends advised us to keep on some little distance farther, to a point where there was a spring in the hills, and excellent camping, to which they would guide us. There we were to rest the remainder of the day, while they would help to select, put into proper shape and pack, everything in the wagon that could be packed. The rest we must be content to leave. As we moved leisurely on to our camping place, they explained more fully the details of our situation—which they understood so much better than we could—and told us what we were to do. There had been two nights of snowstorm at the summit: had there come much more they could not have got through. But the weather had cleared, the snow was fast going off the roads as they came over; and, if no other storm occurred, the pass would be in good order when we reached it. But we must hasten with all possible dispatch, for, when the storms once again set in, they were not likely at that season to give any more chance for crossing the mountains. As to keeping on with the wagon, even supposing the cattle to grow no weaker than now—it would take us two weeks at the least to ascend the Carson Valley to the cañon. That cañon could not in several places be traversed by wheels. Wagons had been taken through; but only by taking them apart and packing, at the most difficult points; which of course could only be done by strong companies with plenty of time. Our only hope, therefore, was to pack. They then went farther into details about packing. The oxen, they said, could easily be made to carry, each, two moderate-sized bundles, if snugly packed and well fastened on. Then the old horse could carry something though not very much. And the mule the young men had brought along, they said must carry most of the provisions.

"And now as to these two mules we brought," continued the chief speaker, "this white one is a perfectly trained, mountain saddle-mule. My wife has rode him for miles, over steep and slippery roads, and he'll be perfectly safe for this lady to ride, with her little girl in front of her. And this dark mule is just as good for carrying packs, and the lady is to have him for her things and the little girl's. Now," he continued, turning to me, "as soon as we stop, and have all had some dinner, you just pick out all the things you care most about, and put them by themselves—you can save out enough for two good-sized packs: he's strong, and understands it—and we'll do them up snug for you, and show the men how to fasten them on safe; and you remember, now, that these two mules are yours till you get through to the gold mines; and all Uncle Sam asks, is, that they shall be brought safely to his boys' headquarters in Sacramento City as soon as possible after you get into California."

Thus, by the wise forethought of our good Government, and the chivalrous management of this faithful agent, I was provided for to a sufficiency that would have looked to me, two hours before, like a fairy-dream. The program for the afternoon was successfully carried out. Everything was arranged for an early morning start; and, at night I lay down to sleep for the last time in the wagon that had proved such a shelter for months past. I remembered well, how dreary it had seemed, on the first night of our journey (which now looked so long ago) to have only a wagon for shelter. Now we were not going to have even that. But, never mind, if we might only reach in safety the other foot of the mountains, all these privations would in their turn look small; and the same rich Providence that had led, and was still so kindly leading us, would, in that new land, perhaps, show us better things than we had seen yet.

So, when morning came, I hailed it with cheerful hope, though with some misgivings, because I had not ridden horseback for several years, and, whenever I had, it had been with side-saddle, and all the usual equipments for lady's riding, and, certainly, with no baby to carry. Now, I was to have only a common Spanish saddle, I must have Mary in front of me, and, it turned out, that several things needed for frequent use would have to be suspended from the pommel of my saddle, in a satchel on one side and a little pail on the other. At first, I was rather awkward, and so afraid Mary would get hurt, that at uneven places in the road I would ask my husband to get up and take her, while I walked. But in a few hours this awkwardness wore off; and the second day of our new style of traveling I rode twenty-five miles, only alighting once or twice for a brief time. Our friends, the government men, had left us the morning we left our wagon; taking the road to the Truckee, where they felt themselves emphatically "due," considering their orders. I have more than once since wished I could see and thank them again; for, grateful as I felt then, I was able to appreciate more highly, a thousandfold, the service they had rendered us when, only ten days after we crossed the summit, the mountains were all blocked with snow, and the stormiest winter California had known for years was fully set in.

About the third day up the Carson, we were overtaken by a small company of men, sent out on some special business which they did not state, from a Western military station; and bound for California. Their animals were exclusively mules, and they were in every way fully equipped. They camped near us, and the commander, whom they called Colonel J——, seemed much impressed with the defenselessness of our condition. Most of the young men shared this feeling more or less, and behaved very gentlemanly. Of course their animals could travel much faster than ours, so we could not hope to join their company. But Colonel J—— suggested that as they had been traveling pretty fast for many days, and the ascent was now becoming more steep, it would be as well for them to make shorter days' rides till the summit was passed; in which case we might, by traveling a little later, camp near them at night, and so be less in danger from Indians. He said they would fire two or three guns when they stopped for the night, so that we might know they were within reach. This was indeed

very acceptable aid; and we prized their company still more, when, on
coming into camp the second night we found they had, during the afternoon, picked up a man whom they found by the roadside, wounded by an
Indian arrow. He had wandered off from his party a few days before, looking for game, had lost his way and had only that day regained the road. He
was hurrying on alone, when an arrow from a thicket struck him and he
fell. The supposition was that the Indians thought him dead, and were prevented from robbery or further violence only by the sudden appearance of
Colonel J——'s company. The wound was painful; but by the good care
given him he gradually recovered.

On the seventeenth of October we reached the head of Carson Valley,
and, just after noon, entered the great cañon. Here the road soon became so
rough and steep as to make it very difficult for me to hold Mary and keep
my seat. The men had hard work to drive the cattle and mules over the boulders at the frequent crossings of the stream, and in between the great masses of rock where the trail sometimes almost disappeared. As the cañon narrowed, the rocky walls towered nearly perpendicular, hundreds of feet; and
seemed in some places almost to meet above our heads. At some of the
crossings it was well nigh impossible to keep the trail, so innumerable were
the boulders; and the scraggy bushes so hid the coming-out place. The days
were shortening fast, and, in this deep gulch, darkness began to come on
early. The animals became more and more restive with the roughness of the
way, and it was hard work to keep them from rushing into a narrow ravine
that occasionally opened, or up one of the steep trails which appeared now
and then, suggesting unpleasant ideas of Indians and wild beasts. If our animals got many steps away we could not find them in the dusk.

The young men had lagged behind most of the afternoon, leaving the
driving mostly to three of us, one of whom had to ride, holding the child.
Just as the shades were beginning to make everything look dim, we came
to a crossing of the creek (which had now become a very small stream),
where on the opposite side instead of the rocky walls we had had, there was
a steep wooded hill up which wound a trail. But that could not be our way,
for it was too steep, besides we had been told to keep the cañon, and we
thought we could dimly trace *our* trail, in the sand between the boulders,
leading up stream. We paused to look closely; but the two mules with their
large packs, one containing nearly all the food of the party, the other the most
valuable goods we possessed, rushed resolutely forward up the creek-bed, and
disappeared among the brush. My husband, who had been carrying Mary

for a while, as I had become tired with the strain, hastily alighted, set her down on a flat rock, told me to take care of my mule for he must follow those animals, and quickly disappeared after them. At the same moment the men came up behind, which started the cattle forward and one of the oxen brushed close by Mary making her fall over into the water. In a moment I was there, had her in my arms, and found she was very little hurt, and her clothes but slightly wet. She was soon soothed; but meanwhile some of the cattle had rushed up the steep trail, and some had scattered among the bushes and boulders all eager to browse. Old Mr. A—— was trying to get together the latter, and young W—— was leading my mule to a convenient place for me to get on, when DeLu who had followed the cattle up the steep trail, called out, "Come on, this is the way!" W—— and the old gentleman both questioned his correctness; but he insisted that the trail became plainer where he was; and when I said I could not ride up so steep a way in the dark, and hold Mary, he said, "Oh we'll come to an easier part pretty soon, you can get her up here afoot, and W—— can lead up the mule and then you can get on. Come, it's the only way."

Thinking, from his positive tone, that he saw something we could not see, W—— and I followed, getting Mary along as well as we could. But, by the time we had climbed awhile, we found the steep growing steeper, and the trail almost disappeared. DeLu stopped, and the two or three cattle who had struggled up, began to tend downward again. It was evident we were lost in the cañon, and had better go no farther in the darkness. I sat down with Mary in my lap, wrapped her closely in my loose sacque and, feeling it a relief to rest instead of climb, soothed her and myself as well as I could; looked at the stars, was thankful there were no signs of storm, and was conjecturing what had become of my husband and the mules, when the sound of a gun echoed through the cañon, followed, soon, by another; and we knew Colonel J——'s party were signaling us. The sound came from the direction in which the mules had disappeared; and so we hoped they and their driver had arrived at camp, and would soon send someone to guide us. We could only account for the lateness of the guns by supposing they had, like ourselves, met with some unusual adventure, or had forgotten. The young men now called down to old Mr. A—— to know if he had the other cattle. He told the number he had been able to get together, and, with those DeLu had, the whole number was complete. Slowly and with much slipping and sliding, DeLu now proceeded to get himself and the oxen down to the creek bed once more. W—— led my mule in the same direction; and

I followed with Mary, who, instinctively, clung close to my shoulder while I supported her with my left arm; and, with my right hand took hold of bushes and branches to break the too-rapid descent. I had not quite reached the bottom when a "Halloa!" was heard. We answered. From the darkness up the cañon help soon appeared, we were once more in line of march, and, in less than an hour, arrived in camp.

The next day we climbed the first of the two ridges at the summit. And now I realized, in earnest, the value of a thoroughly trained mountain mule. In several places the way was so steep that the head of my animal was even with my eyes as I leaned forward with Mary's chief weight on my left arm while I clung with my right hand to the pommel of the saddle, obliged, for the time, to let the mule guide and drive himself. And nobly he did it, never slipping once; while the dark mule did as well with his great load. The other animals had to be driven, urged and kept in the track, while there seemed great danger of their packs being lost or torn; but, near evening, all arrived safely in camp.

That night we slept within a few yards of snow, which lay in a ravine; and water froze in our pans not very far from the fire, which, however, was rather low the last part of the night. But the morning was bright and sunny. "Hope sprang exultant;" for, that day, that blessed nineteenth of October, we were to cross the highest ridge, view the "promised land," and begin our descent into warmth and safety. So, without flinching I faced steeps still steeper than yesterday: I even laughed in my little one's upturned face, as she lay back against my arm, while I leaned forward almost to the neck of the mule, tugging up the hardest places. I had purposely hastened, that morning, to start ahead of the rest; and not far from noon, I was rewarded by coming out, in advance of all the others, on a rocky height whence I looked, *down,* far over constantly descending hills, to where a soft haze sent up a warm, rosy glow that seemed to me a smile of welcome; while beyond, occasional faint outlines of other mountains appeared; and I knew I was looking across the Sacramento Valley.

California, land of sunny skies—that was my first look into your smiling face. I loved you from that moment, for you seemed to welcome me with loving look into rest and safety. However brave a face I might have put on most of the time, I knew my coward heart was yearning all the while for a home-nest and a welcome into it, and you seemed to promise me both. A short time I had on those rocks, sacred to thanksgiving and prayer;

then the others came, and boisterous shouts, and snatches of song made rocks and welkin ring.

We soon began to descend. Not far from the summit, on a small plateau, affording room to camp, and a little timber, we saw traces of fires, and near by, the carcasses of two fine horses evidently not very long dead; while a number of things scattered about looked like hasty flight. We concluded this must have been the scene of disaster of one of those unfortunate parties the relief man had told us of, who were caught in the two nights of snowstorm only about ten days before. And now very cheerily we found our way leading down, and down, and down; so suddenly in some places, that my mule braced his legs and slid. But the next day the descent was not so remarkable; the road became exceedingly dusty; and the spirits of the party flagged somewhat.

We still, each night, made an effort to camp near Colonel J—— and his men, for we had been warned that the Indians had in several instances attempted to attack and rob lone emigrants, while still high up in the mountains; though there would be no danger when we reached the mines. On the night of October twenty-first we unloaded our packs and made our fires within a few rods of our courteous protectors. We had, as usual, made for our own little family a sort of barricade of packs somewhat retired from the others; the men were lying near their fire asleep; and all was still; when a sudden, loud outcry, as of mingled pain and fright followed by other hasty exclamations, and rushing footsteps, and, soon, two or three shots roused us all. We were quickly informed that two Indian arrows had been fired into our neighbors' camp, evidently aimed at the men who were sleeping in the light of their fire. One of the arrows had wounded a man, striking him directly on one of the large ribs, which had prevented its reaching the vitals. The other arrow missed its aim and fell on the ground. Several of the men rushed, armed, into the thicket whence the arrows came, fired, and pursued a short distance. But the enemy knew every turn better than strangers could, and no Indians were to be found. The wounded man proved not to be mortally wounded; and we had the satisfaction of knowing he was improving before we finally parted company—which occurred a day or two after.

On the twenty-fourth of October at evening we reached what in our guidebook was called Pleasant Valley Gold Mines; where we found two or three tents, and a few men with their gold-washing pans. They had been at work there for a while; but said the little "diggings" just there were pretty much "worked out;" and they were going, in a day or two, over to Weaver Creek where, they told us, very fine "prospects had lately been struck," and there was quite a town growing up. That night, we slept, for the first time in several months, without the fear of Indians, or the dread of perils in advance. We rested ourselves and animals for two or three days, and then moved into the village of "Weaverville," of which the miners had told us. This village was made up of tents, many of them very irregularly placed; though in one part, following the trend of the principal ravine, there was, already, something like a row of these primitive dwellings, though at considerable distances apart. We added one to that row, and soon began to gather about us little comforts and conveniences, which made us feel as though we once more had a home. In a few days after we arrived in Weaverville, rain fell heavily, and soon the mountains just above us were blocked by snow. Only one company came through after us; and they barely escaped, by means of good mules. But, with us, lovely, sunny days followed the rainy nights; and, though the season, as a whole, was unusually stormy for California, and doubtless would have been death to any caught at the mountaintops; yet there were intervals that seemed very delightful to those who had spent the preceding winter where the temperature ranged, for many weeks, below zero.

Mark Twain

Samuel Langhorne Clemens (1835–1910)—better known as Mark Twain—was one of the most prolific and celebrated authors of the Gilded Age. His enduring literary reputation may rest on works like Tom Sawyer *and* The Adventures of Huckleberry Finn—*set not in the Far West but along the shores of the Mississippi—but his Western experiences laid the groundwork for his success. He honed his skills as a reporter in Nevada and then moved to California, where he had his first triumph with "The Celebrated Frog of Calaveras County," published in 1867. Suddenly—and very briefly—Clemens was a key figure in a literary scene that included Charles Warren Stoddard, Ina Coolbrith, and Twain's rival, Bret Harte.*

Clemens grew up in Missouri and the young man tried many jobs, including piloting a Mississippi River steamboat and writing short pieces for Midwestern newspapers. When his brother Orion became secretary to the territorial governor of Nevada in 1861, Clemens accompanied him to accept "the sublime position of private secretary under him." In Nevada Clemens prospected for silver before he returned to writing, contributing sketches to a Virginia City newspaper. He also explored the countryside, including the California goldfields. His book Roughing It *recounted these Western experiences—part nostalgia (included his descriptions of life as a San Francisco journalist writing for the* Golden Era, *the* Californian, *and the* Call), *part exaggeration, and part fact. He wasn't primarily interested in portraying the beauty of the Sierra Nevada, but it comes through nevertheless in his inimitable voice, in which the waters of Lake Tahoe are "not merely transparent, but dazzlingly, brilliantly so."* ✒

from Roughing It

It was the end of August, and the skies were cloudless and the weather superb. In two or three weeks I had grown wonderfully fascinated with the curious new country, and concluded to put off my return to "the States" a while. I had grown well accustomed to wearing a damaged slouch hat, blue woolen shirt, and pants crammed into boot-tops, and gloried in the absence of coat, vest, and braces. I felt rowdyish and "bully" (as the historian Josephus phrases it, in his fine chapter upon the destruction of the Temple). It seemed to me that nothing could be so fine and so romantic. I had become an officer of the government, but that was for mere sublimity. The office was an unique sinecure. I had nothing to do and no salary. I was private secretary to his majesty the Secretary and there was not yet writing enough for two of us. So Johnny K—— and I devoted our time to amusement. He was the young son of an Ohio nabob and was out there for recreation. He got it. We had heard a world of talk about the marvelous beauty of Lake Tahoe, and finally curiosity drove us thither to see it. Three or four members of the Brigade had been there and located some timberlands on its shores and stored up a quantity of provisions in their camp. We strapped a couple of blankets on our shoulders and took an ax apiece and started— for we intended to take up a wood ranch or so ourselves and become wealthy. We were on foot. The reader will find it advantageous to go horseback. We were told that the distance was eleven miles. We tramped a long time on level ground, and then toiled laboriously up a mountain about a thousand miles high and looked over. No lake there. We descended on the other side, crossed the valley and toiled up another mountain three or four thousand miles high, apparently, and looked over again. No lake yet. We sat down tired and perspiring, and hired a couple of Chinamen to curse those people who had beguiled us. Thus refreshed, we presently resumed the march with renewed vigor and determination. We plodded on, two or three hours longer, and at last the Lake burst upon us—a noble sheet of blue water lifted six thousand three hundred feet above the level of the sea, and walled in by a rim of snow-clad mountain peaks that towered aloft full three thousand feet higher still! It was a vast oval, and one would have to use up eighty or a hundred good miles in traveling around it. As it lay there with the shadows of the mountains brilliantly photographed upon its still surface, I thought it must surely be the fairest picture the whole earth affords.

We found the small skiff belonging to the Brigade boys, and without loss of time set out across a deep bend of the lake toward the landmarks that signified the locality of the camp. I got Johnny to row—not because I mind exertion myself, but because it makes me sick to ride backwards when I am at work. But I steered. A three-mile pull brought us to the camp just as the night fell, and we stepped ashore very tired and wolfishly hungry. In a "cache" among the rocks we found the provisions and the cooking utensils, and then, all fatigued as I was, I sat down on a boulder and superintended

while Johnny gathered wood and cooked supper. Many a man who had
gone through what I had would have wanted to rest.

It was a delicious supper—hot bread, fried bacon, and black coffee. It was
a delicious solitude we were in, too. Three miles away was a sawmill and
some workmen, but there were not fifteen other human beings throughout
the wide circumference of the lake. As the darkness closed down and the
stars came out and spangled the great mirror with jewels, we smoked med-
itatively in the solemn hush and forgot our troubles and our pains. In due
time we spread our blankets in the warm sand between two large boulders
and soon fell asleep, careless of the procession of ants that passed in through
rents in our clothing and explored our persons. Nothing could disturb the
sleep that fettered us, for it had been fairly earned, and if our consciences
had any sins on them they had to adjourn court for that night, anyway. The
wind rose just as we were losing consciousness, and we were lulled to sleep
by the beating of the surf upon the shore.

It is always very cold on that lakeshore in the night, but we had plenty
of blankets and were warm enough. We never moved a muscle all night, but
waked at early dawn in the original positions, and got up at once, thoroughly refreshed, free from soreness, and brim full of friskiness. There is no
end of wholesome medicine in such an experience. That morning we
could have whipped ten such people as we were the day before—sick ones
at any rate. But the world is slow, and people will go to "water cures" and
"movement cures" and to foreign lands for health. Three months of camp
life on Lake Tahoe would restore an Egyptian mummy to his pristine vigor,
and give him an appetite like an alligator. I do not mean the oldest and driest mummies, of course, but the fresher ones. The air up there in the clouds
is very pure and fine, bracing and delicious. And why shouldn't it be?—it is
the same the angels breathe. I think that hardly any amount of fatigue can
be gathered together that a man cannot sleep off in one night on the sand
by its side. Not under a roof, but under the sky; it seldom or never rains
there in the summertime. I know a man who went there to die. But he
made a failure of it. He was a skeleton when he came, and could barely
stand. He had no appetite, and did nothing but read tracts and reflect on the
future. Three months later he was sleeping out-of-doors regularly, eating all
he could hold, three times a day, and chasing game over mountains three
thousand feet high for recreation. And he was a skeleton no longer, but
weighed part of a ton. This is no fancy sketch, but the truth. His disease was
consumption. I confidently commend his experience to other skeletons.

I superintended again, and as soon as we had eaten breakfast we got in the boat and skirted along the lakeshore about three miles and disembarked. We liked the appearance of the place, and so we claimed some three hundred acres of it and stuck our "notices" on a tree. It was yellow pine timberland—a dense forest of trees a hundred feet high and from one to five feet through at the butt. It was necessary to fence our property or we could not hold it. That is to say, it was necessary to cut down trees here and there and make them fall in such a way as to form a sort of enclosure (with pretty wide gaps in it). We cut down three trees apiece, and found it such heartbreaking work that we decided to "rest our case" on those; if they held the property, well and good; if they didn't, let the property spill out through the gaps and go; it was no use to work ourselves to death merely to save a few acres of land. Next day we came back to build a house—for a house was also necessary, in order to hold the property. We decided to build a substantial log house and excite the envy of the Brigade boys; but by the time we had cut and trimmed the first log it seemed unnecessary to be so elaborate, and so we concluded to build it of saplings. However, two saplings, duly cut and trimmed, compelled recognition of the fact that a still-modester architecture would satisfy the law, and so we concluded to build a "brush" house. We devoted the next day to this work, but we did so much "sitting around" and discussing, that by the middle of the afternoon we had achieved only a halfway sort of affair which one of us had to watch while the other cut brush, lest if both turned our backs we might not be able to find it again, it had such a strong family resemblance to the surrounding vegetation. But we were satisfied with it.

We were landowners now, duly seized and possessed, and within the protection of the law. Therefore we decided to take up our residence on our own domain and enjoy that large sense of independence which only such an experience can bring. Late the next afternoon, after a good long rest, we sailed away from the Brigade camp with all the provisions and cooking utensils we could carry off—borrow is the more accurate word—and just as the night was falling we beached the boat at our own landing.

If there is any life that is happier than the life we led on our timber ranch for the next two or three weeks, it must be a sort of life which I have not read of in books or experienced in person. We did not see a human being but ourselves during the time, or hear any sounds but those that were made by the wind and the waves, the sighing of the pines, and now and then the far-off thunder of an avalanche. The forest about us was dense and cool, the sky above us was cloudless and brilliant with sunshine, the broad lake before us was glassy and clear, or rippled and breezy, or black and storm-tossed, according to Nature's mood; and its circling border of mountain domes, clothed with forests, scarred with landslides, cloven by canyons and valleys, and helmeted with glittering snow, fitly framed and finished the noble picture. The view was always fascinating, bewitching, entrancing. The eye was never tired of gazing, night or day, in calm or storm; it suffered but one grief, and that was that it could not look always, but must close sometimes in sleep.

We slept in the sand close to the water's edge, between two protecting boulders, which took care of the stormy night winds for us. We never took any paregoric to make us sleep. At the first break of dawn we were always up and running footraces to tone down excess of physical vigor and exuberance of spirits. That is, Johnny was—but I held his hat. While smoking the pipe of peace after breakfast we watched the sentinel peaks put on the glory of the sun and followed the conquering light as it swept down among the shadows and set the captive crags and forests free. We watched the tinted pictures grow and brighten upon the water till every little detail of forest, precipice and pinnacle was wrought in and finished, and the miracle of the enchanter complete. Then to "business."

That is, drifting around in the boat. We were on the north shore. There, the rocks on the bottom are sometimes gray, sometimes white. This gives the marvelous transparency of the water a fuller advantage than it has elsewhere on the lake. We usually pushed out a hundred yards or so from shore, and then lay down on the thwarts, in the sun, and let the boat drift by the hour whither it would. We seldom talked. It interrupted the Sabbath stillness, and marred the dreams the luxurious rest and indolence brought. The shore all along was indented with deep, curved bays and coves, bordered by narrow sand-beaches; and where the sand ended, the steep mountainsides rose right up aloft into space—rose up like a vast wall a little out of the perpendicular, and thickly wooded with tall pines.

So singularly clear was the water, that where it was only twenty or thirty feet deep the bottom was so perfectly distinct that the boat seemed floating in the air! Yes, where it was even *eighty* feet deep. Every little pebble was distinct, every speckled trout, every hand's-breadth of sand. Often, as we lay on our faces, a granite boulder, as large as a village church, would start out of the bottom apparently, and seem climbing up rapidly to the surface, till presently it threatened to touch our faces, and we could not resist the impulse to seize an oar and avert the danger. But the boat would float on, and the boulder descend again, and then we could see that when we had been exactly above it, it must still have been twenty or thirty feet below the surface. Down through the transparency of these great depths, the water was not *merely* transparent, but dazzlingly, brilliantly so. All objects seen through it had a bright, strong vividness, not only of outline, but of every minute detail, which they would not have had when seen simply through the same depth of atmosphere. So empty and airy did all spaces seem below us, and so strong was the sense of floating high aloft in mid-nothingness, that we called these boat-excursions "balloon-voyages."

We fished a good deal, but we did not average one fish a week. We could see trout by the thousand winging about in the emptiness under us, or sleeping in shoals on the bottom, but they would not bite—they could see the line too plainly, perhaps. We frequently selected the trout we wanted, and rested the bait patiently and persistently on the end of his nose at a depth of eighty feet, but he would only shake it off with an annoyed manner, and shift his position.

We bathed occasionally, but the water was rather chilly, for all it looked so sunny. Sometimes we rowed out to the "blue water," a mile or two from shore. It was as dead blue as indigo there, because of the immense depth. By official measurement the lake in its center is 1,525 feet deep!

Sometimes, on lazy afternoons, we lolled on the sand in camp, and smoked pipes and read some old well-worn novels. At night, by the camp-fire, we played euchre and seven-up to strengthen the mind—and played them with cards so greasy and defaced that only a whole summer's acquaintance with them could enable the student to tell the ace of clubs from the jack of diamonds.

We never slept in our "house." It never occurred to us, for one thing; and besides, it was built to hold the ground, and that was enough. We did not wish to strain it.

By-and-by our provisions began to run short, and we went back to the old camp and laid in a new supply. We were gone all day, and reached home again about nightfall, pretty tired and hungry. While Johnny was carrying the main bulk of the provisions up to our "house" for future use, I took the loaf of bread, some slices of bacon, and the coffeepot ashore, set them down by a tree, lit a fire, and went back to the boat to get the frying pan.

While I was at this, I heard a shout from Johnny, and looking up I saw that my fire was galloping all over the premises!

Johnny was on the other side of it. He had to run through the flames to get to the lakeshore, and then we stood helpless and watched the devastation.

The ground was deeply carpeted with dry pine needles, and the fire touched them off as if they were gunpowder. It was wonderful to see with what fierce speed the tall sheet of flame traveled! My coffeepot was gone, and everything with it. In a minute and a half the fire seized upon a dense growth of dry manzanita chaparral six or eight feet high, and then the roaring and popping and crackling was something terrific. We were driven to the boat by the intense heat, and there we remained, spellbound.

Within half an hour all before us was a tossing, blinding tempest of flame! It went surging up adjacent ridges—surmounted them and disappeared in the canyons beyond—burst into view upon higher and farther ridges, presently—shed a grander illumination abroad, and dove again—flamed out again, directly, higher and still higher up the mountainside—threw out skirmishing parties of fire here and there, and sent them trailing their crimson spirals away among remote ramparts and ribs and gorges, till as far as the eye could reach the lofty mountain-fronts were webbed as it were with a tangled network of red lava streams. Away across the water the crags and domes were lit with a ruddy glare, and the firmament above was a reflected hell!

Every feature of the spectacle was repeated in the glowing mirror of the lake! Both pictures were sublime, both were beautiful; but that in the lake had a bewildering richness about it that enchanted the eye and held it with the stronger fascination.

We sat absorbed and motionless through four long hours. We never thought of supper, and never felt fatigue. But at eleven o'clock the conflagration had traveled beyond our range of vision, and then darkness stole down upon the landscape again.

Hunger asserted itself now, but there was nothing to eat. The provisions were all cooked, no doubt, but we did not go to see. We were homeless wanderers again, without any property. Our fence was gone, our house burnt down; no insurance. Our pine forest was well scorched, the dead trees all burnt up, and our broad acres of manzanita swept away. Our blankets were on our usual sand-bed, however, and so we lay down and went to sleep. The next morning we started back to the old camp, but while out a long way from shore, so great a storm came up that we dared not try to land. So I baled out the seas we shipped, and Johnny pulled heavily through the billows till we had reached a point three or four miles beyond the camp. The storm was increasing, and it became evident that it was better to take the hazard of beaching the boat than go down in a hundred fathoms of water; so we ran in, with tall whitecaps following, and I sat down in the stern-sheets and pointed her head-on to the shore. The instant the bow struck, a wave came over the stern that washed crew and cargo ashore, and saved a deal of trouble. We shivered in the lee of a boulder all the rest of the day, and froze all the night through. In the morning the tempest had gone down, and we paddled down to the camp without any unnecessary delay. We were so starved that we ate up the rest of the Brigade's provisions, and then set out to Carson to tell them about it and ask their forgiveness. It was accorded, upon payment of damages.

We made many trips to the lake after that, and had many a hair-breadth escape and bloodcurdling adventure which will never be recorded in any history.

John Muir

*John Muir (1838–1914) arrived in San Francisco aboard the steamship
Nebraska on March 27, 1868. The next day Muir and a companion set
out for Yosemite, traveling south to Gilroy, then turning east through Pacheco
Pass. At its summit Muir saw that "the Central Valley, but little trampled or
plowed as yet, was one furred, rich sheet of golden compositae, and the luminous wall of the mountains shone in all its glory. Then it seemed to me the
Sierra should be called not the Nevada, or Snowy Range, but the Range of
Light." Muir would spend the rest of his life climbing its peaks, exploring
its valleys, unlocking its geological secrets, and preserving its beauty. No one
ever did more for the cause of conservation than Muir. Not only did he found
the Sierra Club, but his writing—articles for magazines like* Century *and*
Overland Monthly, *books like* The Mountains of California *and* The
Yosemite—*educated readers about the natural history of the region. Muir
and his works were instrumental in creating the public and political will to
form the National Park System, which assured the protection of Yosemite
and Sequoia.*

*Muir's family came to the United States from Scotland when he was
eleven. He attended the University of Wisconson, but left Madison before
taking a degree. After a walking trip from Indiana to Florida—recorded in
journals that were published after his death as* A Thousand-Mile Walk to
the Gulf—*Muir headed for California. After his first visit to Yosemite, he
went to work as a shepherd. When he was finally able to return, he worked
for James Hutchings, who had opened a hotel in Yosemite Valley, and spent
his free time studying the natural history of the mountains. This "amateur"
geologist was the first to describe the valley's glacial origins, thereby irritating
Josiah Whitney, leader of the state's Geological Survey, who dismissed Muir's
theory in favor of his own, that the valley was formed by a geological cataclysm. Muir was, of course, substantially correct.*

*Muir has an extravagant style, but his literary brinkmanship is saved by
a fine sense of detail. His evident love for his subject sometimes leads him
to personify natural phenomena, often with spiritual overtones: for Muir,
mountains could stand "hushed and waiting like devout worshipers." Here
is his eyewitness description of mountains being reshaped in the 1872 Inyo
earthquake—said to have been even stronger than the San Francisco quake
of 1906.* ✒

from The Yosemite

The avalanche taluses, leaning against the walls at intervals of a mile or two, are among the most striking and interesting of the secondary features of the valley. They are from about three to five hundred feet high, made up of huge, angular, well-preserved, unshifting boulders, and instead of being slowly weathered from the cliffs like ordinary taluses, they were all formed suddenly and simultaneously by a great earthquake that occurred at least three centuries ago. And though thus hurled into existence in a few seconds or minutes, they are the least changeable of all the Sierra soil-beds. Excepting those which were launched directly into the channels of swift rivers, scarcely one of their wedged and interlacing boulders has moved since the day of their creation; and though mostly made up of huge blocks of granite, many of them from ten to fifty feet cube, weighing thousands of tons with only a few small chips, trees and shrubs make out to live and thrive on them and even delicate herbaceous plants—draperia, collomia, zauschneria, etc., soothing and coloring their wild rugged slopes with gardens and groves.

I was long in doubt on some points concerning the origin of these taluses. Plainly enough they were derived from the cliffs above them, because they are of the size of scars on the wall, the rough angular surface of which contrasts with the rounded, glaciated, unfractured parts. It was plain, too, that instead of being made up of material slowly and gradually weathered from the cliffs like ordinary taluses, almost every one of them had been formed suddenly in a single avalanche, and had not been increased in size during the last three or four centuries, for trees three or four hundred years old are growing on them, some standing at the top close to the wall without a bruise or broken branch, showing that scarcely a single boulder had ever fallen among them. Furthermore, all these taluses throughout the range seemed by the trees and lichens growing on them to be of the same age. All the phenomena thus pointed straight to a grand ancient earthquake. But for years I left the question open, and went on from cañon to cañon, observing again and again; measuring the heights of taluses throughout the range on both flanks, and the variations in the angles of their surface slopes; studying the way their boulders had been assorted and related and brought to rest, and their correspondence in size with the cleavage joints of the cliffs from whence they were derived, cautious about making up my mind. But at last all doubt as to their formation vanished.

At half-past two o'clock of a moonlit morning in March, I was awakened by a tremendous earthquake, and though I had never before enjoyed a storm of this sort, the strange thrilling motion could not be mistaken, and I ran out of my cabin, both glad and frightened, shouting, "A noble earthquake! A noble earthquake!" feeling sure I was going to learn something. The shocks were so violent and varied, and succeeded one another so closely, that I had to balance myself carefully in walking as if on the deck of a ship among waves, and it seemed impossible that the high cliffs of the valley could escape being shattered. In particular, I feared that the sheer-fronted Sentinel Rock, towering above my cabin, would be shaken down, and I took shelter back of a large yellow pine, hoping that it might protect me from at least the smaller outbounding boulders. For a minute or two the shocks became more and more violent—flashing horizontal thrusts mixed with a few twists and battering, explosive, upheaving jolts—as if Nature were wrecking her Yosemite temple, and getting ready to build a still better one.

I was now convinced before a single boulder had fallen that earthquakes were the talus-makers and positive proof soon came. It was a calm moonlight night, and no sound was heard for the first minutes or so, save low, muted, underground, bubbling rumblings, and the whispering and rustling of the agitated trees, as if Nature were holding her breath. Then, suddenly, out of the strange silence and strange motion there came a tremendous roar. The Eagle Rock on the south wall, about a half a mile up the Valley, gave way and I saw it falling in thousands of the great boulders I had so long been studying, pouring to the valley floor in a free curve luminous from friction, making a terribly sublime spectacle—an arc of glowing, passionate fire, fifteen hundred feet span, as true in form and as serene in beauty as a rainbow in the midst of the stupendous, roaring rock-storm. The sound was so tremendously deep and broad and earnest, the whole earth like a living creature seemed to have at last found a voice and to be calling to her sister planets. In trying to tell something of the size of this awful sound it seems to me that if all the thunder of all the storms I had ever heard were condensed into one roar it would not equal this rock-roar at the birth of a mountain talus. Think, then, of the roar that arose to heaven at the simultaneous birth of all the thousands of ancient cañon-taluses throughout the length and breadth of the range!

The first severe shocks were soon over, and eager to examine the new-born talus I ran up the valley in the moonlight and climbed upon it before the huge blocks, after their fiery flight, had come to complete rest. They were slowly settling into their places, chafing, grating against one another, groaning, and whispering; but no motion was visible except in a stream of small fragments pattering down the face of the cliff. A cloud of dust particles, lighted by the moon, floated out across the whole breadth of the valley, forming a ceiling that lasted until after sunrise, and the air was filled with the odor of crushed Douglas spruces from a grove that had been mowed down and mashed like weeds.

Remember we are standing on a precipice of nearly three thousand feet. The whole valley and its surroundings are unrolled before us like a map. The river below is as a ribbon of silver, seen only at intervals, winding among the trees, the trees resembling mere shrubs. The grand old sides, and proud head of Tu-tock-ah-nu-lah loom grandly up. Ditto the South Dome, and the Clouds Rest, and the Sentinel Dome, and the Sentinel, with any number of others. In the distance are many snow-covered peaks of the sierras, visible almost to their culminating crest. In the foreground, on our left, is the Ribbon Fall, 3,300 feet above the valley; on our right is the Pohono, or Bridal Veil Fall, 940 feet. Above and back of that stands the Three Graces, 3,600 feet high. If [a] storm has been gathering, perhaps we can see it swoop down "on the wings of the wind" and drape the whole landscape in clouds. At times the entire valley is filled with them, piled layer above layer, stratum above stratum, to the very tops of the mountains, their edges sufficiently light to allow the granite walls to be dimly revealed.

Inspiration Point stands out and up at a somewhat greater altitude than Mount Beatitude, but although the view of the distant sierras is more comprehensive, that of the valley is more limited. The general characteristics of both being similar, there is no necessity for any further remarks. Therefore let us enjoy the scene in peaceful reflection, and when we can say " enough," let us depart on our winding way, and dream of that we have seen.

—J. M. Hutchings, from *Scenes of Wonder and Curiosity in California: A Tourist's Guide to the Yo-semite Valley* (1872)

After the ground began to calm I ran across the meadow to the river to see in what direction it was flowing and was glad to find that *down* the valley was still down. Its waters were muddy from portions of its banks having given way, but it was flowing around its curves and over its ripples and shallows with ordinary tones and gestures. The mud would soon be cleared away and the raw slips on the banks would be the only visible record of the shaking it suffered.

The Upper Yosemite Fall, glowing white in the moonlight, seemed to know nothing of the earthquake, manifesting no change in form or voice, as far as I could see or hear.

After a second startling shock, about half-past three o'clock, the ground continued to tremble gently, and smooth, hollow rumbling sounds, not always distinguishable from the rounded, bumping, explosive tones of the falls, came from deep in the mountains in a northern direction.

The few Indians fled from their huts to the middle of the valley, fearing that angry spirits were trying to kill them; and, as I afterward learned, most of the Yosemite tribe, who were spending the winter at their village on Bull Creek forty miles away, were so terrified that they ran into the river and washed themselves—getting themselves clean enough to say their prayers, I suppose, or to die. I asked Dick, one of the Indians with whom I was acquainted, "What made the ground shake and jump so much?" He only shook his head and said, "No good. No good," and looked appealingly to me to give him hope that his life was to be spared.

In the morning I found the few white settlers assembled in front of the old Hutchings Hotel comparing notes and meditating flight to the lowlands, seemingly as sorely frightened as the Indians. Shortly after sunrise a low, blunt, muffled rumbling, like distant thunder, was followed by another series of shocks, which, though not nearly so severe as the first, made the cliffs and domes tremble like jelly, and the big pines and oaks thrill and swish and wave their branches with startling effect. Then the talkers were suddenly hushed, and the solemnity on their faces was sublime. One in particular of these winter neighbors, a somewhat speculative thinker with whom I had often conversed, was a firm believer in the cataclysmic origin of the valley; and I now jokingly remarked that his wild tumble-down-and-engulfment hypothesis might soon be proved, since these underground rumblings and shakings might be the forerunners of another Yosemite-making cataclysm, which would perhaps double the depth of the valley by swallowing the floor, leaving the ends of the roads and trails dangling three or four thousand feet in the air. Just then came the third series of shocks, and it was fine to see how awfully silent and solemn he became. His belief in the existence of a mysterious abyss, into which the suspended floor of the valley, and all the domes and battlements of the walls might at any moment go roaring down, mightily troubled him. To diminish his fears and laugh him into something like reasonable faith, I said, "Come, cheer up; smile a little and clap your hands, now that kind Mother Earth is trotting us on her knee to amuse us and make us good." But the well-meant joke seemed irreverent and utterly failed, as if only prayerful terror could rightly belong to the wild beauty-making business. Even after all the heavier shocks were over I could do nothing to reassure him. On the contrary, he handed me the keys of his little store to keep, saying that with a companion of like mind he was going to the lowlands to stay until the fate of poor, trembling Yosemite was settled. In vain I rallied them on their fears, calling attention to the strength of the granite walls of our valley home, the very best and solidest masonry in the world, and less likely to collapse and sink than the sedimentary lowlands to which they were looking for safety; and saying that in any case they sometime would have to die, and so grand a burial was not to be slighted. But they were too seriously panic-stricken to get comfort from anything I could say.

During the third severe shock the trees were so violently shaken that the birds flew out with frightened cries. In particular, I noticed two robins flying in terror from a leafless oak, the branches of which swished and quivered as if struck by a heavy battering ram. Exceedingly interesting were the flashing and quivering of the elastic needles of the pines in the sunlight and the waving up and down of the branches while the trunks stood rigid. There was no swaying, waving, or swirling as in wind-storms, but quick, quivering jerks, and at times the heavy tasseled branches moved as if they had all been pressed down against the trunk and suddenly let go, to spring up and vibrate until they came to rest again. Only the owls seemed to be undisturbed. Before the rumbling echoes had died away a hollow-voiced owl began to hoot in philosophical tranquillity from near the edge of the new talus as if nothing extraordinary had occurred, although, perhaps, he was curious to know what all the noise was about. His "hoot-too-hoot-too-whoo" might have meant, "what's a' the steer, kimmer?"

It was long before the valley found perfect rest. The rocks trembled more or less every day for over two months, and I kept a bucket of water on my table to learn what I could of the movements. The blunt thunder in the

depths of the mountains was usually followed by sudden jarring, horizontal thrusts from the northward, often succeeded by twisting, upjolting
movements. More than a month after the first great shock, when I was
standing on a fallen tree up the valley near Lamon's winter cabin, I heard a
distinct bubbling thunder from the direction of Tenaya Cañon. Carlo, a
large intelligent St. Bernard dog standing beside me seemed greatly astonished, and looked intently in that direction with mouth open and uttered a
low *Wouf!* as if saying, "What's that?" He must have known that it was not
thunder, though like it. The air was perfectly still, not the faintest breath of
wind perceptible, and a fine, mellow, sunny hush pervaded everything, in
the midst of which came that subterranean thunder. Then, while we gazed
and listened, came the corresponding shocks, distinct as if some mighty
hand had shaken the ground. After the sharp horizontal jars died away, they
were followed by a gentle rocking and undulating of the ground so distinct
that Carlo looked at the log on which he was standing to see who was
shaking it. It was the season of flooded meadows and the pools about me,
calm as sheets of glass, were suddenly thrown into low ruffling waves.

Judging by its effects, this Yosemite, or Inyo earthquake, as it is sometimes
called, was gentle as compared with the one that gave rise to the grand talus
system of the range and did so much for the cañon scenery. Nature, usually so deliberate in her operations, then created, as we have seen, a new set
of features, simply by giving the mountains a shake—changing not only the
high peaks and cliffs, but the streams. As soon as these rock avalanches fell,
the streams began to sing new songs; for in many places thousands of boulders were hurled into their channels, roughening and half-damming them,
compelling the waters to surge and roar in rapids where before they glided
smoothly. Some of the streams were completely dammed; driftwood, leaves,
etc., gradually filling the interstices between the boulders, thus giving rise
to lakes and level reaches; and these again, after being gradually filled in,
were changed to meadows, through which the streams are now silently
meandering; while at the same time some of the taluses took the places of
old meadows and groves. Thus rough places were made smooth, and
smooth places rough. But, on the whole, by what at first sight seemed pure
confounded confusion and ruin, the landscapes were enriched; for gradually every talus was covered with groves and gardens, and made a finely pro-
portioned and ornamental base for the cliffs. In this work of beauty, every
boulder is prepared and measured and put in its place more thoughtfully
than are the stones of temples. If for a moment you are inclined to regard

these taluses as mere draggled, chaotic dumps, climb to the top of one of them, and run down without any haggling, puttering hesitation, boldly jumping from boulder to boulder with even speed. You will then find your feet playing a tune, and quickly discover the music and poetry of these magnificent rock piles—a fine lesson; and all Nature's wildness tells the same story—the shocks and outbursts of earthquakes, volcanoes, geysers, roaring, thundering waves and floods, the silent uprush of sap in plants, storms of every sort—each and all are the orderly beauty-making love-beats of Nature's heart.

J. Smeaton Chase

*J. Smeaton Chase (1864–1923) came to California in 1890, leaving
behind his native England and a family well established in the business of
books: his father was a publisher and his brother worked for a London bookstore. Lawrence Clark Powell tells us that it is not known what led Chase
to California, perhaps a "quest for health, wealth, and happiness." But he
brought with him a love of nature and travel, passions he indulged in
lengthy horseback trips around his adopted state, recorded in three books:*
California Coast Trails, Yosemite Trails, *and* California Desert Trails.

*Visiting the Sierra on horseback, Chase found this mode of travel well
suited to the close observation of difficult terrain and the sometimes difficult
people who lived there.* ✒

from Yosemite Trails

On a hot, still morning of middle summer I left the Yosemite Valley for a
month's expedition into the High Sierra. The region I expected to travel
would be entirely new to me, so it was advisable to take a guide; and as
there would be no opportunity for refurnishing with provisions until I
reached Mono Lake, on the eastern side of the mountains, it was necessary
to take enough pack animals to carry supplies for two or three weeks.

The problems of guide and pack train solved themselves very satisfacto-
rily, and in this manner: I was returning one day to camp, after compassing,
at the cost of a broken rod, the overthrow of an experienced trout who
had long defied me in a reach of the river a mile or so below the village.
Near the place where we settled our account I came upon a man of a
cheerful and self-helping aspect, who was camped in a little meadow that
ran to the riverbank. In conversation this proved to be one Bodie, who had
been recommended to me as a good man and a capable guide; and before
we parted a "deal" had been arranged whereby he and five animals were
placed at my disposal for the month of July.

Mr. Field, whom I already knew as a pleasant comrade and a thorough
photographer, whose excellent pictures illustrate these pages, was also to

accompany the expedition, completing a triangular (or perhaps it would be fairer to say an octagonal) party.

It was the third of July when Field and I left the valley. The village had broken out in a rash of flags and bunting. Fireworks and a dance were billed to wind up the exercises of the Fourth, and I confess I felt no regret in turning my back upon these festive incongruities.

We drove out on the Big Oak Flat road, bound for Crocker's Station, where Bodie awaited us with the animals. This is the road which, from the southern side of the valley, one sees traced like a white ribbon on the northern cañon wall. I found it on the whole disappointing in the views it offers; but the Bridal Veil Fall was often in sight, and interesting glimpses were opened up of the wide scoop down which the Bridal Veil Creek flows to its famous plunge: while the remarkable fractures of the southern wall of the Merced Cañon would compel the attention of the least geological of men. From this road also El Capitan shows more magnificently than from any other point of view, fronting the west with a vast, doorlike cliff that is truly imposing in its unbroken verticality. But many of the most wonderful features of the valley are not within the view from this side, while from the spot that has been ambitiously named New Inspiration Point, El Capitan itself is completely hidden and only a small segment of the Half Dome is in sight.

Making up, however, for all deficiencies, an unusual haze that day filled the valley with an atmosphere like a vapor of opals, and steeped the landscape in a dreamy beauty, ineffably airy and spiritual. It was like one of those enchanted valleys of our childhood, populated by friendly fairies, gigantic genii, and companionable birds and beasts, where gallant lovers in peach-colored velvet were constantly occupied in rescuing princesses in silver and sky blue.

The summer, moreover, was at its climax of flowers. Every forest opening glinted with cyclamens, columbines, and wallflowers, these last of a peculiar sultry yellow like compressed sunshine. As we rose, the timber changed from yellow pine to spruce, from spruce to sugar pine, then to fir, and lastly to tamarack. At Tamarack Flat we stopped for an hour to rest the team, fagged with a climb of twenty-five hundred feet, and then, after making another rise to Gin Flat (a natural culmination), began the long descent.

The road passes through the Tuolumne Grove of sequoias. While we were paying our homage to some of the most notable trees, we encountered a tall backwoodsman who sat whittling and whistling beside the road.

Your true backwoodsman savors of the forest as a fisherman smells of the
sea, and I was struck by the woodcraftiness, so to speak, of this man's
appearance. He looked like a kind of faun, and his occupation of whittling
seemed almost necessary and symbolic. Long, lean, and shaggy, there was a
fine air of wild instinct about him; he seemed a part of the landscape; and
it was a shock to find him to be after all a prosaic and commercially mind-
ed creature, when, in reply to a remark upon the stateliness of the great
trees that rose around us, he cast a calculating eye over the "General
Lawton," and replied, "Don't know nothin' about that; maybe they's fine,
maybe they ain't. That thar stick will cut up two hunnerd thousand foot of
lumber, board measure. To my thinkin' it's all dad-blasted foolishness that a
feller cain't cut a stick o' timber like that. What's trees, anyway? Ain't they
lumber?" He spat viciously to right and left, throwing up little volcanoes of
dust, and reiterated, "A dad-blasted foolishness, that's what it is: two hunnerd thousand foot, board measure." For some reason, the fact of this iniq-
uitous waste of lumber being estimated by board measure seemed to aggra-
vate the matter intolerably, and he continued dad-blasting and spitting
angrily until, when we parted, quite a range of small craters surrounded
him....

The young sequoias for the first few years of their life show no mark of
their royal nature, but crook and twist about in a particularly ambitionless
manner. Their branchlets sprawl out in a short-sleeved, lanky fashion, and
their heads, as if they were young anthropophagi, "do grow beneath their
shoulders." Standing generally in tangled clumps and thickets, they have an
awkward, schoolboyish air, very different from that of the pines and firs,
which even while crowded in their nurseries show their lineage in an aris-
tocratic trimness.

But after a few decades blood begins to tell. The sequoia becomes conscious of his destiny, and, answering the inward urge, makes for the skies in
a climbing, high-hearted fashion that is fine to behold. Still the family like-
ness does not shine out clearly as they stand mixed in the general forest of
the conifers, all of high birth. They keep yet the thin whiplike branchlets
that grow irregularly from foot to crown, by now bare of foliage, but furred
instead with yellow moss. By the time he reaches his first century of age,
however, being then perhaps eighty feet high, the young tree sloughs his
skin and begins to take on the noble color and habit that mark him at a
glance as a sequoia, of the old nobility of the tree-creation. He "mews his
mighty youth," and casting off with it the undistinguished features of

> What a sight of the falls reflected to the low-hanging moon! The tall trees looked no other but the ghosts or spirits who gathered and talked something wonderful and evil; and what a sound of water, besides that of the fall, which dashed down the river! I felt cold and suddenly hungry when I became conscious of my sad being amid an almost frightening demonstration of Nature, particularly in the night.
> —Yone Noguchi, from *The Story of Yone Noguchi Told by Himself* (1915)

childhood, the trunk, clean, bright, and tapering, which is to bear aloft his massive head through the long procession of the centuries, stands revealed.

By five hundred years the full color is taken, the taper has widened to a slight curve at the foot, and the pointed reticulation of the bark is noticeable. The characteristic shape is now fully marked—the head a sugar-loaf cone, remarkable in its regularity of outline, and the trunk a steadfast column of shining red. Thenceforward they go from strength to strength, ever more glorious and excellent. Their deep-rifted bark clothes them with dignity and age; the great limbs, mossed and lichened, stand out oaklike above and athwart the pines and firs whose dainty tops spire a hundred feet into the air; and still higher, their sumptuous tops are built up in dense bosses of corded foliage. In those high places they bear their multitudinous cones, pendent singly or in twos or threes on stout, bracted stems; till in due time the sun ripens them and coaxes them to open their tight-locked caskets, and the wind, careful old forester, winnows out the flaky seeds and sows them in generous broadcast over the warm forest floor.

When the first millennium is reached the general shape is unchanged, only that the curve at the base is wider, and the lowest limbs are becoming weary and trend downward from the weight of the snows of uncounted winters. Another age passes, and Atlas has planted his feet still wider as he bears up the enormous weight. The symmetry is broken: he has now entered upon middle age, and his individual features are stamped upon him. You may tell Achilles from Agamemnon, and Ajax from Menelaus. Here a thunderbolt has ploughed a heavy furrow, and that fearful scar marks the place where a treelike arm was torn away.

A second millennium passes, with thirty more generations of the sons of men, and the sequoia shows no change but that he has settled at his base into a convex curve, which may be reversed as it enters the ground—a very beautiful form, exhibiting the perfect combination of strength with grace which marks this noblest of trees. From then onward Time has no dominion over him, and the passage of centuries does but mark his inexhaustible fertility and power.

A thunderstorm in this forest is a memorable experience, and one which even enhances the awe of the great sequoias. I was roaming one day about the lower Mariposa Grove, commiserating the tourists who were driven swiftly past on schedule, when I became aware of that quickening of the senses which one feels before a heavy storm. I had noticed an unusual quietness of the population of the brush, the birds going about their concerns with a serious air that was quaint and amusing. The robins in particular foraged silently through the silent woods, passing and repassing one another alternately with that comical appearance of being pushed in jerks from behind, like perambulators. The snowbird's soliloquies were carried on under his breath: even the jay, impudent and voluble in general beyond the wont of birds, refrained himself and pursued his persecutions almost politely.

Suddenly a heavy wind roared overhead, from which the firs and pines recoiled; but I noticed that the sequoias stood stately and unmoving, only their foliage was roughly tossed. Then came a wild slither of lightning, then a crash of thunder, and then the rain came tearing down. For ten minutes the elements were in a paroxysm; lightning thrust and parried, thunder roared incoherent applause, and the rain fell savagely as if it were flung by an angry hand. Then with another burst of wind, that filled the air with sodden tassels of foliage, the storm passed on, and the only sound was that of a hundred rills trilling tiny carillons. When one considers how many times the thunderbolts must have hurtled about these ancient trees it is astonishing that one of them is left standing.

Kenneth Rexroth

In An Autobiographical Novel, *Kenneth Rexroth (1905–1982)
declared that thanks to his long experience of living outdoors, his "poetry
and philosophy of life became what it's now fashionable to call ecological. I
came to think of myself as a microcosm of a macrocosm, related to chipmunks
and bears and pine trees and stars and nebulae and rocks and fossils, as part
of an infinitely interrelated complex of being." Born in Indiana, Rexroth
settled in San Francisco in 1927, largely because he thought few cities in the
world could give such immediate access to mountains and sea. Already well
established as part of the Bay Area avant-garde, Rexroth become associated
with the San Francisco literary renaissance of the 1950s. Though skeptical
that much of the movement was a "public relations invention," he still
acknowledged the achievements of the best of the Beat Generation, especially
Gary Snyder, whose work shows the influence of the older poet.*

*Rexroth nurtured his creative spirit by reading and translating poetry of
the ancient writers of the West and East, influencing his notion of what
poetry is for. Many readers, including critic Morgan Gibson, find in
Rexroth's poetry a strong expression of communion: "Originating as personal vision which becomes verbal, interpersonal communication, poetry functions
as a sacrament, an act of holy union." In the following poems, Rexroth
places himself within the marvelous compass of the Sierra landscape, and the
images he creates place his readers right at his side, a literary community
sharing the warmth of a campfire and the wonder of nature.* ❧

Spring, Sierra Nevada

Once more golden Scorpio glows over the col
Above Deadman Canyon, orderly and brilliant,
Like an inspiration in the brain of Archimedes.
I have seen its light over the warm sea,
Over the coconut beaches, phosphorescent and pulsing;
And the living light in the water
Shivering away from the swimming hand,
Creeping against the lips, filling the floating hair.

Here where the glaciers have been and the snow stays late,
The stone is clean as light, the light steady as stone.
The relationship of stone, ice and stars is systematic and enduring:
Novelty emerges after centuries, a rock spalls from the cliffs,
The glacier contracts and turns grayer,
The stream cuts new sinuosities in the meadow,
The sun moves through space and the earth with it,
The stars change places.
        The snow has lasted longer this year,
Than anyone can remember. The lowest meadow is a lake,
The next two are snowfields, the pass is covered with snow,
Only the steepest rocks are bare. Between the pass
And the last meadow the snowfield gapes for a hundred feet,
In a narrow blue chasm through which a waterfall drops,
Spangled with sunset at the top, black and muscular
Where it disappears again in the snow.
The world is filled with hidden running water
That pounds in the ears like ether;
The granite needles rise from the snow, pale as steel;
Above the copper mine the cliff is blood red,
The white snow breaks at the edge of it;
The sky comes close to my eyes like the blue eyes
Of someone kissed in sleep.
        I descend to camp,
To the young, sticky, wrinkled aspen leaves,
To the first violets and wild cyclamen,
And cook supper in the blue twilight.
All night deer pass over the snow on sharp hooves,
In the darkness their cold muzzles find the new grass
At the edge of the snow.

Fall, Sierra Nevada

This morning the hermit thrush was absent at breakfast,
His place was taken by a family of chickadees;
At noon a flock of humming birds passed south,

Whirling in the wind up over the saddle between
Ritter and Banner, following the migration lane
Of the Sierra crest southward to Guatemala.
All day cloud shadows have moved over the face of the mountain,
The shadow of a golden eagle weaving between them
Over the face of the glacier.
At sunset the half-moon rides on the bent back of the Scorpion,
The Great Bear kneels on the mountain.
Ten degrees below the moon
Venus sets in the haze arising from the Great Valley.
Jupiter, in opposition to the sun, rises in the alpenglow
Between the burnt peaks. The ventriloquial belling
Of an owl mingles with the bells of the waterfall.
Now there is distant thunder on the east wind.
The east face of the mountain above me
Is lit with far off lightnings and the sky
Above the pass blazes momentarily like an aurora.
It is storming in the White Mountains,
On the arid fourteen-thousand-foot peaks;
Rain is falling on the narrow gray ranges
And dark sedge meadows and white salt flats of Nevada.
Just before moonset a small dense cumulus cloud,
Gleaming like a grape cluster of metal,
Moves over the Sierra crest and grows down the westward slope.
Frost, the color and duality of the cloud,
Lies over all the marsh below my campsite.
The wiry clumps of dwarfed whitebark pines
Are smoky and indistinct in the moonlight,
Only their shadows are really visible.
The lake is immobile and holds the stars
And the peaks deep in itself without a quiver.
In the shallows the geometrical tendrils of ice
Spread their wonderful mathematics in silence.
All night the eyes of deer shine for an instant
As they cross the radius of my firelight.
In the morning the trail will look like a sheep driveway,
All the tracks will point down to the lower canyon.
"Thus," says Tyndall, "the concerns of this little place

Are changed and fashioned by the obliquity of the earth's axis,
The chain of dependence which runs through creation,
And links the roll of a planet alike with the interests
Of marmots and of men."

Time Is the Mercy of Eternity

Time is divided into
Seconds, minutes, hours, years,
And centuries. Take any
One of them and add up its
Content, all the world over.
One division contains much
The same as any other.
What can you say in a poem?
Past forty, you've said it all.
The dwarf black oak grows out of
The cliff below my feet. It
May be two hundred years old,
Yet its trunk is no bigger
Than my wrist, its crown does not
Come to my shoulder. The late
Afternoon sun behind it
Fills its leaves with light like
A gem tree, like the wishing
Tree of jewels in the Eastern
Stories. Below it the cliff
Falls sheer away five hundred
Feet to a single burnt pine,
And then another thousand
Feet to a river, noisy
In spate. Off beyond it stretches
Shimmering space, then fold on
Dimmer fold of wooded hills,
Then, hardly visible in
The pulsating heat, the flat

Lands of the San Joaquin Valley,
Boiling with life and trouble.
The pale new green leaves twinkle
In the rising air. A blue
Black, sharp-beaked, sharp-crested jay
Rests for a moment amongst
Them and then plunges off, down
Through the hazy June afternoon.
Far away the writhing city
Burns in a fire of transcendence
And commodities. The bowels
Of men are wrung between the poles
Of meaningless antithesis.
The holiness of the real
Is always there, accessible
In total immanence. The nodes
Of transcendence coagulate
In you, the experiencer,
And in the other, the lover.
When the first blooms come on the
Apple trees, and the spring moon
Swims in immeasurable
Clear deeps of palpable light,
I sit by the waterfall.
The owls call, one beyond the
Other, indefinitely
Away into the warm night.
The moist black rocks gleam faintly.
The curling moss smells of wet life.
The waterfall is a rope
Of music, a black and white
Spotted snake in the moonlit
Forest. The thighs of the goddess
Close me in. The moon lifts into
The cleft of the mountains and a
Cloud of light pours around me like
Blazing perfume. When the moon has
Passed on and the owls are loud in

My ears again, I kneel and drink
The cold, sweet, twisting water.

All day clouds drift up the canyon.
By noon the high peaks are hidden.
Thunder mutters in the distance.
Suddenly the canyon is gone.
My camp on its narrow ledge is
Isolated in swirling mist.
Even the nearby pines grow dim,
And recede into the grayness.
Yellow lightning bursts, like fire through
Smoke, and sets all the mist aglow.
Thunder explodes under my feet.
The rain pours hissing through the
Pine needles. White hailstones fall
Awry between the red pine trunks.
They rattle on my tent. I catch
Some and watch them melt in my hand.
As evening comes, birds ruffle
Their feathers, and fly gingerly
From branch to branch, and sing a few
Notes, while through the orange twilight
Fall green, widely spaced drops of rain.

For three days the clouds have piled up,
And rain has circled the mountains.
For a while it will fall over
Black Rock Pass, and then move across
To the red Kaweahs, and then
On to the white Whitney Range. But
Here by the lake it does not fall,
And the air grows more oppressive.
I swim lazily. Even the
Water seems to be heavier.
The air is full of mosquitoes.
After a listless lunch, I sit
On the bank reading the wise poems

Of Charles Cros. Suddenly the wind
Rises. The tent flaps noisily.
Twigs and dust and pine needles fly
In all directions. Then the wind
Drops and the rain falls on the lake.
The drops chime against the ripples
Like the Japanese glass wind bells
I loved so much as a child.
The rain is gone in an hour.
In the clear evening freshness,
I hear the bell on my donkey,
In his meadow, a mile away.
Nighthawks cry overhead and dive,
Thrumming their wings as they turn.
A deer comes down to the water.
The high passes are closed with snow.
I am the first person in this season.
No one comes by. I am alone
In the midst of a hundred mountains.

Five o'clock, mid-August evening,
The long sunlight is golden
On the deep green grass and bright
Red flowers of the meadow.
I stop where a meander
Of the brook forms a deep pool.
The water is greenish brown,
But perfectly transparent.
A small dense cloud of hundreds
Of midges, no bigger than
My head, hovers over it.
On the bank are two small frogs.
In the water are beetles,
Hydras, water bugs, larvae
Of several insects. On
The surface are water boatmen.
I realize that the color
Of the water itself is

Due to millions of active
Green flecks of life. It is like
Peering into an inkspot,
And finding yourself staring
Out into the Milky Way.
The deep reverberation
Of my identity with
All this plenitude of life
Leaves me shaken and giddy.
I step softly across the
Meadows as the deer lift their
Antlers and idly watch me.

Here on this high plateau where
No one ever comes, beside
This lake filled with mirrored mountains,
The hours and days and weeks
Go by without variation.
Even the rare storms pass over
And empty themselves on the peaks.
There are no fish in the water.
There are few deer or bear in the woods.
Only the bright blue damsel flies
On the reeds in the daytime,
And the nighthawks overhead
In the evening. Suspended
In absolutely transparent
Air and water and time, I
Take on a kind of crystalline
Being. In this translucent
Immense here and now, if ever,
The form of the person should be
Visible, its geometry,
Its crystallography, and
Its astronomy. The good
And evil of my history
Go by. I can see them and
Weigh them. They go first, with all

The other personal facts,
And sensations, and desires.
At last there is nothing left
But knowledge, itself a vast
Crystal encompassing the
Limitless crystal of air
And rock and water. And the
Two crystals are perfectly
Silent. There is nothing to
Say about them. Nothing at all.

Gary Snyder

Gary Snyder (1930–) earned his wilderness credentials early. Born in San Francisco, he grew up in the Pacific Northwest, attending schools in Seattle and Portland. While still in college, he worked as a lumberjack, trail builder, and fire lookout; became expert at mountain climbing; and learned back-country woodsmanship. His first books of poems commemorate some of these experiences: Riprap *is named for "a cobble of stone laid on steep slick rock to make a trail for horses in the mountains." Snyder associated with Beat Generation writers like Jack Kerouac, but was always more deeply drawn to the landscape, partly from temperament and personal experience, partly from his interest in Native American traditions, his study of Zen Buddhism, and his love for the work of Japanese and Chinese poets and landscape artists.*

Snyder has always sought a wholeness of vision, in some ways not unlike two other—and very different—California poets, Robinson Jeffers and Kenneth Rexroth, both of whom Snyder has acknowledged as influences. In his preface for New Nature, *he writes, "Hakuin Zenji puts it 'self-nature that is no nature / ... far beyond mere doctrine.' An open space to move in, with the whole body, the whole mind." The resultant essays and poems are enjoying increasing critical recognition, including honors like the Pulitzer Prize for* Turtle Island *in 1974. In "John Muir on Mt. Ritter" Snyder borrows Muir's own words to create a new version of a famous story.* ✺

John Muir on Mt. Ritter

After scanning its face again and again,
I began to scale it, picking my holds
With intense caution. About half-way
To the top, I was suddenly brought to
A dead stop, with arms outspread
Clinging close to the face of the rock
Unable to move hand or foot
Either up or down. My doom
Appeared fixed. I MUST fall.
There would be a moment of

Bewilderment, and then,
A lifeless rumble down the cliff
To the glacier below.
My mind seemed to fill with a
Stifling smoke. This terrible eclipse
Lasted only a moment, when life blazed
Forth again with preternatural clearness.
I seemed suddenly to become possessed
Of a new sense. My trembling muscles
Became firm again, every rift and flaw in
The rock was seen as through a microscope,
My limbs moved with a positiveness and precision
With which I seemed to have
Nothing at all to do.

Burning the Small Dead

Burning the small dead
          branches
broke from beneath
   thick spreading
          whitebark pine.

          a hundred summers
snowmelt   rock   and air

hiss in a twisted bough.

   sierra granite;
          Mt. Ritter—
          black rock twice as old.

Deneb, Altair

windy fire

The Canyon Wren

for James and Carol Katz

I look up at the cliffs
But we're swept on by   downriver
                    the rafts
Wobble and slide over roils of water
        boulders shimmer
        under the arching stream
Rock walls straight up on both sides.
A hawk cuts across that narrow sky
                    hit by sun,

We paddle forward, backstroke, turn,
Spinning through eddies and waves
Stairsteps of churning whitewater.
        above the roar
        hear the song of a Canyon Wren.

A smooth stretch, drifting and resting.
Hear it again, delicate downward song

        ti ti   ti ti tee tee tee

Descending through ancient beds.
A single female mallard flies upstream—

Shooting the Hundred-Pace Rapids
Su Shih saw, for a moment,
        it all stand still
"I stare at the water:
        it moves with unspeakable slowness"

Dōgen, writing at midnight,
        "mountains flow

        "water is the palace of the dragon
        "it does not flow away."

We beach up at China Camp
Between piles of stone
Stacked there by black-haired miners,
      cook in the dark
      sleep all night long by the stream.

These songs that are here and gone,
Here and gone,
To purify our ears.

The Stanislaus River runs through Central Miwok country and down to the San Joaquin valley. The twists and turns of the river, the layering, swirling stone cliffs of the gorges are cut in nine-million-year-old latites. For many seasons lovers of rocks and water have danced in rafts and kayaks down this dragon-arm of the high Sierra. Not long ago Jim Katz and friends, river runners all, asked me to shoot the river with them, to see its face once more before it goes under the rising waters of the New Melones Dam. The song of the Canyon Wren stayed with us the whole voyage; at China Camp, in the dark, I wrote this poem.

          April 40081, Stanislaus River, Camp 9 to Parrott's Ferry

THE SOUTHERN
DESERT AND BASIN

W ithin its compass Southern California contains three distinct deserts. The northernmost of these is part of the Great Basin, the trans-Sierra portion, thirteen thousand square miles extending east from the Sierra Nevada into Owens Valley and beyond. It includes some of Death Valley, which descends to the lowest spot in the Western Hemisphere at Badwater, 282 feet below sea level. Temperatures here can reach 120 degrees, which makes the appearance of an abundance of wildflowers each spring seem like a natural miracle. South of this is the high desert of the Mojave, the land of the Joshua tree and—at fifteen thousand square miles—California's largest and best-known desert. The Mojave is not usually as hot in the summer as Death Valley or the Colorado Desert, and because of its higher elevations—approaching four thousand feet in some places—it sometimes has a dusting of snow during the winter. The San Gabriel, San Bernardino, and Chocolate Mountains separate the Mojave from the southernmost of California's deserts, the four-thousand-square-mile Colorado, an extension of the blistering Sonoran Desert across the Colorado River in Arizona and Mexico.

Remote areas within these deserts impress their occasional human visitor with an illusion of absolute emptiness. But the familiar phrase "living desert" reminds us that they are far from uninhabited. The deserts are home to bighorn sheep, coyotes, rattlesnakes, desert tortoises, turkey vultures, and all manner of rodents and insects. But these lives are invisible when we survey the vast reaches opening onto desert horizons. For example, at the northern edge of the Saline Valley—between the Inyo Mountains and the Saline Range—the ineffable silence is broken only by slight breezes rustling Mormon tea and desert sage. The valley floor is pale amber; the dark hills rising above it appear black by contrast. Within the valley are an old saltworks, a natural spring, a salt lake, and a long, lonely road meandering through miles and miles of astonishing peace.

Despite the apparent barrenness of the desert landscape, Native Americans had made it their home for generations. Along the Colorado River in the south, the Mojave and Yuma grew corn, beans, pumpkins, and melons in seasonal washes. Further north, the Chemehuevi hunted the small game around the Providence Mountains, supplementing their diet with seeds from mesquite bushes and with produce watered by springs. East of the Sierra were the Paiute of the Owens Valley, hunters and gatherers who lived on pine nuts, roots, seeds, birds, fish, and the jackrabbits and antelope they caught in communal hunts each fall.

The interior deserts were not always as dry as they are today. Fossils of dwarf horses, deer, tapirs, dogs, and even rhinos found in northern Death Valley indicate that the area was wet and wooded over thirty million years ago. Then land west of the San Andreas fault slid to the north, stretching the southern interior, thereby creating new faults, lifting mountain ranges, and dropping valleys. During this period, the Panamint Range moved northwest about fifty miles, causing the adjacent area to sink and form Death Valley. Although no human being could ever have seen this fertile landscape, a Shoshone story seems to describe its destruction: a prideful queen once forced her subjects to build an immense palace and treated them like slaves in her frenzy to complete it. She did not spare even her own daughter, who dropped from fatigue, cursing the queen and her realm. After her daughter's death, "The sun came out with blinding heat and light. Vegetation withered. Animals disappeared. Streams and wells dried up." And once-fertile land became known as "Ground Afire."

The daunting nature of California's deserts did not stop the Spanish. They were looking for an alternative to the long dangerous sea voyages to the Alta California coast, having established a few presidios and missions there. In the late 1760s Francisco Tomás Hermenegildo Garcés had begun pushing north from Sonora, exploring as far as the southern San Joaquin Valley. Captain Juan Bautista de Anza was looking for an overland route when he made the desert crossing in 1774, accompanied by Garcés and another Franciscan, Pedro Font. The crossing depended on the goodwill of the Yuma Indians, with whom Garcés had established an amicable relationship. Unfortunately this relationship did not last. Aggrieved by Spanish mistreatment, the Yuma attacked two mission way stations near the Colorado River in 1781. Among the victims was Garcés, who was traveling with

Spanish soldiers taking a shortcut through Yuma fields. This bloodshed ended overland access to California until after Mexican independence, when the Old Spanish Trail, a caravan route from Santa Fe, New Mexico, began carrying regular traffic to Los Angeles.

Soon, U.S. as well as Mexican travelers were following this dangerous route. Among the earliest was William Manly, whose group—headed for the goldfields—blundered into Death Valley. Manly's account of the adventure has become a mainstay of Western history. Walter Van Tilburg Clark recalls the miseries of the Manly Party in his 1945 novel *The City of Trembling Leaves,* which describes the treacherous beauty of the desert, its sand dunes displaying "clear and lovely wind-ripples, like the water marks on a shallow beach."

After California became part of the United States in 1850, scientific exploration of this untamed region began. In 1870 geologist Joseph LeConte took a trip over Mono Pass to the Great Basin, reporting his observations in *A Journal of Ramblings through the High Sierra of California.* The Owens Valley already had its first settlers by the time LeConte described it. Cattle ranchers had started moving in by 1861 and soon farmers were planting crops along the river. Before Los Angeles laid claim to much of the trans-Sierra water, farmers and ranchers were planning an extensive system of irrigation. Mary Austin moved to Independence when her husband accepted a job as manager of an Owens Valley irrigation project. Her sketches of the region—where "not the law, but the land set the limit"—became the 1903 volume *The Land of Little Rain,* a classic of American nature writing.

The interior deserts also had tremendous mineral potential. There were early silver strikes at places like Calico and the Rand District in the Mojave, while Death Valley became known for its borax, which was transported in sixteen-foot wagons drawn by two horses and eighteen mules, the so-called twenty-mule teams. The establishment of desert mine-camps and the construction of railroads eventually encouraged settlement in these areas.

The Colorado Desert, meanwhile, exerted its own powerful pull on the imagination of writers. John C. Van Dijk, a Rutgers professor of art history, helped to define its allure with his 1901 volume *The Desert: Further Studies in Natural Appearances,* a book which made claims for the purity of light "which falls upon the upper peaks of the Sierra Madre or the uninhabitable wastes of the Colorado Desert." Poet Madge Morris Wagner—whose admirers included the mercurial Joaquin Miller—was also drawn by its stillness: her paean "To the Colorado Desert" declares "The mountain silences have speech, the rivers sing. / Thou answerest never unto anything." The most ambitious attempt to portray the landscape of the Colorado Desert, however, came from the pen of an Englishman, George Wharton James. His best-known book, the 1906 volume *The Wonders of the Colorado Desert,* had drawings and photographs complementing his descriptions.

But the Colorado Desert did not attract only literary interest. Developers wanted to "reclaim" portions of the landscape, to realize a dream of making the desert bloom, that is, produce both crops and profits. One of these men was Charles Rockwood, whose irrigation system in the Imperial Valley overflowed in 1905, filling an ancient lake bed—the Salton Sea— with Colorado River water. Subsequent development brought enough water to create a thriving agricultural area, but the Salton Sea remains as a reminder of nature's power to overwhelm human projects. In 1911 Harold Bell Wright told the story of the reclamation of the Imperial Valley— renaming King's Basin—in his novel *The Winning of Barbara Worth.*

Development has made parts of the desert more attactive to some of its casual visitors and permanent residents. High desert towns like Lancaster and Palmdale are now bedroom suburbs for the crowded Los Angeles Basin. Death Valley offers vacationers deluxe air-conditioned accommodations. Off-road vehicles make miles of desert tracks throughout the interior and dams on the Colorado River hold reservoirs for sport fishing and water skiing. Palm Springs has become a resort community of movie stars and golf courses. This human encroachment is the subject of Norman Mailer's *The Deer Park,* with its air-conditioned interiors dark against the exterior glare.

But even the clamor of civilization cannot destroy this land's quiet, as Aldous Huxley observed in a 1956 essay. With an "enduring transparency," desert "silence persists."

Joseph LeConte

Georgia native Joseph LeConte (1823–1901), first geology professor at a fledgling University of California, led a group of students to the Sierra in 1870. Meeting John Muir in Yosemite Valley, LeConte expressed astonishment at finding a "gentleman of so much intelligence tending a sawmill!" LeConte was one of the earliest subscribers to Muir's theory that Yosemite was formed by glacial forces. Like his friend Muir, LeConte was an energetic explorer of the range. For example, he opened the first high-mountain route from Yosemite to Kings Canyon. LeConte Canyon on the Middle Fork of the Kings River is one of several Sierra landmarks commemorating his trips. He created much-needed maps of the area, the first of which were published in 1893 by the Sierra Club, an organization he served as both charter member and lifelong director.

LeConte's books include his autobiography and Religion and Science, *an attempt to reconcile Darwinism and Christianity, which is said to have influenced Frank Norris. The journal of LeConte's first Sierra visit proves the complementary nature of science and letters. His journal entries contain scientific observations, sometimes even abstracts of the "familiar lecture, or rather talk" on geological subjects. But his disinterested writing constantly gives way to awestruck prose, as in this passage describing the High Sierra to the Great Basin.* ✎

from A Journal of Ramblings

August 13 [1870]. — Cold last night. We had to sleep near the fire, and keep it up during the night. Considerable frost this morning, for we are in the midst of the snows. We got up early, feeling bright and joyous, and enjoyed our breakfast as only mountaineers can. Over Mono Pass, and down Bloody Cañon today. I really dread it, for my horse's sake. Even well-shod horses get their feet and legs cut and bleeding in going down this cañon. My horse, since leaving Yosemite, has lost three shoes, and has already become very tender-footed. Got off by 6 A.M. Sorry, very sorry, to leave our delightful camp here. In commemoration of the delightful time we have spent here, we name it "Camp Dana."

The trail to the summit is a very gentle ascent, the whole way along the margin of a stream. Distance, three or four miles. Saw a deer, but Cobb was not on hand. On the very summit, 10,700 feet high, there is a marshy meadow, from which a stream runs each way: one east, into the Tuolumne, along which we had ascended; the other west, down Bloody Cañon into Mono Lake, along which we expect to descend. Right on the summit, and in Bloody Cañon, we found great masses of snow. The trail passes by their edges and over their surfaces. The trail down Bloody Cañon is rough and precipitous beyond conception. It is the terror of all drovers and packers across the mountains. It descends four thousand feet in two or three miles, and is a mere mass of loose fragments of sharp slate. Our horses' legs were all cut and bleeding before we got down. I really felt pity for my horse, with his tender feet. We all dismounted and led them down with the greatest care. In going down we met a large party of Indians, some on horseback, and some on foot, coming up. We saluted them. In return they invariably whined, "Gie me towaca," "Gie me towaca." They were evidently incredulous when told that none of the party chewed.

The scenery of Bloody Cañon is really magnificent, and, in a scientific point of view, this is the most interesting locality I have yet seen. Conceive a narrow, winding gorge, with black slaty precipices of every conceivable form, fifteen hundred to two thousand feet high on either side. As the gorge descends precipitously, and winds from side to side, we often look from above down into the most glorious amphitheater of cliffs, and from time to time beyond, upon the glistening surface of Mono Lake and the boundless plains, studded with volcanic cones. About one-third way down, in the center of the grandest of these amphitheaters, see! a deep, splendidly clear emerald green lake, three or four times the size of Mirror Lake. It looks like an artificial basin, for its shores are everywhere hard, smooth, polished rock; especially the rim at the lower side is highly polished and finely striated. There can be no doubt that this lake basin has been scooped out by a glacier which once descended this cañon. In fact, glacial action is seen on every side around this lake, and all the way down the cañon and far into the plains below.

The cliffs on each side are scored and polished to the height of one thousand feet or more; projecting knobs in the bottom of the cañon are rounded and scored and polished in a similar manner.

After we had descended the steep slope, and had fairly escaped from the high rocky walls of Bloody Cañon proper; after we had reached the level plain and had prepared ourselves for an extensive view, we found ourselves still confined between two huge parallel ridges of débris five hundred feet high and only half a mile apart, and extending five or six miles out on the plain.

These are the lateral moraines of a glacier which once descended far into the plain toward Mono Lake. A little below the commencement of these moraines, in descending, we found a large and beautiful lake filling the whole cañon. Below this lake the lateral moraines on either side send each a branch which meet each other, forming a crescentic cross-ridge through which the stream breaks. This is evidently a terminal moraine, and the lake has been formed by the damming up of the water of the stream by this moraine barrier.

Below this, or still farther on the plain, I observed several other terminal moraines, formed in a similar way, by curving branches from the lateral moraines. Behind these are no lakes, but only marshes and meadows. These meadows are evidently formed in the same way as the lake; in fact, were lakes, subsequently filled up by deposit.

After getting from these lateral moraines fairly out on the plains, the most conspicuous objects which strike the eye are the extinct volcanoes. There are, I should think, at least twenty of them, with cones and craters as perfect as if they erupted yesterday. Even at this distance, I see that their snow-white, bare sides are composed of loose volcanic ashes and sand, above which projects a distinct rocky crater-rim, some of dark rock, but most of them of light-colored, probably pumice rock. Magnificent views of these cones and of Mono Lake are gotten from time to time, while descending Bloody Cañon. The cones are of all heights, from two hundred to twenty-seven hundred feet above the plain, and the plain itself about five thousand feet above sea level.

We stopped for lunch at a cabin and meadow—a cattle ranch—about five miles from the lake. While our horses grazed, we cooked our dinner as usual, and then proceeded three miles and camped in a fine meadow on the banks of a beautiful stream—Rush Creek.

In riding down to our camp, I observed the terraces of Lake Mono, former water-levels, very distinctly marked, four or five in number. The whole region about Lake Mono, on this side, is covered with volcanic ashes and sand. It is the only soil except in the meadows. Even these seem to have the same soil, only more damp, and therefore more fertile. Scattered about, larger masses of pumice and obsidian are visible. Except in the meadows and along streams, the only growth is the sagebrush. Just before reaching camp, Mr. Muir and myself examined a fine section, made by Rush Creek, of lake and river deposit, beautifully stratified. It consists below of volcanic ashes, carried as sediment and deposited in the lake, and is therefore a true lake deposit, and beautifully stratified. Above this is a drift pebble deposit; the pebbles consisting of granite and slate from the Sierra. Above this again, are volcanic ashes and sand, unstratified, probably blown ashes and sand, or else ejected since the drift. We have therefore certain evidence of eruptions before the drift, and possibly, also, after.

The lake [Mono] is two hundred feet deep, and its sluggish waters are so strong with alkali that if you only dip the most hopelessly soiled garment into them once or twice and wring it out, it will be found as clean as if it had been through the ablest of washerwomen's hands. While we camped there our laundry work was easy. We tied the week's washing astern of our boat, and sailed a quarter of a mile, and the job was complete, all to the wringing out. If we threw the water on our heads and gave them a rub or so, the white lather would pile up three inches high. This water is not good for bruised places and abrasions of the skin. We had a valuable dog. He had raw places on him. He had more raw places on him than sound ones. He was the rawest dog I almost ever saw. He jumped overboard one day to get away from the flies. But it was bad judgment. In his condition, it would have been just as comfortable to jump into the fire. The alkali water nipped him in all the raw places simultaneously, and he struck out for the shore with considerable interest. He yelped and barked and howled as he went—and by the time he got to the shore there was no bark to him—for he had barked the bark all out of his inside, and the alkali water had cleaned the bark all off his outside, and he probably wished he had never embarked in any such enterprise. He ran round and round in a circle, and pawed the earth and clawed the air, and threw double somersets, sometimes backwards and sometimes forwards, in the most extraordinary manner. He was not a demonstrative dog, as a general thing, but rather of a grave and serious turn of mind, and I never saw him take so much interest in anything before. He finally struck out over the mountains, at a gait which we estimated at about 250 miles an hour, and he is going yet. This was about nine years ago. We look for what is left of him along here every day.

—Mark Twain, from *Roughing It* (1872)

In the picture of the view from Mono Lake, I have yet said nothing about the Sierra. The general view of the range from this, the Mono, side is far finer than from the other side. The Sierra rises gradually on the western side for fifty or sixty miles. On the Mono, or eastern, side it is precipitous, the very summit of the range running close to the valley. From this side, therefore, the mountains present a sheer elevation of six or seven thousand feet above the plain. The sunset view of the Sierra, from an eminence near our camp, this evening, was, it seems to me, by far the finest mountain view I have ever in my life seen. The immense height of the chain above the plain, the abruptness of the declivity, the infinitely diversified forms, and the wonderful sharpness and ruggedness of the peaks, such as I have seen nowhere but in the Sierra, and all this strongly relieved against the brilliant sunset sky, formed a picture of indescribable grandeur. As I turn around in the opposite direction, the regular forms of the volcanoes, the placid surface of Lake Mono, with its picturesque islands, and far away in the distance the scarcely visible outlines of the White Mountains, pass in succession before the eye. I enjoyed this magnificent panoramic view until it faded away in the darkness.

From this feast I went immediately to another, consisting of excellent bread, and such delicious mutton chops! If any restaurant in San Francisco could furnish such, I am sure it would quickly make a fortune. Some sentimentalists seem to think that these two feasts are incompatible; that the enjoyment of the beautiful is inconsistent with voracious appetite for mutton. I do not find it so.

After supper I again went out to enjoy the scene by night. As I gazed upon the abrupt slope of the Sierra, rising like a wall before me, I tried to picture to myself the condition of things during the glacial epoch. The long western slope of the Sierra is now occupied by long, complicated valleys, broad and full of meadows, while the eastern slope is deeply graven with short, narrow, steep ravines. During glacial times, therefore, it is evident that the western slope was occupied by long, complicated glaciers, with comparatively sluggish current; while on the east, short, simple parallel ice-streams ran down the steep slope and far out on the level plain. On each side of these protruded icy tongues: the débris brought down from the rocky ravines was dropped as parallel moraines. Down the track of one of these glaciers, and between the outstretched moraine arms, our path lay this morning.

Mary Austin

Mary Austin (1868–1934) wrote thirty-five books, among them the novels
Isadro, A Woman of Genius, *and* The Ford; *she was an outspoken fem-
inist and social critic; and she earned a reputation as an engaging and colorful personality, one of the original Carmel bohemians, a group that included
Jack London, Ambrose Bierce, and George Sterling. Though she lived elsewhere for many years, her sensibility was shaped by California. Its landscape
and native people provided some of her first and finest essays, which were
written for the* Overland Monthly.

*Born and educated in Illinois, Mary Hunter came west in 1888 to live
with her family on a Kern County homestead. While teaching school, she
met and married Stafford Austin, who eventually brought her to the Owens
Valley. In an unhappy marriage and in the afternoon shadows of the eastern
Sierra, Mary Austin found her voice and from her Independence home
broadcast "such news of the land, of its trails and what is astir in them, as
one lover of it can give to another." Such news is the subject of her first
sketch, "The Land of Little Rain," later published in the collection of the
same name. Here Austin captures "the palpable sense of mystery in the
desert air."* ⤴

from The Land of Little Rain

East away from the Sierras, south from Panamint and Amargosa, east and
south many an uncounted mile, is the Country of Lost Borders.

Ute, Paiute, Mojave, and Shoshone inhabit its frontiers, and as far into the
heart of it as a man dare go. Not the law, but the land sets the limit. Desert
is the name it wears upon the maps, but the Indian's is the better word.
Desert is a loose term to indicate land that supports no man; whether the
land can be bitted and broken to that purpose is not proven. Void of life it
never is, however dry the air and villainous the soil.

This is the nature of that country. There are hills, rounded, blunt, burnt,
squeezed up out of chaos, chrome and vermilion painted, aspiring to the
snowline. Between the hills lie high level-looking plains full of intolerable
sun glare, or narrow valleys drowned in a blue haze. The hill surface is

streaked with ash drift and black, unweathered lava flows. After rains water accumulates in the hollows of small closed valleys, and, evaporating, leaves hard dry levels of pure desertness that get the local name of dry lakes. Where the mountains are steep and the rains heavy, the pool is never quite dry, but dark and bitter, rimmed about with the efflorescence of alkaline deposits. A thin crust of it lies along the marsh over the vegetating area, which has neither beauty nor freshness. In the broad wastes open to the wind the sand drifts in hummocks about the stubby shrubs, and between them the soil shows saline traces. The sculpture of the hills here is more wind than water work, though the quick storms do sometimes scar them past many a year's redeeming. In all the Western desert edges there are essays in miniature at the famed, terrible Grand Cañon, to which, if you keep on long enough in this country, you will come at last.

Since this is a hill country one expects to find springs, but not to depend upon them; for when found they are often brackish and unwholesome, or maddening, slow dribbles in a thirsty soil. Here you find the hot sink of Death Valley, or high rolling districts where the air has always a tang of frost. Here are the long heavy winds and breathless calms on the tilted mesas where dust devils dance, whirling up into a wide, pale sky. Here you have no rain when all the earth cries for it, or quick downpours called cloudbursts for violence. A land of lost rivers, with little in it to love; yet a land that once visited must be come back to inevitably. If it were not so there would be little told of it.

This is the country of three seasons. From June on to November it lies hot, still, and unbearable, sick with violent unrelieving storms; then on until April, chill, quiescent, drinking its scant rain and scanter snows; from April to the hot season again, blossoming, radiant, and seductive. These months are only approximate; later or earlier the rain-laden wind may drift up the water gate of the Colorado from the Gulf, and the land sets its seasons by the rain.

The desert floras shame us with their cheerful adaptations to the seasonal limitations. Their whole duty is to flower and fruit, and they do it hardly, or with tropical luxuriance, as the rain admits. It is recorded in the report of the Death Valley expedition that after a year of abundant rains, on the Colorado Desert was found a specimen of amaranthus ten feet high. A year later the same species in the same place matured in the drought at four inches. One hopes the land may breed like qualities in her human offspring, not tritely to "try," but to do. Seldom does the desert herb attain the full stature of the type. Extreme aridity and extreme altitude have the same dwarfing effect, so that we find in the high Sierras and in Death Valley related species in miniature that reach a comely growth in mean temperatures. Very fertile are the desert plants in expedients to prevent evaporation, turning their foliage edgewise toward the sun, growing silky hairs, exuding viscid gum. The wind, which has a long sweep, harries and helps them. It rolls up dunes about the stocky stems, encompassing and protective, and above the dunes, which may be, as with the mesquite, three times as high as a man, the blossoming twigs flourish and bear fruit.

There are many areas in the desert where drinkable water lies within a few feet of the surface, indicated by the mesquite and the bunch grass *(Sporobolus airoides).* It is this nearness of unimagined help that makes the tragedy of desert deaths. It is related that the final breakdown of that hapless party that gave Death Valley its forbidding name occurred in a locality where shallow wells would have saved them. But how were they to know that? Properly equipped it is possible to go safely across that ghastly sink, yet every year it takes its toll of death, and yet men find there sun-dried mummies, of whom no trace or recollection is preserved. To underestimate one's thirst, to pass a given landmark to the right or left, to find a dry spring where one looked for running water—there is no help for any of these things.

Along springs and sunken watercourses one is surprised to find such water-loving plants as grow widely in moist ground, but the true desert breeds its own kind, each in its particular habitat. The angle of the slope, the frontage of a hill, the structure of the soil determines the plant. South-looking hills are nearly bare, and the lower tree-line higher here by a thousand feet. Cañons running east and west will have one wall naked and one clothed. Around dry lakes and marshes the herbage preserves a set and orderly arrangement. Most species have well-defined areas of growth, the best index the voiceless land can give the traveler of his whereabouts.

If you have any doubt about it, know that the desert begins with the creosote. This immortal shrub spreads down into Death Valley and up to the lower timberline, odorous and medicinal as you might guess from the name, wandlike, with shining fretted foliage. Its vivid green is grateful to the eye in a wilderness of gray and greenish white shrubs. In the spring it exudes a resinous gum which the Indians of those parts know how to use with pulverized rock for cementing arrow points to shafts. Trust Indians not to miss any virtues of the plant world!

Nothing the desert produces expresses it better than the unhappy growth of the tree yuccas. Tormented, thin forests of it stalk drearily in the high mesas, particularly in that triangular slip that fans out eastward from the meeting of the Sierras and coastwise hills where the first swings across the southern end of the San Joaquin Valley. The yucca bristles with bayonet-pointed leaves, dull green, growing shaggy with age, tipped with panicles of fetid, greenish bloom. After death, which is slow, the ghostly hollow network of its woody skeleton, with hardly power to rot, makes the moonlight fearful. Before the yucca has come to flower, while yet its bloom is a creamy cone-shaped bud of the size of a small cabbage, full of sugary sap, the Indians twist it deftly out of its fence of daggers and roast it for their own delectation. So it is that in those parts where man inhabits one sees young plants of *Yucca arborensis* infrequently. Other yuccas, cacti, low herbs, a thousand sorts, one finds journeying east from the coastwise hills. There is neither poverty of soil nor species to account for the sparseness of desert growth, but simply that each plant requires more room. So much earth must be preempted to extract so much moisture. The real struggle for existence, the real brain of the plant, is underground; above there is room for a rounded perfect growth. In Death Valley, reputed the very core of desolation, are nearly two hundred identified species.

Above the lower tree-line, which is also the snow-line, mapped out abruptly by the sun, one finds spreading growth of piñon, juniper, branched nearly to the ground, lilac and sage, and scattering white pines.

There is no special preponderance of self-fertilized or wind-fertilized plants, but everywhere the demand for and evidence of insect life. Now where there are seeds and insects there will be birds and small mammals and where these are, will come the slinking, sharp-toothed kind that prey on them. Go as far as you dare in the heart of a lonely land, you cannot go so far that life and death are not before you. Painted lizards slip in and out of rock crevices, and pant on the white hot sands. Birds, hummingbirds even, nest in the cactus scrub; woodpeckers befriend the demoniac yuccas; out of the stark, treeless waste rings the music of the night-singing mockingbird. If it be summer and the sun well down, there will be a burrowing owl to call. Strange, furry, tricksy things dart across the open places, or sit motionless in the conning towers of the creosote. The poet may have "named all the birds without a gun," but not the fairy-footed, ground-inhabiting, furtive, small folk of the rainless regions. They are too many and too swift; how many you would not believe without seeing the footprint tracings in

Walk almost anywhere in the Whites just about any time of the year, and you find yourself in a world completely unlike any other you have ever experienced: a lost world, primeval and dreamlike.

Start on the valley floor, where the roads give out in mazes of gullies and middens of stones. You climb, up the steepening alluvial fans, between minatory cliffs, into the canyons. Sagebrush and shad scale grow on the flinty soil, a parched, knee-high forest that looks as if it is patched together out of barbed wire and parchment. Pass the rusty rubble of an abandoned glory hole and climb the stained rock of a dry waterfall, hand over hand, if you can: the rock is razor-blade-sharp beneath your fingers. There is snow on the peaks above, but down here it is hot, the air touched with fire. A rattlesnake whirs from a heap of stones off to your right....

Up an endless, rotten slope to your left, past a series of evil-looking cliffs, there is easier ground where the first trees, piñon and Utah juniper, appear. It is a completely different realm from the same 6,500- to 9,000-foot altitude zone in the Sierra, across the valley to the [west]. Over there are lush slopes of white fir, red fir, Jeff and lodgepole pine...as different as yang from yin, day from night.

Up above 9,000 feet, you start to get into the mixed forests of limber and bristlecone pines: an environment as clean and intense as those Zen gardens in Japanese temples, with their raked sand, clumped rocks, and twisted bonsai trees....

The last trees thin out and disappear above the 11,500-foot mark. Beyond here, there is nothing but scree, alpine grass, and tundra. You can see forever: the long, long line of Sierra Nevada, pinnacles, crags, glaciers, knife-edges, stretching from hazy Yosemite to the north, to the spike of Mount Whitney to the south; the deep, shadowy pit of the Owens Valley, with the Owens River twisting silver here and there in its depths; the Great Basin, with its boneyard ranges and dead salt seas sunk in their alkalin sockets...And the Whites themselves, the harsh pinnacle of Montgomery to the north, the summits and ridges rolling under your feet to meld into the wild peaks of the Inyos to the south, and Saline, Panamint, and Death Valley beyond....Wilderness without end, brilliant, unknown.

—Rob Schultheis, from *Image*, May 4, 1986

the sand. They are nearly all night workers, finding the days too hot and white. In mid-desert where there are no cattle, there are no birds of carrion, but if you go far in that direction the chances are that you will find yourself shadowed by their tilted wings. Nothing so large as a man can move unspied upon in that country, and they know well how the land deals with strangers. There are hints to be had here of the way in which a land forces new habits on its dwellers. The quick increase of suns at the end of spring sometimes overtakes birds in their nesting and effects a reversal of the ordinary manner of incubation. It becomes necessary to keep eggs cool rather than warm. One hot, stifling spring in the Little Antelope I had occasion to pass and repass frequently the nest of a pair of meadowlarks, located unhappily in the shelter of a very slender weed. I never caught them sitting except near night, but at midday they stood, or drooped above it, half fainting with pitifully parted bills, between their treasure and the sun. Sometimes both of them together with wings spread and half lifted continued a spot of shade in a temperature that constrained me at last in a fellow feeling to spare them a bit of canvas for permanent shelter. There was a fence in that country shutting in a cattle range, and along its fifteen miles of posts one could be sure of finding a bird or two in every strip of shadow; sometimes the sparrow and the hawk, with wings trailed and beaks parted, drooping in the white truce of noon.

If one is inclined to wonder at first how so many dwellers came to be in the loneliest land that ever came out of God's hands, what they do there and why stay, one does not wonder so much after having lived there. None other than this long brown land lays such a hold on the affections. The rainbow hills, the tender bluish mists, the luminous radiance of the spring, have the lotus charm. They trick the sense of time, so that once inhabiting there you always mean to go away without quite realizing that you have not done it. Men who have lived there, miners and cattlemen, will tell you this, not so fluently, but emphatically, cursing the land and going back to it. For one thing there is the divinest air to be breathed anywhere in God's world. Some day the world will understand that, and the little oases on the windy tops of hills will harbor for healing its ailing, house-weary broods. There is promise there of great wealth in ores and earths, which is no wealth by reason of being so far removed from water and workable conditions, but men are bewitched by it and tempted to try the impossible.

You should hear Salty Williams tell how he used to drive eighteen- and twenty-mule teams from the borax marsh to Mojave, ninety miles, with the trail wagon full of water barrels. Hot days the mules would go so mad for drink that the clank of the water bucket set them into an uproar of hideous, maimed noises, and a tangle of harness chains, while Salty would sit on the high seat with the sun glare heavy in his eyes, dealing out curses of pacification in a level, uninterested voice until the clamor fell off from sheer exhaustion. There was a line of shallow graves along that road; they used to count on dropping a man or two of every new gang of coolies brought out in the hot season. But when he lost his swamper, smitten without warning at the noon halt, Salty quit his job; he said it was "too durn hot." The swamper he buried by the way with stones upon him to keep the coyotes from digging him up, and seven years later I read the penciled lines on the pine headboard, still bright and unweathered.

But before that, driving up on the Mojave stage, I met Salty again crossing Indian Wells, his face from the high seat, tanned and ruddy as a harvest moon, looming through the golden dust above his eighteen mules. The land had called him.

The palpable sense of mystery in the desert air breeds fables, chiefly of lost treasure. Somewhere within its stark borders, if one believes reports, is a hill strewn with nuggets; one seamed with virgin silver; an old clayey water-bed where Indians scooped up earth to make cooking pots and shaped them reeking with grains of pure gold. Old miners drifting about the desert edges, weathered into the semblance of the tawny hills, will tell you tales like these convincingly. After a little sojourn in that land you will believe them on their own account. It is a question whether it is not better to be bitten by the little horned snake of the desert that goes sidewise and strikes without coiling, than by the tradition of a lost mine.

And yet—and yet—is it not perhaps to satisfy expectation that one falls into the tragic key in writing of desertness? The more you wish of it the more you get, and in the meantime lose much of pleasantness. In that country which begins at the foot of the east slope of the Sierras and spreads out by less and less lofty hill ranges toward the Great Basin, it is possible to live with great zest, to have red blood and delicate joys, to pass and repass about one's daily performance an area that would make an Atlantic seaboard state, and that with no peril, and, according to our way of thought, no particular difficulty. At any rate, it was not people who went into the desert merely to write it up who invented the fabled Hassaympa, of whose waters, if any drink, they can no more see fact as naked fact, but all radiant with the color of romance. I, who must have drunk of it in my twice seven years' wanderings, am assured that it is worthwhile.

For all the toll the desert takes of a man it gives compensations, deep breaths, deep sleep, and the communion of the stars. It comes upon one with new force in the pauses of the night that the Chaldeans were a desert-bred people. It is hard to escape the sense of mastery as the stars move in the wide clear heavens to risings and settings unobscured. They look large and near and palpitant; as if they moved on some stately service not needful to declare. Wheeling to their stations in the sky, they make the poor world-fret of no account. Of no account you who lie out there watching, nor the lean coyote that stands off in the scrub from you and howls and howls.

William Lewis Manly

*In July of 1849 Vermont native William Lewis Manly (1820–1903) set
out for California, determined to make his fortune in the mines. After following the Oregon Trail to Fort Bridger, on the western side of the Rocky
Mountains, he and six companions decided to try a quicker route to
California. They would float down the Green and Colorado rivers. With
unreliable directions and unlimited optimism, Manly and his group rea-
soned: "If this stream were large enough; if we had a boat; if we knew the
way; if there were no falls or bad places; if we had plenty of provisions; if we
were bold enough [to] set out on such a trip, etc., we might come out at some
point or other on the Pacific Ocean."*

*After wasting time on the ill-advised river trip, Manly and his compan-
ions joined another group going overland to Southern California. They
headed straight into Death Valley—which Manly claims to have named—
where the travelers were stranded. Manly and another man set out to find an
escape route and search for help. Fourteen days later they reached the old
Mission San Fernando, reprovisioned, and returned for their companions.*

*Manly's account of the trip was not published until forty-four years later.
After an earlier manuscript was lost to fire, it took much prodding from
friends before Manly was willing to recount the story. Here is his straight-
forward description of the struggle back to Death Valley for the marooned
group.* ✍

from Death Valley in '49

The range was before us, and we must get to the other side in some way.
We could see the range for a hundred miles to the north and along the base
some lakes of water that must be salt. To the south it got some lower, but
very barren and ending in black, dry buttes. The horses must have food and
water by night or we must leave them to die, and all things considered it
seemed to be the quickest way to camp to try and get up a rough looking
cañon which was nearly opposite us on the other side. So we loaded the
mule and made our way down the rocky road to the ridge, and then left the
Jayhawker's trail, taking our course more south so as to get around a salt lake

which lay directly before us. On our way we had to go close to a steep bluff, and cross a piece of ground that looked like a well-dried mortar bed, hard and smooth as ice, and thus got around the head of a small stream of clear water, salt as brine. We now went directly to the mouth of the cañon we had decided to take, and traveled up its gravelly bed. The horses now had to be urged along constantly to keep them moving and they held their heads low down as they crept along seemingly so discouraged that they would much rather lie down and rest forever than take another step. We knew they would do this soon in spite of all our urging, if we could not get water for them. The cañon was rough enough where we entered it, and a heavy up grade too, and this grew more and more difficult as we advanced, and the rough yellowish, rocky walls closed in nearer and nearer together as we ascended.

A perpendicular wall, or rather rise, in the rocks was approached, and there was a great difficulty to persuade the horses to take exertion to get up and over the small obstruction, but the little mule skipped over as nimbly as a well-fed goat, and rather seemed to enjoy a little variety in the proceedings. After some coaxing and urging the horses took courage to try the extra step and succeeded all right, when we all moved on again, over a path that grew more and more narrow, more and more rocky under foot at every moment. We wound around among and between the great rocks, and had not advanced very far before another obstruction, that would have been a fall of about three feet had water been flowing in the cañon, opposed our way. A small pile of lone rocks enabled the mule to go over all right, and she went on looking for every spear of grass, and smelling eagerly for water, but all our efforts were not enough to get the horses along another foot. It was getting nearly night and every minute without water seemed an age. We had to leave the horses and go on. We had deemed them indispensable to us, or rather to the extrication of the women and children, and yet the hope came to us that the oxen might help some of them out as a last resort. We were sure the wagons must be abandoned, and such a thing as women riding on the backs of oxen we had never seen, still it occurred to us as not impossible and although leaving the horses here was like deciding to abandon all for the feeble ones, we saw we must do it, and the new hope arose to sustain us for farther effort. We removed the saddles and placed them on a rock, and after a few moments' hesitation, moments in which were crowded torrents of wild ideas, and desperate thoughts that were enough to drive reason from its throne, we left the poor animals to their fate and moved along. Just as we were passing out of sight the poor creatures neighed pitifully after us, and one who has never heard the last despairing, pleading neigh of a horse left to die can form no idea of its almost human appeal. We both burst into tears, but it was no use, to try to save them we must run the danger of sacrificing ourselves, and the little party we were trying so hard to save.

We found the little mule stopped by a still higher precipice or perpendicular rise of fully ten feet. Our hearts sank within us and we said that we should return to our friends as we went away, with our knapsacks on our backs, and the hope grew very small. The little mule was nipping some stray blades of grass and as we came in sight she looked around to us and then up the steep rocks before her with such a knowing, intelligent look of confidence, that it gave us new courage. It was a strange wild place. The north wall of the cañon leaned far over the channel, overhanging considerably, while the south wall sloped back about the same, making the wall nearly parallel, and like a huge crevice descending into the mountain from above in a sloping direction.

We decided to try to get the confident little mule over this obstruction. Gathering all the loose rocks we could we piled them up against the south wall, beginning some distance below, putting up all those in the bed of the stream and throwing down others from narrow shelves above we built a sort of inclined plane along the walls gradually rising till we were nearly as high as the crest of the fall. Here was a narrow shelf scarcely four inches wide and a space of from twelve to fifteen feet to cross to reach the level of the crest. It was all I could do to cross this space, and there was no foundation to enable us to widen it so as to make a path for an animal. It was forlorn hope but we made the most of it. We unpacked the mule and getting all our ropes together, made a leading line of it. Then we loosened and threw down all the projecting points of rocks we could above the narrow shelf, and every piece that was likely to come loose in the shelf itself. We fastened the leading line to her and with one above and one below we thought we could help her to keep her balance, and if she did not make a misstep on that narrow way she might get over safely. Without a moment's hesitation the brave animal tried the pass. Carefully and steadily she went along, selecting a place before putting down a foot, and when she came to the narrow ledge leaned gently on the rope, never making a sudden start or jump, but cautiously as a cat moved slowly along. There was now no turning back for her. She must cross this narrow place over which I had to creep on hands and knees, or be dashed down fifty feet to a certain death. When the worst place was reached she stopped and hesitated, looking back as well as she could. I was ahead with the rope, and I called encouragingly to her and talked to her a little. Rogers wanted to get all ready and he said, "holler" at her as loud as he could and frighten her across, but I thought the best way to talk to her gently and let her move steadily.

I tell you, friends, it was a trying moment. It seemed to be weighed down with all the trails and hardships of many months. It seemed to be the time when helpless women and innocent children hung on trembling balance between life and death. Our own lives we could save by going back, and sometimes it seemed as if we would perhaps save ourselves the additional sorrow of finding them all dead to do so at once. I was so nearly in despair that I could not help bursting in tears, and I was not ashamed of the weakness. Finally Rogers said, "Come Lewis" and I gently pulled the rope, calling the little animal, to make a trial. She smelled all around and looked over every inch of the strong ledge, then took one careful step after another over the dangerous place. Looking back I saw Rogers with a very large stone in his hand, ready to "holler" and perhaps kill the poor beast if she stopped. But she crept along trusting to the rope to balance, till she was halfway across, then another step or two, when calculating the distance closely she made a spring and landed on a smooth bit of sloping rock below, that led up to the highest crest of the precipice, and safely climbed to the top, safe and sound above the falls. The mule had no shoes and it was wonderful how her little hoofs clung to the smooth rock. We felt relieved. We would push on and carry food to the people: we would get them through some way; there could be no more hopeless moment than the one just past, and we would save them all.

It was the work of a little while to transfer the load up the precipice, and pack the mule again, when we proceeded. Around behind some rocks only a little distance beyond this place we found a small willow bush and enough good water for a camp. This was a strange cañon. The sun never shown down to the bottom in the fearful place where the little mule climbed up, and the rocks had a peculiar yellow color. In getting our provisions up the precipice, Rogers went below and fastened the rope while I pulled them up. Rogers wished many times we had the horses up safely where the mule was, but a dog could hardly cross the narrow path and there was no hope. Poor brutes, they has been faithful servants, and we felt sorrowful enough at their terrible fate.

We had walked two days without water, and we were wonderfully refreshed as we found it here. The way up this cañon was very rough and the bed full of sharp broken rocks in loose pieces which cut through the bottoms of our moccasins and left us with bare feet upon the acute points and edges. I took off one of my buckskin leggins, and gave it to Rogers, and with the other one for myself we fixed the mocassins with them as well as we could, which enabled us to go ahead, but I think if our feet had been shod with steel those sharp rocks would have cut through.

Starting early we made the summit about noon, and from here we could see the place where we found a water hole and camped the first night after we left the wagons. Down the steep cañon we turned, the same one in which we had turned back with the wagons, and over the sharp broken pieces of volcanic rock that formed our only footing we hobbled along with sore and tender feet. We had to watch for the smoothest place for every step, and then moved only with the greatest difficulty. The Indians could have caught us easily if they had been around for we must keep our eyes on the ground constantly and stop if we looked up and around. But we at last got down and camped on some spot where we had set out twenty-five days before to seek the settlements. Here was the same little water hole in the sand plain, and the same strong sulphur water which we had to drink the day we left. The mule was turned loose dragging the same piece of rawhide she had attached to her when we purchased her, and she ranged and searched faithfully for food finding little except the very scattering bunches of sagebrush. She was industrious and walked around rapidly picking here and there, but at dark came into camp and lay down close to us to sleep.

There was no sign that anyone had been here during our absence, and if the people had gone to hunt a way out, they must either have followed the Jayhawker's trail or some other one. We were much afraid that they might have fallen victims to the Indians. Remaining in camp so long it was quite likely they had been discovered by them and it was quite likely they had been murdered for the sake of the oxen and camp equipage. It might be that we should find the hostiles waiting for us when we reached the appointed camping place, and it was small show for two against a party. Our mule and her load would be a great capture for them. We talked a great deal and said a great many things at that campfire for we knew we were in great danger, and we had many doubts about the safety of our people, that would soon be decided, and whether for joy or sorrow we could not tell.

From this place, as we walked along, we had a wagon road to follow, in soft sand, but not a sign of a human footstep could we see, as we marched toward this, the camp of the last hope. We had the greatest fears the people had given up our return and started out for themselves and that we should follow on, only to find them dead or dying. My pen fails me as I try to tell the feelings and thoughts of this trying hour. I can never hope to do so, but if the reader can place himself in my place, his imagination cannot form a picture that shall go beyond reality.

We were some seven or eight miles along the road when I stopped to fix my moccasin while Rogers went slowly along. The little mule went on ahead of both of us, searching all around for little bunches of dry grass, but always came back to the trail again and gave us no trouble. When I had started up again I saw Rogers ahead leaning on his gun and waiting for me, apparently looking at something on the ground. As I came near enough to speak I asked what he had found and he said "Here is Captain Culverwell, dead." He did not look much like a dead man. He lay upon his back with arms extended wide, and his little canteen, made of two powder flasks, lying by his side. This looked indeed as if some of our saddest forbodings were coming true. How many more bodies should we find? Or should we find the camp deserted, and never find a trace of the former occupants....

One hundred yards now to the wagons and still no sign of life, no positive sign of death, though we looked carefully for both. We fear that perhaps there are Indians in ambush, and with nervous irregular breathing we counsel what to do. Finally Rogers suggested that he had two charges in this shot gun and I seven in the Coll's rifle, and that I fire one of mine and await results before we ventured any nearer....And now both closely watching the wagons I fired the shot. Still as death and not a move for a moment, and then as if by magic a man came out from under a wagon and stood up looking all around, for he did not see us. Then he threw up his arms high over his head and shouted, "The boys have come," "The boys have come!"

Walter Van Tilburg Clark

Walter Van Tilburg Clark (1909–1971) set his best-known work—his 1940 novel, The Ox-Bow Incident—*in Nevada cattle country, but he established firm California credentials with an earlier project, his 1934 master's thesis on Robinson Jeffers. Clark was already an admirer of his poetry before meeting Jeffers at Tor House. "Now," says Max Westbrook, "he came to like the man, his famous [T]or House, and his beloved and rugged California coast." Clark shared with Jeffers the belief that human beings need to see themselves as a part of the natural world, and he made this a major theme of* The City of Trembling Leaves, *the coming-of-age story of Tim Hazard, a composer living in Reno, Nevada.*

Clark grew up in Reno. Born in Maine, he moved west when his father was appointed president of the University of Nevada. Clark eventually took B.A. and M.A. degrees there before moving on to the University of Vermont, where the Jeffers thesis earned him a second M.A. He married and had two children, established a distinguished teaching career, and wrote poetry and fiction. Clark eventually moved to California, where he taught creative writing at San Francisco State, before returning to the University of Nevada as writer-in-residence in 1962. He published a third novel, The Track of the Cat, *and wrote at least two more (without submitting them to publishers), as well as many finely crafted short stories. He once remarked that "landscape is character, not background. It is not a stage. It's an active agent." Nowhere in Clark's work is this more evident than in the desperate trip Tim Hazard makes through Death Valley, tracking his self-destructive friend Lawrence Black.* ❧

from The City of Trembling Leaves

Tim drank deeply, bathed his face and neck, wet down the sacks over the beer, filled Jeremiah's radiator, and drove on. What had been only an occasional worry about Lawrence before was now a constant fear, which sometimes rose almost to panic. He cursed himself for having stayed so long in Baker. That adventure would make the kind of story Lawrence loved, a story of encouragement against all the headline thinking, the Napoleonic gluttonies, the Sargasso Seas of the spirit. It wouldn't seem trivial to Lawrence, but now it seemed nearly a betrayal, at best a good passage in the wrong place. His imagination, in spite of him, began to scour the valley, finding Lawrence roving mad, or fallen, or missing him behind the warped mirrors of the heat. He remembered tales of the suffering and doom of people much better fixed than Lawrence was to fight the valley, and the hot, arid wind beating in around Jeremiah's windshield, the pummeling of the sun, the blinding light which ricocheted from white earth made the tales real. There were the pioneers who had named the valley. They had slowly followed their bad guide across the worst deserts of Nevada and into this trap. They had come out on the other side at last, but on foot, with their boots torn, their eyes nearly boiled in their heads, and carrying nothing but their firearms and the strips of evil, dried meat which were all that remained of their animals. The wagons had been burnt to cure the meat, and the bones, and the iron hubs and rims, left behind in the dunes. The valley had been unknown then, of course, but much later the drivers and swampers of twenty-mule borax teams, men who knew the valley like the palms of their hands, had died in the sun, and their animals with them, or gone mad and attacked each other. And someone had told him about two men who had tried to come up the valley on motorcycles, before the road was paved. The next travelers to take the road had found the motorcycles, their tires exploded and their paint scorched and flaking off. Then, far apart in the barrens, they had found the two skeletons, as clean and ashy as if they had been there for a century. Probably the vultures first, and after that the sun. One claim of the old-timers kept coming back to him with a peculiarly ter- rible force, because it was easy to believe that Lawrence's imagination might do that to him. The old-timers said that heat-crazy wanderers had been trailed by their clothes, which they peeled off and left behind them, and had been found wading naked, sometimes even making the arm motions of swimmers, through their visions of deep water. It was hard to believe that such things could happen now, with cars, and paved roads, and the water holes marked, but everything in this wilderness of light said they could. Even at this hour, when the sun was well down toward the western moun- tains, Tim jumped if his elbow touched the metal of Jeremiah's door, and great areas of the valley floor were invisible behind the heat waves. High and near on the east rose the crenelated cliffs of the Funeral Range, black and dull red, like slowly cooling iron, and with long, gray strata tilted across them. The cliffs were softened, as if by smoke from smoldering fires along their bases, and purple shadows were beginning to give them form behind the haze. Jeremiah couldn't be pushed any faster, though, and besides, it wouldn't do to hurry through the dunes. If there were footprints leading out into the dunes, he mustn't miss them.

Still, as the minutes passed, and the dunes flowed smoothly by, showing only their clear and lovely wind-ripples, like the water marks on a shallow beach, and the shadow of the western range extended its slow blessing, Tim began to feel relieved and glad. Some car they hadn't seen from the ranch must have come through and picked Lawrence up. Lawrence was probably sitting in the shade at Stove-Pipe Wells Hotel right now, with a cold beer in one hand and a pebble in the other, thinking and watching the light change and the shadows come. Better yet, he didn't have a beer. He was sitting there thinking that in a few minutes he would go and get a beer. Then Tim would stagger up to him, lugging the magnificent tub. He would set the tub down before Lawrence without a word, and watch Lawrence's face as he came to understand what was in it.

This was such an engrossing vision that Tim didn't realize he'd seen the tracks until Jeremiah had gone a hundred yards past them. The dream-success vanished, and the fears returned and multiplied. He backed Jeremiah to the point where the tracks began, and stopped him, and got out slowly, his knees shaking. Yes, they were the tracks of one person, going in a widely wavering line up the high side of the dune before him and out of sight over the top. He didn't like that wavering. It might be just the result of climbing switch-back in the loose sand, but it might not, too. He knelt by the first tracks and examined them closer, but the sliding sand had left only smooth indentations. Anyone might have made them. He climbed to the top of the first dune. A sea of dunes came into view beyond it, and the tracks went on across them, disappearing in each trough, and reappearing, much smaller, upon the flank of the next dune, until they dwindled into a single, fine thread and ended on the crest of another high dune. At least the tracks were going somewhere. The points at which they topped the dunes lay along a nearly straight line.

Tim stood staring across the dunes, trying to think what to do. There was no use following the trail off into the sand at this hour, with no idea how far it went. That was what he felt like doing, and he felt like trying to run, too, which would be equally foolish. He looked all around, as if he might see something which would give him an answer. Nothing moved except, very slowly, the shadows of the dunes, and the tiny shadows seeping in behind the ripples. Repeatedly, he peered ahead at the point where the tracks disappeared. The silence over the dunes rang like bells in his head. He stared beyond the dunes at the mountains, and was suddenly profoundly discouraged and frightened by their immense indifference and by the distance to which they had retreated when he thought of walking toward them. But it was looking at those mountains which gave him the answer. The pass went up through there, through Boundary Canyon, to Beatty. He remembered that he had passed the junction with the Beatty road not far back. He thought where he was, and knew that Lawrence had headed off across the dunes to reach the wells.

He ran back down to Jeremiah and climbed in and started him off. It wasn't far across those dunes between the road and the cutoff, anyway. If Lawrence wasn't at the wells, and the tracks didn't come out there, he could

Even if you can't tell a tufa from a tule, everyone seems to want to tell a story, or be in one, about Death Valley. At best, the anthropologists estimate, Death Valley supported a hundred Indians. Now up to thirty thousand tourists turn up for the long weekends of the annual forty-niner encampment, and the yearly total approaches three-quarters of a million. In the books and pamphlets that fill the shelves in the Death Valley Museum you can find enshrined the naturalist's Death Valley, the geologist's, the ethnologist's, the western historian's, the nostalgia buff's—each adding a few grains to the same experiences, tall tales, facts, and myths. There's even an "archaeology of litter" that allows us to determine when a particular bottle was dropped in the waste—by the nature of the glass, the way the bottle cap was attached, and what material it was made of.

Thinking about the valley's enigmatic rock formations and its many petroglyphs, I wondered if the Indians might have responded to a similar necessity. Bruce Chatwin in *Songlines* talks about the immense pattern of songs and myths by which the Aboriginals, without any written language, map Australia. Geologists have noticed some places in the Panamints where the rocks have been altered into semigeometrical forms. Perhaps within the present-day songs and stories of the descendants of the natives of Death Valley there is a similarly hidden map of ancient water holes and game routes, burial grounds and food stores.

—Leo Braudy, "Renewing the Edge," from *Roots and Branches* (1991)

return to where the tracks began, and follow them as far as he had to before it got dark. He came to the cutoff and swung into it. When he saw the sign and the stand-pipe, he stopped Jeremiah at the edge of the road. A man was there, squatting on his hunkers, like a desert Indian, near the stand-pipe. He had a faded blue jacket drawn up over his head and shoulders, and his arms dangled over his knees, so that his long hands touched the ground. Beside his right hand there was an open tomato can with a fresh label on it. While Tim was climbing over Jeremiah's door, the squatting man realized that he had heard a motor, and had heard it stop. He drew the jacket slowly back from his face and looked at Tim and Jeremiah. The red sunlight shone direct-ly against his face, making a glitter in the deep eye-sockets, and showing up the stubble of black beard, the swollen lips, and the sweaty shine of the skin, like polished dark wood, or wet metal. It was the face of a desperate, per-haps a dangerous man, but just the same, it was also Lawrence's face.

George Wharton James

George Wharton James (1858–1923) came to the West from his native England in the 1870s, traveling the Methodist circuit as a preacher in frontier Nevada. Later he assumed a pastorate in Long Beach, suffered through a divorce—a scandal fueled by the unlikely and salacious accusations of his English wife—and was expelled from the Church. Armed with his own brand of idealism and endless reserves of energy, James set aside his misfortunes and eventually became a public lecturer. Southern California and the Southwest became his special interests, and when he turned to writing he drew upon them for his subjects. His books include A Tourist's Guide Book to Southern California, In and Out of the California Missions, *and* Through Ramona's Country, *in which he revisits the settings of Helen Hunt Jackson's famous novel.*

James's most enduring work is The Wonders of the Colorado Desert, *all-inclusive as attested by the subtitle: "Its Rivers and Its Mountains, Its Canyons and Its Springs, Its Life and Its History, Pictured and Described." This book invites comparison with another portrait of the area,* California Desert Trails, *also written by an Englishman, J. Smeaton Chase. James, whose prose often seems dated, writes in the more oratorical style. But James came to the Colorado Desert first, hence the freshness of his impressions. Here he renders the "marvelous" tints and hues of the desert.* ✒

from The Wonders of the Colorado Desert

In all ordinary conditions the colors of the desert are well defined and distinct. Especially are the shadows strong and vivid. The blacks remind one of the shadows cast by the mountain ranges on the moon, when observed through a powerful telescope.

During the sandstorms the mountains that shut in the northwestern end of the desert undergo marvelous transformations. The atmosphere becomes charged with fine sand and dust particles upon which the sun reflects and plays as the clouds that intervene between it and the dust allow. Late in the afternoon this dust becomes luminous with a half-transparent color-light that glows and shines and makes the whole mountainside appear as a veritable mountain of transfiguration; as if the "glory of the Lord" shone upon it. One feels in looking at it that he is on holy ground and must not only take his shoes from his feet but uncover his head in awesome reverence.

Then, if his attention be called away, and he look again fifteen minutes later, the divine glow has gone, and a sullen, bluish, sodden effect takes its place. The sand-veil is there, but no longer illumined by the sun. A little later, and it becomes a misty purple, and night finally curtains it with its darker shades.

The sun is just rising over the Chocolate range. For an hour the eastern sky has been a changing glory of orange, fiery red, and madder brown. Now as the sun bursts over the hills and floods the desert the range to the left is outlined with such distinctness as to suggest a black silhouette on a white background; but the color is royal Tyrian purple instead of black, and the background a luminous pearly opalescence that shades off into the pure blue seen only over desert and southern ocean skies.

At this early hour the light shining at so low an angle reveals the different ridges of the San Bernardino range with a vividness that is startling to one who has seen them before only in the direct light of noon. Now each ridge stands forth as clear and distinct in its own individuality as can be. The "pip, pip, pip" of the quail is heard on every hand; the wild deluge of song of the mockingbird; the cheery warble of the linnet; and from the distance the faint crow of the domestic rooster calling his family out to gather the early worm.

The peculiar lighting of these early sunrise hours well repays much and careful watching. The beams of light strike through certain passes in the mountains, flooding slopes and peaks and ridges beyond with patches of vivid light and color, while other places are kept in shadow by the arresting of the sun's beams by giant mural faces or higher peaks close at hand.

How the delicate tints of the desert appeal to you seen in contrast with the strong colors! Here are the browns, grays, reds, and greens of the mountains, with the greens and purples which shade into blackness, and stand out vividly against the pure white of the snowy peaks beyond. Then there are the deep black gashes of the canyons, with here and there a patch of delicate pea-green showing that trees are growing near running water in the mouths of the canyons.

At dawn, and equally at sundown, everything seems bathed in a soft greenish gold atmosphere giving to animals, moving figures of men, silent wagons, gently waving trees a peculiarly mysterious appearance that one can hardly describe and that is never felt or seen away from the desert.

Harold Bell Wright

Harold Bell Wright (1872–1944) was an accomplished writer by the time he moved to California to become the pastor for the Redlands Christian Church. Born to a struggling family in upstate New York, Wright had to go to work at eleven, when his mother died. He became an itinerant painter, but found a new calling after he dropped in on an Ohio meeting of the Disciples of Christ. Pastor Wright published That Printer of Udell's, *which was built on the theme of "practical Christianity," and other religious works followed.*

When ill health forced Wright to give up his ministry in Redlands, he turned to writing full-time. He bought land in El Centro, built a writing studio, and became one of the Southwest's most popular novelists. His best-known work, The Winning of Barbara Worth, *is set in Wright's back-yard, the Colorado Desert. Wright renamed his California locations: for example, the Imperial Valley became King's Basin, San Diego became San Felipe. But there is no mistaking his carefully crafted landscapes. In the following selection, Jefferson Worth oversees the huge King's Basin, soon to become a battleground between Eastern land profiteers and locals seeking a better life.* ✒

from The Winning of Barbara Worth

When day broke over the topmost ridges of No Man's Mountains, Jefferson Worth's outfit was ready to move. The driver of the lighter rig with its four broncos set out for San Felipe. On the front seat of the big wagon Texas Joe picked up his reins, sorted them carefully, and glanced over his shoulder at his employer. "All set?"

"Go ahead."

"You, Buck! Molly!" The lead mules straightened their traces. "Jack! Pete!" As the brake was released with a clash and rattle of iron rods, the wheelers threw their weight into their collars and the wagon moved ahead.

Grim, tireless, world-old sentinels, No Man's Mountains stood guard between the fertile land on their seaward side and the desolate forgotten wastes of the east. They said to the country of green life, of progress and growth and civilization, that marched to their line on the west, "Halt!" and it stopped. To the land of lean want, of gray death, of gaunt hunger, and torturing thirst, that crept to their feet on the other side, "Stop!" and it came no farther. With no land to till, no mineral to dig, their very poverty was their protection. With an air of grim finality, they declared strongly that as they had always been they would always remain; and, at the beginning of my story, save for that one, slender, man-made trail, their hoary boast had remained unchallenged.

Steadily, but with frequent rests on the grades, Jefferson Worth's outfit climbed toward the summit and a little before noon gained the pass. The loud, rattling rumble of the wagon as the tires bumped and ground over the stony, rock-floored way, with the sharp ring and clatter of the iron-shod hoofs of the team, echoed, echoed, and echoed again. Loudly, wildly, the rude sounds assaulted the stillness until the quiet seemed hopelessly shattered by the din. Softly, tamely, the sounds drifted away in the clear distance; through groves of live oak, thickets of greasewood, juniper, manzanita and sage; into canyon and wash; from bluff and ledge; along slope and spur and shoulder; over ridge and saddle and peak; fainting, dying—the impotent sounds of man's passing sank into the stillness and were lost. When the team halted for a brief rest it was in a moment as if the silence had never been broken. Grim, awful, the hills gave no signs of man's presence, gave that creeping bit of life no heed.

At Mountain Spring—a lonely little pool on the desert side of the huge wall—they stopped for dinner. When the meal was over, Texas Joe, with the assistance of Pat, filled the water barrels, while the boy busied himself with the canteen and the Seer and Jefferson Worth looked on.

"'Tis a dhry counthry ahead, I'm thinkin'," remarked the Irishman inquiringly as he lifted another dripping bucket.

"Some," returned Tex. "There are three water holes between here and the river where there's water sometimes. Mostly, though, when you need it worst, there ain't none there, an' I reckon a dry water hole is about the most discouragin' proposition there is. They'll all be dry this trip. There wasn't nothin' but mud at Wolf Wells when we come through last week."

Again the barren rocks and the grim, forbidding hills echoed the loud sound of wheel and hoof. Down the steep flank of the mountain, with screaming, grinding brakes, they thundered and clattered into the narrow hallway of Devil's Canyon with its sheer walls and shadowy gloom. The little stream that trickled down from the tiny spot of green at the spring tried bravely to follow but soon sank exhausted into the dry waste. A cool wind, like a draft through a tunnel, was in their faces. After perhaps two hours of this the way widened out, the sides of the canyon grew lower with now and then gaps and breaks. Then the walls gave way to low, rounded hills, through which the winding trail lay—a bed of sand and gravel—and here and there appeared clumps of greasewood and cacti of several varieties.

At length they passed out from between the last of the foothills and sud-denly—as though a mighty curtain were lifted—they faced the desert. At their feet the mesa lay in a blaze of white sunlight, and beyond and below the edge of the bench the vast King's Basin country.

At the edge of the mesa Texas halted his team and the little party looked out and away over those awful reaches of desolate solitude. The Seer and Pat uttered involuntary exclamations. Jefferson Worth, Texas, and Abe were silent, but the boy's thin features were aglow with eager enthusiasm, and the face of the driver revealed an interest in the scene that years of familiarity could not entirely deaden, but the gray mask of the banker betrayed no emotion.

In that view, of such magnitude that miles meant nothing, there was not a sign of man save the one slender thread of road that was so soon lost in the distance. From horizon to horizon, so far that the eye ached in the effort to comprehend it, there was no cloud to cast a shadow, and the deep sky poured its resistless flood of light upon the vast dun plain with savage fury, as if to beat into helplessness any living creature that might chance to be caught thereon. And the desert, receiving that flood from the wide, hot sky, mysteriously wove with it soft scarfs of lilac, misty veils of purple and filmy curtains of rose and pearl and gold; strangely formed with it wide lakes of blue rimmed with phantom hills of red and violet—constantly changing, shifting, scene on scene, as dream pictures shift and change.

Norman Mailer

Norman Mailer (1923–) is one of the most celebrated writers of his genera-tion, as well as one of the most controversial. His first novel, The Naked and the Dead, *which drew on Mailer's experience in the Pacific during World War II, earned him instant recognition. But the works that followed met mixed response, and critics—ever willing to speculate about the causes of imaginative failure—blamed the decline on Mailer's stormy personal life and the energy he wasted creating the "hipster" persona, which he described in an essay called "The White Negro."*

His writing became more compelling as it blurred the distinction between fact and fiction. In The Armies of the Night *Mailer reported on a mas-sive 1967 protest against the Vietnam War, describing his experiences from two separate perspectives. It earned him a National Book Award and a Pulitzer Prize. He won his second Pulitzer with another nonfiction narra-tive,* The Executioner's Song, *about a convict named Gary Gilmore and the controversy surrounding his execution. In the meantime, Mailer helped to secure the release of Jack Henry Abbot, a convict-turned-author who commit-ted another murder shortly after he was freed. Mailer has never ducked trou-ble: he wrote* The Prisoner of Sex *and become a bête noir for American feminism in the seventies; recently he took on Christianity in* The Gospel According to the Son, *Jesus' first-person account of his life on earth and death on the cross.*

Early in his career Mailer wrote a California novel, the only entry in what he had planned as a series. The Deer Park *is set in a resort that Mailer calls "Desert D'Or," in an improbable world of cocktail lounges and jungle foliage springing out of the Colorado Desert.* 🖎

from The Deer Park

In the cactus wild of Southern California a distance of two hundred miles from the capital of cinema, as I choose to call it, is the town of Desert D'Or. There I went from the Air Force to look for a good time. Some time ago.

Almost everybody I knew in Desert D'Or had had an unusual career, and it was the same for me. I grew up in a home for orphans. Still intact at the age of twenty-three, wearing my flying wings and a first lieutenant's uniform, I arrived at the resort with fourteen thousand dollars, a sum I picked up via a poker game in a Tokyo hotel room while waiting with other fliers for our plane home. The curiosity is that I was never a gambler, I did not even like the game, but I had nothing to lose that night, and maybe for such a reason I accepted the luck of my cards. Let me leave it at that. I came out of the Air Force with no place to go, no family to visit, and I wandered down to Desert D'Or.

Built since the Second World War, it is the only place I know which is all new. A long time ago, Desert D'Or was called Desert Door by the prospectors who put up their shanties at the edge of its oasis and went into the mountains above the desert to look for gold. But there is nothing left of those men; when the site of Desert D'Or was chosen, none of the old shacks remained.

No, everything is in the present tense, and during the months I stayed at the resort, I came to know it in a way we can know few places. It was a town built out of no other obvious motive than commercial profit and so no sign of commerce was allowed to appear. Desert D'Or was without a main street, and its stores looked like anything but stores. In those places which sold clothing, no clothing was laid out, and you waited in a modern living room while salesmen opened panels in the wall to exhibit summer suits, or held between their hands the blooms and sprays of a tropical scarf. There was a jewelry store built like a cabin cruiser: from the street one peeped through a porthole to see a thirty-thousand-dollar necklace hung on the silver antlers of a piece of driftwood. None of the hotels—not the Yacht Club, nor the Debonair, not the Yucca Plaza, the Sandpiper, the Creedmor, nor the Desert D'Or Arms—could even be seen from outside. Put behind cement-brick fences or wooden palings, one hardly came across a building which was not green, yellow, rose, orange, or pink, and the approach was hidden by a shrubbery of bright flowers. You passed through the gate to the Yacht Club, the biggest and therefore the most exclusive hotel in the resort, and followed its private road which twisted through the grounds for several hundred yards, expecting a mansion at the end, but came instead to no more than a carport, a swimming pool in the shape of a free-form coffee table with curved-wall cabañas and canasta tables, and a set of lawn-tennis courts, the only lawn in all that part of Southern California. At night, along yellow sidewalks which crossed a winding artificial creek, lit up with Japanese lanterns strung to the tropical trees, you could wander by the guest bungalows scattered along the route, their flush pastel-colored doors another part of the maze of the arrangement.

I blew a piece of my fourteen-thousand-dollar fortune and stayed at the Yacht Club until I picked the house I was to rent for the rest of my stay in Desert D'Or. I could describe that house in detail, but what would be the use? It was like most of the houses in the resort; it was modern, ranch-style, of course, with light furniture and rugs which felt like poodle wool, and it had a garden and a wall which went around the garden, the standard fault of Desert D'Or architecture; along the desert table, the walls were made of glass to have a view of mesa-colored sand and violet mountains, but the houses were so close to each other that the builders had to fence them in, and the result was like living in a room whose walls are mirrors. In fact, my house had a twenty-foot mirror which faced the wall of plate-glass window. No matter where I stood in the living room, I could never miss the sight of my rented garden with its desert flowers and the lone yucca tree.

During the dry season which lasted for nine months of the year, the resort was parched by the sun. Every twilight the spray from a thousand sprinklers washed dust and sand from the gray foliage; morning and afternoon the sun scorched the sap from the plants and the desert circled the resort, its cacti standing on the horizon while croppings of dusty rock gathered like scavengers in the distance. The blue sky burnt on the pale desert. It would come on me at times that Desert D'Or was a place where no trees bear leaves. The palms and the yuccas lifted a foliage of tufts and fans and fronds and shoots but never leaves, and on some of the roads where tall palms lined the way, their dead fronds hung from the trunk like an ostrich's muff.

During the off-season, most of the activity took place in the bars. The bars were a village in the town, or at least a kind of main street in the absence of any other, yet they were as different from the warm front of Desert D'Or as the inside of one's body is separate from the surface of one's skin. Like so many other places in Southern California, the bars, cocktail lounges, and nightclubs were made to look like a jungle, an underwater grotto, or the lounge of a modern movie theater. The Cerulean Room, to take an example, had an irregular space of rose-orange walls and booths of yellow leatherette under the influence of a dark blue ceiling. Above the serving bar with its bank of bottles, its pyramids of citrus fruit, a smoky-yellow false ceiling reflected into the mirror behind the bar and colored the etching of a half-nude girl which had been cut into the glass. Drinking in that atmosphere, I never knew whether it was night or day, and I think that kind of uncertainty got into everybody's conversation. Men lacquered with liquor talked to other men who were sober, stories were started and never finished. On a typical afternoon in the air-cooled midnight of the bar, you could see a fat old man in a Palm Beach suit talking to a young girl with orange lipstick and the deep suntan of Desert D'Or, the girl more interested in the old gent than the gentleman in her. Promoters and tourists, middle-aged women with new-colored hair, and high school kids who had com-peted in running hot-rods across the desert, were jammed together. The talk was made up of horses, stories of parties the night before, and systems for roulette. Running along the heavy beat of a third-rate promotor trying to raise money, there would come the solo shriek of one hysterical blond or another, who seemed to be laughing in that tune which goes, "I'm dumb, I'm dumb, but you're a scream."

In such a way, afternoon was always passing into night, and drunken nights into the dawn of a desert morning. One seemed to leave the the-atrical darkness of afternoon for the illumination of night, and the sun of Desert D'Or became like the stranger who the drunk imagines to be fol-lowing him. So I spent my first few weeks doing little more than pick up the bar checks of all those small sharp prospectors for pleasure from the capital, and in the capsule biography by which most of the people knew one another, I was understood to be an Air Force pilot whose family was wealthy and lived in the East, and I even added the detail that I had a bro-ken marriage and drank to get over it. As a story it was reasonable enough to pass, and I sometimes believed what I said and tried to take the cure in the very real sun of Desert D'Or with its cactus, its mountain, and the bright green foliage of its love and its money.

Aldous Huxley

Born in England and educated at Oxford, Aldous Huxley (1894–1963) is known primarily for his 1932 science fiction novel, Brave New World, *a satirical look at people who have become prisoners of their technology, surrendering their individuality to "Community, Identity, Stability." A prolific writer, he was already well known when he moved to Los Angeles in 1937. There he continued producing novels, short stories, and poetry—as well as screenplays such as* Pride and Prejudice *and* Jane Eyre—*until his death from cancer.*

Anthony Burgess claimed that it was Huxley who "helped to equip the contemporary novel with a brain." And part of this talent as a novelist may derive from his skill as an essayist. According to critic Frederick J. Hoffman, "the characters of his creation stumble, swagger, or are carried through his novels, supported almost always by the essayist." Huxley wrote scores of essays—of "every size and shape and color," as he put it—on any subject that appealed to his imagination. His experiments with mescaline, chronicled in The Doors of Perception, *formed only part of his spiritual quest in California. This quest also took him to the Mojave Desert, where he found much that was disturbing.* 🦗

from Tomorrow and Tomorrow and Tomorrow

The facts of silence and emptiness are traditionally the symbols of divine immanence—but not, of course, for everyone, and not in all circumstances. "Until one has crossed a barren desert, without food or water, under a burning tropical sun, at three miles an hour, one can form no conception of what misery is." These are the words of a gold seeker, who took the southern route to California in 1849. Even when one is crossing it at seventy miles an hour on a four-lane highway, the desert can seem formidable enough. To the forty-niners it was unmitigated hell. Men and women who are at her mercy find it hard to see in Nature and her works any symbols but those of brute power at the best and, at the worst, of an obscure and mindless malice. The desert's emptiness and the desert's silence reveal what we may call their spiritual meanings only to those who enjoy some measure of physiological security. The security may amount to no more than St. Anthony's hut and daily ration of bread and vegetables, no more than Milarepa's cave and barley meal and boiled nettles—less than what any sane economist would regard as the indispensable minimum, but still security, still a guarantee of organic life and, along with life, of the possibility of spiritual liberty and transcendental happiness.

But even for those who enjoy security against the assaults of the environment, the desert does not always or inevitably reveal its spiritual meanings. The early Christian hermits retired to the Thebaid because its air was purer, because there were fewer distractions, because God seemed nearer there than in the world of men. But, alas, dry places are notoriously the abode of unclean spirits, seeking rest and finding it not. If the immanence of God was sometimes more easily discoverable in the desert, so also, and all too frequently, was the immanence of the devil. St. Anthony's temptations have become a legend, and Cassian speaks of "the tempests of imagination" through which every newcomer to the eremitic life had to pass. Solitude, he writes, makes men feel "the many-winged folly of their souls [...]; they find the perpetual silence intolerable, and those whom no labor on the land could weary, are vanquished by doing nothing and worn out by the long duration of their peace." *Be still, and know that I am God;* be still, and know that *you* are the delinquent imbecile who snarls and gibbers in the basement of every human mind. The desert can drive men mad, but it can also help them to become supremely sane.

The enormous drafts of emptiness and silence prescribed by the eremites are safe medicine only for a few exceptional souls. By the majority the desert should be taken either dilute or, if at full strength, in small doses. Used in this way, it acts as a spiritual restorative, as an anti-hallucinant, as a de-tensioner and alterative.

In his book, *The Next Million Years,* Sir Charles Darwin looks forward to thirty thousand generations of ever more humans pressing ever more heavily on ever dwindling resources and being killed off in ever increasing numbers by famine, pestilence and war. He may be right. Alternatively, human ingenuity may somehow falsify his predictions. But even human ingenuity will find it hard to circumvent arithmetic. On a planet of limited area, the more people there are, the less vacant space there is bound to be. Over and above the material and sociological problems of increasing population, there is a serious psychological problem. In a completely homemade environment, such as is provided by any great metropolis, it is as hard to remain sane as it is in a completely natural environment such as the desert or the forest. O Solitude, where are thy charms? But, O Multitude, where are *thine?* The most wonderful thing about America is that, even in these middle years of the twentieth century, there are so few Americans. By taking a certain amount of trouble you might still be able to get yourself eaten by a bear in the state of New York. And without any trouble at all you can get bitten by a rattler in the Hollywood hills, or die of thirst, while wandering through an uninhabited desert, within a hundred and fifty miles of Los Angeles. A short generation ago you might have wandered and died within only a hundred miles of Los Angeles. Today the mounting tide of humanity has oozed through the intervening canyons and spilled out into the wide Mojave. Solitude is receding at the rate of four and a half kilometers per annum.

And yet, in spite of it all, the silence persists. For this silence of the desert is such that casual sounds, and even the systematic noise of civilization, cannot abolish it. They coexist with it—as small irrelevances at right angles to an enormous meaning, as veins of something analogous to darkness within an enduring transparency. From the irrigated land come the dark gross sounds of lowing cattle, and above them the plovers trail their vanishing threads of shrillness. Suddenly, startlingly, out of the sleeping sagebrush there bursts the shrieking of coyotes—Trio for Ghoul and Two Damned Souls. On the trunks of cottonwood trees, on the wooden walls of barns and houses, the woodpeckers rattle away like pneumatic drills. Picking one's way between the cactuses and the creosote bushes one hears, like some tiny whirring clockwork, the soliloquies of invisible wrens, the calling, at dusk, of the nightjays and even occasionally the voice of Homo sapiens—six of the species in a parked Chevrolet, listening to the broadcast of a prize fight, or else in pairs necking to the delicious accompaniment of Crosby. But the light forgives, the distances forget, and this great crystal of silence, whose base is as large as Europe and whose height, for all practical purposes, is infinite, can coexist with things of a far higher order of discrepancy than canned sentiment or vicarious sport. Jet planes, for example—the stillness is so massive that it can absorb even jet planes. The screaming crash mounts to its intolerable climax and fades again, mounts as another of the monsters rips through the air, and once more diminishes and is gone. But even at the height of the outrage the mind can still remain aware of that which surrounds it, that which preceded and will outlast it.

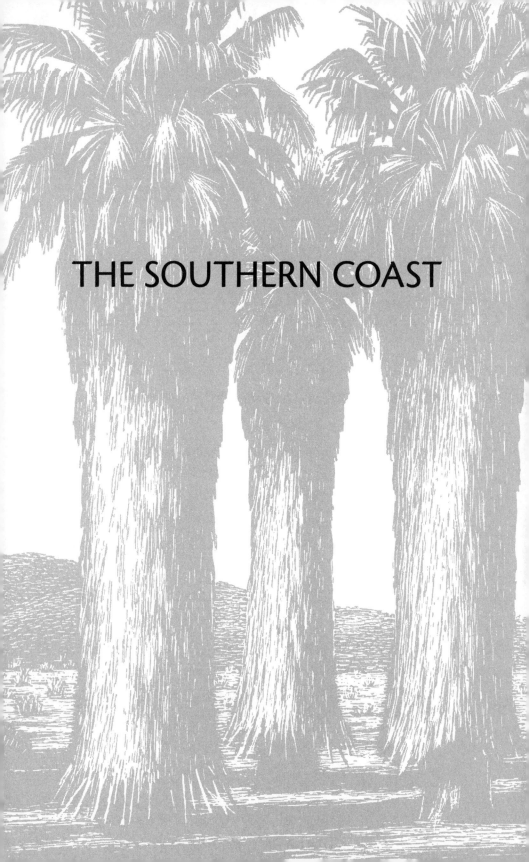

THE SOUTHERN COAST

M ore than any other region of California, the southern coast bears the imprint of its inhabitants, half the population of the state squeezed into an area roughly the size of Belgium. If you want to see how this kind of human concentration can affect the landscape, go to a point overlooking Los Angeles on a clear night: the turnout along Mulholland Drive or the parapets of Griffith Park Observatory. A striking view, and what is most striking is the impression of order: street lamps strung out along endless avenues and boulevards, bright pinpoints tracing near-perfect rectangles; incandescent ribbons of car lights, narrow and precise, streaming along the freeways; glowing windows of homes and businesses, as neatly arranged as tokens on a Monopoly board. Somewhere below are parks and vacant lots, backyards, and green spaces, bits of earth not yet covered by concrete or asphalt. But these are unilluminated and therefore invisible patches within the dominating pattern of the cityscape.

California's southern coast traces an arc curving east from Point Arguello, then south to the Mexican border. The region is separated from the rest of the state by densely forested mountains: the Transverse Ranges to the north—the Santa Ynez, Santa Monica, San Gabriel, and San Bernardinos, and by the Peninsular Ranges to the east—the San Jacinto and Santa Rosas. Between these steep mountains and the sea are the beaches and interior valleys of Santa Barbara and Ventura counties, the Los Angeles lowlands—most of Los Angeles and Orange counties and western San Bernardino and Riverside counties—and coastal San Diego, the south state's only natural harbor.

Much of the low terrain is semiarid, originally supporting two plant communities: chaparral on the coast, bunchgrass and oak in the interior valleys. Runoff from the surrounding mountains feeds rivers like the Los

Angeles, San Gabriel, and Santa Ana, but the region's low rainfall meant they ran dry in the summer even before they were altered for flood control and water storage. Resource-poor Southern California would have been an odd place for development but for its Mediterranean climate, the mild weather Carey McWilliams describes as its one natural asset, "predictable to the point of monotony," thereby attracting "unlimited resources of manpower and wealth."

Before Spanish settlement, Native Americans thrived in this mild climate. To the north, the Chumash lived in villages on the coast and on the Channel Islands (where Juan Cabrillo found them in 1542—the first California natives encountered by Europeans). To the south were the Gabrielino, who inhabited the mainland around present-day Los Angeles and also San Clemente and Catalina islands. Both groups hunted marine mammals (the Chumash also fished, using canoes made from wooden planks) and harvested acorns, berries, and cactus fruit.

As these original inhabitants knew, nature does not always smile on the area. Southern California is earthquake country, where the San Andreas Fault interrupts its six-hundred-and-fifty-mile run (from Imperial to Mendocino county) to shift directions. The resulting pressure in this area, which is fissured with many more faults, can generate up to ten thousand earthquakes a year. The Gabrielinos explained them with a story as elegant and imaginative as any contemporary geological theory:

> Long ago, before there were people, there was only water.
> Great Spirit decided to make a beautiful land. He spotted a
> giant turtle and decided to make an island on its back. But
> one back wasn't enough, so the Great Spirit summoned his six
> brothers, placed all seven turtles together, and built the land on
> their shells. But the turtles began to argue about which way to
> swim. Three swam west and four swam east, making the land
> above shake. Whenever they argue, Turtle Island shakes again.

Besides earthquakes, two other problems come with the southern coast's terrain: a pair of weather patterns linked to the landscape. Temperature inversions often trap pollution and marine fog to produce smog, particularly in summer. Although the problem was aggravated by modern technology—especially the emissions from internal combustion engines—the phenomenon was first recorded by Cabrillo. He observed that smoke from Indian campfires rose just a few hundred feet before spreading out, so he called San Pedro Bay La Bahía de los Fumos, a name that is still apt. In autumn, offshore winds sometimes bring relief by shoving the marine layer out to sea. But inland winds offer little relief. The hot, dry Santa Ana winds, which cut through mountain passes from the Mojave, not only fan brushfires, they "curl your hair and make your nerves jump and your skin itch," said Raymond Chandler in 1938. Three decades later Joan Didion described the same sharp edge to the Santa Ana wind, as well as its special place in the local imagination.

Permanent Spanish settlement in Southern California began at San Diego in 1769. The Spanish pushed north from there to establish seven missions connected by the famous El Camino Real (which took almost the same route as today's Highway 101). Los Angeles—a small ranching community—was settled in 1781, with Spanish land grants establishing ranchos that produced hides and tallow. This Mexican wealth brought Yankee traders to California, among them seaman Richard Henry Dana, who landed in Santa Barbara in 1835.

Cattle raising remained the chief industry in Southern California for at least a decade after the state joined the Union. Reformer and writer Helen Hunt Jackson describes this period in *Ramona,* bemoaning the "Americans pouring in, at all points, to reap the advantages of their new possessions." As the cattle market waned, Southern Californians shifted to farming, planting crops like apples, pears, figs, olives, lemons, and oranges. And surveyor William H. Brewer noted in 1860, "All that is wanted to naturally make [Los Angeles] a paradise is *water,* more *water.*" The south state would not solve that problem until the next century. But with the controversial acquisition of water from the Owens Valley and the con-struction of a huge system of aqueducts to bring even more water from the Colorado River and the north, the Southern California landscape changed forever. When Sarah Bixby Smith was a girl in the 1870s, Los Angeles was at the end of its "Adobe Days": sidewalks were already replacing brush and wildflowers in the growing city.

The Southern Coast soon started to attract health seekers, especially after the Southern Pacific reached Los Angeles in 1876. Charles Nordhoff targeted part of an 1872 book, *California for Health, Pleasure, and Residence,* to invalids, promising that Southern California is "remarkably mild and healing." The health rush was the first of a number of population "booms" fueled by new opportunities, later to include tourism and the motion picture industry. Fifteen oil fields were discovered in the Los

Angeles Basin between 1917 and 1929, just in time to feed Americans' appetite for petroleum products as the automobile industry grew. After World War I the region became an important center for the defense industry and the military, which established several Army and Navy bases and some key facilities in San Diego. To support its population growth, Southern California imported water and power and developed a freeway network that now links the entire sprawling region. "Autopia," as Rayner Banham calls it, "is now a single comprehensible place, a coherent state of mind, a complete way of life."

This remarkable expansion brought remarkable opportunities for writers. Southern California caught the attention of Edwin Markham—author of "Man with a Hoe," one of the most anthologized poems about the working class—who escaped to "California the Wonderful" in 1914. Besides the pull of its warm climate, writers also felt the pull of the movies, of the Hollywood life. F. Scott Fitzgerald's Pat Hobby stories and Nathaniel West's *The Day of the Locust* portrayed the seedier side of an industry that attracted such talents as William Faulkner and Christopher Isherwood (one of the few Los Angeles émigrés with any appreciation for the "real nature" of California).

In fact, it is the real nature of the place that seems so much at issue in Southern California, where Hollywood movies and Orange County theme parks provide fantasy alternatives to real life. Charles Bukowski and Keven Hearle have insisted on this real world in poems that return Los Angeles life to its basis, to the water that comes down in winter torrents or comes from sprinklers on suburban lawns.

And despite the population pressures that have remade so much of the region's landscape into a cityscape—an artificial world where the illusion of perpetual comfort and convenience prevails over the uncertainties of reality—some of the Southern Coast has escaped development. Some of Southern California is still rural: the Santa Ynez Mountains, for example, are still ranch country. Jane Hollister Wheelwright returns to her childhood home there and describes a canyon where there are still juncos and linnets and flycatchers—and no need for a lawn. And at the edge of the continent, there are still places, as Gretel Ehrlich tells us, where the land meets the sea as it always has.

Richard Henry Dana

In his sophomore year at Harvard, Richard Henry Dana (1815–1882) suffered eye damage from a bout of measles and could not read without pain. To recover his health, he left his studies and went to sea. In 1834 he joined the crew of the Pilgrim, *a brig bound for California with Yankee goods to exchange for cowhides. Dana was nineteen years old, the well-schooled son of an upper-crust Boston family, and almost wholly ignorant of the harsh realities of a sailor's life. Aboard ship he found himself a virtual captive, subject to a master who was finally discharged for brutality. Dana kept a journal of his voyage, describing the seafaring life and the people and places he visited. That journal was lost when Dana returned to Boston in 1836, but it seems that "the memory of his experiences—and perhaps of their formation in the lost journal—was vivid," as Thomas Philbrick has noted, "for he completed a draft of the book, comprising all but the first and last chapters, in a period of six months"—a remarkable feat for the man who could not bear to read when he set sail.*

*Two Years Before the Mast was a best-seller—it sold ten thousand copies the first year and is still in print. He wrote other books—*The Seaman's Friend *and* To Cuba and Back, a Vacation Voyage—but *Dana felt this description of California life and landscape was his best achievement. He became a successful attorney and enjoyed a minor political career, but in 1871 he told his son that his life had been "a failure compared to what I might and ought to have done. My great success—my book—was a boy's work done before I came to the bar." Boy's work or no,* Two Years Before the Mast *provides a fine picture of the remote Mexican province just opening up to U.S. merchants.* 🖎

from Two Years Before the Mast

Upper California has the seat of its government at Monterey, where is also the customhouse, the only one on the coast, and at which every vessel intending to trade on the coast must enter its cargo before it can commence its traffic. We were to trade upon this coast exclusively, and therefore expected to go to Monterey at first; but the captain's orders from home were to put in at Santa Barbara, which is the central port of the coast, and wait there for the agent who lives there, and transacts all the business for the firm to which our vessel belonged.

The bay, or, as it was commonly called, the canal [channel] of Santa Barbara, is very large, being formed by the mainland on one side (between Point Conception on the north and Point St. Buena Ventura on the south), which here bends in like a crescent, and three large islands opposite to it and at the distance of twenty miles. This is just sufficient to give it the name of a bay, while at the same time it is so large and so much exposed to the southeast and northwest winds, that it is little better than an open roadstead; and the whole swell of the Pacific Ocean rolls in here before a southeaster, and breaks with so heavy a surf in the shallow waters, that it is highly dangerous to lie near in to the shore during the southeaster season, that is, between the months of November and April.

This wind (the southeaster) is the bane of the coast of California. Between the months of November and April (including a part of each), which is the rainy season in this latitude, you are never safe from it, and accordingly, in the ports which are open to it, vessels are obliged, during these months, to lie at anchor at a distance of three miles from the shore, with slip-ropes on their cables, ready to slip and go to sea at a moment's warning. The only ports which are safe from this wind are San Francisco and Monterey in the north, and San Diego in the south.

As it was January when we arrived, and the middle of the southeaster season, we accordingly came to anchor at the distance of three miles from the shore, in eleven fathoms water, and bent a slip-rope and buoys to our cables, cast off the yard arm gaskets from the sails, and stopped them all with rope-yarns. After we had done this, the boat went ashore with the captain, and returned with orders to the mate to send a boat ashore for him at sundown. I did not go in the first boat, and was glad to find that there was another going before night; for after so long a voyage as ours had been, a few hours is long to pass in sight and out of reach of land. We spent the day on board in the usual avocations; but as this was the first time we had been without the captain, we felt a little more freedom, and looked about us to see what sort of a country we had got into, and were to spend a year or two of our lives in.

In the first place, it was a beautiful day, and so warm that we had on straw hats, duck trowsers, and all the summer gear; and as this was midwinter, it spoke well for the climate; and we afterwards found that the thermometer never fell to the freezing point throughout the winter, and that there was very little difference between the seasons, except that during a long period of rainy and southeasterly weather, thick clothes were not uncomfortable.

The large bay lay about us, nearly smooth, as there was hardly a breath of wind stirring, though the boat's crew who went ashore told us that the long groundswell broke into a heavy surf on the beach. There was only one vessel in the port—a long, sharp brig of about three hundred tons, with raking masts and very square yards, and English colors at her peak. We afterwards learned that she was built at Guayaquil, and named the *Ayacucho*, after the place where the battle was fought that gave Peru her independence, and was now owned by a Scotchman named Wilson, who commanded her, and was engaged in the trade between Callao, the Sandwich Islands, and California. She was a fast sailer, as we frequently afterwards perceived, and had a crew of Sandwich Islanders on board. Beside this vessel there was no object to break the surface of the bay. Two points ran out as the horns of the crescent, one of which—the one to the westward—was low and sandy, and is that to which vessels are obliged to give a wide berth when running out for a southeaster; the other is high, bold, and well wooded, and, we were told, has a mission upon it, called Santa Buenaventura, from which the point is named. In the middle of this crescent, directly opposite the anchoring ground, lie the mission and town of Santa Barbara, on a low, flat plain, but little above the level of the sea, covered with grass, though entirely without trees, and surrounded on three sides by an amphitheater of mountains, which slant off to the distance of fifteen or twenty miles. The mission stands a little back of the town, and is a large building, or rather collection of buildings, in the center of which is a high tower, with a belfry of five bells; and the whole, being plastered, makes quite a show at a distance, and is the mark by which vessels come to anchor. The town lies a little nearer to the beach—about half a mile from it—and is composed of one-story houses built of brown clay—some of them plastered—with red tiles on the roofs. I should judge that there were about a hundred of them; and in the midst of them stands the presidio, or fort, built of the same materials, and apparently but little stronger. The town is certainly finely situated, with a bay in front, and an amphitheater of hills behind. The only thing which diminishes its beauty is that the hills have no large trees upon them, they having been all burnt by a great fire which swept them off about a dozen years before, and they had not yet grown up again. The fire was described to me by an inhabitant, as having been a very terrible and magnificent sight. The air of the whole valley was so heated that the people were obliged to leave the town and take up their quarters for several days upon the beach.

Just before sundown the mate ordered a boat's crew ashore, and I went as one of the number. We passed under the stern of the English brig, and had a long pull ashore. I shall never forget the impression which our first landing on the beach of California made upon me. The sun had just gone down; it was getting dusky; the damp night wind was beginning to blow, and the heavy swell of the Pacific was setting in, and breaking in loud and high "combers" upon the beach. We lay on our oars in the swell, just outside of the surf, waiting for a good chance to run in, when a boat, which had put off from the *Ayacucho* just after us, came alongside of us, with a crew of dusky Sandwich Islanders, talking and hallooing in their outlandish tongue. They knew that we were novices in this kind of boating, and waited to see us go in. The second mate, however, who steered our boat, determined to have the advantage of their experience, and would not go in first. Finding at length how matters stood, they gave a shout, and taking advantage of a great comber which came swelling in, rearing its head, and lifting up the stern of our boat nearly perpendicular, and again dropping it in the trough, they gave three or four long and strong pulls, and went in on top of the great wave, throwing their oars overboard, and as far from the boat as they could throw them, and jumping out the instant that the boat touched the beach, and then seizing hold of her and running her up high and dry upon the sand. We saw at once how it was to be done, and also the necessity of keeping the boat "stern on" to the sea; for the instant the sea should strike upon her broadside or quarter, she would be driven up broadside on, and capsized. We pulled strongly in, and as soon as we felt that the sea had got hold of us and was carrying us in with the speed of a racehorse, we threw the oars as far from the boat as we could, and took hold of the gunwale, ready to spring out and seize her when she struck, the officer using his utmost strength to keep her stern on. We were shot up upon the beach like an arrow from a bow, and seizing the boat, ran her up high and dry, and soon picked up our oars, and stood by her, ready for the captain to come down.

Finding that the captain did not come immediately, we put our oars in the boat, and leaving one to watch it, walked about the beach to see what we could of the place. The beach is nearly a mile in length between the two points, and of smooth sand. We had taken the only good landing-place, which is in the middle; it being more stony toward the ends. It is about twenty yards in width from high-water mark to a slight bank at which the soil begins, and so hard that it is a favorite place for running horses. It was growing dark, so that we could just distinguish the dim outlines of the two vessels in the offing; and the great seas were rolling in, in regular lines, growing larger and larger as they approached the shore, and hanging over the beach upon which they were to break, when their tops would curl over and turn white with foam, and, beginning at one extreme of the line, break rapidly to the other, as a long card-house falls when the children knock down the cards at one end. The Sandwich Islanders, in the meantime, had turned their boat round, and ran her down into the water, and were loading her with hides and tallow. As this was the work in which we were soon to be engaged, we looked on with some curiosity. They ran the boat into the water so far that every large sea might float her, and two of them, with their trousers rolled up, stood by the bows, one on each side, keeping her in her right position. This was hard work; for beside the force they had to use upon the boat, the large seas nearly took them off their legs. The others were running from the boat to the bank, upon which, out of the reach of the water, was a pile of dry bullocks' hides, doubled lengthwise in the middle, and nearly as stiff as boards. These they took upon their heads, one or two at a time, and carried down to the boat, where one of their number stowed them away. They were obliged to carry them on their heads, to keep them out of the water, and we observed that they had on thick woolen caps. "Look here, Bill, and see what you're coming to!" said one of our men to another who stood by the boat. "Well, D[ana]," said the second mate to me, "this does not look much like Cambridge College, does it? This is what I call 'head work.'" To tell the truth, it did not look very encouraging.

After they had got through with the hides, they laid hold of the bags of tallow (the bags are made of hide, and are about the size of a common meal bag), and lifting each upon the shoulders of two men, one at each end, walked off with them to the boat, and prepared to go aboard. Here, too, was something for us to learn. The man who steered, shipped his oar and stood up in the stern, and those that pulled the after oars sat upon their benches, with their oars shipped, ready to strike out as soon as she was afloat. The two men at the bows kept their places; and when, at length, a large sea came in and floated her, seized hold of the gunwale, and ran out with her till they were up to their armpits, and then tumbled over the gunwale into the bows, dripping with water. The men at the oars struck out, but it wouldn't do; the sea swept back and left them nearly high and dry. The two fellows jumped out again; and the next time they succeeded better, and, with the help of a deal of outlandish hallooing and bawling, got her well off. We watched them till they were out of the breakers, and saw them steering for their vessel, which was now hidden in the darkness.

The sand of the beach began to be cold to our bare feet; the frogs set up their croaking in the marshes, and one solitary owl, from the end of the distant point, gave out his melancholy note, mellowed by the distance, and we began to think that it was high time for "the old man," as the captain is generally called, to come down. In a few minutes we heard something coming towards us. It was a man on horseback. He came up on the full gallop, reined up near us, addressed a few words to us, and receiving no answer, wheeled round and galloped off again. He was nearly as dark as an Indian, with a large Spanish hat, blanket cloak or surreppa [serape], and leather leggins, with a long knife stuck in them. "This is the seventh city that ever I was in, and no Christian one neither," said Bill Brown. "Stand by!" said Tom, "you haven't seen the worst of it yet." In the midst of this conversation the captain appeared; and we winded the boat round, shoved her down, and prepared to go off. The captain, who had been on the coast before and "knew the ropes," took the steering oar, and we went off in the same way as the other boat. I, being the youngest, had the pleasure of standing at the bow, and getting wet through. We went off well, though the seas were high. Some of them lifted us up, and sliding from under us, seemed to let us drop through the air like a flat plank upon the body of the water. In a few minutes we were in the low, regular swell, and pulled for a light, which, as we came up, we found had been run up to our trysail gaff.

Coming aboard, we hoisted up all the boats, and diving down into the forecastle, changed our wet clothes, and got our supper. After supper the sailors lit their pipes (cigars, those of us who had them), and we had to tell all we had seen ashore. Then followed conjectures about the people ashore, the length of the voyage, carrying hides, etc., etc., until eight bells, when all hands were called aft, and the "anchor watch" set. We were to stand two in a watch, and as the nights were pretty long, two hours were to make a watch. The second mate was to keep the deck until eight o'clock, and all hands were to be called at daybreak, and the word was passed to keep a bright lookout, and to call the mate if it should come on to blow from the southeast. We had also orders to strike the bells every half hour through the night, as at sea. My watchmate was John, the Swedish sailor, and we stood from twelve to two, he walking the larboard side, and I the starboard. At daylight all hands were called, and we went through the usual process of washing down, swabbing, etc., and got breakfast at eight o'clock. In the course of the forenoon, a boat went aboard of the *Ayacucho* and brought off a quarter of beef, which made us a fresh bite for dinner. This we were glad enough to have, and the mate told us that we should live upon fresh beef while we were on the coast, as it was cheaper here than the salt. While at dinner, the cook called, "Sail ho!" and coming on deck, we saw two sails coming round the point. One was a large ship under top-gallant sails, and the other a small hermaphrodite brig. They both backed their topsails and sent boats aboard of us. The ship's colors had puzzled us, and we found that she was from Genoa, with an assorted cargo, and was trading on the coast. She filled away again, and stood out, being bound up the coast to San Francisco. The crew of the brig's boat were Sandwich Islanders, but one of them, who spoke a little English, told us that she was the *Loriotte,* Captain Nye, from Oahu, and was engaged in the [hide-and-tallow] trade. She was a lump of a thing—what the sailors call a butter-box. This vessel, as well as the *Ayacucho,* and others which we afterwards saw engaged in the same trade, have English or Americans for officers, and two or three before the mast to do the work upon the rigging, and to rely upon for seamanship, while the rest of the crew are Sandwich Islanders, who are active, and very useful in boating.

The three captains went ashore after dinner, and came off again at night. When in port, everything is attended to by the chief mate; the captain, unless he is also supercargo, has little to do, and is usually ashore much of his time. This we thought would be pleasanter for us, as the mate was a good-natured man and not very strict. So it was for a time, but we were worse off in the end; for wherever the captain is a severe, energetic man, and the mate is wanting in both these qualities, there will always be trouble. And trouble we had already begun to anticipate. The captain had several times found fault with the mate, in presence of the crew; and hints had been dropped that all was not right between them. When this is the case, and the captain suspects that his chief officer is too easy and familiar with the crew, then he begins to interfere in all the duties, and to draw the reins more taut, and the crew have to suffer.

Helen Hunt Jackson

In the course of her active career, social critic Helen Hunt Jackson (1830–1885) published poems, travel sketches, children's stories, and essays. In 1881 she published A Century of Dishonor, *an indictment of the U.S. government for its faithless treatment of seven Native American tribes. And a year before her death in 1885, she published a novel meant to awaken the uncaring public to the plight of the mission Indians. Jackson lived just long enough to think her arrow missed its mark. She responded to a favorable review in the* Atlantic Monthly *with despair, "Not one word for my Indians! I put my heart and soul in the book for them. It is a dead failure." The readers of Jackson's most enduring work saw it as a romantic tale of vanishing cultures. The moral of* Ramona *had been overwhelmed by Jackson's imagination.*

Ramona tells the tragic tale of the virtuous and beautiful Ramona Ortegna, daughter of a Scotsman and an Indian woman, and the handsome and equally virtuous Allesandro Assis, an itinerant Indian laborer. While not entirely predictable, the plot is highly conventional, not much more than a frame for Jackson's exposé of the ruthless treatment of mission Indians by land-hungry Americans. Ramona's lasting appeal comes from Jackson's creation of an idyll of rancho life in a still-pastoral California. Here we follow the novel's venerable priest on his walk to the rancho of Ramona's guardian. ✒︎

from Ramona

...Father Salvierderra drew near the home of the Señora Moreno late in the afternoon of one of those midsummer days of which Southern California has so many in spring. The almonds had bloomed and the blossoms fallen; the apricots also, and the peaches and pears; on all the orchards of these fruits had come a filmy tint of green, so light it was hardly more than a shadow on the gray. The willows were vivid light green, and the orange groves dark and glossy like laurel. The billowy hills on either side [of] the valley were covered with verdure and bloom—myriads of low blossoming plants, so close to the earth that their tints lapped and overlapped on each other, and on the green of the grass, as feathers in fine plumage overlap each other and blend into a changeful color.

The countless curves, hollows, and crests of the coast-hills in Southern California heighten these chameleon effects of the spring verdure; they are like nothing in nature except the glitter of a brilliant lizard in the sun or the iridescent sheen of a peacock's neck.

Father Salvierderra paused many times to gaze at the beautiful picture. Flowers were always dear to the Franciscans. St. Francis himself permitted all decorations which could be made of flowers. He classed them with his brothers and sisters, the sun, moon, and stars—and all members of the sacred choir praising God.

It was melancholy to see how, after each one of these pauses, each fresh drinking in of the beauty of the landscape and the balmy air, the old man resumed his slow pace, with a long sigh and his eyes cast down. The fairer this beautiful land, the sadder to know it lost to the Church—alien hands reaping its fullness, establishing new customs, new laws. All the way down the coast from Santa Barbara he had seen, at every stopping-place, new tokens of the settling up of the country—farms opening, towns growing; the Americans pouring in, at all points, to reap the advantages of their new possessions. It was this which had made his journey heavy-hearted, and made him feel in approaching the Señora Moreno's, as if he were coming to one of the last sure strongholds of the Catholic faith left in the country.

When he was within two miles of the house, he struck off from the highway into a narrow path that he recollected led by a shortcut through the hills, and save nearly a third of the distance. It was more than a year since he had trod this path, and as he found it growing fainter and fainter, and more and more overgrown with the wild mustard, he said to himself, "I think no one can have passed through here this year."

As he proceeded he found the mustard thicker and thicker. The wild mustard in Southern California is like that spoken of in the New Testament, in the branches of which the birds of the air may rest. Coming up out of the earth, so slender a stem that dozens can find starting-point in an inch, it darts up, a slender straight shoot, five, ten, twenty feet, with hundreds of the fine feathery branches locking and interlocking with all the other hundreds around it, till it is an inextricable network like lace. Then it bursts into yellow bloom still finer, more feathery and lacelike. The stems are so infinitesimally small, and of so dark a green, that at a short distance they do not show, and the cloud of blossom seems floating in the air; at times it looks like golden dust. With a clear blue sky behind it, as it is often seen, it looks like a golden snowstorm. The plant is a tyrant and a nuisance—the terror of the farmer; it takes riotous possession of a whole field in a season; once in, never out; for one plant this year, a million the next; but it is impossible to wish that the land were freed from it. Its gold is as distinct a value to the eye as the nugget gold is in the pocket.

Father Salvierderra soon found himself in a veritable thicket of these delicate branches, high above his head, and so interlaced that he could make headway only by slowly and patiently disentangling them, as one would disentangle a skein of silk. It was a fantastic sort of dilemma, and not unpleasing. Except that the Father was in haste to reach his journey's end, he would have enjoyed threading his way through the golden meshes. Suddenly he heard faint notes of singing. He paused—listened. It was the voice of a woman. It was slowly drawing nearer, apparently from the direction in which he was going. At intervals it ceased abruptly, then began again; as if by a sudden but brief interruption, like that made by question and answer. Then, peering ahead through the mustard blossoms, he saw them waving and bending, and heard sounds as if they were being broken. Evidently someone entering on the path from the opposite end had been caught in the fragrant thicket as he was. The notes grew clearer, though still low and sweet as the twilight notes of the thrush; the mustard branches waved more and more violently; light steps were now to be heard. Father Salvierderra

---

Another thing that made the air in Whittier special, to my inner nose anyway, were the great fields of wild mustard that almost surrounded us. It grew on the hills, of course. But between us and Los Angeles were long stretches of open meadows, and in the spring they were dazzling, like pale yellow gold. They sent up a wild sweet blast of perfume, an invitation almost, hinting of strange pleasures not yet understood. As we tooled sedately on a Sunday, in our open Model-T, toward Los Angeles or perhaps the Busch Gardens in Pasadena and got past Pio Pico's crumbling White House and over the Rio Hondo Bridge, the fields opened out on either side of us and rolled as far as we could see. There was the little village of Montebello, and from then on to the outskirts of Los Angeles, with its peculiar Chinese and Greek cemeteries, its huge brick Catholic orphanage, there was nothing but gold. On a still day, the air was so little moved by our cutting slowly through it that the honeyed heavy perfume almost drugged us.

—M. F. K. Fisher, from *To Begin Again: Stories and Memoirs, 1908–1929*

stood still as one in a dream, his eyes straining forward into the golden mist of blossoms. In a moment more came, distinct and clear to his ear, the beautiful words of the second stanza of Saint Francis's inimitable lyric, "The Canticle of the Sun."

> Praise be to thee, O Lord, for all thy creatures,
> and especially for our brother the Sun—
> who illuminates the day, and by his beauty
> and splendor shadows forth unto us thine.

"Ramona!" exclaimed the Father, his thin cheeks flushing with pleasure. "The blessed child!"

William H. Brewer

William H. Brewer (1828–1910) was the first man selected by Josiah Whitney for the Geological Survey of California. Like his chief, Brewer was an Easterner, a Yale graduate who had studied in Europe. Before returning to Yale to teach agriculture in 1864, Brewer traveled around the state as Whitney's main assistant and the leader of his field parties. Throughout this period Brewer wrote to his brother in New York describing his activities. Seventy years after their composition, his letters were arranged by Francis P. Farquhar to create an exceptional travelogue.

Brewer, who had both scientific training and literary skill, often displayed an emotional response to the landscape. On the day before his thirty-fifth birthday and alone near Mount Shasta, he reported, "I gazed on it for hours as I lay there, not with the awe that I did two days ago, but with even more admiration." Much of his tour inspired such delight, but Brewer also detailed its gritty side, the fierce afternoon winds of the Salinas Valley, "filled with dry dust and sand," the tarantulas that got into a man's boots overnight. Here Brewer—newly arrived in California—describes the Los Angeles Basin, a "gentle slope" from the Pacific to the mountains. ✍

from Up and Down California

In camp at Los Angeles. December 7 — Well, we are in camp. It is a cold rainy night, but I can hardly realize the fact that you at home are blowing your fingers in the cold, and possibly sleighing, while I am sitting here in a tent, without fire, and sleeping on the ground in blankets, in this month. We are camped on a hill near the town, perhaps a mile distant, a pretty place.

Los Angeles is a city of some three and a half or four thousand inhabitants, nearly a century old, a regular old Spanish-Mexican town, built by the old padres, Catholic Spanish missionaries, before the American independence. The houses are but one story, mostly built of adobe or sunburnt brick, with very thick walls and flat roofs. They are so low because of earthquakes, and the style is Mexican. The inhabitants are a mixture of old Spanish, Indian, American, and German Jews; the last two have come in lately. The language of the natives is Spanish, and I have commenced learning it. The only thing they appear to excel in is riding, and certainly I have never seen such riders.

Here is a great plain, or rather a gentle slope, from the Pacific to the mountains. We are on this plain about twenty miles from the sea and fifteen from the mountains, a most lovely locality; all that is wanted naturally to make it a paradise is *water,* more *water.* Apples, pears, plums, figs, olives, lemons, oranges, and "the finest grapes in the world," so the books say, pears of two and a half pounds each, and such things in proportion. The weather is soft and balmy—no winter, but a perpetual spring and summer. Such is Los Angeles, a place where "every prospect pleases and only man is vile."

As we stand on a hill over the town, which lies at our feet, one of the loveliest views I ever saw is spread out. Over the level plain to the southwest lies the Pacific, blue in the distance; to the north are the mountains of the Sierra Santa Monica; to the south, beneath us, lies the picturesque town with its flat roofs, the fertile plain and vineyards stretching away to a great distance; to the east, in the distance, are some mountains without name, their sides abrupt and broken, while still above them stand the snow-covered peaks of San Bernardino. The effect of the pepper, fig, olive, and palm trees in the foreground, with the snow in the distance, is very unusual.

This is a most peculiar climate, a mingling of the temperate with the tropical. The date palm and another palm grow here, but do not fruit, while the olive, fig, orange, and lemon flourish well. The grapes are famous, and the wine of Los Angeles begins to be known even in Europe.

We got in camp on Tuesday, December 4. We had been invited to a ranch and vineyard about nine miles east, and went with a friend on Tuesday evening. It lies near San Gabriel Mission, on a most beautiful spot, I think even finer than this. Mr. Wilson, our host, uneducated, but a man of great force of character, is now worth a hundred or more thousand dollars and lives like a prince, only with less luxury. His wife is finely educated and refined, and his home to the visitor a little paradise. We were received with the greatest cordiality and were entertained with the greatest hospitality. A touch of the country and times was indicated by our rig—I was dressed in colored woolen shirt, with heavy navy revolver (loaded) and huge eight-inch bowie knife at my belt; my friend the same; and the clergyman who took us out in his carriage carried along his rifle, he said for game, yet owned that it was "best to have arms after dark."

Here let me digress. This southern California is still unsettled. We all continually wear arms—each wears both bowie knife and pistol (navy revolver), while we have always for game or otherwise a Sharp's rifle, Sharp's carbine, and two double-barrel shotguns. Fifty to sixty murders per year have been common here in Los Angeles, and some think it odd that there has been no violent death during the two weeks that we have been here. Yet with our care there is no considerable danger, for as I write this there are at least six heavy loaded revolvers in the tent, besides bowie knives and other arms, so we anticipate no danger. I have been practicing with my revolver and am becoming expert.

Well, to return to my story, and to Mr. Wilson's. We found a fine family, with two lovely young ladies. The next day, Wednesday, December 5, we went up into the mountain, followed up a canyon (gorges are called cañons or canyons), and then separated. I climbed a hill two and a half thousand or more feet, very steep and rocky, gathered some plants, and had one of the most magnificent views of my life—the plain, and the ocean beyond. The girls went with us into the canyon, but did not climb higher. After our climb and a lunch, a ride of eight miles over the fields (for no fences obstruct the land) brought us back; then dinner and return here. We had a delightful time—I ought to say "we" were the field assistant Mr. Ashburner and I. We will try to visit them again when Professor Whitney comes.

It is cold, wet, and cheerless, so good night! Rain patters on the tent and dribbles within.

Sarah Bixby Smith

Sarah Bixby Smith (1871–1935) hailed from the most prominent family in Southern California. Sarah's father and two uncles came west from Maine and went from being sheep ranchers to the biggest landowners in the Los Angeles area, with property in several counties, even on oil-rich Signal Hill. But to judge from Adobe Days—*Smith's memoir of growing up on a ranch and in the "small and humble town" of Los Angeles—the family's steadily increasing wealth interested her less than such things as banana transplants and tarantulas, two of her more exotic subjects.*

Despite her family's financial security—and her evident generosity— Sarah Bixby Smith suffered more than her share of personal loss. Her first husband—Congregationalist minister Arthur Maxon Smith—left her for a young parishioner, and her second husband—author and Los Angeles Times literary editor Paul Jordan-Smith—left her for his cousin. "Characteristically," says Kevin Starr in Material Dreams, *"she refused to be bitter over this abandonment by the man whose children she had supported and whom she had kept in such comfortable circumstances....Ironically, she, not he, was to write the better-known book." Here is a selection from her fond reminiscence of the city's early days.* ✍

from Adobe Days

Los Angeles was about ninety years old and I about one when we first met, neither of us, I am afraid, taking much notice of the other. For over twenty years San Francisco had been a city, a most interesting and alive city, making so much stir in the world that people forgot that Los Angeles was the older; that her birth has been ordained by the governor and attended with formal rites of the church and salutes from the military way back in 1781, when the famous revolution on the East Coast was just drawing to a successful close. Until the stirring days of '49, San Francisco was insignificance on sand hills. Then her rise was sudden and glorious and the Queen of the Angels was humble. But she was angelic only in name. She was a typical frontier town with primitive, flat-roofed dwellings of sun-dried bricks, much like those built in ancient Assyria or Palestine. Saloons and gambling houses were out of proportion in number, and there were murders every day. The present crime wave is nothing in comparison.

My father first saw Los Angeles in January 1854, when he was camped with his sheep on the Rancho San Pasqual; his arrival was a few months later than that of Mr. Harris Newmark, who, in his book *Sixty Years in Southern California,* so vividly describes the village as he found it.

By the time I knew it there had been a great change. There were some sidewalks, water was piped to the houses, gas had been introduced; several public school buildings had been built; there were three newspapers, the *Star,* the *Express,* and the *Herald.* The public library had been founded—it occupied rooms in the Downey Block where the Federal Building now stands. Compared with what it had been twenty years before, Los Angeles was a modern, civilized city; compared with what it is now, it was a little frontier town. At school I once learned its population to be 11,311.

We lived first on Temple Street, near Charity. Once Los Angeles boasted Faith and Hope streets as well, but only Hope remains, for Faith has turned to Flower, and Charity masquerades as Grand.

Next door to us lived a Jewish family whose girls sat on the front porch and amazed me by crocheting on Sunday. I had not known that any Jews existed outside the Bible. Perhaps this family was the nucleus for the present large colony of Hebrews that now fills the neighborhood.

Temple Street was new and open for only a few blocks. Bunker Hill Avenue was the end of the settlement, a roof of scattered houses along the ridge fringing the sky. Beyond that we looked over empty, grassy hills to the mountains. Going down the first hillside and over towards Beaudry's reservoir for a picnic, I once found maidenhair ferns under some brush, and was frightened by what sounded like a rattlesnake—probably only a cicada. Court Street disappeared in a hollow at Hope, where a pond was made interesting by a large flock of white ducks.

Across the street from us on top of a hill that is now gone, at the head of a long flight of wide steps, stood "The Horticultural Pavilion," destroyed a few years later by fire. It was replaced by Hazard's Pavilion, an equally barn-like, wooden building on the site of the present Philharmonic Auditorium. The first Pavilion held county fairs, conventions, and operas. It was in this place that I once had a great disappointment, for when I was hearing *Pinafore* a child ahead of me suddenly coughed and whooped, and I was removed with haste just at the most entrancing moment. The opera had been put on in London first in the spring of '78. It had reached Los Angeles by '79, and we reveled in its wit and melody with the rest of the world.

Here, I once saw a strange instrument, a box into which one could speak and be heard half a mile away at a similar contraption—a very meek and lowly promise of our present telephone system.

At this fair, where there were exhibited fruits, jellies and cakes, quilts and long strings of buttons, when the mania for collecting them was at its height, I remember that some ladies, interested in the new Orphans' Home, served New England dinners—coffee, doughnuts, and beans. Among them were my mother and Mrs. Dan Stevens, two slender, dark-haired young women, wearing colonial costume and high combs—my mother, who so soon after left this world, and Mrs. Stevens, still among us, loved and honored for her many good works.

It may have been at this same time that all Los Angeles turned out to welcome President and Mrs. Hayes and the party of senators and cabinet officials who accompanied them. Earlier in the day there had been speaking at the grandstand built in front of the Baker Block, and a reception had been given to Mrs. Hayes and the ladies accompanying her in the parlors of the fashionable St. Elmo Hotel, still standing, but no longer fashionable. However, the great event for us in this connection was in the Pavilion where a little boy who had brought a bouquet for Mrs. Hayes suffered from stage fright, and my small sister, standing near the platform, was substituted. She marched serenely across the stage, delivered the flowers, was kissed by the president and returned safely—I am sure it was the most lime-lighty occasion of Nan's modest life. And, showing how bitter the political feeling of the day was, our little neighbor who was similarly gowned in pale blue silk and black velvet, resented very much being mistaken for the "little girl whom the president kissed." Her family, Southern Democrats, had come to look at "the man who held Tilden's rightful place," but refused to shake his hand as they passed by.

Speaking of politics recalls the wonderful torchlight processions of a later period when I, with my cousins, shouting little Republicans, perched on the fence at their residence on the corner of Second and Broadway and delightedly recognized our fathers under the swinging, smoky lights.

I happened to be in Maine during the Blaine-Cleveland campaign and once rode upon a train to which Mr. Blaine's special car was attached. It interested me to see that when he got out at one station for a hasty cup of coffee at a lunch counter, he poured the hot liquid into his saucer to drink.

Was that doing politics, being one of the people, or was it simply that the mouth of a presidential candidate is as susceptible to heat as that of an ordinary mortal? I was much edified, as I was not accustomed to saucer-drinking. When the train reached Boston towards midnight, it was met by a most gorgeous torchlight parade and a blare of music.

When Garfield died, Los Angeles had a memorial service and a long daylight procession headed by a "Catafalque," (a large float, gruesomely black), on which one of my schoolmates, Laura Chauvin, rode to represent, I suppose, a mourning angel. Later its black broadcloth draperies were used to make souvenirs and sold for some deserving cause. We purchased a pin-ball the size of a dollar, decorated with a green and white embroidered thistle— a curious memento of a murdered president.

But I have been lured by memories of processions, as is a small boy by martial music, away from my ordered account of where I have lived in Los Angeles. The second year we moved to the Shepherd house (so-called because of its owner), where presently my brother, Llewellyn Bixby, Junior, in direct answer to my prayers, came through the ceiling of the front bedroom straight into the apron of Mrs. Maitland—a two-day-late birthday present for me. So I was told. My skeptical faculty was dormant.

This house still stands at the top of the precipice made by the cutting of First Street between Hill and Olive streets.

The lot in front was very steep, with zig-zag paths and terraces, in one of which was a grove of banana trees, where fruit formed, but, owing to insufficient heat, never ripened well. Do you know the cool freshness of the furled, new, pale green leaves? Or how delightful it is to help the wind shred the old ones into fringe? One by one the red and gray covers for the circled blossoms drop, and make fetching little leather caps for playing children.

In those days the hill had not been hacked away to make streets, and where now is a great gash to let First Street through there was then a breezy, open hilltop, whereon grew brush and wildflowers. The poppies in those days were eschscholtzias (the learning to spell the name was a feat of my eighth year) and were not subjected to the ignominy of being painted with poinsettias on fringed-leather souvenirs for tourists. The yellow violets were gallitas, little roosters, perhaps because in the hands of children they fought to the death, their necks hooked together until one or the other was decapitated. The brodiaeas, or wild hyacinths, sometimes now called "rubber-necks," were then known to us all by the name cocomitas. I have been unable to find the derivation of this word, or even find it in

print, but I spell it as it used to sound, and I like to think that it meant little coconuts, a diminutive from coco, but the etymologically wise cannot,
because of the *m* in the middle of the word. But nature favors me, for the
bulbs look like tiny hairy coconuts, and are good eating, with an odd sweet-
ish taste. They were a much valued article of Indian food.

Between the weeds and bushes there were bare spots of ground where,
by careful searching, one might find faint circles about the size of a "two-
bit" piece. Wise ones knew that these marked the trapdoors of tarantula
nests. It was sport to try to pry one open, with mother spider holding it
closed. We young vandals would dig out the nests, interested for a moment
in the silky lining and the tiny babies and then would throw away the
wrecked home of the gorgeous black velvet creatures that did no harm on
the open hillside.

At this house Harry and I conducted an extensive "essence factory," collecting old bottles far and near, and filling them with varicolored liquids,
obtained by soaking or steeping different flowers and leaves. We used to
drink the brew made from eucalyptus leaves. The pepper infusion was pale,
like tea; that made from old geraniums was of a horrible odor—hence we
liked to inveigle innocent grown folks into smelling it. The cactus solution
was thick, like castor oil, and we considered it our most valuable product,
having arrived thus early at the notion that difficulty of preparation adds to
the cost of a manufactured article.

North of us were several houses containing children—and here I found
my first girl playmates—Grace and Susie, Bertha and Eileen. The level street
at Court and Hill—protected on three sides by grades too steep for horses,
was our safe neighborhood playground. I never go through the tunnel that
now has pierced the hill without hearing, above the roar of the Hollywood
car, the patter of flying feet, the rhythms of the witch dances, the thud-thud
of hop-scotch, the shouting boys and girls defending goals in Prisoner's
Base, the old, old song of London Bridge, or the "Intry mintry cutry corn"
that determined who was "it" for the twilight game of Hide-and-Seek—
and then the varied toned bells in the hands of mothers who called the
children home.

Edwin Markham

Oregon-born Edwin Markham (1852–1940) grew up in San José and Vacaville, and worked as a cowboy, a blacksmith, and a sheepman before attending Christian College in Santa Rosa and the San José Normal School. Then in 1899 the schoolteacher wrote "The Man with the Hoe" and became one of the best-known writers of his time. Inspired by a painting by Jean-François Millet, the poem describes a farmer whose grim existence makes him "dead to rapture and despair/A thing that grieves not and that never hopes." Originally published in the San Francisco Examiner, *Markham's poem was translated into forty languages, eventually earning him over two hundred thousand dollars.*

After the success of the poem, which lent its title to a collection of verse, Markham moved to New York and soon published Lincoln and Other Poems, *which was praised by Jack London, another working-class sympathizer. Markham never repeated that first great success, but he enjoyed a long and productive literary career. Among his volumes are an anthology of California songs and stories, and the forthrightly titled* California the Wonderful, *in which Markham travels statewide to create vivid historical and geographical portraits for his readers.* ❧

from California the Wonderful

A FLIGHT INTO THE CLOUDS

While skirting the outlands, a half hour from the heart of Los Angeles, you come upon a remarkable achievement of engineering—the Mount Lowe Railway, the first in California to lift the traveler to the clouds.

Will you take a flight to the clouds? Then ride out through the gardens and orchards and bloom-bright towns and brilliant poppy banks, and mount the cable car at Rubio Canyon, above Pasadena, and sweep skyward.

Up there, standing on the triple-crowned summit, you are looking out on the blue of the Pacific that is melting into the blue of the sky. Santa Monica, Venice, Redondo, Long Beach, with their bathers and fishermen, are a flight of shore towns fading toward the south. Farther out in the luminous sea lies Santa Catalina, the top of a broad mountain peak lifted out of the deep ocean floor. Mysterious caves are there, and dells and winding mossy ways: there, too, is Avalon!

Beautiful valleys stretch below you—the San Gabriel, La Canyada and the San Fernando, once tinted long ago with wildflowers and roved over by the buccaneer bees, but now all covered with groves and gardens of the most highly specialized tillage in the world. Yonder lies Los Angeles, spread out and serene. Here lies Hollywood with her groups of beautiful homes. And there, farther away, are Pomona, Ontario, Riverside, San Bernardino, with their green fields, stately avenues, clustered roofs, while the mountains look down upon them from quiet skies. And here, closer at hand, lies Pasadena, "the crown of the valley," a charming little city of exquisite homes in the midst of gardens—bowers of vines, leagues of blossoms, colonnades of palms and magnolias—a city set on the hills, whose light has gone out over the world.

SANTA BARBARA BY THE SEA

One hundred miles northwest of Los Angeles lies Santa Barbara on the shore, in the midst of an amphitheater of hills. Looking toward the ocean, you behold some twenty miles away the Channel Islands, like dolphins sleeping in the sun. And, ensphering them all, is the blue crystal of the sky expanding over the blue crystal of the sea; while out of this luminous immensity come little tender breezes stealing in with the lotus-rest without the lotus-languor.

About four miles inland stand the purpling Santa Ynez Mountains curving with a gesture of protection about the sequestered city. Little flowery valleys are folded into the landscape; and in all of them, as in the city herself, are balconied and bowered homes, touched with architectural beauty borrowed from many lands and melting harmoniously into the lines of cliff and canyon. As we move through these expanses of loveliness, these garden glories, these balmy airs, we think of Capri...Seville...Samoa.

Here upon the hills we find new gardens lifting their crowns of beauty not far from old strange gardens that have brightened this shore for over a hundred years. Let us wander into one of these newer miracles of beauty, the garden of a poet, whose song, "The Rosary," has won its way to many hearts. His garden is a poem in flowers; and, hidden behind a bloom-bright wall of stone, it stretches over a Santa Ynez hill, lying open to sun and dew, like a slope in Tuscany. In front, and among the boulders left by old glaciers, blue

African lilies and pink amaryllis scatter flashes of color. Elsewhere the boulders of the garden are softened and subdued by a wilderness of ferns and vines and creeping things. In the spring of the year, the pergola is looped with clusters of purple wistaria, amethystine chains swaying and breathing odor. Acacias and live oaks shade the walk that winds on to a fountain where the waterlilies are moored and silent in their ancient dreaming.

We find in the midst of the city the buildings of the old mission founded in 1787 "to draw into the Apostolic net the multitude of gentiles." The colonnade, the campo santo and the cathedral are places of visitation. The cathedral doorsteps are worn into grooves by the sandals and slippers and bared feet that came and went in the long ago.

This old structure ("a fountain and a shrine" beside the sea) would have been dear to Poe, the poet of mournful remembrance. It is simple, massive, dignified, and its austere quiet sends a noble hush upon the loud clamors of our century. Robert Haven Schauffler, musing upon rose-buried Santa Barbara, catches for us the wistful loveliness of the twin-towered mission in its irised garden, behind the wall of passionflowers. Here is a sketch of it from his poet pen:

> Perhaps one never realizes the full poetry of Santa Barbara Mission until he has knelt some misty evening on the steps of the softly-plashing mission fountain, and looked out onto the spray of peppers and seen how soft and spiritual the church facade becomes in the veiled light of the arcs that are like so many little moons. On such a night one grows aware of the wonder of these broad shadows thrown by these pilasters that go to almost nothing in the common light of day; but are now transformed with as poignant a sorcery as ever gleamed from the front of a Notre Dame or an Amiens. One feels how majestically the towers lose themselves in the night; and then, glancing downward, he finds the whole wonder given back [from the glass of the water], but more faintly, like the dream of a dream.

We feel in this quiet city the atmosphere of an old cathedral town, and mingled with that atmosphere is a fragrance from the serene Spanish life of the early years. The old Spanish home of the De la Guerras is still standing with its tiles and patio—a hacienda renowned for old-time hospitality; and sprinkled here and there in picturesque nooks we find the humble adobe homes of the Mexicans.

Christopher Isherwood

When Christopher Isherwood (1904–1986) settled in California in 1939, he was already a seasoned traveler and successful author. After Cambridge and a short stint at medical school, Isherwood moved to Berlin for four years, an experience that eventually led to The Berlin Stories, *inspiration for the musical* Cabaret. *Before coming to the United States, Isherwood also traveled to China with W. H. Auden—with whom he had written several plays—and the two recorded their trip in* Journey to War. *His remarkably prolific writing career continued in Los Angeles, where Isherwood produced more fiction, including* Down There on a Visit *and* A Single Man, *and collaborated on many screenplays.*

He also edited the Hindu magazine Vedanta and the West *after being introduced (by Aldous Huxley) to Swami Prabhavananda, who later teamed with Isherwood on a translation of the* Bhagavad Gita. *Isherwood's religious views—his feeling that "our real nature is to be at one with life, with consciousness, with everything else in the universe"—exerted a subtle influence on his work, creating what scholar Alan Wilde describes as a "sense of communion…with all human beings following their many paths to the truth." From* Exhumations, *"Los Angeles"—one of Isherwood's numerous essays—communicates this vision with its consciousness of the "untamed, undomesticated, aloof, prehistoric landscape" around the city.* 🖎

from Exhumations

In order to get the worst possible first impression of Los Angeles one should arrive there by bus, preferably in summer and on a Saturday night. That is what I did, eight years ago, having crossed the country via Washington, New Orleans, El Paso, Albuquerque and Flagstaff, Arizona. As we passed over the state line at Needles (one of the hottest places, outside Arabia, in the world) a patriotic lady traveler started to sing "California, here I come!" In America you can do this kind of thing unselfconsciously on a long-distance bus: a good deal of the covered wagon atmosphere still exists. Nevertheless, the effect was macabre. For ahead of us stretched the untidy yellow desert, quivering in its furnace-glare, with, here and there, among the rocks at the roadside, the rusty skeleton of an abandoned automobile, modern counterpart of the pioneer's dead mule. We drove forward into the Unpromising Land.

Beyond the desert, the monster market-garden begins: thousands of acres of citrus groves, vineyards, and flat fields planted with tomatoes and onions. The giant billboards reappear. The Coca Cola advertisement: "Thirst ends here." The girl telling her friend: "He's tall, dark…and owns a Ford V-8." The little towns seem almost entirely built of advertisements. Take these away, you feel, and there would be scarcely anything left: only drugstores, filling stations and unpainted shacks. And fruit: Himalayas of fruit. To the European immigrant, this rude abundance is nearly as depressing as the desolation of the wilderness. The imagination turns sulky. The eye refuses to look and the ear to listen.

Downtown Los Angeles is at present one of the most squalid places in the United States. Many of the buildings along Main Street are comparatively old but they have not aged gracefully. They are shabby and senile, like nasty old men. The stifling sidewalks are crowded with sailors and Mexicans, but there is none of the glamor of a port and none of the charm of a Mexican city. In twenty-five years this section will probably have been torn down and rebuilt; for Los Angeles is determined to become at all costs a metropolis. Today, it is still an uncoordinated expanse of townlets and suburbs, spreading wide and white over the sloping plain between the mountains and the Pacific Ocean. The Angeleno becomes accustomed to driving great distances in his car between his work, his entertainment and his home: eighty miles a day would not be very unusual. Most people have a car or the use of one. It is an essential, not a luxury, for the bus services are insufficient and there is no subway. I would scarcely know how to "show" Los Angeles to a visitor. Perhaps the best plan would be to drive quite aimlessly, this way and that, following the wide streets of little stucco houses, gorgeous with flowering trees and bushes—jacaranda, oleander, mimosa and eucalyptus—beneath a technicolor sky. The houses are ranged along communal lawns, unfenced, staring into each other's bedroom windows, without even a pretense of privacy. Such are the homes of the most inquisitive nation in the world; a nation which demands, as its unquestioned right, the minutest details of the lives of its movie stars, politicians and other public men. There is nothing furtive or unfriendly about this American curiosity, but it can sometimes be merciless.

It should not be supposed, from what I have written above, that the architecture of Los Angeles is uniform or homogeneous. On the contrary, it is strongly, and now and then insanely, individualistic. Aside from all the conventional styles—Mexican, Spanish, French Chateau, English Tudor, American Colonial and Japanese—you will find some truly startling freaks: a witch's cottage with nightmare gables and eaves almost touching the ground, an Egyptian temple decorated with hieroglyphics, a miniature medieval castle with cannon on the battlements. Perhaps the influence of the movies is responsible for them. Few of the buildings look permanent or entirely real. It is rather as if a gang of carpenters might be expected to arrive with a truck and dismantle them next morning.

North of Hollywood rises a small steep range of hills. In the midst of the city, they are only half-inhabited; many of their canyons are still choked with yuccas, poison oak and miscellaneous scrub. You find rattlesnakes there and deer and coyotes. At dusk, or in the first light of dawn, the coyotes can be mistaken for dogs as they come trotting along the trail in single file, and it is strange and disconcerting to see them suddenly turn and plunge into the undergrowth with the long, easy leap of the wild animal. Geologically speaking, the Hollywood hills will not last long. Their decomposed granite breaks off in chunks at a kick and crumbles in your hand. Every year the seasonal rains wash cartloads of it down into the valley.

In fact, the landscape, like Los Angeles itself, is transitional. Impermanence haunts the city, with its mushroom industries—the aircraft perpetually becoming obsolete, the oil which must one day be exhausted, the movies which fill America's theatres for six months and are forgotten. Many of its houses—especially the grander ones—have a curiously disturbing atmosphere, a kind of psychological dankness which smells of anxiety, overdrafts, uneasy lust, whisky, divorce, and lies. "Go away," a wretched little ghost whispers from the closet, "go away before it is too late. I was vain. I was silly. They flattered me. I failed. You will fail, too. Don't listen to their promises. Go away. Now, at once." But the new occupant seldom pays any attention to such voices. Indeed he is deaf to them, just as the pioneers were deaf to the ghosts of the goldfields. He is quite sure that he knows how to handle himself. He will make his pile; and he will know when to stop. No stupid mistakes for *him*. No extravagance, no alimony, no legal complications....And then the lawyer says: "Never mind all that small print: it doesn't mean a thing. All you have to do is sign here." And he signs.

California is a tragic country—like Palestine, like every Promised Land. Its short history is a fever-chart of migrations—the land rush, the gold rush, the oil rush, the movie rush, the Okie fruit-picking rush, the wartime rush to the aircraft factories—followed, in each instance, by counter-migrations of the disappointed and unsuccessful, moving sorrowfully homeward. You will find plenty of people in the Middle West and in the East who are very bitter against California in general and Los Angeles in particular. They complain that the life there is heartless, materialistic, selfish. But emigrants to El Dorado have really no right to grumble. Most of us come to the Far West with somewhat cynical intentions. Privately, we hope to get something for nothing—or, at any rate, for very little. Well, perhaps we shall. But if we don't, we have no one to blame but ourselves.

The movie industry—to take the most obvious example—is still very like a gold-mining camp slowly and painfully engaged in transforming itself into a respectable, ordered community. Inevitably, the process is violent. The anarchy of the old days, with every man for himself and winner take the jackpot, still exercises an insidious appeal. It is not easy for the writer who earns eight thousand dollars a week to make common cause with his colleague who only gets two hundred fifty. The original tycoons were not monsters; they were merely adventurers, in the best and worst sense of the word. They had risked everything and won—often after an epic and ruthless struggle—and they thought themselves entitled to every cent of their winnings. Their attitude toward their employees, from stars down to stagehands, was possessive and paternalistic. Knowing nothing about art and very little about technique, they did not hesitate to interfere in every stage of film production—blue-pencilling scripts, dictating casting, bothering directors and criticizing camera angles. The specter of the Box Office haunted them night and day. This was their own money, and they were madly afraid of losing it. "There's nothing so cowardly," a producer once told me, "as a million dollars." The paternalist is a sentimentalist at heart, and the sentimentalist is always potentially cruel. When the studio operatives ceased to rely upon their bosses' benevolence and organized themselves into unions, the tycoon became an injured papa, hurt and enraged by their ingratitude. If the boys did not trust him—well, that was just too bad. He knew what was good for them, and to prove it he was ready to use strike breakers and uniformed thugs masquerading as special police. But the epoch of the tycoons is now, happily, almost over. The financier of today has learnt that it pays better to give his artists and technicians a free hand, and to concentrate his own energies on the business he really understands; the promotion and distribution of the finished product. The formation of independent units within the major studios is making possible a much greater degree of cooperation between directors, writers, actors, composers, and art directors. Without being childishly optimistic, one can foresee a time when quite a large proportion of Hollywood's films will be entertainment fit for adults, and when men and women of talent will come to the movie colony not as absurdly overpaid secretaries resigned to humoring their employers but as responsible artists free and eager to do their best. Greed is, however, only one of two disintegrating forces which threaten the immigrant's character: the other, far more terrible, is sloth. Out there, in the eternal lazy morning of the Pacific, days slip away into months, months into years; the seasons are reduced to the faintest nuance by the great central fact of the sunshine; one might pass a lifetime, it seems, between two yawns, lying bronzed and naked on the sand. The trees keep their green, the flowers perpetually bloom, beautiful girls and superb boys ride the foaming breakers. They are not always the same boys, girls, flowers, and trees; but that you scarcely notice. Age and death are very discreet there; they seem as improbable as the Japanese submarines which used to lurk up and down the coast during the war and sometimes sink ships within actual sight of the land. I need not describe the deluxe, parklike cemeteries which so hospitably invite you to the final act of relaxation: Aldous Huxley has done this classically already in *After Many a Summer*. But it is worth recalling one of their advertisements, in which a charming, well-groomed elderly lady (presumably risen from the dead) assured the public: "It's better at Forest Lawn. *I speak from experience.*"

To live sanely in Los Angeles (or, I suppose, in any other large American city) you have to cultivate the art of staying awake. You must learn to resist (firmly but not tensely) the unceasing hypnotic suggestions of the radio, the billboards, the movies and the newspapers; those demon voices which are forever whispering in your ear what you should desire, what you should fear, what you should wear and eat and drink and enjoy, what you should think and do and be. They have planned a life for you—from the cradle to the grave and beyond—which it would be easy, fatally easy, to accept. The least wandering of the attention, the least relaxation of your awareness, and already the eyelids begin to droop, the eyes grow vacant, the body starts to move in obedience to the hypnotist's command. Wake up, wake up—before you sign that seven-year contract, buy that house you don't really want, marry that girl you secretly despise. Don't reach for the whisky, that won't help you. You've got to think, to discriminate, to exercise your own free will and judgment. And you must do this, I repeat, without tension, quite ration-ally and calmly. For if you give way to fury against the hypnotists, if you smash the radio and tear the newspapers to shreds, you will only rush to the other extreme and fossilize into defiant eccentricity. Hollywood's two polar types are the cynically drunken writer aggressively nursing a ten-year-old reputation and the theatrically self-conscious hermit who strides the boulevard in sandals, homemade shorts and a prophetic beard, muttering against the Age of the Machines.

An afternoon drive from Los Angeles will take you up into the high mountains, where eagles circle above the forests and the cold blue lakes, or out over the Mojave Desert, with its weird vegetation and immense vistas. Not very far away are Death Valley, and Yosemite, and the Sequoia Forest with its giant trees which were growing long before the Parthenon was built; they are the oldest living things in the world. One should visit such places often, and be conscious, in the midst of the city, of their surrounding presence. For this is the real nature of California and the secret of its fascination; this untamed, undomesticated, aloof, prehistoric landscape which relentlessly reminds the traveler of his human condition and the circumstances of his tenure upon the earth. "You are perfectly welcome," it tells him, "during your short visit. Everything is at your disposal. Only, I must warn you, if things go wrong, don't blame me. I accept no responsibility. I am not part of your neurosis. Don't cry to me for safety. There is no home here. There is no security in your mansions or your fortresses, your family vaults or your banks or your double beds. Understand this fact, and you will be free. Accept it, and you will be happy."

Charles Bukowski

The life and work of Charles Bukowski (1920–1994) have been hard for critics to pigeonhole. He has been called a Beat or a "Meat School poet," for his tough, macho verse. But Bukowski had no interest in schools, movements, or ideologies; as Gay Brewer comments: "Bukowski was obscene, resilient, and sui generis." In recent years Bukowski's literary reputation has climbed out of the gutter: he used to be no more than a cult writer famous for an obsession with booze and sex, now his poetry and fiction are seen as falling squarely within "the American tradition of the maverick," as one reviewer assessed his new status.

Bukowski's work is often autobiographical, painfully honest, and explicit. His family moved to the United States from Germany when he was two, and Bukowski grew up in Depression-era Los Angeles. It was a harsh childhood at the hands of an abusive father, an experience that figures in much of his writing. He tried Los Angeles City College briefly and then traveled and tried various jobs, including stock boy, dishwasher, factory worker, and postal clerk. Unsuccessful as a writer, he started drinking heavily, which eventually led to a bleeding ulcer, a hospital visit—and an unrepentant return to the bottle. Most of these experiences made their way into his writing, which came out regularly after the 1959 publication of Flower, Fist, and Bestial Wail, *a book of poems. Over forty other volumes followed, including the novels* Factotum *and* Ham on Rye *and the screenplay for* Barfly, *the 1987 film-biography that brought him new fame. Although "we ain't got no money, honey, but we got rain" was written late in Bukowski's career, it deals with his Los Angeles childhood, with its wildly arbitrary storms.* ✎

we ain't got no money, honey, but we got rain

call it the greenhouse effect or whatever
but it just doesn't rain like it
used to.

I particularly remember the rains of the
depression era.
there wasn't any money but there was
plenty of rain.

it wouldn't rain for just a night or
a day,
it would RAIN for 7 days and 7
nights
and in Los Angeles the storm drains
weren't built to carry off that much
water
and the rain came down THICK and
MEAN and
STEADY
and you HEARD it banging against
the roofs and into the ground
waterfalls of it came down
from the roofs
and often there was HAIL
big ROCKS OF ICE
bombing
exploding
smashing into things
and the rain
just wouldn't
STOP
and all the roofs leaked—
dishpans,
cooking pots
were placed all about;
they dripped loudly
and had to be emptied
again and
again.

the rain came up over the street curbings,
across the lawns, climbed the steps and

entered the houses.
there were mops and bathroom towels,
and the rain often came up through the
toilets: bubbling, brown, crazy, whirling,
and the old cars stood in the streets,
cars that had problems starting on a
sunny day,
and the jobless men stood
looking out the windows
at the old machines dying
like living things
out there.

the jobless men,
failures in a failing time
were imprisoned in their houses with their
wives and children
and their
pets.
the pets refused to go out
and left their waste in
strange places.

the jobless men went mad
confined with
their once beautiful wives.
there were terrible arguments
as notices of foreclosure
fell into the mailbox.
rain and hail, cans of beans,
bread without butter; fried
eggs, boiled eggs, poached
eggs; peanut butter
sandwiches, and an invisible
chicken
in every pot.

my father, never a good man
at best, beat my mother
when it rained
as I threw myself
between them,
the legs, the knees, the
screams
until they
separated.

"I'll kill you," I screamed
at him. *"You hit her again
and I'll kill you!"*

*"Get that son-of-a-bitching
kid out of here!"*

"no, Henry, you stay with
your mother!"

all the households were under
siege but I believe that ours
held more terror than the
average.

and at night
as we attempted to sleep
the rains still came down
and it was in bed
in the dark
watching the moon against
the scarred window
so bravely
holding out
most of the rain,
I thought of Noah and the
Ark
and I thought, it has come

again.
we all thought
that.

and then, at once, it would
stop.
and it always seemed to
stop
around 5 or 6 a.m.,
peaceful then,
but not an exact silence
because things continued to
drip
    drip
        drip

and there was no smog then
and by 8 a.m.
there was a
blazing yellow sunlight,
Van Gogh yellow—
crazy, blinding!
and then
the roof drains
relieved of the rush of
water
began to expand
in the warmth:
PANG! PANG! PANG!

and everybody got up
and looked outside
and there were all the lawns
still soaked
greener than green will ever
be
and there were the birds
on the lawn

CHIRPING like mad,
they hadn't eaten decently
for 7 days and 7 nights
and they were weary of
berries
and
they waited as the worms
rose to the top,
half-drowned worms.
the birds plucked them
up
and gobbled them
down; there were
blackbirds and sparrows.
the blackbirds tried to
drive the sparrows off
but the sparrows,
maddened with hunger,
smaller and quicker,
got their
due.

the men stood on their porches
smoking cigarettes,
now knowing
they'd have to go out
there
to look for that job
that probably wasn't
there, to start that car
that probably wouldn't
start.

and the once beautiful
wives
stood in their bathrooms
combing their hair,
applying makeup,

trying to put their world back
together again,
trying to forget that
awful sadness that
gripped them,
wondering what they could
fix for
breakfast.

and on the radio
we were told that
school was now
open.
and
soon
there I was
on the way to school,
massive puddles in the
street,
the sun like a new
world,
my parents back in that
house,
I arrived at my classroom
on time.

Mrs. Sorenson greeted us
with, "we won't have our
usual recess, the grounds
are too wet."

"AW!" most of the boys
went.

"but we are going to do
something special at
recess," she went on,
"and it will be
fun!"

well, we all wondered
what that would
be
and the two hour wait
seemed a long time
as Mrs. Sorenson
went about
teaching her
lessons.

I looked at the little
girls, they all looked so
pretty and clean and
alert,
they sat still and
straight
and their hair was
beautiful
in the California
sunshine.

then the recess bell rang
and we all waited for the
fun.

then Mrs. Sorenson told
us:
"now, what we are going to
do is we are going to tell
each other what we did
during the rainstorm!
we'll begin in the front
row and go right around!
now, Michael, you're
first! . . ."

well, we all began to tell
our stories, Michael began

and it went on and on,
and soon we realized that
we were all lying, not
exactly lying but mostly
lying and some of the boys
began to snicker and some
of the girls began to give
them dirty looks and
Mrs. Sorenson said,
"all right, I demand a
modicum of silence
here!
I am interested in what
you did
during the rainstorm
even if you
aren't!"

so we had to tell our
stories and they *were*
stories.

one girl said that
when the rainbow first
came
she saw God's face
at the end of it.
only she didn't say
which end.

one boy said he stuck
his fishing pole
out the window
and caught a little
fish
and fed it to his
cat.

almost everybody told
a lie.
the truth was just
too awful and
embarrassing to
tell.
then the bell rang
and recess was
over.

"thank you," said Mrs.
Sorenson, "that was very
nice.
and tomorrow the grounds
will be dry
and we will put them
to use
again."

most of the boys
cheered
and the little girls
sat very straight and
still,
looking so pretty and
clean and
alert,
their hair beautiful
in a sunshine that
the world might
never see
again.

Joan Didion

Born in Sacramento, Joan Didion (1934–) grew up in the Central Valley and then went to the University of California in Berkeley. After her graduation in 1956, she worked at Vogue *for eight years, a job she got by winning its Prix de Paris. While with that magazine, she wrote her first novel,* Run River, *set in the Sacramento Valley. Returning to California with her husband, writer John Gregory Dunne, she did a series of essays about the West Coast, which were published as* Slouching Towards Bethlehem *in 1968, earning her wide acclaim. She continues to produce nonfiction articles and books, including* The White Album *and* After Henry, *as well as novels, such as* Play It as It Lays, A Book of Common Prayer, Democracy, *and* The Last Thing He Wanted, *and screenplays (with her husband), among them* Up Close and Personal, *based on the life of reporter Jessica Savitch.*

"Nobody writes better English prose than Joan Didion," said New York Times *reviewer John Leonard, voicing a fairly widespread opinion. By placing herself at the center of many of her essays, she can be flatly honest about her feelings. One of these is a passion for "total control," which she reveals in "Holy Water," confessing to a wish to run the California State Water Project Operations Control Center. In the following selection Didion uses a relentlessly edgy style to convey her sense of Los Angeles's leaching winds.* ✥

from Slouching Towards Bethlehem

There is something uneasy in the Los Angeles air this afternoon, some unnatural stillness, some tension. What it means is that tonight a Santa Ana will begin to blow, a hot wind from the northeast whining down through the Cajon and San Gorgonio passes, blowing up sandstorms out along Route 66, drying the hills and the nerves to the flash point. For a few days now we will see smoke back in the canyons, and hear sirens in the night. I have neither heard nor read that a Santa Ana is due, but I know it, and almost everyone I have seen today knows it too. We know it because we feel it. The baby frets. The maid sulks. I rekindle a waning argument with the telephone company, then cut my losses and lie down, given over to whatever it is in the air. To live with the Santa Ana is to accept, consciously or unconsciously, a deeply mechanistic view of human behavior.

I recall being told, when I first moved to Los Angeles and was living on an isolated beach, that the Indians would throw themselves into the sea when the bad wind blew. I could see why. The Pacific turned ominously glossy during a Santa Ana period, and one woke in the night troubled not only by the peacocks screaming in the olive trees but by the eerie absence of surf. The heat was surreal. The sky had a yellow cast, the kind of light sometimes called "earthquake weather." My only neighbor would not come out of her house for days, and there were no lights at night, and her husband roamed the place with a machete. One day he would tell me that he had heard a trespasser, the next a rattlesnake.

"On nights like that," Raymond Chandler once wrote about the Santa Ana, "every booze party ends in a fight. Meek little wives feel the edge of the carving knife and study their husbands' necks. Anything can happen." That was the kind of wind it was. I did not know then that there was any basis for the effect it had on all of us, but it turns out to be another of those cases in which science bears out folk wisdom. The Santa Ana, which is named for one of the canyons it rushes through, is a foehn wind, like the foehn of Austria and Switzerland and the hamsin of Israel. There are a number of persistent malevolent winds, perhaps the best known of which are the mistral of France and the Mediterranean sirocco, but a foehn wind has distinct characteristics: it occurs on the leeward slope of a mountain range and, although the air begins as a cold mass, it is warmed as it comes down the mountain and appears finally as a hot dry wind. Whenever and wherever a foehn blows, doctors hear about headaches and nausea and allergies, about "nervousness," about "depression." In Los Angeles some teachers do not attempt to conduct formal classes during a Santa Ana, because the children become unmanageable. In Switzerland the suicide rate goes up during the foehn, and in the courts of some Swiss cantons the wind is considered a mitigating circumstance for crime. Surgeons are said to watch the wind, because blood does not clot normally during a foehn. A few years ago an Israeli physicist discovered that not only during such winds, but for the ten or twelve hours which precede them, the air carries an unusually high ratio of positive to negative ions. No one seems to know exactly why that should be; some talk about friction and others suggest solar disturbances. In any case the positive ions are there, and what an excess of positive ions does, in the simplest terms, is make people unhappy. One cannot get much more mechanistic than that.

Easterners commonly complain that there is no "weather" at all in Southern California, that the days and the seasons slip by relentlessly, numbingly bland. That is quite misleading. In fact the climate is characterized by infrequent but violent extremes: two periods of torrential subtropical rains which continue for weeks and wash out the hills and send subdivisions

The climate of Southern California is palpable: a commodity that can be labeled, priced, and marketed. It is not something that you talk about, complain about, or guess about. On the contrary, it is the most consistent, the least paradoxical factor in the environment. Unlike climates the world over, it is predictable to the point of monotony. In its air-conditioned equability, it might well be called "artificial." The climate is the region. It has attracted unlimited resources of manpower and wealth, made possible intensive agricultural development, and located specialized industries, such as motion pictures. It has given the region its rare beauty. For the charm of Southern California is largely to be found in the air and the light. Light and air are really one element: indivisible, mutually interacting, thoroughly interpenetrated. Without the ocean breezes, the sunlight would be intolerable; without the sunlight and imported water, virtually nothing would grow in the region.

When the sunlight is not screened and filtered by the moisture-laden air, the land is revealed in all its semiarid poverty. The bald, sculptured mountains stand forth in a harsh and glaring light. But let the light turn soft with ocean mist, and miraculous changes occur. The bare mountain ranges, appallingly harsh in contour, suddenly become wrapped in an entrancing ever-changing loveliness of light and shadow; the most commonplace objects assume a matchless perfection of form; and the land itself becomes a thing of beauty. The color of the land is in the light and the light is somehow artificial and controlled. Things are not killed by the sunlight, as in a desert; they merely dry up. A desert light brings out the sharpness of points, angles, and forms. But this is not a desert light nor is it tropical, for it has neutral tones. It is Southern California light, and it has no counterpart in the world.

—Carey McWilliams, from *Southern California Country: An Island on the Land* (1946)

sliding toward the sea; about twenty scattered days a year of the Santa Ana, which, with its incendiary dryness, invariably means fire. At the first prediction of a Santa Ana, the Forest Service flies men and equipment from northern California into the southern forests, and the Los Angeles Fire Department cancels its ordinary non-firefighting routines. The Santa Ana caused Malibu to burn the way it did in 1956, and Bel Air in 1961, and Santa Barbara in 1964. In the winter of 1966–67 eleven men were killed fighting a Santa Ana fire that spread through the San Gabriel Mountains.

Just to watch the front-page news out of Los Angeles during a Santa Ana is to get very close to what it is about the place. The longest Santa Ana period in recent years was in 1957, and it lasted not the usual three or four days but fourteen days, from November 21 until December 4. On the first day twenty-five thousand acres of the San Gabriel Mountains were burning, with gusts reaching one hundred miles an hour. In town, the wind reached Force 12, or hurricane force, on the Beaufort scale; oil derricks were toppled and people ordered off the downtown streets to avoid injury from flying objects. On November 22 the fire in the San Gabriels was out of control. On November 24 six people were killed in automobile accidents, and by the end of the week the *Los Angeles Times* was keeping a box score of traffic deaths. On November 26 a prominent Pasadena attorney, depressed about money, shot and killed his wife, their two sons, and himself. On November 27 a South Gate divorcee, twenty-two, was murdered and thrown from a moving car. On November 30 the San Gabriel fire was still out of control, and the wind in town was blowing eighty miles an hour. On the first day of December four people died violently, and on the third the wind began to break.

It is hard for people who have not lived in Los Angeles to realize how radically the Santa Ana figures in the local imagination. The city burning is Los Angeles's deepest image of itself: Nathanael West perceived that, in *The Day of the Locust*; and at the time of the 1965 Watts riots what struck the imagination most indelibly were the fires. For days one could drive the Harbor Freeway and see the city on fire, just as we had always known it would be in the end. Los Angeles weather is the weather of catastrophe, of apocalypse, and, just as the reliably long and bitter winters of New England determine the way life is lived there, so the violence and the unpredictability of the Santa Ana affect the entire quality of life in Los Angeles, accentuate its impermanence, its unreliability. The wind shows us how close to the edge we are.

Kevin Hearle

Kevin Hearle (1958–) can trace his family's West Coast roots back to the gold rush. He was born in California and has lived here all his life, except for a brief stint at the University of Iowa where he got an M.F.A. from the Writers' Workshop, returning to Santa Cruz for his Ph.D. in literature. He serves on the board of the Steinbeck Newsletter *and edited the Viking Portable book,* The Grapes of Wrath: Text and Criticism. *He has served as poetry coeditor for* Quarry West *and published his first book of poems in 1994,* Each Thing We Know Is Changed Because We Know It, *which was a finalist for the National Poetry Series, the Yale Series of Younger Poets, and the Pushcart Prize.*

Hearle brings a geographical perspective to his poems—he has lived in both north and south state—as well as a historical one. Familiar-seeming objects sometimes conjure California's strange story: a favorite seashell from his childhood can evoke the history of the state's exploration. Even common names evoke the past, since California is a place "where everything had to be named twice / to survive: / where Hangtown became Placerville, / where La Brea couldn't hold its bones / in Spanish, but had to be redundant / and bilingual— / The La Brea Tar Pits...." The work of time and humanity upon the Southern California landscape are obvious in the following poems. ☙

Each Thing We Know Is Changed Because We Know It

A eucalyptus has its implications
where I come from: it means the autumn winds
return each year like brushfires from the desert,
return as dry reminders of the oaks
whose place this was: the valley oak, blue oak,
and the oracle which thrive on little water.
And eucalyptus means the orange groves
once flourished here, that rivers were diverted,
that winter was denied and smoke hung low
over the valley the night of the first frost—

smudgepots warming and darkening the sky.
And eucalyptus means that people lived here;
the flesh tones of the mottled trunk, the bark
in strips that dry and curl and fall to the ground
mean that my mother's family would walk,
through walnut orchards and orange groves, to church—
Saturday nights, three women, three generations,
bound for the revival meeting, each collecting
more friends as she went further south through town.
And eucalyptus leaves, silver, scythe-like,
shaken down by the wind, the tree still tall,
scented the questions that my mother asked
when her senile grandmother would get out
of the house, walk south through the orchards, south
right through downtown, straight to the water tower.
Dark letters spilled across it six foot tall—
SANTA ANA SANTA ANA, high
and circular, the water named the town.
Great-grandmother would stand beneath it—no words
she could recall to call herself—just waiting,
for what she didn't know, and trying on names.

Water and Power

> It is true that nearly 40 percent of Los
> Angeles' water goes for outside uses
> such as lawns, gardens, swimming
> pools, and public parks... but such
> amenities are at the heart of Los
> Angeles' way of life.
> —Remi Nadeau

Despite your thousand pious gigolo suburbs;
and even though I know the lies the angels tell the living
in Los Angeles—the way history eclipses history here
and passes into fable—this is my heritage: the land of the lawn

and the home of the sprinkler head. Oh, I have wasted my time
detesting the soap kings and the chewing gum barons—
so much time on the real estate men planning their floral parades
and football games. They were nothing;
each one mortal and pitiful. It is the lawn which has survived,
and which I hate. I do not think they would have come—
the bacon and ham millionaires of Illinois,
the five and dime rich merchants of Ohio—if
there hadn't been lawns for the making. Without dichondra
they would not have boarded the pullman cars for Pasadena
or Santa Barbara. If not for the sprinkler heads,
which made an arid land seem green and neatly divisible,
the railroad speculators could not have brought Iowa west,
in square lots, to the Pacific. And, without the millions
from Cedar Falls and Council Bluffs and Keokuk,
the banks would not have come—like locusts over Egypt—
with their New Yorkers spreading legends of a lost city
of true intelligence, benevolence, culture
and pastrami. The apostles of the Empire State
rehearsing their litany of things which *were better back there,*
but entering their whiny exile in ever greater numbers,
and each one wanting lawns. Never mind the seasons without rain
or the water wasted on St. Augustine; they must have lawns.
Lawns, so the people, we, the people, can move on,
(each moving van an absolution) believing
in new towns whose names sound more chaste—"Mission Viejo;"
in offramps more green—"Ventura," "Garden Grove;"
and, in—"Salsipuedes," "Los Feliz"—lives perhaps
more sibilant than what we've left behind.
Damn the lawns. Damn the sprinkler heads which feed them.
Damn the pipes and aqueducts that feed the sprinklers
that feed the lawns that feed the thirst for green and land,
and damn the dams which feed on river valleys so far away
voracious angels need never dream they once were green.

In the spring of 1931, on a lawn in Glendale, California, a man was bracing trees. It was a tedious job, for he had first to prune dead twigs, then wrap canvas buffers around weak branches, then wind rope slings over the buffers and tie them to the trunks, to hold the weight of the avocados that would ripen in the fall. Yet, although it was a hot afternoon, he took his time about it, and was conscientiously thorough, and whistled. He was a smallish man, in his middle thirties, but in spite of the stains on his trousers, he wore them with an air. His name was Herbert Pierce. When he had finished with the trees, he raked the twigs and dead branches into a pile, carried them back to the garage, and dropped them in a kindling box. Then he got out a mower and mowed the lawn. It was a lawn like thousands of others in southern California: a patch of grass in which grew avocado, lemon, and mimosa trees, with circles of spaded earth around them. The house, too, was like others of its kind: a Spanish bungalow, with white walls and red-tile roof. Now, Spanish houses are a little outmoded, but at the time they were considered high-toned, and this one was as good as the next, and perhaps a little bit better.

The mowing over, he got out a coil of hose, screwed it to a spigot, and proceeded to water. He was painstaking about this too, shooting the water all over the trees, down on the spaded circles of earth, over the tiled walk, and finally on the grass. When the whole place was damp and smelled like rain, he turned off the water, pulled the hose through his hand to drain it, coiled it, and put it in the garage. Then he went around front and examined his trees, to make sure the water hadn't drawn the slings too tight. Then he went into the house.

—James M. Cain, from *Mildred Pierce* (1934)

Jane Hollister Wheelwright

The property known as the Hollister Ranch—actually five ranches totaling thirty-nine thousand acres—had been part of the Hollister family for generations. The largest stretch of land covered twenty-five thousand acres west of Santa Barbara; it ran south along the coast from Point Conception to five miles past Gaviota at the foot of the Santa Ynez mountains. When John James Hollister died in 1961, the family was forced to sell this valuable property, but not before his daughter, Jane Hollister Wheelwright, (1905–) returned for a visit. She had gone far: she had lived in China and London with her husband, had founded the first Jungian training center in San Francisco, had prepared herself by writing Death of a Woman. *Now she wanted to better understand how the land had influenced her, why "love of land can transcend human love, as it did for my father and grandfather." Wheelwright roamed the "hills and mesas and canyons" of her childhood home, taking notes that would eventually become* The Ranch Papers: A California Memoir.

May Sarton sees this book as "a work of art relying almost entirely on concrete description," and she is right. Wheelwright explains how she arrived at these vivid descriptions: "to find the telling words I would have to proceed blindly. I would have to sustain the chaos and undifferentiated jumble of feelings turned loose. I would have to believe, as the Chumash did, that there were ordering forces in the offing." Here her memories start to take shape. 🖎

from The Ranch Papers

In June, after my father's death, I was at last free to roam the coast ranch—to look around in my own way. This first lonely visit was unannounced although I was virtually the head of the family by then. No one was there to meet me—not even the ranch hands. I had none of the honor and recognition given automatically to El Patrón. The ranch seemed deserted. I was being deliberately avoided.

Wandering aimlessly, I found myself walking into the canyon that stretched in back of the old family home. An unexpectedly peaceful feeling came over me. It came from the stillness under the great oaks. The disappointment at seeing no one quickly faded. At least the land was there to greet me.

I walked instinctively to where my twin brother and I had gone as small children. It was our outermost limit of adventure when we were little. Because our parents were too busy to concern themselves with us, we could mark our own boundaries. The place had become special long ago; it was ours, we had discovered it—the waterfall that spills over the great ledge of rock a mile or more into the canyon. It would be my objective that day as it had been in my childhood.

I went farther into Bulito Canyon along the dry creekbed where there were cattle trails under the dark ceiling of interlacing tree branches. It was cool and pleasant in the deep shade of the live oaks, and it gave me the brief chance to savor a past free from family turmoil. Our falls appeared around the bend. They were smaller and more intimate than I remembered. Water trickled down from a pool fed by a thin stream, which skipped down the rock face from far above, from a high ground of oaks and shrubs. The cattle had churned up the mud.

When I sat on the sandstone, the silence came in force. It was an old friend from long ago and lifted my feelings of heaviness. It was good to be quiet, in spite of the thoughts and feelings that had piled up in the aftermath of my father's long life. To still them I deliberately called up memories that might point to what I needed to know and felt was asking to be known. I knew memories would focus me on what lay ahead. This land and my memories were inextricable.

Silence is another form of sound. I recalled how at times it rang in my ears, and I thought how as a child I had to listen carefully. We always stopped to listen. It had become a habit—no sound in the wild country was ever left uninterpreted.

The June quiet for the first time seemed different. It was not as I remembered it from earliest times—a caress, a great soft cloak drawn lightly around you. Instead it conveyed a sense of pressure. There was the suppression of sound that always happens when an intruder enters. I had never before noted the difference.

In the past, even when I walked into the dark wooded canyon as quietly as I could, I knew I would see nothing. It was no different this time. The place was apparently uninhabited, yet I had the feeling that many pairs of eyes were observing my slightest movement. I was right; I was being watched. From experience, too, I knew that once I sat quietly and waited long enough the whole place would come back to its busy, curious, noisy life—a life ordered within its disorder. Only the coyote, who follows like a dog, would never honor me by coming into view.

That day, after first settling in, only small alarms interrupted the stillness. I sat higher on the sandstone ledge to recollect a few of the conflicting feelings and to try to sort them with the help of nature's overall plan. This spot was a vantage point from which I could survey a fair distance down the creek and along the canyon flats to the reservoir. An overwhelming impulse to record what I was to see came over me. Completely fitting the resolve I had made, it came from that vague earlier need to articulate what had been taken for granted all my life. I wanted to get some bearings from a sense of the totality that the ranch was, and especially to stop the unpleasant sense of floating in the vacuum that my father's death had left. There was, besides, an anticipation of overwhelming problems created by his long life; spanning the era of profitable cattle ranching and modern times when cattle no longer paid, we were faced with the need for radical changes in our operation.

Unexpectedly, giant frogs, which until then had been camouflaged against the sandstone, flopped from out of nowhere into the pool. Deep, hollow and refreshing, their sounds were clean against the still water as they echoed against the sheer wall. I counted them as they jumped—one after the other, as though clocked by an unseen presence. They were part of my settling further into the scene.

Several blushing, red-headed linnets, otherwise known as house finches, and a small speckled thrush, with light spots on an earth-brown body, appeared in the circle of the falls. The sound of a relaxed trickle of water came from the moss-slicked rock face. The buzz of linnets' wings echoed briefly against the high semicircle of overhead sandstone that looked more like hardened mud. A canyon wren appeared, tiny and perfect. He flipped his tail like a pointer, this way, then that, his head low on his tip-tilted body as though by habit he was prone to look under things. His dainty song penetrated the silence. For the moment my troubles would have to wait. Looking around I saw orderly rows of delicately shining, black-stemmed maidenhair ferns lodged in the seeping dampness of the green moss at the base of the wall. Reflecting brightly in the water, they made a broad fringe. Two poplar branches rubbed together in the slight breeze. The familiarity of the sounds successfully merged the immediacy of the moment with a distant past.

I heard the liquid *shreeee* of a rufous-sided towhee on the opposite bank. Dressed up in black, orange, and white, he looked at me out of startling red eyes. From the distance came the sad undulating message of a lonely mourning dove. I was becoming one with these creatures. The far past continued blending into the present; it would not be put down. Old reflexes had been lying there waiting.

Belonging at last brought with it a peaceful feeling. Experiencing the vast world of sounds and sights that had always been there, lodged in the outer reaches of my awareness, was like coming home. I wondered why I had never before consciously focused on this place. It then occurred to me that, as children, we were never encouraged to report on our day's activities. We were unaccustomed to putting our experiences into words. Instead we had indulged (or escaped into?) secret lives of our own, and were filled with happenings left undigested deep down in us. We had been in a constant state of uncommunicated excitement. It was as though day after day we had what hunters called "buck fever"—the tremor that overtakes the novice when he is at last faced by his quarry. Our quarry was the unexpected minute-to-minute, day-to-day manifestation of nature. But, much later, I discovered that we were the hunted and nature was the hunter.

Gretel Ehrlich

Gretel Ehrlich (1946–) is a native Californian, born in Santa Barbara. She attended Bennington College; the University of California, Los Angeles Film School; and the New School for Social Research. In 1976 Ehrlich went to Wyoming to make a PBS documentary on sheepherders—and she stayed on. She worked on sheep and cattle ranches and wrote about the place, in the nonfiction The Solace of Open Spaces *and* Islands, the Universe, Home, *the novel* Heart Mountain, *and in* Drinking Dry Clouds: Stories from Wyoming. *She has also contributed work to magazines like* Harpers, Time Magazine, Antaeus, *and* Outside *and published several volumes of poetry, notably* Arctic Heart: A Poem Cycle.

In 1994, Ehrlich published A Match to the Heart, *a personal account of a near-death experience and its aftermath. She and her dogs were walking on Ehrlich's Wyoming ranch when she was struck by lightning. Her recovery from the emotional and physical damage involved visits to family and friends in California, where she took long, quiet nature walks. As her careful observations reaffirm her sense of the connectedness of all things, Ehrlich rediscovers that "everything in nature invites us constantly to be what we are."* 🐾

from A Match to the Heart

In the morning I followed Sam's map of smells to rock piles, tide pools. He had been timid at first, then grew bold: the beach was his domain. I tried to imagine how his olfactory sense opened every inch of ground for him—successive explosions at each step, widening into a map of the world, but what a map: guano, salt, fish scale, seal fur, tar, and the mineral smell of sand. The beach was near the town of Carpinteria, named by Spaniards for the Chumash Indians they saw there—the carpenters—who were building their seaworthy canoes called tomols, sealing them with the asphaltum that still oozes from a nearby cliff and piles up into a hill of black bubble gum on which sea lions bark and lounge as if waiting for the tomols to return.

Though Sam is no bloodhound—he'd rather look at a band of sheep and lick his chops than smell the guano of any seagull—when the water went out, his nose took me to the edge of the shore, to exposed rock. Tide pools are another kind of gap—an edge between batholith and lithosphere, ocean and earth. They are ecotones, in-between places like those clefts in the brain and the rug-pulled-out limbos in our lives where, ironically, much richness occurs.

Down boulders, across sand, between clumps of kelp, Sam's paw prints in wet sand were dark asterisks on the map marking the trail. That day the beach was a bed of black rock hung with the slanted roofs of barnacles, mussels, and the limpets' pink volcano shells, and pocked with smooth basins catching the green splash of waves. Each pool of water held an image of the sun; each sun was a lake of daylight, and when the shine of the rock started to fade as it dried, another wave splashed it bright.

A tide pool is a kind of meadow: rocks bared by low tides are strewn with red algae and green mermaid's hair—seagrass, surfgrass and eelgrass—which is brushed back and forth in undulating waves. In the splash zone, village life seems to prevail: both shelled and soft creatures hide under rocks, between rocks, or fasten themselves to rocks in colonies, rigid in sweeping waters and in the continual flux of tides. Barnacles, anemones, jellyfish, starfish, sponges, hydroids, worms, chitons, mussels, clams, snails, octopuses, shrimps, crabs, lobsters, sea spiders, urchins, sea squirts and salps, algae, kelp, lichens, and grasses—all crowd together in urban densities. Aggregate anemones often live in concentrations of three thousand individuals per square meter of rock; they are marine apartment dwellers.

A tide pool is perhaps the one place where creatures can prosper by becoming completely sedentary and permanently attached. Barnacles spend their youths floating free before coming home to a rock and, once glued, they never leave again, never have to go in search of food because room service is provided by the waves bringing it to them. They merely extend legs to capture floating plankton; these legs are also the apparatus through which they breathe. Mussels are "gill-netters." They catch prey, pump water, and breathe through fleshy tubes that extend from the rear of their hinged shell.

Because sessile creatures—ones that are permanently attached—are unable to "go with the flow," they thrive on extremes: they're either underwater or desiccating in hot sun. To avoid drying up during low tide, periwinkles and limpets keep so tightly closed that their respiration stops. They literally hold their breath until covered by water again.

A regimen of daily walks took me into the middle of January. With each high tide more sand was removed, more rocks exposed, more sea creatures revealed. In dense fog a single red starfish, bright on wet sand, was the only thing visible and seemed to stand for the whole unseen galaxy. Up close they're less than romantic. If barnacles and mussels represent tenacity—not only are they unmoving, but also very long-lived—then starfish are known for their voraciousness. Known as the "walking stomachs of the deep," they eat continually, devouring everything in their path: oysters, clams, barnacles, and they sift through sand and mud for any bits of bottom garbage and carrion.

A starfish eats by pushing his stomach out through his mouth, located at the center of his body. That's how greedy it is: it eats everything whole, shell and all. And just so nothing is missed, the branching tubes in the arms, where its eyes and respiratory system are located, are put to work picking up any dropped morsels. The efficiency of the starfish's stomach is twofold: waste products are ejected from the same opening through which the meal was ingested.

Brittle stars, blood stars, ocher stars, leather stars, variable and shallow-water sand stars—the ones seen around here—as well as thirty-six hundred other species, all start out as one of thousands of eggs shed from the under-arms of a mother/father (they are hermaphroditic). Once released, they glue themselves to kelp. From "stardust" they turn into odd-shaped punctuation marks until the rays finally emerge; they grow from stardust to gluttony in a matter of weeks.

Sea stars, as biologists like to call them, since they're not fish, have an extremely complex nervous system and are famous for regenerating lost arms. They can cast off a wounded ray and regrow a new one, or else grow a whole new body if part of the central disk is included in the cut-off arm. With such powers, starfish numbers could get out of control, but this problem is solved by sex changes—no operation needed. Males can turn into females, and vice versa, an art that regulates population dynamics.

As I poked through tide pools, Sam began stalking shorebirds. He never hurt one, rarely even chased them, just sneaked up on them, wishing they were sheep or cows. Sandpipers, sanderlings, phalaropes, plovers, godwits, curlews, and pelicans flew in front of him as he ran, circling around over the water and landing behind him. On one of those days I stumbled on something shaped like a tiny leaf, though it felt alive, like an animal in my hand. Animal or vegetable? Less than half an inch high, soft like a cut-off earlobe, with a purple stem, tiny volcano-shaped pores, and a calcium carbonate "skeleton" made of microscopic spicules, it later proved to be a white fan sponge, severed from its other friends: the urn, macaroni, and crumb-of-bread sponges, the purple, yellow, orange, and free-living sponges.

Sam's paw marks and my footprints crisscrossed that of a snail, which secretes a mucous trail to trap plankton and small creatures, then reels in the trail to feed on the catch. We came upon spotted nudibranchs that looked like bits of body parts, unshelled, skinned, globs of flesh exposed to sea and air. They were easy to spot near the sponges, because that's what they dine on.

Nearby were brown sea hares, which look nothing like a rabbit but are in the mollusk family—a type of snail. They lay their eggs in long strings that get wound up into spongy yellow balls the size of grapefruit and contain as many as a million eggs apiece. When the larvae hatch, in ten days or so, the young swim free, but most are quickly eaten. This is rather fortunate because if they weren't the population of brown hares would exceed the combined populations of animal life on the entire earth in only two or three years.

Fertility, gluttony, tenacity, and a who-cares-who-does-what-to-whom sex life—that's what typifies creatures of the intertidal zone. No sinner has had a life as rigid and voluptuous as the tube snail, which lives clustered and unmoving, its shells growing entwined, or the sea cucumber, whose water and oxygen are pumped in and out of its anus, or the vaginal-looking aggregate anemone, which stings its prey with a paralyzing toxin and reproduces by splitting in half lengthwise, generating two individuals of the same sex.

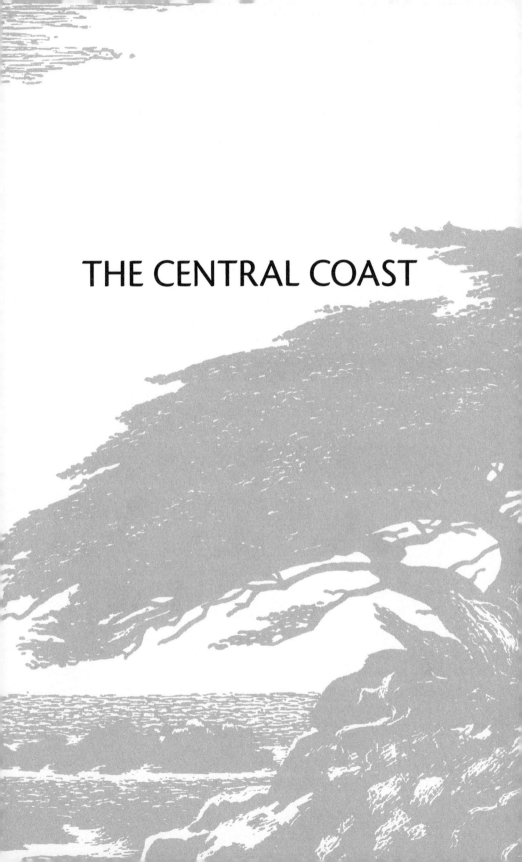

THE CENTRAL COAST

To get a feel for the landscape of the Central Coast region, imagine the Santa Lucia Range as its backbone, 125 miles long, stretching northwest between Morro and Monterey bays. The western slope of this mountain range is the steepest coastal slope in the contiguous United States. Roads and trails through it cling to a mountainside that plunges dramatically toward the roiling surf of ocean coves or rises as dramatically to dark redwood canyons—with few grassy terraces, except Monterey's wide coastal plain, in between.

The eastern slope of the range has the gentler face. Sun-speckled mixtures of oak, tan oak, and madrone gather beneath towering volcanic peaks; river valleys shelter pastures and farms, meadows and fields that change color with the seasons. The moderating influence of the Pacific Ocean is weaker on this side of the range, so the landscape is drier and its seasons more pronounced, with frosts in winter and scorching summer heat.

The Native Americans who lived here before the Spanish arrived—the Esselen, the Salinan, the Ohlone—took what they needed from the bounty around them. They followed the seasons and knew the land, a way of life preserved in their stories. Coyote taught them: "You will have acorn mush for your food. You will gather acorns and you will have acorn bread to eat. Go down to the ocean and gather seaweed that you may eat it… And at low tide pick abalones and mussels to eat." They hunted and gathered seals and bird eggs, salmon and wild game, surviving droughts and floods and earthquakes.

The first Spanish explorers soon learned what the Native Americans already knew, that this was an extraordinary place, a land of bobcat and mountain lion, grizzly bear and wolf; a sky haunted with hawks and vultures. Juan Cabrillo sailed past the Santa Lucia Range in 1542, reporting that "there are mountains which seem to reach the heavens, and the sea beats on them; sailing along close to land, it appears as though they would fall on the ships." In 1769 Gaspar de Portolá and the Franciscan Juan Crespí became the first Europeans to see *Sequoia sempervirens,* the coast redwood, which they called palo colorado. The following year they returned to Monterey with Junípero Serra, who founded a mission on the Carmel River, giving the Spanish a precarious foothold on the Central Coast. In 1774 and 1775 Juan Bautista de Anza and diarist Pedro Font traveled overland to the area and described the obstacles to Spanish settlement—the "high and broken" mountains—and its obvious advantages—among them, salmon "so large that I saw one six palms long." Anza's assessment: "counting both the coasts and the interior districts and their respective climates, I have seen no other region so advantageous as this for the raising of all kinds of stock."

Following his prediction of "good commerce," Spanish soldiers and missionaries pressed deeper into the region, moving across the Santa Lucia Ridge to the San Antonio and the Salinas river valleys (this latter being ninety miles of fertile land between the Gabilan Range and the Sierra de Salinas). As the mission system expanded, it nearly destroyed the region's indigenous population. As the rancho system expanded, it destroyed the region's predator population. Huge land grants encouraged settlement after Mexican independence in 1822, and cattle ranchers anxious to protect their herds—and a short-lived trade in tallow and hides—hunted and poisoned grizzly bears to regional extinction. Mountain lions still roam the hills (though sightings are rare) as do bobcats, coyotes, wild pigs, and deer, but bear and wolves had disappeared by the twentieth century.

Monterey was the capital of California under Spanish and Mexican rule and so became a cultural center, but wilderness remained close by. After California became part of the United States, a handful of settlers homesteaded the Monterey coast, building redwood shelters and raising livestock. But most settlers preferred to go inland to King City, at the southern end of Salinas Valley and on the Southern Pacific line, where it was easier for them to secure mail and supplies.

Because access was so difficult to the rugged country south of Monterey, the area resisted change and remained unspoiled. Its wild landscape attracted many artists and writers, among them Robert Louis Stevenson, who included the Monterey Peninsula in his travels. But it was the Carmel bohemians who established the area's reputation—Jack London, Mary

Austin, Ambrose Bierce, and poet George Sterling, who hosted parties on
the stunning local beaches. Sterling grew lyrical about the coast in his
own poetry, but felt that his friend Robinson Jeffers described the landscape most eloquently, evoking a place of "superfluous beauty," a site "crying out for tragedy." While Robinson brought the splendid isolation of
Big Sur to readers in his poems, his wife Una penned a lovely memoir of
their mountain home. So thoroughly did Robinson Jeffers make this coast
his own that other writers, who have included Walter Van Tilburg Clark,
Henry Miller, and poet Bernice Zamora, the latter in direct response to his
mastery, can hardly describe its landscape without invoking him.

Jeffers may have commanded Carmel and Big Sur, but J. Smeaton Chase
encompassed the whole western slope of the Santa Lucia Range in his
1911 tour. And a few decades later John Steinbeck claimed its eastern valleys and Monterey—the more inhabited areas—as *his* territory. It was
Steinbeck who recorded the area's rapid transformation by agriculture in
the decades that followed. Salinas and San Antonio valleys had been farmed
since Spanish days. Mission fathers had planted corn and wheat and raised
livestock, and Mexican ranchers had expanded the land supporting cattle.
But U.S. technology pumped energy into farming. Railroads made wheat
growing practical. Refineries made sugar beets a cash crop. In this century
Salinas turned into the "U.S. Lettuce Capital;" Castroville, near the coast,
became synonymous with artichokes, Watsonville with strawberries. Soon
even grape growers and vineyards appeared in Monterey County.

What was Salinas Valley like before the big growers took over? John
Steinbeck draws on not-very-distant memories in *East of Eden:* "When
my grandfather came into the valley, the mustard was so tall that a man
on horseback showed only his head above the yellow flowers. On the
uplands the grass would be strewn with buttercups, with hen-and-chickens,
with black-centered yellow violets. And a little later in the season there
would be red and yellow stands of Indian paintbrush. These were the
flowers of the open places exposed to the sun."

But the lee side of the Santa Lucia Range has more valleys than one,
and some still cast their rural spell. Jolon Valley, setting for Steinbeck's *To a
God Unknown,* is such a place. Though split by a county highway that
climbs into the foothills and follows the path of Jolon Creek—not much
more than a dry cut in the valley floor during the summer—it seems
barely touched by modern life. Still graced by great oaks that spread their
giant limbs to shade the grass around them, the rolling landscape vibrates

only to the secret whispers of the wind. And there is at least one more such peaceful valley: Tassajara, visited by James D. Houston, reenacting a youthful search for "something more primal, more essential" and finding at least "some simplicity, some silence, the memory of wildness."

Pedro Font

Pedro Font (–1781) was chaplain of Mexico's second overland expedition to Alta California. In 1774 Juan Bautista de Anza had traveled to the Monterey coast from the presidio in Tubac, Arizona. The next year he set out on a similar journey, this time "to escort some families with whom to occupy and settle the port of San Francisco," as Font explains in his diary. The priest recorded travel distances, with the names and locations of landmarks, in a short log of the trip that he later expanded to provide a more detailed version of its events.

Herbert Eugene Bolton, who translated the nine Anza diaries and retraced expedition routes nearly a century and a half later, stated that Font's longer diary was "unsurpassed in all the long history of exploration in the Western Hemisphere." Font, who was ill throughout the journey, was "pessimistic and irritable," according to Bolton. His diary records "that he found Indians disgusting, that he was not always pleased with the weather or the country over which he traveled, [and] even that he sometimes complained about [De] Anza." His discomfort led to a sharp appraisal of the rough coastal landscape. Here Font describes two hard days' travel. ❧

from Font's Complete Diary

Monday, March 4. — I said Mass and bade good-bye to my fellow countrymen, Father Cavaller and his two companions, who were in every way very demonstrative. We set out from the mission of San Luís Obispo at nine o'clock in the morning, and at a quarter to five in the afternoon halted at a place called La Assumpción on the banks of the Monterey River, below its junction with the Santa Margarita River, having traveled some ten leagues, about one to the northeast, four to the north, one to the northnorthwest, two to the northwest, and two to the west-northwest.[1] ...

---

1. The route was northeast for a league, up San Luís Creek, over Cuesta Pass, down Santa Margarita Creek, past Santa Margarita to [the] Salinas River, past Atascadero a short distance, to La Assumpción, where camp was made. The Puerto Dulce mentioned by Font was Carquinez Strait and Suisun Bay.

On setting out we at once entered a long canyon through which flows a pretty arroyo. It is very shady and all along it there are various trees, among which I saw some beautiful laurels. Ascending the canyon we crossed a spur of the range which runs out from the Sierra de Santa Lucía and joins another range which we kept on our right, and behind which are the tulares. This last range continues clear to the mouth of the Puerto Dulce at the extremity of the Puerto de San Francisco, where it ends. Then we descended among some hills and very green meadows with their arroyos, which form the Santa Margarita River, where we arrived after going five leagues, there being a small village at this place. From here we went as far as the campsite through level country, which is like a valley, having on the left the Sierra de Santa Lucía and on the right the other sierra mentioned. All the road and all these plains are full of very large, tall oaks having good and large acorns. Likewise there are many sycamores and pines bearing good pine nuts with hard shells and so leafy that their branches, which begin near the ground and, tapering toward the top, end almost in a conical point. High up in the sierras are seen large numbers of spruce and other trees. Along here there are some birds which they call carpenters, which make round holes in the trunks of the oaks. In each hole they insert an acorn so neatly that it can be taken out only with difficulty, and in this way they make their harvest and store, some of the oaks being all dotted with the acorns in their trunks.

Tuesday, March 5. — I said Mass. In the morning the weather was fair. A little before we set out a messenger arrived from San Luís with letters written by the fathers so that we might take them to the mission of El Carmelo. They did not write them during the day when we were there, because they were talking with us; for they are so lonesome and so far apart that it is a rare day when they see anybody. We set out from La Assumpción at quarter to nine in the morning and at quarter past four in the afternoon we halted on the banks of the San Antonio River at the place called the First Ford, having traveled some ten leagues, about three nearly to the north, five to the northwest, and two to the west-northwest.[2]...

---

2. They followed the Salinas to Paso Robles. Here they swung northwest over the hills along Oak Flat Road (Paso de los Robles) to San Marcos Creek, then nearly north to the Nacimiento River about at Nacimiento Ranch, thence to the Primer Vado, or first ford of San Antonio River, about at King Well.

On setting out we without difficulty crossed the Monterey River, which, because it has rained little this year, was not swollen, though it has few fords and is usually miry. We traveled some three leagues near the river, and then after five more leagues we arrived at the Nacimiento River, which farther down joins the San Antonio River, this in turn joining the Monterey River. Finally we arrived at the campsite, which is on the banks of the San Antonio River, at the beginning of a long valley through which this rivers runs and emerges from the Sierra de Santa Lucía, from which also run the other rivers which I have named. At this place we were molested somewhat by fleas. We had already felt them at the missions but not so much as here, because here they are very hungry, lean, and have hard bills, and they were not few in number. These fleas appear to be a plague in those lands, especially when the weather gets a little warm, so that they are to be found not only in the houses and huts but also in the fields and on the roads, and wherever one halts they are right on hand.

Robert Louis Stevenson

Robert Louis Stevenson made the most of his brief stay in California. After a visit to this strange curving spit of land along the Central Coast—which he described in "The Old Pacific Capital"—the Monterey Peninsula's thickets of twisted trees and "hot wind" were transplanted to Treasure Island. The mood of menace he creates in that 1882 novel can already be felt in this portrait of Monterey, in which Stevenson conveys an oddly prescient sense of the threats to its beauty. ✒

from Old and New Pacific Capitals

The Bay of Monterey has been compared by no less a person than General Sherman to a bent fishing-hook; and the comparison, if less important than the march through Georgia, still shows the eye of a soldier for topography. Santa Cruz sits exposed at the shank; the mouth of the Salinas River is at the middle of the bend; and Monterey itself is cozily ensconced beside the barb. Thus the ancient capital of California faces across the bay, while the Pacific Ocean, though hidden by low hills and forest, bombards her left flank and rear with never-dying surf. In front of the town, the long line of sea-beach trends north and northwest, and then westward to enclose the bay. The waves which lap so quietly about the jetties of Monterey grow louder and larger in the distance; you can see the breakers leaping high and white by day; at night the outline of the shore is traced in transparent silver by the moonlight and the flying foam; and from all round, even in quiet weather, the low, distant, thrilling roar of the Pacific hangs over the coast and the adjacent country like smoke above a battle.

These long beaches are enticing to the idle man. It would be hard to find a walk more solitary and at the same time more exciting to the mind. Crowds of ducks and seagulls hover over the sea. Sandpipers trot in and out by troops after the retiring waves, trilling together in a chorus of infinitesimal song. Strange sea-tangles, new to the European eye, the bones of whales, or sometimes a whole whale's carcass, white with carrion-gulls and poisoning the wind, lie scattered here and there along the sands. The waves come in slowly, vast and green, curve their translucent necks, and burst with a surprising uproar, that runs, waxing and waning, up and down the long keyboard of the beach. The foam of these great ruins mounts in an instant to the ridge of the sand glacis, swiftly fleets back again, and is met and buried by the next breaker. The interest is perpetually fresh. On no other coast that I know shall you enjoy, in calm, sunny weather, such a spectacle of Ocean's greatness, such beauty of changing color, or such degrees of thunder in the sound. The very air is more than usually salt by this Homeric deep.

Inshore, a tract of sand-hills borders on the beach. Here and there a lagoon, more or less brackish, attracts the birds and hunters. A rough, spotty undergrowth partially conceals the sand. The crouching, hardy live oaks flourish singly or in thickets—the kind of wood for murderers to crawl among—and here and there the skirts of the forest extend downward from the hills with a floor of turf and long aisles of pine trees hung with Spaniard's Beard. Through this quaint desert the railway cars drew near to Monterey from the junction at Salinas City—though that and so many other things are now forever altered—and it was from here that you had the first view of the old township lying in the sands, its white windmills bickering in the chill, perpetual wind, and the first fogs of the evening drawing drearily around it from the sea.

The one common note of all this country is the haunting presence of the ocean. A great faint sound of breakers follows you high up into the inland cañons; the roar of water dwells in the clean, empty rooms of Monterey as in a shell upon the chimney; go where you will, you have but to pause and listen to hear the voice of the Pacific. You pass out of the town to the southwest, and mount the hill among pine woods. Glade, thicket, and grove surround you. You follow winding sandy tracks that lead nowither. You see a deer; a multitude of quail arises. But the sound of the sea still follows you as you advance, like that of wind among the trees, only harsher and stranger to the ear; and when at length you gain the summit, out breaks on every hand and with freshened vigor that same unending, distant, whispering rumble of the ocean; for now you are on the top of Monterey peninsula, and the noise no longer only mounts to you from behind along the beach towards Santa Cruz, but from your right also, round by Chinatown and Pinos lighthouse, and from down before you to the mouth of the Carmelo river. The whole woodland is begirt with thundering surges. The silence that immediately surrounds you where you stand is not so much broken as it is haunted by this distant, circling rumor. It sets your senses upon edge; you strain your attention; you are clearly and unusually conscious of small sounds near at hand; you walk listening like an Indian hunter; and that voice of the Pacific is a sort of disquieting company to you in your walk.

When once I was in these woods I found it difficult to turn homeward. All woods lure a rambler onward; but in those of Monterey it was the surf that particularly invited me to prolong my walks. I would push straight for the shore where I thought it to be nearest. Indeed, there was scarce a direction that would not, sooner or later, have brought me forth on the Pacific. The emptiness of the woods gave me a sense of freedom and discovery in these excursions. I never in all my visits met but one man. He was a Mexican, very dark of hue, but smiling and fat, and he carried an axe, though his true business at that moment was to seek for straying cattle. I asked him what o'clock it was, but he seemed neither to know nor care; and when he in his turn asked me for news of his cattle, I showed myself equally indifferent. We stood and smiled upon each other for a few seconds, and then turned without a word and took our several ways across the forest.

One day—I shall never forget it—I had taken a trail that was new to me. After a while the woods began to open, the sea to sound nearer hand. I came upon a road, and, to my surprise, a stile. A step or two farther, and, without leaving the woods, I found myself among trim houses. I walked through street after street, parallel and at right angles, paved with sward and dotted with trees, but still undeniable streets, and each with its name posted at the corner, as in a real town. Facing down the main thoroughfare— "Central Avenue," as it was ticketed—I saw an open-air temple, with benches and sounding-board, as though for an orchestra. The houses were all tightly shuttered; there was no smoke, no sound but of the waves, no moving thing. I have never been in any place that seemed so dreamlike. Pompeii is all in a bustle with visitors, and its antiquity and strangeness deceive the imagination; but this town had plainly not been built above a year or two, and perhaps had been deserted overnight. Indeed it was not so much like a deserted town as like a scene upon the stage by daylight, and with no one on the boards. The barking of a dog led me at last to the only house still occupied, where a Scots pastor and his wife pass the winter alone in this empty theater. The place was "The Pacific Campgrounds, the Christian Seaside Resort." Thither, in the warm season, crowds come to enjoy a life of teetotalism, religion, and flirtation, which I am willing to think blameless and agreeable. The neighborhood at least is well selected. The Pacific booms in front. Westward is Point Pinos, with the lighthouse in a wilderness of sand, where you will find the lightkeeper playing the piano,

making models and bows and arrows, studying dawn and sunrise in amateur oil-painting, and with a dozen other elegant pursuits and interests to
surprise his brave, old-country rivals. To the east, and still nearer, you will
come upon a space of open down, a hamlet, a haven among rocks, a world
of surge and screaming seagulls. Such scenes are very similar in different climates; they appear homely to the eyes of all; to me this was like a dozen
spots in Scotland. And yet the boats that ride in the haven are of strange
outlandish design; and, if you walk into the hamlet you will behold cos-
tumes and faces, and hear a tongue, that are unfamiliar to the memory. The
joss-stick burns, the opium pipe is smoked, the floors are strewn with slips
of colored paper—prayers, you would say, that had somehow missed their
destination—and a man guiding his upright pencil from right to left across
the sheet writes home the news of Monterey to the Celestial Empire.

The woods and the Pacific rule between them the climate of this
seaboard region. On the streets of Monterey, when the air does not smell
salt from the one, it will be blowing perfumed from the resinous treetops
of the other. For days together a hot, dry air will overhang the town, close
as from an oven, yet healthful and aromatic in the nostrils. The cause is not
far to seek, for the woods are afire, and the hot wind is blowing from the
hills. These fires are one of the great dangers of California. I have seen from
Monterey as many as three at the same time, by day a cloud of smoke, by
night a red coal of conflagration in the distance. A little thing will start
them, and, if the wind be favorable, they gallop over miles of country faster
than a horse. The inhabitants must turn out and work like demons, for it is
not only the pleasant groves that are destroyed; the climate and the soil are
equally at stake, and these fires prevent the rains of the next winter and dry
up perennial fountains. California has been a land of promise in its time,
like Palestine; but if the woods continue so swiftly to perish, it may become,
like Palestine, a land of desolation.

To visit the woods while they are languidly burning is a strange piece of
experience. The fire passes through the underbrush at a run. Every here and
there a tree flares up instantaneously from root to summit, scattering tufts
of flame, and is quenched, it seems, as quickly. But this last is only in semblance. For after this first squiblike conflagration of the dry moss and twigs,
there remains behind a deep-rooted and consuming fire in the very entrails
of the tree. The resin of the pitch pine is principally condensed at the base
of the bole and in the spreading roots. Thus, after the light, showy, skirmishing flames, which are only as the match to the explosion, have already

scampered down the wind into the distance, the true harm is but beginning for this giant of the woods. You may approach the tree from one side, and see it, scorched indeed from top to bottom, but apparently survivor of the peril. Make the circuit, and there, on the other side of the column, is, a clear mass of living coal, spreading like an ulcer; while underground, to their most extended fiber, the roots are being eaten out by fire, and the smoke is rising through the fissures to the surface. A little while and, without a nod of warning, the huge pine tree snaps off short across the ground and falls prostrate with a crash. Meanwhile the fire continues its silent business; the roots are reduced to a fine ash; and long afterwards, if you pass by, you will find the earth pierced with radiating galleries, and preserving the design of all these subterranean spurs, as though it were the mold for a new tree instead of the print of an old one. These pitch pines of Monterey are, with the single exception of the Monterey cypress, the most fantastic of forest trees. No words can give an idea of the contortion of their growth; they might figure without change in a circle of the nether hell as Dante pictured it; and at the rate at which trees grow, and at which forest fires spring up and gallop through the hills of California, we may look forward to a time when there will not be one of them left standing in that land of their nativity. At least they have not so much to fear from the axe, but perish by what may be called a natural although a violent death; while it is man in his short-sighted greed that robs the country of the nobler redwood. Yet a little while and perhaps all the hills of seaboard California may be as bald as Tamalpais.

I have an interest of my own in these forest fires, for I came so near to lynching on one occasion, that a braver man might have retained a thrill from the experience. I wished to be certain whether it was the moss, that quaint funereal ornament of Californian forests, which blazed up so rapidly when the flame first touched the tree. I suppose I must have been under the influence of Satan, for instead of plucking off a piece for my experiment, what should I do but walk up to a great pine tree in a portion of the wood which had escaped so much as scorching, strike a match, and apply the flame gingerly to one of the tassels. The tree went off simply like a rocket; in three seconds it was a roaring pillar of fire. Close by I could hear the shouts of those who were at work combating the original conflagration. I could see the wagon that had brought them tied to a live oak in a piece of open; I could even catch the flash of an axe as it swung up through the underwood into the sunlight. Had anyone observed the result of my experiment,

my neck was literally not worth a pinch of snuff; after a few minutes of passionate expostulation I should have been run up to a convenient bough.

To die for faction is a common evil;
But to be hanged for nonsense is the devil.

I have run repeatedly, but never as I ran that day. At night I went out of
town, and there was my own particular fire, quite distinct from the other,
and burning, as I thought, with even greater vigor.

But it is the Pacific that exercises the most direct and obvious power
upon the climate. At sunset, for months together, vast, wet, melancholy fogs
arise and come shoreward from the ocean. From the hilltop above
Monterey the scene is often noble, although it is always sad. The upper air
is still bright with sunlight; a glow still rests upon the Gabelano [Gabilan]
Peak; but the fogs are in possession of the lower levels; they crawl in scarves
among the sand-hills; they float, a little higher, in clouds of a gigantic size
and often of a wild configuration; to the south, where they have struck the
seaward shoulder of the mountains of Santa Lucia, they double back and
spire up skyward like smoke. Where their shadow touches, color dies out of
the world. The air grows chill and deadly as they advance. The tradewind
freshens, the trees begin to sigh, and all the windmills in Monterey are
whirling and creaking and filling their cisterns with the brackish water of
the sands. It takes but a little while till the invasion is complete. The sea, in
its lighter order, has submerged the earth. Monterey is curtained in for the
night in thick, wet, salt, and frigid clouds, so to remain till day returns; and
before the sun's rays they slowly disperse and retreat in broken squadrons to
the bosom of the sea. And yet often when the fog is thickest and most chill,
a few steps out of the town and up the slope, the night will be dry and
warm and full of inland perfume.

Robinson Jeffers

Robinson Jeffers (1887–1962) has been called one of the most notable American poets of his generation. And also "the most widely-read unread poet." But anyone who cares about the future should read his work, since it reveals a special sensitivity, Loren Eiseley feels, "to those aspects of nature which contribute to the creation and maintenance of human dignity and which are sadly threatened in our time."

Jeffers was born in Pittsburgh, the son of a theology professor who led his family around Europe before settling in Pasadena in 1903. Jeffers graduated from Occidental College and went on to study medicine at the University of Southern California and forestry at the University of Washington. He met his future wife in a German class at USC. Una Call Custer was the wife of a prominent Los Angeles attorney. He eventually agreed to a divorce, and Robinson and Una were married in 1913, a year after the publication of Robinson's first book, Flagons and Apples, a volume of love verse. In 1914 the couple moved to Carmel and started exploring the coast in the rambling hikes she dubbed "pilgrimages." Deeply affected by the rugged beauty of the Central Coast, Jeffers began to develop a mature verse in which he sought to express the "transhuman magnificence" of nature. Shifting "emphasis and significance from man to not-man" meant adopting a new perspective which Jeffers called "Inhumanism." That attitude influenced all of his later work, including prose pieces and a famous 1947 Broadway adaptation of Medea, as well as his many short lyric and long narrative poems—the best inspired by the beauty of Carmel and Big Sur. 🐍

Continent's End

At the equinox when the earth was veiled in a late rain, wreathed with
   wet poppies, waiting spring,
The ocean swelled for a far storm and beat its boundary, the ground-swell
   shook the beds of granite.

I gazing at the boundaries of granite and spray, the established sea-marks,
   felt behind me

Mountain and plain, the immense breadth of the continent, before me the
mass and doubled stretch of water.

I said: You yoke the Aleutian seal-rocks with the lava and coral sowings
that flower the south,
Over your flood the life that sought the sunrise faces ours that has followed
the evening star.

The long migrations meet across you and it is nothing to you, you have
forgotten us, mother.
You were much younger when we crawled out of the womb and lay in
the sun's eye on the tideline.

It was long and long ago; we have grown proud since then and you have
grown bitter; life retains
Your mobile soft unquiet strength; and envies hardness, the insolent
quietness of stone.

The tides are in our veins, we still mirror the stars, life is your child, but
there is in me
Older and harder than life and more impartial, the eye that watched
before there was an ocean.

That watched you fill your beds out of the condensation of thin vapor
and watched you change them,
That saw you soft and violent wear your boundaries down, eat rock, shift
places with the continents.

Mother, though my song's measure is like your surf-beat's ancient rhythm
I never learned it of you.
Before there was any water there were tides of fire, both our tones flow
from the older fountain.

Evening Ebb

The ocean has not been so quiet for a long while; five night-herons
Fly shorelong voiceless in the hush of the air
Over the calm of an ebb that almost mirrors their wings.
The sun has gone down, and the water has gone down
From the weed-clad rock, but the distant cloud-wall rises. The ebb
   whispers.
Great cloud-shadows float in the opal water.
Through rifts in the screen of the world pale gold gleams and the evening
Star suddenly glides like a flying torch.
As if we had not been meant to see her; rehearsing behind
The screen of the world for another audience.

The Place For No Story

The coast hills at Sovranes Creek;
No trees, but dark scant pasture drawn thin
Over rock shaped like flame;
The old ocean at the land's foot, the vast
Gray extension beyond the long white violence;
A herd of cows and the bull
Far distant, hardly apparent up the dark slope;
And the gray air haunted with hawks:
This place is the noblest thing I have ever seen. No imaginable
Human presence here could do anything
But dilute the lonely self-watchful passion.

Fire On The Hills

The deer were bounding like blown leaves
Under the smoke in front of the roaring wave of the brushfire;
I thought of the smaller lives that were caught.
Beauty is not always lovely; the fire was beautiful, the terror

Of the deer was beautiful; and when I returned
Down the black slopes after the fire had gone by, an eagle
Was perched on the jag of a burnt pine,
Insolent and gorged, cloaked in the folded storms of his shoulders.
He had come from far off for the good hunting
With fire for his beater to drive the game; the sky was merciless
Blue, and the hills merciless black,
The sombre-feathered great bird sleepily merciless between them.
I thought, painfully, but the whole mind,
The destruction that brings an eagle from heaven is better than mercy.

Una Jeffers

The second favorite poet of Una Jeffers (1884–1950) was William Butler
Yeats, and, like him, she had a passion for Irish towers. After she moved to a
bare bluff above Carmel with Robinson Jeffers, her husband built her one: a
stone-walled, four-story edifice complete with parapet walls commanding a
magnificent view of the rocky cove below and foggy Point Lobos to the
south. For Jeffers it was more than a romantic gesture. It was a lasting gift
for the woman he would memorialize as a falcon in "Hungerfield." They
called it Hawk Tower, a reminder of the birds of prey that figure in Jeffers'
verse and a monument to Una's strength of character and keen intelligence.

The couple lived in Tor House, which ran more or less under Una's direction, James Karman tells us in his study of Robinson Jeffers. She made breakfast, took care of their twin sons, and made sure that Robinson spent mornings productively—on his poetry. But Robinson was not the only writer at
work. Una had a scholar's training—capped by a University of Southern
California graduate degree in philosophy—which may have prepared her for
the correspondence she maintained with ever more friends and literary con-
tacts. In 1935 Horace and Edna Lyon conceived of a book that would marry
Jeffers' verse to Lyon's photographs, thus enhancing the enjoyment of readers
unfamiliar with the Jefferses' settings. Una was enthusiastic, suggesting locations for photos and selecting lines from poems. In 1938 she and her husband each wrote a foreword for the book. The project languished until 1971,
when Skrimshaw Press brought out an edition that included her marvelous
foreword, a description of "Jeffers Country" in which Una—in the words of
poet Mark Jarman—"makes love to the landscape she writes about." ✦

from Jeffers Country

Looking southward from our headland we see beyond the mouth of the
Carmel River the gentle rounded outlines of the Santa Lucia Mountains,
bright green with pasture and dark with thickets of chaparral and sage. One
yellowed ivory scar marks the quarry where, long ago, Indians hewed out
blocks of chalkstone to build the Spanish mission church, San Carlos del
Rio Carmelo. The mountains look serenely lovely, with no hint of the

magnificent and menacing face they turn toward the sea. This range, narrow but rising in double or triple ridges, stretches southward along the coast for a hundred miles.

The river too is quiet, except when winter floods rage down the valley to battle the waves across the sandbar, or surge out in a tremendous bore through new-cut channels. At most times it spreads out like a placid lake, and trickles into the adjoining water-meadows. Here among reeds and tough grasses the pools reflect every changing hue of sky and clouds, and the shadow of the hills lies darkly. The air is full of birdsongs, and the plop-plop of game birds that rest in their flights and feed here—ducks and geese and wild swans, with the local herons and passing egret—every day a different group. But a myriad of gulls are constant on the sand-spits by the open water. They fish and swirl on flashing white wings; sometimes, before storm, they float high aloft for hours, weaving great complicated circles in some precise ritual. Unwieldy pelicans feed here too, and row away to their sea-rocks on heavy wings.

The coast road, the great San Simeon Highway, crosses the river just beyond the mission. It was completed in 1937, a hundred miles of road; its construction consumed seventeen years of labor and eight million dollars, indicative of the difficult terrain. Beyond, no longer gentle now, the mountains hurry to the sea in great precipices, slashed by canyons, only seldom flattening to a few acres of possible plowland. Cattle, pasturing for centuries where they could, have left the welts of their hoof-tracks crisscrossing many a steep hillside. Canyons, gushing springs and streams, are thickly wooded with redwoods and pines, laurels, tan oaks, maples and sycamores, and, high up, the rosy-barked madrones. Near the Little Sur River there are dunes, whose drifting sands defy any boundaries of the road. Beyond, the Point Sur lighthouse sits atop a rock like St. Michael's Mount off Cornwall. From three hundred and fifty feet above the sea the powerful lens and bellowing siren warn mariners that many a stout ship has broken up along this terrible shore, which mile after mile is jagged with sharp cliffs and narrow inlets with only an occasional furlong of white-sanded beach, inaccessible from above. Lashing waves roll in, incredibly green and blue beyond the foam, menacing and gray in storm. Color, *color* on land and sea, greens and tawny yellows, and the millefleurs tapestry. Name the flowers to conjure up the colors—blues of wild lilac and lupin, larkspur and iris and blue-eyed grass; gold of poppies and yarrow and the yellow lupin, wild pansies and wallflowers; and white heather, white wild lilac, candle-white yucca, and sometimes snow-on-the-mountain. Flashing bird wings too, red-winged blackbirds and golden finches, blue jays and hummingbirds, darting red and emerald. And high above, arrogant hawks hover, marsh hawks and sparrow hawks, redtails and peregrine falcons. Vultures too peering down, and a rare pair of eagles. Even on sunny days there will be a vagrant wisp of luminous fog creeping like a live thing in and out the canyons.

Long ago I read in Dorothy Wordsworth's *Journal* an observation of hers in some remote highland glen. She was "conscious of the interest man gives to nature, and still more, the dignity nature gives to man." They enhance each other; we have realized their interplay as we have walked and ridden over this coast land, meditating on remote farmhouses, evidences of formerly vigorous and self-sustained life. Only a heart of horn could fail to quicken to the mute tokens around a deserted farm, old cart wheels and antique gear, faded calico rags, a caved-in well, clumps of ragged geranium and the

Big Sur has a climate of its own and a character all its own. It is a region where extremes meet, a region where one is always conscious of weather, of space, of grandeur, and of eloquent silence. Among other things, it is the meeting place of migratory birds coming from north and south. It is said, in fact, that there is a greater variety of birds to be found in this region than in any other part of the United States. It is also the home of the redwoods; one encounters them on entering from the north and one leaves them on passing southward. At night one can still hear the coyote howling, and if one ventures beyond the first ridge of mountains one can meet up with mountain lions and other beasts of the wild. The grizzly bear is no longer to be found here, but the rattlesnake is still to be reckoned with. On a clear, bright day, when the blue of the sea rivals the blue of the sky, one sees the hawk, the eagle, the buzzard soaring above the still, hushed canyons. In summer, when the fogs roll in, one can look down upon a sea of clouds floating listlessly above the ocean; they have the appearance, at times, of huge iridescent soap bubbles, over which, now and then, may be seen a double rainbow. In January and February the hills are greenest, almost as green as the Emerald Isle. From November to February are the best months, the air fresh and invigorating, the skies clear, the sun still warm enough to take a sunbath.

—Henry Miller, from *Big Sur and the Oranges of Hieronymus Bosch* (1957)

startling clarity of calla lilies. Never unkempt, however long lost, these cold flowers rise on high stems out of shining leaves. And the many abandoned enterprises: old sawmills, the tottering buildings at Notley's Landing, where once great loads of redwood and tan bark went out on ships; the coal mine up Mal Paso, where only a hump hidden by thistles indicates the slide that covered its mouth and twenty Chinese workmen as well. Other random diggings too, where men have vainly sought the lost gold mine of the padres; or sought the loot buried by the bandits, Vásquez and Murietta.

Up Mill Creek was the most extensive of the old enterprises, limekilns, whose output slid on skips down to the sea on a steel cable slung high above the canyon. No road goes to the kilns, only a broken trail crossing and recrossing a tumbling stream, whose fords were washed away long ago. A traveler treads precariously across on broken tree trunks, or leaps from the tall white kilns smothered with vines and poison oak. Redwoods pushed through the walls and tilted the floors of the house, empty save for a broken bench or table, or a rusty iron stove. In one house the portrait of an old lady startled us. It was one of those old-fashioned crayon enlargements common enough in the nineties, framed heavily in machine-carved wood with metal embellishments. From her position on the floor, propped against a sagging door, the old lady looked at us with prim and steadfast eyes. Her sensitive mouth and neat garb were curiously arresting in that situation. Afterwards we often speculated about her plight, and sensed the forest growth closing in, the wild creatures brushing against her. Years went by. Once more we journeyed to the kilns, and Horace Lyon with us. The lady awaited our coming. We lifted her to a broken window, and Horace photographed her there. On an impulse I sent the picture with a note to *Time*, which published it with the caption "Santa Lucia Lady—who is she?" Other people found her interesting, too, for I received letters about her from all over the country, and at last one from an old lady in Ohio, identifying this picture of her mother and explaining its mysterious abandonment.

Horace Lyon caught the atmosphere at the kiln, as he has of many places in this region, toward which he seems to have a peculiarly sympathetic relationship. No other person, either with lens or paints, has approached his understanding of its drama and stark terror and beauty. If ill luck ever pushed us from this place of our choice, Robin and I would certainly carry away with us, among our best treasures, this series of Horace Lyon's photographs of "Jeffers Country."

Bernice Zamora

Bernice Zamora (1938–) is not really a landscape writer. Her poems more often explore the boundaries between two cultures: "one private, interior, womanly, and communal, in the Chicano sense, and another that some would label public, academic, intellectual, and male," according to Nancy Vogely. Zamora bridges these cultures and their literary traditions while she explores the relationship between self and community.

Zamora grew up in Aguilar, Colorado, attended Catholic schools, married, and had two children. Later she attended Southern Colorado University and Colorado State University at Fort Collins and began writing poetry. Her first book, Restless Serpents, *was published in 1976; her second book,* Releasing Serpents, *appeared eighteen years later. In the intervening years Zamora moved to California, earned a Ph.D. from Stanford, worked in the Chicano movement, and became a respected university teacher. She has recently moved back to Colorado, abandoning academic life to reconnect with family and continue to write. Zamora goes back to the beginning in "Pico Blanco," which is the center of creation according to the Esselen natives—whose voices seem to echo through this apostrophe directed at Robinson Jeffers.* ✍

Pico Blanco

On your "steep sea-wave of marble,"
I stand—mad Cassandra, screeching
perhaps, but straining my eyes
to catch a glimpse of the "great king,
cold and austere," or the "pale
hunchback shuffling along corridors,"
or Azevedo's three giant Indians
stepping over the Ventana Mountains.
These are the stewards of *your* estate.
You will, I hope, entertain the blond
harlot while I search for mine.
Never mind cousin Christ. He will
rise above America's adoration for
blood in the corners.

"Poor bitch," you say. Indeed I am,
but I am not mumbling to my people
or to my gods. I am chipping the
crust of the Pico Blanco.
Your stewards could help—or you,
Jeffers; then you and I could vacillate
breaking the crust—You and I, Jeffers.

John Steinbeck

John Steinbeck (1902–1968) lived on both sides of the Santa Lucia Range. Born in Salinas, he moved to the Monterey Peninsula after he published his first novel, Cup of Gold, *in 1929. His knowledge of the region and its working people are obvious throughout his work, in novels like* Tortilla Flat *and* Cannery Row, *which take place in Monterey, as well as in other writings, such as the novel* East of Eden *and the short story collection* The Long Valley, *which have inland locales. In 1962 Steinbeck became the only California writer ever to receive the Nobel Prize for Literature. His most celebrated work (the Pulitzer Prize–winner in 1939) is* The Grapes of Wrath, *the powerful story of an Oklahoma family traveling to California to escape dust-bowl poverty.*

Steinbeck's second novel, To a God Unknown, *is the story of Joseph Wayne, a farmer who homesteads a portion of a small valley that Steinbeck calls Nuestra Señora. The "long valley of Our Lady" was based on the Jolon, an interior valley nestled against the Santa Lucia slopes about twenty miles east of King City, where Steinbeck spent boyhood summers on his uncle's ranch.* To a God Unknown *took him five years to complete; with it Steinbeck made a fit start on capturing the spirit of his country, "one of those pregnant places from which come wonders."* 🐾

from To a God Unknown

After a time of wandering, Joseph came to the long valley called Nuestra Señora, and there he recorded his homestead. Nuestra Señora, the long valley of Our Lady in central California, was green and gold and yellow and blue when Joseph came into it. The level floor was deep in wild oats and canary mustard flowers. The river San Francisquito flowed noisily in its bouldered bed through a cave made by its little narrow forest. Two flanks of the Coast Range held the valley of Nuestra Señora close, on one side guarding it against the sea, and on the other against the blasting winds of the great Salinas Valley. At the far southern end a pass opened in the hills to let out the river, and near this pass lay the church and the little town of Our Lady. The huts of Indians clustered about the mud walls of the church, and

although the church was often vacant now and its saints were worn and part
of its tile roof lay in a shattered heap on the ground, and although the bells
were broken, the Mexican Indians still lived near about and held their fes-
tivals, danced La Jota on the packed earth and slept in the sun.

When his homestead was recorded, Joseph set out for his new home. His
eyes glittered with excitement under his broad-brimmed hat and he sniffed

When he'd first returned to California the previous summer, he'd made a
pilgrimage down the coast in his pickup, cutting over the Santa Lucia range
at Nacimiento Summit. He'd parked for a few minutes beneath the big
Monterey pines at the top, remembering his father walking into the shadows of the trees twenty years before to cut his hair, mourning Attis, his
other son. He remembered the last time he and Attis had climbed down
the steep trail below the summit to fish the headwaters of the San Antonio
River, the summer before Attis went to Vietnam.

Then he'd started the pickup and driven down into the wild Jolon Valley
and south on little back roads through country where they'd hunted deer
and quail. The grass had been thick and brown beneath the trees of the
foothills, alive with ground squirrels, and meadowlarks had lined the fence
posts. Finally, he'd taken the one-lane gravel road that led to their first
house in California.

It was still there, tucked far back up a narrow cleft in the coast range, a
little white house with flaking paint and slanting foundation, with a bare
dirt yard where a half dozen brown-and-white chickens still scratched. In
the hillside behind the house he could see a depression where, when he was
seven and Attis nine, they had dug a cave, finding at the bottom two arrow-
heads of obsidian and flint and a little white stone doll. In thirty-five years,
nothing about the house had changed. The canyon was as still as the inside
of a kiva. Not even a bird made a sound or mark against the sky. In the big
black oak at the edge of the yard, a few rotten boards still suggested the rec-
tangle of the tree fort he'd built with Attis. The thick buckbrush and manzanita through which they'd squirmed with slingshots and beebee guns still
rose on both sides of the canyon walls, and the wild oats were tall and gold-
en between the thickets on the hillside.

—Louis Owens, from *Bone Game: A Novel* (1994)

at the valley hungrily. He wore new jeans with a circle of brass buttons around the waist, a blue shirt, and a vest for the sake of the pockets. His high-heeled boots were new and his spurs shone like silver. An old Mexican was trudging painfully in to Our Lady. His face lighted up with pleasure when Joseph drew near. He removed his hat and stepped aside. "Is there a fiesta some place?" he asked politely.

Joseph laughed with delight. "I have a hundred and sixty acres of land up the valley. I'm going to live on it."

The old walker's eyes lighted on the rifle which, in its scabbard, lay snugly under Joseph's leg. "If you see a deer, señor, and if you kill that deer, remember old Juan."

Joseph rode on, but he called back over his shoulder, "When the house is built I'll make a fiesta. I'll remember you then, Old Juan."

"My son-in-law plays the guitar, señor."

"Then he'll come too, Old Juan."

Joseph's horse walked quickly along, swishing with its hoofs through the brittle oak leaves; the iron shoes rang against protruding stones. The path went through the long forest that bordered the river. As he rode, Joseph became timid and yet eager, as a young man is who slips out to a rendezvous with a wise and beautiful woman. He was half-drugged and overwhelmed by the forest of Our Lady. There was a curious femaleness about the interlacing boughs and twigs, about the long green cavern cut by the river through the trees and the brilliant underbrush. The endless green halls and aisles and alcoves seemed to have meanings as obscure and promising as the symbols of an ancient religion. Joseph shivered and closed his eyes. "Perhaps I'm ill," he said. "When I open my eyes I may find that all this is delirium and fever." As he rode on and on the fear came upon him that this land might be the figure of a dream which would dissolve into a dry and dusty morning. A manzanita branch whipped his hat off and dropped it on the ground, and, when Joseph dismounted he stretched his arms and leaned down to pat the earth with his hand. There was a need in him to shake off the mood that had fallen upon him. He looked up to the treetops where the sun flashed on trembling leaves, where the wind sang huskily. When he mounted his horse again he knew that he could never lose the feeling for the land. The crying leather of his saddle, the jingle of his spur chains, the rasping of the horse's tongue over the bit-roller sang the high notes over the land's throbbing. Joseph felt that he had been dull and now suddenly was sensitized; had been asleep and was awakened. Far in the back of his mind lay the feeling that he was being treacherous. The past, his home and all the events of his childhood were being lost, and he knew he owed them the duty of memory. This land might possess all of him if he were not careful. To combat the land a little, he thought of his father, of the calm and peace, the strength and eternal rightness of his father, and then in his thought the difference ended and he knew that there was no quarrel, for his father and this new land were one. Joseph was frightened then. "He's dead," he whispered to himself. "My father must be dead."

The horse had left the river's forest now to follow a smooth rounded track that might have been made by a python's body. It was an ancient game trail made by the hoofs and pads of lonely fearful animals that had followed the track as though they loved even the ghosts of company. It was a trail of innumerable meanings. Here it swung wide to avoid a large oak with one thick overhanging limb where long ago a lion had crouched and made its kill and left its scent to turn the trail aside: here the track went carefully around a smooth rock whereon a rattlesnake habitually sunned its cold blood. The horse kept to the center of the trail and heeded all its warnings.

Now the path broke into a broad grassy meadow, in the center of which a colony of live oaks grew like a green island in a lake of lighter green. As Joseph rode toward the trees he heard an agonized squealing, and turning the grove's shoulder he came in sight of a huge boar with curved tusks and yellow eyes and a mane of shaggy red hair. The beast sat on its haunches and tearingly ate the hindquarters of a still-squealing little pig. In the distance a sow and five other little pigs bounded away, crying their terror. The boar stopped eating and set its shoulders when Joseph rode into its line of scent. It snorted and then returned to the dying pig, which still squealed piercingly. Joseph jerked up his horse. His face contracted with anger and his eyes paled until they were almost white. "Damn you," he cried. "Eat other creatures. Don't eat your own people." He pulled his rifle from its scabbard and aimed between the yellow eyes of the boar. And then the barrel lowered and a firm thumb let down the hammer. Joseph laughed shortly at himself. "I'm taking too great power into my hands," he said. "Why he's the father of fifty pigs and he may be the source of fifty more." The boar wheeled and snorted as Joseph rode on by.

Now the trail skirted a long side hill densely protected by underbrush—blackberry, manzanita, and scrub oak so thickly tangled that even the rabbits had to make little tunnels through it. The trail forced its way up the long narrow ridge and came to a belt of trees, tan oak and live oak and white oak.

Among the branches of the trees a tiny white fragment of mist appeared and delicately floated along just over the treetops. In a moment another translucent shred joined it, and another and another. They sailed along like a half-materialized ghost, growing larger and larger until suddenly they struck a column of warm air and rose into the sky to become little clouds. All over the valley the flimsy little clouds were forming and ascending like the spirits of the dead rising out of a sleeping city. They seemed to disappear against the sky, but the sun was losing its warmth because of them. Joseph's horse raised its head and sniffed the air. On top of the ridge stood a clump of giant madrone trees, and Joseph saw with wonder how nearly they resembled meat and muscles. They thrust up muscular limbs as red as flayed flesh and twisted like bodies on the rack. Joseph laid his hand on one of the branches as he rode by, and it was cold and sleek and hard. But the leaves at the ends of the horrible limbs were bright green and shiny. Pitiless and terrible trees, the madrones. They cried with pain when burnt.

Joseph gained the ridgetop and looked down on the grasslands of his new homestead where the wild oats moved in silver waves under a little wind, where the patches of blue lupins lay like shadows in a clear lucent night, and the poppies on the side hills were broad rays of sun. He drew up to look at the long grassy meadows in which clumps of live oaks stood like perpetual senates ruling over the land. The river with its mask of trees cut a twisting path down through the valley. Two miles away he could see, beside a gigantic lonely oak, the white speck of his tent pitched and left while he went to record his homestead. A long time he sat there. As he looked into the valley, Joseph felt his body flushing with a hot fluid of love. "This is mine," he said simply, and his eyes sparkled with tears and his brain was filled with wonder that this should be his. There was pity in him for the grass and the flowers; he felt that the trees were his children and the land his child. For a moment he seemed to float high in the air and to look down upon it. "It's mine," he said again, "and I must take care of it."

The little clouds were massing in the sky; a legion of them scurried to the east to join the army already forming on the hill line. From over the western mountains the lean gray ocean clouds came racing in. The wind started up with a gasp and sighed through the branches of the trees. The horse stepped lightly down the path toward the river again, and often it raised its head and sniffed at the fresh sweet odor of the coming rain. The cavalry of clouds had passed and a huge black phalanx marched slowly in from the sea with a tramp of thunder. Joseph trembled with pleasure in the promised violence. The river seemed to hurry along down its course, to chatter excitedly over the stones as it went. And then the rain started, fat lazy drops splashing on the leaves. Thunder rolled like caissons over the sky. The drops grew smaller and thicker, raked through the air and hissed in the trees. Joseph's clothing was soaked in a minute and his horse shone with water. In the river the trout were striking at tumbled insects and all the tree trunks glistened darkly.

The trail left the river again, and as Joseph neared his tent the clouds rolled backward from the west to the east like a curtain of gray wool and the late sun sparkled on the washed land, glittered on the grass blades and shot sparks into the drops that lay in the hearts of wildflowers. Before his tent Joseph dismounted and unsaddled the horse and rubbed its wet back and shoulders with a cloth before he turned the tired beast loose to graze. He stood in the damp grass in front of his tent. The setting sun played on his brown temples and the evening wind ruffled his beard. The hunger in his eyes became rapaciousness as he looked down the long green valley. His possessiveness became a passion. "It's mine," he chanted. "Down deep it's mine, right to the center of the world." He stamped his feet into the soft earth. Then the exultance grew to be a sharp pain of desire that ran through his body in a hot river. He flung himself face downward on the grass and pressed his cheek against the wet stems. His fingers gripped the wet grass and tore it out, and gripped again. His thighs beat heavily on the earth.

The fury left him and he was cold and bewildered and frightened at himself. He sat up and wiped the mud from his lips and beard. "What was it?" he asked himself. "What came over me then? Can I have a need that great?" He tried to remember exactly what had happened. For a moment the land had been his wife. "I'll need a wife," he said. "It will be too lonely here without a wife." He was tired. His body ached as though he had lifted a great rock, and the moment of passion had frightened him.

Over a little fire before his tent he cooked his meager supper, and when the night came he sat on the ground and looked at the cold white stars, and he felt a throbbing in his land. The fire died down to coals and Joseph heard the coyotes crying in the hills, and he heard the little owls go shrieking by, and all about him he heard the field mice scattering in the grass. After a while the honey-colored moon arose behind the eastern ridge. Before it was clear of the hills, the golden face looked through bars of pine trunks. Then for a moment a black sharp pine tree pierced the moon and was withdrawn as the moon arose.

J. Smeaton Chase

*J. Smeaton Chase visited the Central Coast in the course of his longest
California horseback trip—he traveled from El Monte in southern
California, reached the Pacific at Malibu, and turned north along the coast
to Oregon. On an earlier trip he had traveled south from El Monte to San
Diego. He described both trips in* California Coast Trails, *which many
consider the best volume in his travel trilogy. Here Chase paints a detailed
portrait of the coastal face of the Santa Lucia Range.* ❧

from California Coastal Trails

It was a Saturday afternoon when I left Pacific Valley. A few miles up coast
the view was closed by the promontory of Lopez Point, on the hither side
of which is a stream called Mill Creek, where I proposed camping for
Sunday. The afternoon was bright for a change, and I traveled slowly, reve-
ling in the romping wind and the splendid color-play of the sea. The mountains again rose abruptly from the shore in folds of faded gold that were
swept by flying cloud-shadows and checkered with clear-blocked masses of
timber in cañon and on crest. Again I longed to be a painter—a *great*
painter, one to whom the subjectiveness, the spirituality, of color should be
known, and who might transcribe this fine fragment of Nature in all its
material and immaterial beauty. There is a largeness and freedom about this
little-visited coast that puts the mind under stimulus, and almost rids one of
that deadly incubus of experience which so sadly dulls the edge of our
impressions.

At Mill Creek I found one of the "landings" which take the place of harbors on this rocky coast—a crane, cable, and windlass by which freight is
sent up or down between cliff and water. I found my friends from the ranch
at work at a pile of redwood timbers which they were about to raft down
to their own landing. There is no lack of variety in the occupations of the
settlers on the coast of the Santa Lucia. "Tools and the man" will be the text
of the Virgil of this region. I made camp beside the creek, but the pasturage
was so scanty that it was necessary to take Anton a mile farther, to where a
Mexican lived from whom I might buy hay. Here Anton was accommodated

in the stable, and when, after a pleasant chat, I returned to camp, I carried back a sizable venison steak, pressed upon me by the good people.

The fog was unusually dense at night, and by morning my blankets were soaking. I kept up a roaring fire for comfort till noon, when the weather cleared, and the rest of the day was spent in seeking shady places for relief from the sun. The creek was full of trout, and two hours of the evening sufficed to catch my breakfast and enough to make a fair return for my venison.

The trail next day continued to wind along the cliff, diving every half-mile or so into a wooded cañon and giving a charming alternation of land- and seascape. If the course of this trail were drawn in bird's-eye fashion it would show a surprising serpentine, and the ratio of air-line distance to actual traveling would be a remarkable one if it were calculated.

In one of the cañons I found the home of an old settler. It made an inviting appearance, with its garden of herbs and flowers and its half-acre of fruits and vegetables. A boy was cleaning a rifle by the gate, and through the open door I could see the owner of the place; a man of so little curiosity that, although I may easily have been the first passerby for a week, he neither asked nor cared to see who the traveler might be. Usually, the arrival of a stranger would bring out all hands and a host of questions.

In another and deeper cañon, known as Limekiln Cañon, I came upon the remains of a considerable building filled with machinery, all now fallen into wreck. The place was a wilderness of ferns, flowers, and noble red-woods, and I had to resist a strong inclination to camp there, backed by Anton on the score of a scanty cropping of green fodder. The climb out was long and strenuous, but Anton did himself credit, and, indeed, I had constant reason to congratulate myself on the exchange I had made.

After some miles of steady traveling my next landmark came in sight far ahead, a farmhouse set high up on the hillside. It was always a relief to find that I was on the right track, for besides being little traveled the trails are much complicated with cattle-trails. The house proved to be also the post office of Lucia, the farthest outpost of the postal service in this direction. Here (on Monday) I mailed letters which, after lying here until Saturday, would be taken to Gorda, where they would wait until the following Saturday before starting for Jolon and the inhabited world.

Now began another stiff climb, compensated by fine expansive views to seaward. I was astonished to find a school up here on this lonely moun-tainside. The scholars had just been dismissed and were playing round the neat little building. Of the ten or twelve I saw while I stopped to chat with them, all but two were Mexican—a fact which helped to explain there being so many children within range, for Mexican families are apt to be a good deal larger than American, and three little homes might easily contribute a dozen or more youngsters of school age.

A couple of miles farther on I came on one such home—a picturesque, weather-beaten house shaded by fruit trees whose size showed a probable age of some forty years. A tall, white-haired old man who was sitting in the porch came forward and greeted me in Spanish as I reined up, inquiring whether I would not dismount. I was glad to do so, and passed a pleasant half-hour with him and his eldest son. Again I found that the mere mention of having friendly acquaintance with a compatriot was enough to ensure the kindest reception.

It was late afternoon when I got my directions for the next ranch, where I intended to stay for the night. Crossing the deep cañon of Vicente Creek, the trail bore steadily up the mountainside until it must have reached a height of well over two thousand feet. In the cañons hereabouts the tan-bark oak *(Quercus densiflora),* that curious link between oak and chestnut, grows freely, and the gathering and shipping of the bark formerly made a considerable industry here, as it still does along the coast farther north. At one spot, known as Tan-Bark Camp, I noticed the remains of a large abandoned encampment.

Higher still, and near the crest, I came into a region of magnificent yellow pines and redwoods. It was sundown, and the view was a remarkable one. The sun shone level, and with a strange bronze hue, through a translucent veil of fog. Below the fog the surface of the ocean was clear, and was flooded with gorgeous purple by the sunset. On the high crest where I stood, a clear, warm glory bathed the golden slopes of grass and lighted the noble trees as if for some great pageant. There was a solemnity in the splendor, an unearthly quality in the whole scene; that kept me spellbound and bareheaded until, fatefully, imperceptibly, the sun had set.

The situation of Gamboa's Ranch is superb, the very finest I know. The house, an old and picturesque one, hangs like an aerie on the mountainside, which here is so high and steep that one looks down upon the vast expanse of ocean as if from a two- or three-thousand-foot cliff. Downs of rich grassland fill the view to north, south, and east, with great pines clothing every ridge and hollow. The fog seldom reaches to this height; yet its coolness tempers the summer, and the climate forms a perfect combination of the sea, mountain, and forest elements.

The "boys" were away driving cattle across the mountains, but the wife, a pretty Mexican woman, made me welcome, and after a supper of venison with frijoles and tortillas, entertained the hired man and me with a phonograph medley of favorite Spanish airs. It was something of a shock to find that even these farthest recesses of the mountains had not escaped the terrible machine, which I suppose by now is rousing the echoes of Nova Zembla and the Mountains of the Moon. I slept under an apple tree in the orchard, which was festooned throughout with ropes of venison "jerky." During the deer season, venison is as much a staple of these mountaineers as potatoes are all the year to dwellers in town.

A mile or two beyond Gamboa's is the Arroyo Grande, one of the deepest cañons of the range. I had been but little on horseback since we entered this rougher country, wishing to spare Anton as much as possible: a point of necessity, indeed, for the trail was almost always either steep in grade or lay along slopes sharp enough to make the consequences of a stumble something more than annoying. I now led Anton carefully down the stairlike descent, which took us from open grassy slopes, through a region of flowery brush, into a shadowy cañon of redwoods with a lively stream. Here again it was a trial that the total absence of forage forbade camping, for otherwise the place was superlative for the purpose. Half a mile farther on we crossed the north fork of the same stream, where I had to endure a similar tantalization. Then came a long, hard climb out, with alternate blaze of open hillside and slumberous shade of cañon.

These changes are startlingly sudden throughout this region. From steep-walled clefts filled with silent companies of straight-stemmed trees and roofed with a green firmament of foliage, one passes without warning to breezy hillsides of sun-scorched grass or brittle gray sage and buckwheat, where, far below, the greatest of oceans stretches from the line of the cliff, out, and away, to infinitude and China.

The country hereabouts was marked everywhere with an unconscionable tangle of cattle-paths, among which it was quite impossible to keep the trail. I knew that I needed to keep well up on the mountain, but with a mile of steep slant to guess on I was soon hopelessly at fault. Moreover, the slope was cut vertically by rocky, brush-filled gullies which bothered Anton greatly. Several times I had to build or cut a way for him. He was behaving so bravely and sagaciously that when, at one place, after I had spent half an hour in building trail, he pointedly refused to trust himself to it, I thought it best to defer to his instinct and waive the point, though to round the head of the gully meant another hard climb. As it was, he received some cuts about the knees, hocks, and feet, and I looked at him with compunction when, at last, we picked up a more likely trail, and rested for ten minutes to recuperate and repair damages.

Far ahead, and nearly at shore level, I could see a tumbledown mess of corrals and cabins which I knew must mark an abandoned ranch called Dolan's. I had been advised to camp there, on account of there being water and a little pasturage; but when we reached the place it looked so woebegone and generally uninviting that, fagged as we both were, I resolved to push on to some more desirable spot. So on we marched for weary miles, now, fortunately, over a better trail, and at last, rounding the head of another deep cañon, came to Little's Springs, otherwise known as Slate's.

Here I found a comfortable, old-fashioned house where I could put up for the night. In fact, the place makes some claim to rank as a resort, by virtue of its medicinal springs, though no guests were in evidence, nor any token of either expectation or accommodation for them. A quarter of a mile from the house I found a couple of tents pitched on a ledge of rock halfway down the hundred-foot bluff. In them were bathtubs to which hot sulphur water was led from springs that break out all along the cliff. Tents and tubs had been hauled up with windlass and cable from the vessel that brought them down from San Francisco, and then had been lowered over the cliff onto the ledge near the springs. It was an enjoyable experience to bathe thus, as it were, in midair, with gulls screaming all around and breakers roaring fifty feet below.

Fog again enveloped us when we started next morning. I was told that the trail from this place was an official one, being kept up by the county, and I communicated the news to Anton for his consolation. It kept close along the cliff, as I could tell by the sound of the surf and the cries of seabirds far below. It was very interesting to travel thus, as was often the case, in company with unseen comrades, beauties, or dangers. Once I heard a company of land-birds singing away merrily in some bush in the fog below me. It had a charming sound, reminding one of

> ...magic casements opening on the foam
> Of perilous seas in fairy lands forlorn.

I often wished I were some small fraction of a Keats myself, to put the beauty of such little incidents into felicitous phrase.

Now and then a rift in the vapor showed for a moment the dull gray gleam of the combers as they plunged shoreward, or the dark fringe of rocks, forever pushing back the wash of the sea. In the cañons the fog made a strange white gloom, dense but luminous, through which great stems of trees stood up like pillars in some Dantean temple of shades. Sometimes a group of wind-twisted trees showed weirdly through the mist, as if peering up from under their matted thatches of foliage in dread of some portentous stroke. Every cañon had its stream, filling the air with a monotone that would have been ghostly but for the cheerful notes of the ouzels. The presence of that gay little water-sprite is as genial as August sunshine.

About midday the fog broke away, revealing, far up the coast, a prominent headland which I set down as Point Sur. It revealed also my trail, stretching like a pleated ribbon along the mountain, high above the sea, on and on to vanishing point. At the head of one of the cañons I found a snug little place kept by two old bachelors who have carved out a narrow strip of ground on the rooflike slope above the creek. I stopped for a rest and a chat, and gained a little sidelight on the conditions of life along this coast from the three piles of magazines, each reaching from floor to ceiling of their living room, or about two hundred feet, board measure, of compressed literature, which they keep for reading matter in winter, when for weeks together the trails may be impassable. At the mouth of this cañon the creek makes a spectacular drop direct into the ocean, like some Norwegian stream falling into a fjord.

The trees are inhabited by the most charming birds. Our ornithologist stuffed several varieties of sparrows, blue jays, titmice, speckled woodpeckers, and troupiales. Among the birds of prey, we observed the white-headed eagle, the large and small falcon, the goshawk, the sparrow hawk, the black vulture, the large owl, and the raven.

In the ponds and on the seacoast are found the duck, the gray and white pelican with yellow tufts, different species of gulls, cormorants, curlews, ring plovers, small water hens, and herons. Lastly, we killed and stuffed a bee-eater, which ornithologists have supposed to be peculiar to the old continent.

—Jean François de la Pérouse, from *Life in a California Mission* (1786)

In the next large cañon there was a huddle of decayed buildings with the remains of an orchard. As there was fair pasturage I resolved to camp, a special attraction being the fine redwoods that grew along the creek. I had never until then found an opportunity of making camp among these trees, though at one time or another I have hobnobbed with almost all the other members of the California conifers, from tidewater to timberline. I unsaddled at the foot of a genial-looking monster, picketed Anton in knee-high wild oats, and ate my supper under the eyes of a covey of quail that perched on an old rail fence nearby and discussed me in almost human tones. The occasion justified a campfire of the best, and I passed a long evening cheerful with reminiscences of bygone nights among the forests of the greater California Sierra.

The squirrels and jays were aroused at first daylight by the smoke of my breakfast-fire; but when we were ready to start, it seemed to me that I had hardly done due honor to my first redwood camp, so I took off Anton's saddle and smoked a couple more leisurely pipes. Then in peaceful mood we set out. The ocean lay under the usual shroud of fog, but on our high path the sun shone warm and bright, and the morning was gay with birds and butterflies. A rattlesnake that was out for an early breakfast, and crossed the trail in front of us, left his body to the buzzards as a sarcastic commentary on the adage of the bird and the worm. Tracks of deer were numerous about every creek and spring, and once, when we had just crossed the trail of a mountain lion, Anton became so excited that I had no doubt he scented the animal somewhere close at hand.

The redwoods in the cañons were finer than any I had yet seen, some of them quite wonderful in their straight, stately symmetry. The older branches of the largest trees were recurved, and hung for thirty or forty feet close about the stem. In places the sun's rays could hardly pass through the high roof of foliage, and I moved among the gray and purple pillars subdued to "a green thought in a green shade," as someone has put it. Anton's sensations apparently took the same hue. His pasturage the past night had not been over-luxurious, and he neglected no mouthful of verdure that came in his way. I wished I could introduce him to one of those mountain meadows where in former years I had often seen my animals half-smothered in juicy grasses.

Late afternoon found us at Castro's Ranch, a comfortable, old-fashioned place, the terminus of wagon travel at the northern end of the Santa Lucias, as San Simeon is at the southern. The distance between them is about sixty miles in an air-line, but must be two or three times as much in actual traveling distance by the trails. I received a genial welcome from these excellent people, and made up Anton's arrears of hay and grain.

Dogs, cats, and geese made the place lively with companionable sounds, and an orchard of peaches and apples formed an acceptable incident. I was lodged in a tiny, white-curtained room opening on a flowery jungle of garden, and at supper was plied with venison, frijoles, and tortillas, with vegetable adjuncts, to which I had long been a stranger, in notable array.

James D. Houston

James D. Houston (1933–) was born and schooled in the Bay Area. He earned an M.A. from Stanford University in 1962 before being named its Wallace Stegner creative writing fellow for 1967–68, the first of many such honors at colleges throughout the United States. Houston's work, which has received numerous awards, includes the novels Gig, Continental Drift, *and* Love Life, *as well as the non-fiction* Farewell to Manzanar *(cowritten with his wife, Jeanne Wakatsuki Houston) and* Californians: Searching for the Golden State, *containing interviews with residents of every region in the state.*

His home-state's place on the Pacific Rim fascinates Houston. He and his wife traveled to Japan, Hawaii, Bali, and the Ryukyus for In the Ring of Fire: A Pacific Basin Journey. *His experiences of East and West are integrated during his visit to a Zen monastery in California.* ✍

A Coast Range Sutra

There is a place not far from here where the final edge of America's wilderness meets Asia. Down in the deepest canyon in the wild country behind Big Sur, where boar are hunted and lions still roam, there is a zendo, a meditation hall, and a wooden gong hanging from a rope. When you hear the mallet ringing wood on wood in the predawn air, you could swear you're somewhere in the mountains of Japan.

Once or twice a year we go down there, my wife and I. For each of us the trip into the Santa Lucias is a little pilgrimage to a serene and protected place that is also an emblematic place.

Her background happens to be Japanese. Tubs of hot spring water always revive connections to her early years growing up near Inglewood, where her father farmed row crops on land now covered by the runways of L.A. International. They had an outdoor tub, a furo, heated from below by a wood-fueled fire. At the end of the day her family would come in off the fields and gather there to sit and sweat and talk and soak away the aches and pains.

For me these are trips into the kind of terrain my father and I used to hike through together. He was a man from east Texas who kept rifles and loved to hunt, though I later realized that the chance to get out of San Francisco and wander a while in open country was at least as important for him as bringing down a deer to carry home. I never took to the killing. I'm not sure why. Maybe it was growing up a city kid. Maybe if we had truly needed the meat it would have been a different story. But thanks to him I discovered the many pleasures of the long Coast Range, the boot crunch of soil under still madrones, the curl of rusty bark under arid, pale blue sky.

Somehow all of these things inhabit the atmosphere of Tassajara Canyon. Wild boar. Mountain lion. Temple gong. Jay squawk. Creek tumble. Black robe. Morning sutra. Steam curl in the morning fog. Madrone and oak and manzanita. Sitting buddha. Logging road....

We follow the Carmel River inland, with tawny ridges humping above condo clusters and white-railed corrals. The valley narrows to a thickly wooded corridor, and then the semirural feel gives way to dry and rolling hills. Twenty miles in we take a winding road south to the end of the pavement, where we park our car and catch the mountain shuttle van, a workhorse Ford with nine seats and four-wheel drive and many gears. They call it "The Tassajara Stage," harking back to the days a hundred years ago when a horse and wagon traveled three times a week over this same tortuous fourteen-mile track.

Heading farther south, we climb past the scars of old fires, with blackened limbs still poking through the newer growth, and here and there a tree trunk split by lightning. The dust billows out behind, while the ridges roll away in both directions, east toward the Salinas Valley, west toward the unseen ocean, and no habitat visible now, just the gorges, the ribs of granite, and slopes furred with live oak, manzanita, pine.

In low gear for the zigzag descent we drop from five thousand feet, honking on the blind curves, and arrive at last at a long dusty clearing lined with dusty cars and pickups, and pull into the canyon/oasis where it's already hot, a dry desert heat, though the canyon is green and the creek gushes through it. The heat itself slows you down, says take your time, take your time.

The cabin is simple, old redwood siding, with a double mattress on the floor, two wooden chairs, a small chest of drawers, kerosene lamps, no electricity, screens for windows, or translucent plastic tarp, so the sound of the creek, the dripping rush of it, is always there, indoors and out, all day and night, contained and amplified within the canyon's narrow, rocky walls.

Within two miles of the Pacific rounding
this long bay, sheening the light for miles
inland, floating its fog through redwood rifts and over
strawberry and artichoke fields, its bottomless mind
returning always to the same rocks, the same cliffs, with
ever-changing words, always the same language
—this is where I live now. If you had known me
once, you'd still know me now though in a different
light and life. This is no place you ever knew me.
But it would not surprise you
to find me here, walking in fog, the sweep of the great ocean
eluding me, even the curve of the bay, because as always
I fix on the land. I am stuck to earth. What I love here
is old ranches, leaning seaward, lowroofed spreads between rocks
small canyons running through pitched hillsides
live oaks twisted on steepness, the eucalyptus avenue leading
to the wrecked homestead, the fogwreathed heavy-chested cattle
on their blond hills. I drive inland over roads
closed in wet weather, past shacks hunched in the canyons
roads that crawl down into darkness and wind into light
where trucks have crashed and riders of horses tangled
to death with lowstruck boughs. These are not the roads
you knew me by. But the woman driving, walking, watching
for life and death, is the same.
        —Adrienne Rich, from *An Atlas of the Difficult World: Poems 1988–1991*

We change into the robes we picked up on our trip to Japan. Yukata for me. Kimono for Jeanne. Geometrical patterns of blue on white, diagonals and diamonds, sashes at the waist. Put the shoes away, and step into slippers, and shuffle along the swept path toward the bathhouse, passing other cottages like the one we've rented, survivors from the days when this was a hunting and fishing retreat. Now yellow green bamboo rises next to some of the walls. Reed fencing lines the path, and retaining walls of fitted stone. Small settings of creek-rolled stones have been arranged next to the steps of the cottages, giving each entryway the look of a little Japanese garden. Slippers and getas have been left outside the doors.

Past the meditation hall, past the cookhouse, an arching bridge crosses over the creek. An American trout stream. An Asian footbridge, made of carefully crafted, curving wood. At the far side a small altar is waiting, with incense sticks, a new blossom, a figure of the Buddha. We pause and bow, which is a way of honoring that place in each of us where the universe resides, the still center that links us all. This figure has found its way to the wilderness creekside from India, by way of China, Japan, San Francisco— serene man sitting with his feet in his lap and his hands folded. Not such a bad idea, that kind of serenity. Not such a bad ideal. If you can get to it. Or close to it. If only every once in a while.

The next step is down into the heat and steam piped up from the mineral springs that have bubbled here for longer than anyone can remember, and said to be the richest springs in the United States. In these waters thirty-two minerals have been identified, among them sulfur, sodium, calcium, magnesium, potassium, iron. Drop the robe. Slide into the wide tub lined with tile. This time of day I have the men's side to myself. Beyond the wall I can hear women talking. Like the creek sound, their voices punctuate the stillness. Don't move too much. Moving makes currents, and the scalding currents hurt. Let the surface turn to glass. Smell rocks in the water, a faint sulfur whiff. Heat to the neck. To the chin. As long as I can stand it. Then down a rocky path to the little reservoir of cold mountain water three feet deep, backed beyond the low stone dam. Plunge in and feel the fingerlings poking at my feet and legs, tiny fishlets come to investigate, darting in the cold, cold creek.

Splash out, and head for the tubs again, for more heat.

More cold.

More heat.

More cold.

Dry off. Slow down. At the altar, we bow again to the Buddha, and the little hand-lettered sign that sums it up:

> With all beings
> I wash body and mind
> Free of dust
> Pure and shining
> Within and without.

Walk back along the path, under a canopy of limbs and leaves, the granite walls rising, catching light.

Below the cabin, next to a creekside sycamore, someone has placed a battered chair, a weatherworn wooden chair that looks older than the cabins, and that is the place to sit awhile and listen. No phones down here. No radio. No TV. No boom box from the guy in the next lane or from a garage across the way. No cars inside the compound. No ads. No neon. No e-mail or Internet or fax for urgent messages. Just this dry heat under oaks and sycamores, the steady tumble of the creek, the squawk of jays coming to see who's here and check for random scraps of food, with a breeze along the water from time to time to riffle leaves that send sparks of sunlight through the canyon shade. When the alder leaves quiver, a softer light splashes upward, mountain strobe light rippled by the creek god's hidden hand.

Waking early I hear the sound of water against the far wall of our cabin, like bacon sizzling on a grill. Jeanne will sleep until the chill is off the air and then head straight for the baths, to get in a soak before breakfast. I have a morning pilgrimage in mind, up to the spot where they've erected a memorial to the man who first imagined this old-time mountain resort could be transformed into a Zen retreat and monastery.

His name was Shunryu Suzuki Roshi. Born in Japan in 1905, he came to the United States at the age of fifty-three. They say he was a small and very private fellow, both humble and forceful, instructing more by example than by words. He'd been trained in the Soto Zen tradition, and going to America was, for many years, his dream. When he was invited to become the priest at a San Francisco Buddhist temple, in 1958, he readily accepted. Before long he had founded the San Francisco Zen Center which, in 1967, acquired this acreage in Tassajara Canyon. It was the first Zen monastery to be established anywhere in the world outside Asia.

Four years later Suzuki Roshi passed away, having spent the final months of his life right here, gardening, lecturing, preparing himself and his followers for his death. In the style and feel of what this place has become, in the gardens, in the very joints of the carpentry, his example and his spirit live on.

Yesterday, in the office, I was checking through the shelf of books and pamphlets they keep for browsers, and I heard someone behind the counter say that after his cremation, his ashes had been divided, with some buried here and some buried in Japan. Though I've been to the canyon a dozen times, I'd never heard this mentioned. It took me by surprise, caused my forearm hairs to prickle.

"Dividing the ashes," I said, "that's quite a statement."

"He felt such strong ties to both places," this woman replied. She wore a collarless shirt, round glasses, brown hair cropped close.

"Do you know where in Japan?"

"Where he came from, I think. But I'm not sure about the details. You'd have to ask someone who's been around here longer than I have."

At this early hour the jays are quiet. Sutras spill from the zendo in low-voiced Japanese. When the voices fade behind me, there is only the creek. From the road I take a narrow footpath that begins a steady climb through live oak and bay and sycamore. A couple of switchbacks, another climb, then I pass below an overhang into a small clearing of raked gravel, under an umbrella of oak limbs, the kind of space that requires you to stop and pay attention. Someone has already been up here this morning. The tine marks look fresh. The ground itself says walk with care.

A low retaining wall of fitted stones is built against the farther embankment. In front of it stands a chunk of granite about four feet high, roughly triangular, with a flat side facing out. The stone is gray with a greenish cast. From the top, a coating of white, like thick paint or white lava, seems ready to spill. A streak of white cuts across the flat face of the stone like a vein just under the skin, or a lightning streak. Where did it come from? I wonder. There is movement in this stone, an uncarved, unaltered piece of natural sculpture that is stationary and fixed, yet somehow catches and conveys the flow and energy of life.

Around it, smaller stones make an altar, where pale green mandalas of lichen cling. On the flat place in front of these stones, a metal vase holds a bamboo stem, some wildflowers, and next to it an incense bowl.

This slightly sculpted place has the feel of the garden we saw in Japan, behind the Zen temple at Dazaifu, outside Fukuoka, though it is more surprising, somehow more remarkable, since this little space has been cleared at the very edge of raw wilderness. Here and there, young trees rise through the gravel, so that the space is open yet not empty of vegetation. With its canopy of limbs it is in fact just one step away from the rugged terrain you see beyond the trees, the steep ridges higher up with their rocky outcroppings, the empty arroyos veering off through cliffs of scrub oak and manzanita.

The centerpiece, the quietly majestic hunk of living stone, is *of* that terrain, still connected to it, though set apart now, singled out, to honor the pioneering roshi. This shrine also honors and recognizes all that surrounds it here, the singularity of every other stone, each leaf, each life, each day, each bird trill in the morning air, each moment in the midst of the cosmic pond that has no beginning and no end.

THE CENTRAL VALLEY

The Great Central Valley, which stretches almost four hundred and fifty miles through California's interior, is formed by the conjunction of two large valleys, the Sacramento in the north and the San Joaquin in the south. Draining these depressions are major rivers that join to form the Sacramento Delta, a vast watershed of islands and freshwater channels flowing into the saltier waters of Suisun Bay in the San Francisco Bay estuary. This huge valley, which can be as much as seventy-five miles wide, includes grassland, riparian forests, tule marshes, chaparral, and acres and acres of farmland—nut and fruit orchards, vineyards, rice paddies, vegetable and cotton fields. The extensive cultivation makes it almost impossible to imagine the flower-strewn valley, "little trampled or plowed," that greeted John Muir over a hundred and twenty years ago.

Before John Muir ever set foot in the Central Valley, it was home to many groups of Native Americans, who favored areas near reliable sources of water and away from extremes of valley heat (temperatures can hover above 100° for days on end). Among the Central Valley natives were the Wintu of the Coast Ranges and the western Sacramento Valley, the Maidu of the eastern Sacramento Valley, and the Miwok and the Yokuts of the San Joaquin. The valley's many habitats yielded abundant food— besides the staple acorns, the chaparral regions provided deer; the grasslands, antelope; and the rivers, salmon and other fish—even though much of the region (especially the southern end) is arid. Despite their dry climate, low-lying regions are subject to flooding in wet years, when there is heavy runoff from the Sierra snowpack, a natural hazard that the native people always respected. A Maidu legend tells of a Sacramento Valley flood that "covered the land so deep that none could measure. Many fled and many more were drowned. Frogs and salmon chased the Indians beneath the water and ate them. Only two Indians escaped to the foothills." The Great Man blessed these two, the ancestors of a mighty nation whose chief—after nine sleeps on a hill above the flooded valley—asked the Great Man to let the water flow away from the valley of his ancestors. According to the legend, "The Great Man opened the side of the mountain, and all the floodwater flowed away into the big water." The gap that the Great Man created saved the valley for the native people, but it also gave later newcomers access to the interior of Alta California.

In 1772 Juan Crespí glimpsed the Sacramento Delta and the Central Valley from a vantage point near Mount Diablo. He reported that "the land opened into a great plain as level as the palm of the hand, the quarters from northwest to southeast, all level land as far as the eye could reach." The Spanish sent a few exploratory parties to the Central Valley, but never had sufficient numbers to establish missions or permanent settlements there. After independence, the Mexican government started awarding land grants in the Sacramento Valley, many to U.S. citizens. Visits to the interior increased as did reports on its character. Commodore Charles Wilkes, who led an important exploratory and scientific expedition, noted such an abundance of game, especially elk, in the Sacramento Valley that it "almost exceeds belief." Others, including trapper Jedediah Smith and emigrant John Bidwell, were struck by the numbers of grizzly bears, whose strength and ferocity were not proof against human predation.

New U.S. settlers focused on running cattle to supply meat for miners joining the gold rush. Agriculture seemed out of the question in this hot dry terrain. William H. Brewer reported whirlwinds of dust in his survey of early California. The end of the gold rush and the effects of overgrazing led settlers to try raising grain. Farming started in the Sacramento Valley, which had slightly heavier rainfall and a river to carry the crop to market. Construction of the Southern Pacific Valley Line, begun in 1871, allowed the expansion of agriculture north and south, providing a major theme of Great Valley writing.

At the turn of the century, novelist Frank Norris was obsessed with his "Epic of the Wheat," describing the plowing of the San Joaquin Valley as an assault on the earth—beautiful, moving, and brutal. Wilma Elizabeth McDaniel described farmworkers in California's heartland in poems that rival *The Grapes of Wrath* as literary chronicles of the Okie experience. Gary Soto, a Mexican-American, responded to the extremes of the landscape while working the San Joaquin fields. Today, Norris's vision of a phalanx of horse-drawn plows has been replaced by the startling specter of reaping machines in Sherley Anne Williams's poetry.

The railroad changed the valley, fostering the growth of the farms and cities strung along its tracks, with townships sometimes named for Southern Pacific executives. But the valley's landscape was even more drastically affected by the state's water control projects. The California Aqueduct cuts a long concrete swath south from the Sacramento Delta to Los Angeles, with reservoirs storing water in the foothills. The entire system helps to keep valley crops wet and ancient drainage basins—notably Lake Tulare in the southern San Joaquin Valley—mostly dry. Such large-scale technology may have given Californians some control over their environment, but it has its limit, as William Saroyan demonstrates when his uncle tries to farm on land "away over to hell and gone," and as Gerald Haslam sees, when an ancient lake persists in this archmodern landscape.

Throughout most of the Great Central Valley, air conditioners do tame the summer heat; control projects do manage—though not entirely defeat—seasonal flooding; and farms and ranches do thrive upon irrigation and mechanization. But so far, as many of its writers have testified, nothing has been invented—save, perhaps, a comfortable wool sweater with a shawl collar—that can loosen the grip of the clammy, bone-chilling fog that often sinks into the Valley in winter.

Tule fog—named for the bulrushes that grow in low-lying marshy areas—forms when the surrounding mountains trap cold air, creating an inversion layer. In early winter, when this dense, ground-hugging fog may not burn off for days, "the heart will not quicken," writes Selma-born poet William Everson. This Depression-era sentiment endures in more recent works by valley residents, in other writers who have felt firsthand the affective grip of the tule fog. Among them is essayist David Mas Masumoto, who imagines his family farmhouse "cutting through the gray mist like a lost ship"—an oppressive image, recalling the Maidu legend of the valley flood, human beings powerless before an enveloping natural force. But there is always spring, when wild and orchard flowers again bring bursts of color to California's vast interior basin.

William H. Brewer

When Surveyor William H. Brewer returned to the San Joaquin Valley after a two-year absence, he found it devastated by drought. (For more on William Brewer, see page 240). 🖎

from Up and Down California

Under a tree, Tulare Plain. Sunday, June 5 [1864] — Monday, May 30, we came on to San Luis de Gonzaga Ranch, at the eastern entrance of the pass. Our road lay over the mountains. They are perfectly dry and barren, no grass—here and there a poor gaunt cow is seen, but what she gets to eat is very mysterious.

As we cross the summit the Sierra Nevada should be in view, with its sharp outline and cool snows; but not so—we look out on the dry plain, which becomes more indistinct and finally fades away into the hazy air, shutting out like a veil all that lies beyond. The wind blows heavily over the pass, and we descend to the San Luis Ranch. The wind is so high that we can build no fire, so we cook in the dirty kitchen. Dust fills the air—often we cannot see fifty yards in any direction—it covers everything. We cook our dinner, but before it can be eaten we cannot tell its color because of the dirt that settles on it. Our food is gritty between our teeth, and as we drink out our cups of tea we find a deposit of fine sand in the bottom. Dirt, dirt, dirt—eyes full, face dirty, whole person feeling dirty and gritty.

All around the house it looks desolate. Where there were green pastures when we camped here two years ago, now all is dry, dusty, bare ground. Three hundred cattle have died by the miserable water hole back of the house, where we get water to drink, and their stench pollutes the air.

This ranch contains eleven square leagues, or over seventy-six square miles. In its better days it had ten thousand head of cattle, besides the horses needed to manage them. Later it became a sheep ranch, and two years ago, when we camped here, it fed sixteen thousand sheep besides some few thousand cattle. Now, owing to the drought, there is no feed for cattle, and not over one thousand sheep, if that, can be kept through the summer. The last of the cattle, about one thousand head, were lately sold for $1,500, or only $1.50 each! Such is the effect of the drought on one ranch.

We spent a miserable night there, the wind and dust almost preventing sleep, and paid $14 in gold for the hay that our seven animals ate.

May 31 we came on to Lone Willow, a stage station out on the plain, where there has been a sheep ranch until the present year. The ride was over the plain, which is utterly bare of herbage. No green thing greets the eye, and clouds of dust fill the air. Here and there are carcasses of cattle, but we see few living ones—not twenty during the day, where nearly as many thousands could have been seen two years ago. There is a sinkhole of alkaline water, by which stands the "lone willow," the only tree for many a weary mile. Our camp here is as dirty, dusty, and miserable as the last. There is a well that supplies water for drinking that is poorer than any you ever tasted, yet quite good for the region.

June 1 we came on to Firebaugh's Ferry, on the San Joaquin, twenty-five miles. Portions of this day's ride, for miles together, not a vestige of herbage of any kind covered the ground; in other places there was a limited growth of wire grass or alkali grass, but not enough to make it green. Yet cattle live here—we passed numbers during the day, and countless carcasses of dead animals. We camped at Firebaugh's, where we got hay for our animals and took a grateful bath in the cold San Joaquin. The bad water, dust, alkali, and our change of diet begin to tell on the boys, but all are cheerful.

June 2, to Fresno City. For the first ten miles the ground was entirely bare, but then we came on green plains, green with fine rushes, called wire grass, and some alkali grass. The ground is wetter and cattle can live on the rushes and grass. We now came on thousands of them that have retreated to this feed and have gnawed it almost into the earth.

The air is very clear this day—on the one side the Coast Range loomed up, barren and desolate, its scorched sides furrowed into canyons, every one of which was marvelously distinct; on the other side the distant sierra, its cool snows glistening in the sun and mocking us on our scorching trail. We camped by a slough of stinking, alkaline water, which had the color of weak coffee. It smelled bad and tasted worse, and our poor animals drank it protesting. We drank well water which looked better and tasted better, but I think it smelled worse. But in this dry, hot, and dusty air we must drink, and drink much and often.

At Fresno City we got barley but no hay. I cannot conceive of a much worse place to live, unless it be the next place where we stopped; yet here a *city* was laid out in early speculative times, streets and public squares figure on paper and on the map, imaginary bridges cross the stinking sloughs, and pure water gushes from artesian wells that have never been sunk.

June 3 we came on to Elkhorn Station, an old overland station. We came southeast across the plain. The day was hot, as usual, but not so clear. The mountains were invisible through the dusty air; the perfectly level plain stretched away on every side to the horizon, and seemed as boundless and as level as the ocean. It is, in fact, sixty miles wide at this place, and neither tree, nor bush, nor house breaks the monotony. Thus we slowly plodded our weary way over it, league after league, day after day. During the entire day we saw beyond us, behind us, sometimes all around, the deceitful mirage. I never cease to wonder at this phenomenon, although it has been so long a familiar thing. It looks so like water, its surface gently rippled by the wind, clear and sparkling, trees and mountains as vividly reflected in it as in genuine lakes! But it always vanishes as you approach it—heated air, and not cool water, we find in its place.

When we neared the San Joaquin River, we saw about twenty elk. We had approached quite close to them, but had not seen them at once, and they were hurrying away through a low swale, or dry slough, which paralleled the river. I will always remember how quickly they disappeared and how clever they were at making use of the cover. There were a few oak trees near, and they kept these between us and themselves. They lowered their heads with their horns against their necks and shoulders and sneaked along as rapidly as a horse could run.

We also saw some tracks along the river that my daddy said were made by bear. They must have been grizzlies, as I have found since that they were the only bear along the San Joaquin.

The most amusing sight I remember on the plains before we reached the San Joaquin River was a large flock of sandhill cranes. We passed within forty yards of some of them and they hardly noticed us. Quite a large group of them were holding a sort of powwow. They would all jabber a while and then they would do a sort of fandango. We laughed at them for a long while, they were so sober and earnest about it

—Thomas Jefferson Mayfield, from *Indian Summer: Traditional Life Among the Choinumne Indians of California's San Joaquin Valley* (1928)

During these days whirlwinds stalked over the plain. The high winds I spoke of as occurring near Pacheco's Pass ceased. Fitful, often hot puffs blew first this way and then that, giving rise to little whirlwinds that looked like waterspouts at sea, moving for a time over the plain, then breaking and vanishing. They were continually about us during the heat of the day. Sometimes they were slender columns of dust but a few feet in diameter and several hundred feet high; at others the columns were larger. Sometimes they were like cones with bases upward; then again they would break and throw out branches which fell down on all sides with beautiful effect—all the time moving over the plain, some slowly, some swiftly. It is not uncommon to see a dozen of these at once, and I have counted twenty-seven at one time.

We camped at Elkhorn Station, nearly in the center of the plain. There is some feed here, and a well supplies the cattle with water, poor though it is. Again we got barley, but no hay.

Here a calamity befell us. I was awakened at about midnight by our mule, Jim. He was sick and in a terrible agony. Poor feed, change of diet, bad water, alkali, dust, heat—all had probably combined to produce the result. We watched with him all night, bled him, gave him such remedies as we thought best under the circumstances, but at six o'clock in the morning he died. He was our most valuable animal, a most excellent mule, worth $150 or $200. He had been a faithful beast, was very sagacious and very true, and had been with us since we started at Los Angeles, nearly four years ago. I did not think that I could feel so sad over the death of any animal as I did over that faithful old mule, who has been our companion for so long a time and under such varied circumstances. He died near the house. I hired a man to drag him away. We left him out on the plain to the vultures and coyotes, both of which species are fat this year, for the starving cattle have been their harvest. Luckily a wagon from this place was going into Visalia and I sent in his saddle and pack.

June 4, yesterday, we came on here to Kings River. Here we struck good water again, good hay for our animals, and fine oak trees for shade. And what a relief! We are again in good spirits. Last night, again, we had a campfire, and the boys sang songs.

John Muir

John Muir's love of nature was not restricted to the mountains. He was almost equally ravished by his first sight of the florious Central Valley, which he remembers here, in "The Bee-Pastures." (For more on John Muir, see page 155). ✌︎

from The Mountains of California

When California was wild, it was one sweet bee-garden throughout its entire length, north and south, and all the way across from the snowy Sierra to the ocean.

Wherever a bee might fly within the bounds of this virgin wilderness—through the redwood forests, along the banks of the rivers, along the bluffs and headlands fronting the sea, over valley and plain, park and grove, and deep, leafy glen, or far up the piny slopes of the mountains—throughout every belt and section of climate up to the timberline, bee-flowers bloomed in lavish abundance. Here they grew more or less apart in special sheets and patches of no great size, there in broad, flowing folds hundreds of miles in length—zones of polleny forests, zones of flowery chaparral, stream-tangles of rubus and wild rose, sheets of gold compositae, beds of violets, beds of mint, beds of bryanthus and clover, and so on, certain species blooming somewhere all the year round.

But of late years plows and sheep have made sad havoc in these glorious pastures, destroying tens of thousands of the flowery acres like a fire, and banishing many species of the best honey-plants to rocky cliffs and fence-corners, while, on the other hand, cultivation thus far has given no adequate compensation, at least in kind; only acres of alfalfa for miles of the richest wild pasture, ornamental roses and honeysuckles around cottage doors for cascades of wild roses in the dells, and small, square orchards and orange groves for broad mountain-belts of chaparral.

The Great Central Plain of California, during the months of March, April, and May, was one smooth, continuous bed of honey-bloom, so marvelously rich that, in walking from one end of it to the other, a distance of more than four hundred miles, your foot would press about a hundred flowers at every step. Mints, gilias, nemophilas, castilleias, and innumerable compositae were so crowded together that, had ninety-nine percent of them been taken away, the plain would still have seemed to any but Californians extravagantly flowery. The radiant, honeyful corollas, touching and overlapping, and rising above one another, glowed in the living light like a sunset sky—one sheet of purple and gold, with the bright Sacramento pouring through the midst of it from the north, the San Joaquin from the south, and their many tributaries sweeping in at right angles from the mountains, dividing the plain into sections fringed with trees.

Along the rivers there is a strip of bottom-land, countersunk beneath the general level, and wider toward the foothills, where magnificent oaks, from three to eight feet in diameter, cast grateful masses of shade over the open, prairielike levels. And close along the water's edge there was a fine jungle of tropical luxuriance, composed of wild-rose and bramble bushes and a great variety of climbing vines, wreathing and interlacing the branches and trunks of willows and alders, and swinging across from summit to summit in heavy festoons. Here the wild bees reveled in fresh bloom long after the flowers of the dried plain had withered and gone to seed. And in midsummer, when the "blackberries" were ripe, the Indians came from the mountains to feast—men, women, and babies in long, noisy trains, often joined by the farmers of the neighborhood, who gathered this wild fruit with commendable appreciation of its superior flavor, while their home orchards were full of ripe peaches, apricots, nectarines, and figs, and their vineyards were laden with grapes. But, though these luxuriant, shaggy riverbeds were thus distinct from the smooth, treeless plain, they made no heavy dividing lines in general views. The whole appeared as one continuous sheet of bloom bounded only by the mountains.

When I first saw this central garden, the most extensive and regular of all the bee-pastures of the state, it seemed all one sheet of plant gold, hazy and vanishing in the distance, distinct as a new map along the foothills at my feet.

Descending the eastern slopes of the Coast Range through beds of gilias and lupins, and around many a breezy hillock and bush-crowned headland, I at length waded out into the midst of it. All the ground was covered, not with grass and green leaves, but with radiant corollas, about ankle-deep next the foothills, knee-deep or more five or six miles out. Here were bahia, madia, madaria, burrielia, chrysopsis, corethrogyne, grindelia, etc., growing in close social congregations of various shades of yellow, blending finely with the purples of clarkia, orthocarpus, and oenothera, whose delicate petals were drinking the vital sunbeams without giving back any sparkling glow.

Because so long a period of extreme drought succeeds the rainy season, most of the vegetation is composed of annuals, which spring up simultaneously, and bloom together at about the same height above the ground, the general surface being but slightly ruffled by the taller phacelias, penstemons, and groups of *Salvia carduacea,* the king of the mints.

Sauntering in any direction, hundreds of these happy sun-plants brushed against my feet at every step, and closed over them as if I were wading in liquid gold. The air was sweet with fragrance, the larks sang their blessed songs, rising on the wing as I advanced, then sinking out of sight in the polleny sod, while myriads of wild bees stirred the lower air with their monotonous hum—monotonous, yet forever fresh and sweet as everyday sunshine. Hares and spermophiles showed themselves in considerable numbers in shallow places, and small bands of antelopes were almost constantly in sight, gazing curiously from some slight elevation, and then bounding swiftly away with unrivaled grace of motion. Yet I could discover no crushed flowers to mark their track, nor, indeed, any destructive action of any wild foot or tooth whatever.

The great yellow days circled by uncounted, while I drifted toward the north, observing the countless forms of life thronging about me, lying down almost anywhere on the approach of night. And what florious botanical beds I had! Oftentimes on awaking I would find several new species leaning over me and looking me full in the face, so that my studies would begin before rising.

About the first of May I turned eastward, crossing the San Joaquin River between the mouths of the Tuolumne and Merced, and by the time I had reached the Sierra foothills most of the vegetation had gone to seed and become as dry as hay.

All the seasons of the great plain are warm or temperate, and bee-flowers are never wholly wanting; but the grand springtime—the annual resurrection—is governed by the rains, which usually set in about the middle of November or the beginning of December. Then the seeds, that for six months have lain on the ground dry and fresh as if they had been gathered into barns, at once unfold their treasured life. The general brown and purple of the ground, and the dead vegetation of the preceding year, give place to the green of mosses and liverworts and myriads of young leaves. Then one species after another comes into flower, gradually overspreading the green with yellow and purple, which lasts until May.

The "rainy season" is by no means a gloomy, soggy period of constant cloudiness and rain. Perhaps nowhere else in North America, perhaps in the world, are the months of December, January, February, and March so full of bland, plant-building sunshine. Referring to my notes of the winter and spring of 1868–69, every day of which I spent out-of-doors, on that section of the plain lying between the Tuolumne and Merced rivers, I find that the first rain of the season fell on December eighteenth. January had only six rainy days—that is, days on which rain fell; February three, March five, April three, and May three, completing the so-called rainy season, which was about an average one. The ordinary rainstorm of this region is seldom very cold or violent. The winds, which in settled weather come from the northwest, veer round into the opposite direction, the sky fills gradually and evenly with one general cloud, from which the rain falls steadily, often for days in succession, at a temperature of about 45 or 50 degrees.

More than seventy-five percent of all the rain of this season came from the northwest, down the coast over southeastern Alaska, British Columbia, Washington, and Oregon, though the local winds of these circular storms blow from the southeast. One magnificent local storm from the northwest fell on March twenty-first. A massive, round-browed cloud came swelling and thundering over the flowery plain in most imposing majesty, its bossy front burning white and purple in the full blaze of the sun, while warm rain poured from its ample fountains like a cataract, beating down flowers and bees, and flooding the dry watercourses as suddenly as those of Nevada are flooded by the so-called "cloudbursts." But in less than half an hour not a trace of the heavy, mountainlike cloud-structure was left in the sky, and the bees were on the wing, as if nothing more gratefully refreshing could have been sent them.

By the end of January four species of plants were in flower, and five or six mosses had already adjusted their hoods and were in the prime of life; but the flowers were not sufficiently numerous as yet to affect greatly the general green of the young leaves. Violets made their appearance in the first week of February, and toward the end of this month the warmer portions of the plain were already golden with myriads of the flowers of rayed compositae.

This was the full springtime. The sunshine grew warmer and richer, new plants bloomed every day; the air became more tuneful with humming wings, and sweeter with the fragrance of the opening flowers. Ants and

U.S. 99 in fact passes through the richest and most intensely cultivated agricultural region in the world, a giant outdoor hothouse with a billion-dollar crop. It is when you remember the valley's wealth that the monochromatic flatness of its towns takes on a curious meaning, suggests a habit of mind some would consider perverse. There is something in the valley mind that reflects a real indifference to the stranger in his air-conditioned car, a failure to perceive even his presence, let alone his thoughts or wants. An implacable insularity is the seal of these towns. I once met a woman in Dallas, a most charming and attractive woman accustomed to the hospitality and social hypersensitivity of Texas, who told me that during the four war years her husband had been stationed in Modesto, she had never once been invited inside anyone's house. No one in Sacramento would find this story remarkable ("She probably had no *re*latives there," said someone to whom I told it), for the valley towns understand one another, share a peculiar spirit. They think alike and they look alike. *I* can tell Modesto from Merced, but I have visited there, gone to dances there; besides, there is over the main street of Modesto an arched sign which reads:

Water—Wealth

Contentment—Health

There is no such sign in Merced.

—Joan Didion, from *Slouching Towards Bethlehem* (1961)

ground squirrels were getting ready for their summer work, rubbing their benumbed limbs, and sunning themselves on the husk-piles before their doors, and spiders were busy mending their old webs, or weaving new ones.

In March, the vegetation was more than doubled in depth and color; claytonia, calandrinia, a large white gilia, and two nemophilas were in bloom, together with a host of yellow compositae, tall enough now to bend in the wind and show wavering ripples of shade.

In April, plant life, as a whole, reached its greatest height, and the plain, over all its varied surface, was mantled with a close, furred plush of purple and golden corollas. By the end of this month, most of the species had ripened their seeds, but undecayed, still seemed to be in bloom from the numerous corollalike involucres and whorls of chaffy scales of the compositae. In May, the bees found in flower only a few deep-set liliaceous plants and eriogonums.

June, July, August, and September is the season of rest and sleep—a winter of dry heat—followed in October by a second outburst of bloom at the very driest time of the year. Then, after the shrunken mass of leaves and stalks of the dead vegetation crinkle and turn to dust beneath the foot, as if it has been baked in an oven, *Hemizonia virgata,* a slender, unobtrusive little plant, from six inches to three feet high, suddenly makes its appearance in patches miles in extent, like a resurrection of the bloom of April. I have counted upward of three thousand flowers, five-eighths of an inch in diameter, on a single plant. Both its leaves and stems are so slender as to be nearly invisible, at a distance of a few yards, amid so showy a multitude of flowers. The ray and disk flowers are both yellow, the stamens purple, and the texture of the rays is rich and velvety, like the petals of garden pansies. The prevailing wind turns all the heads round to the southeast, so that in facing northwestward we have the flowers looking us in the face. In my estimation, this little plant, the last born of the brilliant host of compositae that glorify the plain, is the most interesting of all. It remains in flower until November, uniting with two or three species of wiry eriogonums, which continue the floral chain around December to the spring flowers of January. Thus, although the main bloom and honey season is only about three months long, the floral circle, however thin around some of the hot, rainless months, is never completely broken.

How long the various species of wild bees have lived in this honey-garden, nobody knows; probably ever since the main body of the present flora gained possession of the land, toward the close of the glacial period. The first brown honeybees brought to California are said to have arrived in San Francisco in March 1853. A beekeeper by the name of Shelton purchased a lot, consisting of twelve swarms, from someone at Aspinwall, who had brought them from New York. When landed at San Francisco, all the hives contained live bees, but they finally dwindled to one hive, which was taken to San José. The little immigrants flourished and multiplied in the bountiful pastures of the Santa Clara Valley, sending off three swarms the first season. The owner was killed shortly afterward, and in settling up his estate, two of the swarms were sold at auction for $105 and $110 respectively. Other importations were made, from time to time, by way of the isthmus and though great pains were taken to insure success, about one-half usually died on the way. Four swarms were brought safely across the plains in 1859, the hives being placed in the rear end of a wagon, which was stopped in the afternoon to allow the bees to fly and feed in the floweriest places that were within reach until dark, when the hives were closed.

In 1855, two years after the time of the first arrivals from New York, a single swarm was brought over from San José, and let fly in the Great Central Plain. Bee-culture, however, has never gained much attention here, notwithstanding the extraordinary abundance of honey-bloom, and the high price of honey during the early years. A few hives are found here and there among settlers who chanced to have learned something about the business before coming to the state. But sheep, cattle, grain, and fruit raising are the chief industries, as they require less skill and care, while the profits thus far have been greater. In 1856 honey sold here at from one and a half to two dollars per pound. Twelve years later the price had fallen to twelve and a half cents. In 1868 I sat down to dinner with a band of ravenous sheep-shearers at a ranch on the San Joaquin, where fifteen or twenty hives were kept, and our host advised us not to spare the large pan of honey he had placed on the table, as it was the cheapest article he had to offer. In all my walks, however, I have never come upon a regular bee-ranch in the Central Valley like those so common and so skilfully managed in the southern counties of the state. The few pounds of honey and wax produced are consumed at home, and are scarcely taken into account among the coarser products of the farm. The swarms that escape from their careless owners have a weary, perplexing time of it in seeking suitable homes. Most of them make their way to the foothills of the mountains, or to the trees that line the banks of the rivers, where some hollow log or trunk may be found. A friend of mine, while out hunting on the San Joaquin, came upon an old coon trap, hidden among some tall grass, near the edge of the river, upon which he sat down to rest. Shortly afterward his attention was attracted to a crowd of angry bees that were flying excitedly about his head, when he discovered that he was sitting upon their hive, which was found to contain more than two hundred pounds of honey. Out in the broad, swampy delta of the Sacramento and San Joaquin rivers, the little wanderers have been known to build their combs in a bunch of rushes, or stiff, wiry grass, only slightly protected from the weather, and in danger every spring of being carried away by floods. They have the advantage, however, of a vast extent of fresh pasture, accessible only to themselves.

The present condition of the Grand Central Garden is very different from that we have sketched. About twenty years ago, when the gold placers had been pretty thoroughly exhausted, the attention of fortune-seekers—not home-seekers—was, in great part, turned away from the mines to the fertile plains, and many began experiments in a kind of restless, wild agriculture. A load of lumber would be hauled to some spot on the free wilderness, where water could be easily found, and a rude box-cabin built. Then a gang plow was procured, and a dozen mustang ponies, worth ten or fifteen dollars apiece, and with these hundreds of acres were stirred as easily as if the land had been under cultivation for years, tough, perennial roots being almost wholly absent. Thus a ranch was established, and from these bare wooden huts, as centers of desolation, the wild flora vanished in ever-widening circles. But the arch destroyers are the shepherds, with their flocks of hoofed locusts, sweeping over the ground like a fire, and trampling down every rod that escapes the plow as completely as if the whole plain were a cottage garden–plot without a fence. But notwithstanding these destroyers, a thousand swarms of bees may be pastured here for every one now gathering honey. The greater portion is still covered every season with a repressed growth of bee-flowers, for most of the species are annuals, and many of then are not relished by sheep or cattle, while the rapidity of their growth enables them to develop and mature their seeds before any foot has time to crush them. The ground is, therefore, kept sweet, and the race is perpetuated, though only as a suggestive shadow of the magnificence of its wildness.

The time will undoubtedly come when the entire area of this noble valley will be tilled like a garden, when the fertilizing waters of the mountains, now flowing to the sea, will be distributed to every acre, giving rise to prosperous towns, wealth, arts, etc. Then, I suppose, there will be few left, even among botanists, to deplore the vanished primeval flora. In the meantime, the pure waste going on—the wanton destruction of the innocents—is a sad sight to see, and the sun may well be pitied in being compelled to look on.

Frank Norris

Frank Norris (1870–1902) found his vocation as a novelist early. When he was fourteen, he moved with his parents from Chicago to San Francisco. After studies in France and at the University of California, Berkeley, he moved east in 1894 to study at Harvard. As a nondegree student there, he did a class project that eventually evolved into his best-known work, McTeague. *This 1899 tale of the demise of a brutal, degenerate San Francisco dentist was shaped by Norris's idea of the "novel with a purpose": a work that "proves something, draws conclusions from a whole congeries of forces, social tendencies, race impulses, devotes itself not to the study of men but of man."*

After McTeague, *Norris conceived a new project, an "Epic of the Wheat," meant to illustrate, says critic Frank Lundy, "the fundamental issues of American life by an examination of the production, distribution, and consumption of wheat." Norris's untimely death from peritonitis prevented him from fulfilling his plan, but he did finish the first two installments,* The Octopus *and* The Pit. *Although Norris imported some of the landmarks from Hollister,* The Octopus *takes place in the southern San Joaquin Valley. The novel contains a fictionalized version of the Mussel Slough tragedy, an 1880 gunfight that erupted over land disputes between the Southern Pacific and local farmers who felt the railroad was gouging them. Embedded in this plot are fine depictions of Central Valley farmland with its limitless horizons.* ✒

from The Octopus

On the Quien Sabe ranch, in one of its western divisions, near the line fence that divided it from the Osterman holding, Vanamee was harnessing the horses to the plow to which he had been assigned two days before, a stableboy from the division barn helping him.

Promptly discharged from the employ of the sheep raisers after the lamentable accident near the Long Trestle, Vanamee had presented himself to Harran, asking for employment. The season was beginning; on all the ranches work was being resumed. The rain had put the ground into admirable condition for plowing, and Annixter, Broderson, and Osterman all had their gangs at work. Thus, Vanamee was vastly surprised to find Los Muertos idle, the horses still in the barns, the men gathering in the shade of the bunk-house and eating-house, smoking, dozing, or going aimlessly about, their arms dangling. The plows for which Magnus and Harran were waiting in a fury of impatience had not yet arrived, and since the management of Los Muertos had counted upon having these in hand long before this time, no provision had been made for keeping the old stock in repair; many of these old plows were useless, broken, and out of order; some had been sold. It could not be said definitely when the new plows would arrive. Harran had decided to wait one week longer, and then, in case of their non-appearance, to buy a consignment of the old style of plow from the dealers in Bonneville. He could afford to lose the money better than he could afford to lose the season.

Failing of work on Los Muertos, Vanamee had gone to Quien Sabe. Annixter, whom he had spoken to first, had sent him across the ranch to one of his division superintendents, and this latter, after assuring himself of Vanamee's familiarity with horses and his previous experience—even though somewhat remote—on Los Muertos, had taken him on as a driver of one of the gang plows, then at work on his division.

The evening before, when the foreman had blown his whistle at six o'clock, the long line of plows had halted upon the instant, and the drivers, unharnessing their teams, had taken them back to the division barns—leaving the plows as they were in the furrows. But an hour after daylight the next morning the work was resumed. After breakfast, Vanamee, riding one horse and leading the others, had returned to the line of plows together with the other drivers. Now he was busy harnessing the team. At the division blacksmith shop—temporarily put up—he had been obliged to wait while one of his lead horses was shod, and he had thus been delayed quite five minutes. Nearly all the other teams were harnessed, the drivers on their seats, waiting for the foreman's signal.

"All ready here?" inquired the foreman, driving up to Vanamee's team in his buggy.

"All ready, sir," answered Vanamee, buckling the last strap.

He climbed to his seat, shaking out the reins, and turning about, looked back along the line, then all around him at the landscape inundated with the brilliant glow of the early morning.

The day was fine. Since the first rain of the season, there had been no other. Now the sky was without a cloud, pale blue, delicate, luminous, scintillating with morning. The great brown earth turned a huge flank to it, exhaling the moisture of the early dew. The atmosphere, washed clean of dust and mist, was translucent as crystal. Far off to the east, the hills on the other side of Broderson Creek stood out against the pallid saffron of the horizon as flat and as sharply outlined as if pasted on the sky. The campanile of the ancient Mission of San Juan seemed as fine as frost work. All about between the horizons, the carpet of the land unrolled itself to infinity. But now it was no longer parched with heat, cracked and warped by a merciless sun, powdered with dust. The rain had done its work; not a clod that was not swollen with fertility, not a fissure that did not exhale the sense of fecundity. One could not take a dozen steps upon the ranches without the brusque sensation that underfoot the land was alive; roused at last from its sleep, palpitating with the desire of reproduction. Deep down there in the recesses of the soil, the great heart throbbed once more, thrilling with passion, vibrating with desire, offering itself to the caress of the plow, insistent, eager, imperious. Dimly one felt the deep-seated trouble of the earth, the uneasy agitation of its members, the hidden tumult of its womb, demanding to be made fruitful, to reproduce, to disengage the eternal renascent germ of Life that stirred and struggled in its loins.

The plows, thirty-five in number, each drawn by its team of ten, stretched in an interminable line, nearly a quarter of a mile in length, behind and ahead of Vanamee. They were arranged, as it were, en echelon, not in file—not one directly behind the other, but each succeeding plow its own width farther in the field than the one in front of it. Each of these plows held five shears, so that when the entire company was in motion, one hundred and seventy-five furrows were made at the same instant. At a distance, the ploughs resembled a great column of field artillery. Each driver was in his place, his glance alternating between his horses and the foreman nearest at hard. Other foremen, in their buggies or buckboards, were at intervals along the line, like battery lieutenants. Annixter himself, on horseback, in boots and campaign hat, a cigar in his teeth, overlooked the scene.

The division superintendent, on the opposite side of the line, galloped past to a position at the head. For a long moment there was a silence. A sense of preparedness ran from end to end of the column. All things were ready, each man in his place. The day's work was about to begin.

Suddenly, from a distance at the head of the line came the shrill trilling of a whistle. At once the foreman nearest Vanamee repeated it, at the same time turning down the line, and waving one arm. The signal was repeated, whistle answering whistle, till the sounds lost themselves in the distance. At once the line of plows lost its immobility, moving forward, getting slowly under way, the horses straining in the traces. A prolonged movement rippled from team to team, disengaging in its passage a multitude of sounds— the click of buckles, the creak of straining leather, the subdued clash of machinery, the cracking of whips, the deep breathing of nearly four hundred horses, the abrupt commands and cries of the drivers, and, last of all, the prolonged, soothing murmur of the thick brown earth turning steadily from the multitude of advancing shears.

The plowing thus commenced, continued. The sun rose higher. Steadily the hundred iron hands kneaded and furrowed and stroked the brown, humid earth, the hundred iron teeth bit deep into the Titan's flesh. Perched on his seat, the moist living reins slipping and tagging in his hands, Vanamee, in the midst of this steady confusion of constantly varying sensation, sight interrupted by sound, sound mingling with sight, on this swaying, vibrating seat, quivering with the prolonged thrill of the earth, lapsed to a sort of pleasing numbness, in a sense, hypnotized by the weaving maze of things in which he found himself involved. To keep his team at an even, regular gait, maintaining the precise interval, to run his furrows as closely as possible to those already made by the plow in front—this for the moment was the entire sum of his duties. But while one part of his brain, alert and watchful, took cognizance of these matters, all the greater part was lulled and stupefied with the long monotony of the affair.

The plowing, now in full swing, enveloped him in a vague, slow-moving whirl of things. Underneath him was the jarring, jolting, trembling machine; not a clod was turned, not an obstacle encountered, that he did not receive the swift impression of it through all his body, the very friction of the damp soil, sliding incessantly from the shiny surface of the shears, seemed to reproduce itself in his fingertips and along the back of his head. He heard the horse hoofs by the myriads crushing down easily, deeply, into the loam, the prolonged clinking of trace-chains, the working of the smooth brown flanks in the harness, the clatter of wooden hames, the champing of bits, the click of iron shoes against pebbles, the brittle stubble of the surface ground crackling and snapping as the furrows turned, the sonorous, steady breaths wrenched from the deep, laboring chests, strap-bound, shining with sweat, and all along the line the voices of the men talking to the horses. Everywhere there were visions of glossy brown backs, straining, heaving, swollen with muscle; harness streaked with specks of froth, broad, cup-shaped hoofs, heavy with brown loam, men's faces red with tan, blue overalls spotted with axle-grease; muscled hands, the knuckles whitened in their grip on the reins, and through it all the ammoniacal smell of the horses, the bitter reek of perspiration of beasts and men, the aroma of warm leather, the scent of dead stubble—and stronger and more penetrating than everything else, the heavy, enervating odor of the upturned, living earth.

At intervals, from the tops of one of the rare, low swells of the land, Vanamee overlooked a wider horizon. On the other divisions of Quien Sabe the same work was in progress. Occasionally he could see another column of plows in the adjoining division—sometimes so close at hand that the subdued murmur of its movements reached his ear; sometimes so distant that it resolved itself into a long, brown streak upon the gray of the ground. Farther off to the west on the Osterman ranch other columns came and went, and, once, from the crest of the highest swell on his division, Vamamee caught a distant glimpse of the Broderson ranch. There, too, moving specks indicated that the plowing was underway. And farther away still, far off there beyond the fine line of the horizons, over the curve of the globe, the shoulder of the earth, he knew were other ranches, and beyond these others, and beyond these still others, the immensities multiplying to infinity.

Everywhere throughout the great San Joaquin, unseen and unheard, a thousand plows up-stirred the land, tens of thousands of shears clutched deep into the warm, moist soil.

It was the long stroking caress, vigorous, male, powerful, for which the Earth seemed panting. The heroic embrace of a multitude of iron hands, gripping deep into the brown, warm flesh of the land that quivers responsive and passionate under this rude advance, so robust as to be almost an assault, so violent as to be veritably brutal. There, under the sun and under the speckless sheen of the sky, the wooing of the Titan began, the vast primal passion, the two world forces, the elemental Male and Female, locked in a colossal embrace, at grapples in the throes of an infinite desire, at once terrible and divine, knowing no law, untamed, savage, natural, sublime.

William Everson

As a young man William Everson (1912–1994) happened upon the poetry
of Robinson Jeffers, and was so struck with Jeffers' essential power and his
uncompromising vision that Everson determined that he too would become a
poet: "It was an intellectual awakening and a religious conversion in one."
Everson soon married his high school sweetheart, planted a vineyard, and
began to write. Much of the early poetry of this Central Valley native—he
was born in Sacramento and raised in Selma—was rooted in his experience
as a farmer, close to the land.

Everson registered as a conscientious objector during World War II and spent
the war years working in Northwest lumber camps. Not only did he continue
to write, he helped found the Camp Waldport Untide Press. His first marriage ended after the war and Everson gave up his farm. He eventually
remarried and moved to the Bay Area, where he learned more about letter-
press printing. As part of Kenneth Rexroth's literary circle in San Francisco,
Everson found his poetry receiving more notice. When Everson converted
to Catholicism and joined the Dominican order as lay member Brother
Antoninus, he continued to write deeply moving autobiographical verse and
practice the art of fine handpress printing. The essays he wrote on Jeffers during this period provide extraordinarily sensitive readings of the elder poet's
work. In 1969, after eighteen years in the religious order, Everson returned
to secular life. In 1971 he became poet-in-residence at the University of
California, Santa Cruz, where he established the Lime Kiln Press.

The changes in Everson's life were reflected in his work, with his Central
Valley and wartime poetry giving way to the devotions he wrote as Brother
Antoninus. Among the collections of his poems are The Veritable Years:
Poems 1949-1966 and Man-Fate: The Swan-Song of Brother
Antoninus, which includes "Tendril in the Mesh," explaining the poet's
renunciation of his vows. Everson died in 1994 having achieved a national
reputation as a poet, scholar, and printer. The following poems were written
while he still lived in the Central Valley. ✒︎

Winter Ploughing

Before my feet the ploughshare rolls the earth,
Up and over,
Splitting the loam with a soft tearing sound.
Between the horses I can see the red blur of a far peach orchard,
Half obscured in drifting sheets of morning fog.
A score of blackbirds circles around me on shining wings.
They alight beside me, and scramble almost under my feet
In search of upturned grubs.
The fragrance of the earth rises like tule-pond mist,
Shrouding me in impalpable folds of sweet, cool smell,
Lulling my senses to the rhythm of the running plough,
The jingle of the harness,
And the thin cries of the gleaming, bent-winged birds.

Fog

The gray mask of the fog, the pale plate of the sun,
The dark nudeness of the stripped trees
And no motion, no wave of the branch:
The sun stuck in the thick of the sky and no wind to move it.
The sagged fence and the field
Do not remember the lark or her mate or the black lift of
    the rising crows.
The eye sees and absorbs; the mind sees and absorbs;
The heart does not see and knows no quickening.
There has been fog for a month and nothing has moved.
The eyes and the brain drink it, but nothing has moved
    for a number of days,
And the heart will not quicken.

San Joaquin

This valley after the storms can be beautiful beyond the telling,
Though our city-folk scorn it, cursing heat in the summer and
  drabness in winter,
And flee it: Yosemite and the sea.
They seek splendor; who would touch them must stun them;
The nerve that is dying needs thunder to rouse it.

I in the vineyard, in green-time and dead-time, come to it dearly,
And take nature neither freaked nor amazing,
But the secret shining, the soft indeterminate wonder.
I watch it morning and noon, the unutterable sundowns,
And love as the leaf does the bough.

Clouds

Over the coastal ranges slight and indefinite clouds
Moved in to sunrise, rode up the west;
Toward noon the change of the wind strung them to furrows.
Sundown flared late, the close and heavy twilight of August
  hooded the fields.
They were broken to fragments, and were burnt on the growth
  of the gathering night,
When Venus blazed west and went down.

So common a beauty: the workers over the wide fields hardly looked up.
Under the great arching sky of the valley the clouds are across us,
The trade of the routes of the upper air,
Their temporal splendor hawked on the wind for some listless eve.

Cirrus and stratus: the fringe of the distant storms of the sea;
December wanes and the nimbus are driving.
They are scattered by dawns, or are killed on the heavy fists
  of the peaks;
But the wind breeds them west forever

Oh Fortunate Earth

Now afternoon's running.
There are men moving singly and slow, pruning dead growth.
In the cold south-falling light there are teams moving.
High up killdeer, crying, flash white from the breast as the
    sun takes them.

You can see from this hillock towns and their smoke on them,
    roads shining,
And miles under the thrusting sight the slumbrous earth.
That beauty shadows the heart,
Till evil and violence and the tragic splendor of the crashing world
Die on the mind, as thunder fades over a sleeper.
In islanded calmness, in the deep quiet, spirit nor blood will
    awake to the drum,
Perfectly tuned to the heavy mood that breeds in the valley.

"Oh fortunate earth, you must find someone to make you
    bitter music…"
No chanting of mine lures the talons down.
These places rare, and too dear.
The world is the plunder of hawks.

.

William Saroyan

William Saroyan (1908–1981) won the Pulitzer Prize in 1940 for his drama The Time of Your Life. *The Fresno native, high school dropout, and former telegrapher took the unusual step of refusing the cash award. During his long career he won many other honors, including an Academy Award for the script of* The Human Comedy. *But Saroyan remained an independent: "I have never been subsidized, I have never accepted money connected with a literary prize or award, I have never been endowed, and I have never received a grant or fellowship." Saroyan wrote "There is nothing wrong with [financial] security. But I prefer another kind. I prefer to recognize the truth that I must work, and to believe that I can." And work Saroyan did, producing novels, plays, essays, and hundreds of short stories, many of them based on the Fresno he knew while growing up.*

Saroyan—who was one of the best-known and busiest writers of his day—is now "one of the most underappreciated of all major California authors," says fellow Central Valley native Gerald Haslam. This is a great loss to readers, since Saroyan's work—especially the best of his short stories—endows "the large comic world" of Fresno with a bittersweet warmth. Here is just such an autobiographical story. 🦢

from My Name Is Aram

My uncle Melik was just about the worst farmer that ever lived. He was too imaginative and poetic for his own good. What he wanted was beauty. He wanted to plant it and see it grow. I myself planted over one hundred pomegranate trees for my uncle one year back there in the good old days of poetry and youth in the world. I drove a John Deere tractor too, and so did my uncle. It was all pure aesthetics, not agriculture. My uncle just liked the idea of planting trees and watching them grow.

Only they wouldn't grow. It was on account of the soil. The soil was desert soil. It was dry. My uncle waved at the six hundred and eighty acres of desert he had bought and he said in the most poetic Armenian anybody ever heard, Here in this awful desolation a garden shall flower, fountains of cold water shall bubble out of the earth, and all things of beauty shall come into being.

Yes, sir, I said.

I was the first and only relative to see the land he had bought. He knew I was a poet at heart, and he believed I would understand the magnificent impulse that was driving him to glorious ruin. I did. I knew as well as he that what he had purchased was worthless desert land. It was away over to hell and gone, at the foot of the Sierra Nevada mountains. It was full of every kind of desert plant that ever sprang out of dry hot earth. It was overrun with prairie dogs, squirrels, horned toads, snakes, and a variety of smaller forms of life. The space over this land knew only the presence of hawks, eagles, and buzzards. It was a region of loneliness, emptiness, truth, and dignity. It was nature at its proudest, driest, loneliest, and loveliest.

My uncle and I got out of the Ford roadster in the middle of his land and began to walk over the dry earth.

This land, he said, is my land.

He walked slowly, kicking into the dry soil. A horned toad scrambled over the earth at my uncle's feet. My uncle clutched my shoulder and came to a pious halt.

What is that animal? he said.

That little tiny lizard? I said.

That mouse with horns, my uncle said. What is it?

I don't know for sure, I said. We call them horny toads.

The horned toad came to a halt about three feet away and turned its head.

My uncle looked down at the small animal.

Is it poison? he said.

To eat? I said. Or if it bites you?

Either way, my uncle said.

I don't think it's good to eat, I said. I think it's harmless. I've caught many of them. They grow sad in captivity, but never bite. Shall I catch this one?

Please do, my uncle said.

I sneaked up on the horned toad, then sprang on it while my uncle looked on.

Careful, he said. Are you sure it isn't poison?

I've caught many of them, I said.

I took the horned toad to my uncle. He tried not to seem afraid.

A lovely little thing, isn't it? he said. His voice was unsteady.

Would you like to hold it? I said.

No, my uncle said. You hold it. I have never before been so close to such a thing as this. I see it has eyes. I suppose it can see us.

I suppose it can, I said. It's looking up at you now.

My uncle looked the horned toad straight in the eye. The horned toad looked my uncle straight in the eye. For fully half a minute they looked one another straight in the eye and then the horned toad turned its head aside and looked down at the ground. My uncle sighed with relief.

A thousand of them, he said, could kill a man, I suppose.

They never travel in great numbers, I said. You hardly ever see more than one at a time.

A big one, my uncle said, could probably bite a man to death.

They don't grow big, I said. This is as big as they grow.

They seem to have an awful eye for such small creatures, my uncle said. Are you sure they don't mind being picked up?

I suppose they forget all about it the minute you put them down, I said.

Do you really think so? my uncle said.

I don't think they have very good memories, I said.

My uncle straightened up, breathing deeply.

Put the little creature down, he said. Let us not be cruel to the innocent creations of Almighty God. If it is not poison and grows no larger than a mouse and does not travel in great numbers and has no memory to speak of, let the timid little thing return to the earth. Let us be gentle toward these small things which live on the earth with us.

Yes, sir, I said.

I placed the horned toad on the ground.

Gently now, my uncle said. Let no harm come to this strange dweller on my land.

The horned toad scrambled away.

These little things, I said, have been living on soil of this kind for centuries.

Centuries? my uncle said. Are you sure?

I'm not sure, I said, but I imagine they have. They're still here, anyway.

My uncle looked around at his land, at the cactus and brush growing out of it, at the sky overhead.

What have they been eating all this time? he shouted.

I don't know, I said.

What would you say they've been eating? he said.

Insects, I guess.

Insects? my uncle shouted. What sort of insects?

Little bugs, most likely, I said. I don't know their names. I can find out tomorrow at school.

We continued to walk over the dry land. When we came to some holes in the earth my uncle stood over them and said, What lives down there?

Prairie dogs, I said.

What are *they?* he said.

Well, I said, they're something like rats. They belong to the rodent family.

What are all these things doing on my land? my uncle said.

They don't know it's your land, I said. They've been living here a long while.

I don't suppose that horny toad ever looked a man in the eye before, my uncle said.

I don't think so, I said.

Do you think I scared it or anything? my uncle said.

I don't know for sure, I said.

If I did, my uncle said, I didn't mean to. I'm going to build a house here some day.

I didn't know that, I said.

Of course, my uncle said. I'm going to build a magnificent house.

It's pretty far away, I said.

It's only an hour from town, my uncle said.

If you go fifty miles an hour, I said.

It's not fifty miles to town, my uncle said. It's thirty-seven.

Well, you've got to take a little time out for rough roads, I said.

I'll build me the finest house in the world, my uncle said. What else lives on this land?

Well, I said, there are three or four kinds of snakes.

Poison or non-poison? my uncle said.

Mostly non-poison, I said. The rattlesnake is poison, though.

Do you mean to tell me there are *rattlesnakes* on this land? my uncle said.

This is the kind of land rattlesnakes usually live on, I said.

How many? my uncle said.

Per acre? I said. Or on the whole six hundred and eighty acres?

Per acre, my uncle said.

Well, I said, I'd say there are about three per acre, conservatively.

Three per acre? my uncle shouted. Conservatively?

Maybe only two, I said.

How many is that to the whole place? my uncle said.

Well, let's see, I said. Two per acre. Six hundred and eighty acres. About fifteen hundred of them.

Fifteen hundred of them? my uncle said.

An acre is pretty big, I said. Two rattlesnakes per acre isn't many. You don't often see them.

What else have we got around here that's poison? my uncle said.

I don't know of anything else, I said. All the other things are harmless. The rattlesnakes are pretty harmless too, unless you step on them.

All right, my uncle said. You walk ahead and watch where you're going. If you see a rattlesnake, don't step on it. I don't want you to die at the age of eleven.

Yes, sir, I said. I'll watch carefully.

We turned around and walked back to the Ford. I didn't see any rattlesnakes on the way back. We got into the car and my uncle lighted a cigarette.

I'm going to make a garden of this awful desolation, he said.

Yes, sir, I said.

I know what my problems are, my uncle said, and I know how to solve them.

How? I said.

Do you mean the horny toads or the rattlesnakes? my uncle said.

I mean the problems, I said.

Well, my uncle said, the first thing I'm going to do is hire some Mexicans and put them to work.

Doing what? I said.

Clearing the land, my uncle said. Then I'm going to have them dig for water.

Dig where? I said.

Straight down, my uncle said. After we get water, I'm going to have them plow the land and then I'm going to plant.

What are you going to plant? I said. Wheat?

Wheat? my uncle shouted. What do I want with wheat? Bread is five cents a loaf. I'm going to plant pomegranate trees.

How much are pomegranates? I said.

Pomegranates, my uncle said, are practically unknown in this country.

Is that all you're going to plant? I said.

I have in mind, my uncle said, planting several other kinds of trees.

Peach trees? I said.

About ten acres, my uncle said.

How about apricots? I said.

By all means, my uncle said. The apricot is a lovely fruit. Lovely in shape, with a glorious flavor and a most delightful pit. I shall plant about twenty acres of apricot trees.

I hope the Mexicans don't have any trouble finding water, I said. Is there water under this land?

Of course, my uncle said. The important thing is to get started. I shall instruct the men to watch out for rattlesnakes. Pomegranates, he said. Peaches. Apricots. What else?

Figs? I said.

Thirty acres of figs, my uncle said.

How about mulberries? I said. The mulberry tree is a very nice-looking tree.

Mulberries, my uncle said. He moved his tongue around in his mouth. A nice tree, he said. A tree I knew well in the old country. How many acres would you suggest?

About ten, I said.

All right, he said. What else?

Olive trees are nice, I said.

Yes, they are, my uncle said. One of the nicest. About ten acres of olive trees. What else?

Well, I said, I don't suppose apple trees would grow on this kind of land.

I suppose not, my uncle said. I don't like apples anyway.

He started the car and we drove off the dry land on to the dry road. The car bounced about slowly until we reached the road and then we began to travel at a higher rate of speed.

One thing, my uncle said. When we get home I would rather you didn't mention this *farm* to the folks.

Yes, sir, I said. (*Farm?* I thought. *What farm?*)

I want to surprise them, my uncle said. You know how your grandmother is. I'll go ahead with my plans and when everything is in order I'll take the whole family out to the farm and surprise them.

Yes, sir, I said.

Not a word to a living soul, my uncle said.

Yes sir, I said.

Well, the Mexicans went to work and cleared the land. They cleared about ten acres of it in about two months. There were seven of them. They worked with shovels and hoes. They didn't understand anything about anything. It all seemed very strange, but they never complained. They were being paid and that was the thing that counted. They were two brothers and their sons. One day the older brother, Diego, very politely asked my uncle what it was they were supposed to be doing.

Señor, he said, please forgive me. Why are we cutting down the cactus?

I'm going to farm this land, my uncle said.

The other Mexicans asked Diego in Mexican what my uncle had said and Diego told them.

They didn't believe it was worth the trouble to tell my uncle he couldn't do it. They just went on cutting down the cactus.

The cactus, however, stayed down only for a short while. The land which had been first cleared was already rich again with fresh cactus and brush. My uncle made this observation with considerable amazement.

It takes deep plowing to get rid of cactus, I said. You've got to plow it out.

My uncle talked the matter over with Ryan, who had a farm-implement business. Ryan told him not to fool with horses. The modern thing to do was to turn a good tractor loose on the land and do a year's work in a day.

So my uncle bought a John Deere tractor. It was beautiful. A mechanic from Ryan's taught Diego how to operate the tractor, and the next day when my uncle and I reached the land we could see the tractor away out in the desolation and we could hear it booming in the awful emptiness of the desert. It sounded pretty awful. It *was* awful. My uncle thought it was wonderful.

Progress, he said. There's the modern age for you. Ten thousand years ago, he said, it would have taken a hundred men a week to do what the tractor's done today.

Ten thousand years ago? I said. You mean yesterday.

Anyway, my uncle said, there's nothing like these modern conveniences.

The tractor isn't a convenience, I said.

What is it, then? my uncle said. Doesn't the driver sit?

He couldn't very well stand, I said.

Any time they let you sit, my uncle said, it's a convenience. Can you whistle?

Yes, sir, I said. What sort of a song would you like to hear?

Song? my uncle said. I don't want to hear any song. I want you to whistle at that Mexican on the tractor.

What for? I said.

Never mind what for, my uncle said. Just whistle. I want him to know we are here and that we are pleased with his work. He's probably plowed twenty acres.

Yes, sir, I said.

I put the second and third fingers of each hand into my mouth and blew with all my might. It was good and loud. Nevertheless, it didn't seem as if Diego had heard me. He was pretty far away. We were walking toward him anyway, so I couldn't figure out why my uncle wanted me to whistle at him.

Once again, he said.

I whistled once again, but Diego didn't hear.

Louder, my uncle said.

This next time I gave it all I had, and my uncle put his hands over his ears. My face got very red, too. The Mexican on the tractor heard the whistle this time. He slowed the tractor down, turned it around, and began plowing straight across the field toward us.

Do you want him to do that? I said.

It doesn't matter, my uncle said.

In less than a minute and a half the tractor and the Mexican arrived. The Mexican seemed very delighted. He wiped dirt and perspiration off his face and got down from the tractor.

Señor, he said, this is wonderful.

I'm glad you like it, my uncle said.

Would you like a ride? the Mexican asked my uncle.

My uncle didn't know for sure. He looked at me.

Go ahead, he said. Hop on. Have a little ride.

Diego got on the tractor and helped me on. He sat on the metal seat and I stood behind him, holding him. The tractor began to shake, then jumped, and then began to move. It moved swiftly and made a good deal of noise. The Mexican drove around in a big circle and brought the tractor back to my uncle. I jumped off.

All right, my uncle said to the Mexican. Go back to your work.

The Mexican drove the tractor back to where he was plowing.

My uncle didn't get water out of the land until many months later. He had wells dug all over the place, but no water came out of the wells. Of course he had motor pumps too, but even then no water came out. A water specialist named Roy came out from Texas with his two younger brothers and they began investigating the land. They told my uncle they'd get water for him. It took them three months and the water was muddy and there wasn't much of it. There was a trickle of muddy water. The specialist told my uncle matters would improve with time and went back to Texas.

Now half the land was cleared and plowed and there was water, so the time had come to plant.

We planted pomegranate trees. They were of the finest quality and very expensive. We planted about seven hundred of them. I myself planted a hundred. My uncle planted quite a few. We had a twenty-acre orchard of pomegranate trees away over to hell and gone in the strangest desolation anybody ever saw. It was the loveliest-looking absurdity imaginable and my uncle was crazy about it. The only trouble was, his money was giving out. Instead of going ahead and trying to make a garden of the whole six hundred and eighty acres, he decided to devote all his time and energy and money to the pomegranate trees.

Only for the time being, he said. Until we begin to market the pomegranates and get our money back.

Yes, sir, I said.

I didn't know for sure, but I figured we wouldn't be getting any pomegranates to speak of off those little trees for two or three years at least, but I didn't say anything. My uncle got rid of the Mexican workers and he and I took over the farm. We had the tractor and a lot of land, so every now and then we drove out to the farm and drove the tractor around, plowing up cactus and turning over the soil between the pomegranate trees. This went on for three years.

One of these days, my uncle said, you'll see the loveliest garden in the world in this desert.

The water situation didn't improve with time, either. Every once in a while there would be a sudden generous spurt of water containing only a few pebbles and my uncle would be greatly pleased, but the next day it would be muddy again and there would be only a little trickle. The pomegranate trees fought bravely for life, but they never did get enough water to come out with any fruit.

There were blossoms after the fourth year. This was a great triumph for my uncle. He went out of his head with joy when he saw them.

Nothing much ever came of the blossoms, though. They were very beautiful, but that was about all. Purple and lonely.

That year my uncle harvested three small pomegranates.

I ate one, he ate one, and we kept the other one up in his office.

The following year I was fifteen. A lot of wonderful things had happened to me. I mean, I had read a number of good writers and I'd grown as tall as my uncle. The farm was still our secret. It had cost my uncle a lot of money, but he was always under the impression that very soon he was going to start marketing his pomegranates and get his money back and go on with his plan to make a garden in the desert.

The trees didn't fare very well. They grew a little, but it was hardly noticeable. Quite a few of them withered and died.

That's average, my uncle said. Twenty trees to an acre is only average. We won't plant new trees just now. We'll do that later.

He was still paying for the land, too.

The following year he harvested about two hundred pomegranates. He and I did the harvesting. They were pretty sad-looking pomegranates. We packed them in nice-looking boxes and my uncle shipped them to a wholesale produce house in Chicago. There were eleven boxes.

We didn't hear from the wholesale produce house for a month, so one night my uncle made a long-distance phone call. The produce man, D'Agostino, told my uncle nobody wanted pomegranates.

How much are you asking per box? my uncle shouted over the phone.

One dollar, D'Agostino shouted back.

That's not enough, my uncle shouted. I won't take a nickel less than five dollars a box.

They don't want them at one dollar a box, D'Agostino shouted.

Why not? my uncle shouted.

They don't know what they are, D'Agostino shouted.

What kind of a business man are you anyway? my uncle shouted. They're pomegranates. I want five dollars a box.

I can't sell them, the produce man shouted. I ate one myself and I don't see anything so wonderful about them.

You're crazy, my uncle shouted. There is no other fruit in the world like the pomegranate. Five dollars a box isn't half enough.

What shall I do with them? D'Agostino shouted. I can't sell them. I don't want them.

I see, my uncle whispered. Ship them back. Ship them back express collect.

The phone call cost my uncle about seventeen dollars.

So the eleven boxes came back.

My uncle and I ate most of the pomegranates.

The following year my uncle couldn't make any more payments on the land. He gave the papers back to the man who had sold him the land. I was in the office at the time.

Mr. Griffith, my uncle said, I've got to give you back your property, but I would like to ask a little favor. I've planted twenty acres of pomegranate trees out there on that land and I'd appreciate it very much if you'd let me take care of those trees.

Take care of them? Mr. Griffith said. What in the world for?

My uncle tried to explain, but couldn't. It was too much to try to explain to a man who wasn't sympathetic.

So my uncle lost the land, and the trees, too.

About three years later he and I drove out to the land and walked out to the pomegranate orchard. The trees were all dead. The soil was heavy again with cactus and desert brush. Except for the small dead pomegranate trees the place was exactly the way it had been all the years of the world.

We walked around in the orchard for a while and then went back to the car.

We got into the car and drove back to town.

We didn't say anything because there was such an awful lot to say, and no language to say it in.

Wilma Elizabeth McDaniel

The sharecropper family of Wilma Elizabeth McDaniel (1918–) left Oklahoma for California's Central Valley in 1936. The part-Cherokee girl had already started writing and kept at it through hard years as a farm-worker. After years of recording her poems on envelopes and grocery bags, she published her first book in 1973 and has published more than a dozen since. Her poems often speak of her people, the Okies, of their labor in California, of their love for their new home. Fellow Central Valley writer Gerald Haslam pays high praise to her economical verse: "True to place, true to people, yet powerfully universal, Wilma's language is as vernacular as what you might hear in a Central Valley shopping mall and her subjects are as palpable as breath itself." ✎

Dustbowl Doxology

Sweet
it was
is now
and ever shall be sweet
in memory
of wild walnut trees
at the spot
where curving banks
hugged
the faithful Merced River
and the sound of young
Sunday picnic voices
drifted downstream

The Flower Lover

The visitors had been talking
about baseball, but somehow
Uncle Bart switched off to the
subject of flowers
jumped right in with, "Folks
if you really want to see a sight
take that Yokohl Valley Drive
why the roadsides and low spots
are alive with monkeyflowers
little yellow monkey faces
and beds of buttercups
and if you take that drive to
Woodlake
the lupine will knock you out
shimmery shiny blue alive
and poppies just popping gold.
It's a calling card from the Almighty
I tell you from my heart."
And his son tried to shut him up
"Dad, not everyone is as crazy
as you over California wildflowers."

Viewing Kern County Desolation

Uncle Phylo
made a mournful
face
and sounded even
sadder
when he said Them
builders has ruined
this land
not even room
for a jackrabbit to hide

First Spring in California, 1936

The Okies wrapped their
cold dreams in army blankets
and patchwork quilts
and slept away the foggy
winter nights of 1935

From doorways of tents
and hasty shacks
now and then a boxcar
they watched for spring
as they would watch for
the Second Coming of Christ

And saw the Valley change
from skim milk blue
still needing sweaters
to palest green that filled
their eyes with hope

As they waited for odd jobs
the Valley burst forth
with one imperial color
poppies flung their gold
over acres of sand
like all the bankers in California
gone raving mad

Women wept in wonder
and hunted fruit jars to can
the precious flowers
in case next year
did not produce a bumper crop

Gary Soto

Mexican-American Gary Soto (1952–) was a farm laborer before enrolling at California State University, Fresno, where he studied with Philip Levine. He moved to the University of California, Irvine, to earn his M.F.A. Besides contributing to numerous periodicals, among them Poetry, New Republic, Paris Review, Nation, *and the* New Yorker, *Soto has authored or edited many books (including prose and poetry aimed at younger readers), most completed while serving in various teaching positions. In 1993 he gave up the classroom in order to write full-time.*

Soto's first book of poems, The Elements of San Joaquin, *conveys his great sympathy for the farmworker, depicting both the harsh conditions and the beauty of the valley landscape.* ✒

Field

The wind sprays pale dirt into my mouth
The small, almost invisible scars
On my hands.

The pores in my throat and elbows
Have taken in a seed of dirt of their own.

After a day in the grape fields near Rolinda
A fine silt, washed by sweat,
Has settled into the lines
On my wrists and palms.

Already I am becoming the valley,
A soil that sprouts nothing
For any of us.

Wind

A dry wind over the valley
Peeled mountains, grain by grain,
To small slopes, loose dirt
Where red ants tunnel.

The wind strokes
The skulls and spines of cattle
To white dust, to nothing,

Covers the spiked tracks of beetles,
Of tumbleweed, of sparrows
That pecked the ground for insects.

Evenings, when I am in the yard weeding,
The wind picks up the breath of my armpits
Like dust, swirls it
Miles away

And drops it
On the ear of a rabid dog,
And I take on another life.

When you got up this morning the sun
Blazed an hour in the sky,

A lizard hid
Under the curled leaves of manzanita
And winked its dark lids.

Later, the sky grayed,
And the cold wind you breathed
Was moving under your skin and already far
From the small hives of your lungs.

Stars

At dusk the first stars appear.
Not one eager finger points toward them.
A little later the stars spread with the night
And an orange moon rises
To lead them, like a shepherd, toward dawn.

Sun

In June the sun is a bonnet of light
Coming up,
Little by little,
From behind a skyline of pine.

The pastures sway with fiddle-neck
Tassels of foxtail.

At Piedra
A couple fish on the river's edge,
Their shadows deep against the water.
Above, in the stubbled slopes,
Cows climb down
As the heat rises
In a mist of blond locusts,
Returning to the valley.

Fog

If you go to your window
You will notice a fog drifting in.

The sun is no stronger than a flashlight.
Not all the sweaters
Hung in closets all summer

Could soak up this mist. The fog:
A mouth nibbling everything to its origin,
Pomegranate trees, stolen bicycles,

The string of lights at a used-car lot,
A Pontiac with scorched valves.

In Fresno the fog is passing
The young thief prying a window screen,
Graying my hair that falls
And goes unfound, my fingerprints
Slowly growing a fur of dust—

One hundred years from now
There should be no reason to believe
I lived.

Rain

When autumn rains flatten sycamore leaves,
The tiny volcanos of dirt
Ants raised around their holes,
I should be out of work.

My silverware and stack of plates will go unused
Like the old, my two good slacks
Will smother under a growth of lint

And smell of the old dust
That rises
When the closet door opens or closes.

The skin of my belly will tighten like a belt
And there will be no reason for pockets.

Daybreak

In this moment when the light starts up
In the east and rubs
The horizon until it catches fire,

We enter the fields to hoe,
Row after row, among the small flags of onion,
Waving off the dragonflies
That ladder the air.

And tears the onions raise
Do not begin in your eyes but in ours,
In the salt blown
From one blister into another;

They begin in knowing
You will never waken to bear
The hour timed to a heart beat,
The wind pressing us closer to the ground.

When the season ends,
And the onions are unplugged from their sleep,
We won't forget what you failed to see,
And nothing will heal
Under the rain's broken fingers.

Sherley Anne Williams

Sherley Anne Williams (1944–) is probably best known for her novel Dessa
Rose, *the story of a pregnant slave jailed for murdering the white man who
killed her lover. This realistic depiction of slavery brought Williams popular
success. But this professor of African-American literature at the University of
California, San Diego, had already earned critical acclaim for* Give Birth to
Brightness: A Thematic Study in Neo-Black Literature *and* The
Peacock Poems, *a collection of autobiographical poems nominated for a
National Book Award.*

*Born in Fresno, Williams grew up in the Central Valley. She worked in
fruit orchards and cotton fields with her father, who died when she was seven,
and her mother, who died nine years later. Williams eventually entered
Fresno State College, where she earned her B.A. in 1966, going on to
Howard and Brown to earn her M.A. in 1972.*

Some of the poems in her collection Some One Sweet Angel Chile
*examine the life of singer Bessie Smith, while others look back at Williams'
own life.* ❧

The Green-Eyed Monsters
of the Valley Dusk

sunset knocks the edge from the
day's heat, filling the Valley
with shadows: Time for coming
in getting on; lapping fields
lapping orchards like greyhounds
racing darkness to mountain
rims, land's last meeting with still
lighted sky.

This is a car
I watched in childhood, streaking
the straightaway through the dusk
I look for the ghost of that

girl in the mid–summer fields
whipping past but what ghosts lurk
in this silence are feelings
not spirit not sounds.

Bulbous
lights approach in the gloom
hovering briefly between
memory and fear, dissolve
into fog lamps mounted high
on the ungainly bodies
of reaping machines: Time
coming in. Time getting on.

from california light

1. North County

The freeway is a river
of light rounding the base of
Mt. Soledad, its distant
drone a part of the night. I've
watched in the darkness as the
river dimmed to the fitful
passing of solitary
cars and heard the coyotes
in the canyon crying their
survival to the strange land

I booted up one day, walked
out across the mesa that
fronts along my place till the
land was a shallow cup around
me and the houses were lost
in the distance on its
rim. The plants were the only

life I saw—muted greens dry
browns bursts of loud purple and
lighter blues, brilliant in the
spring light; something rustled the
undergrowth; a jet murmured
in the softly clabbered sky.

The Indian dead are here
buried beneath Spanish place
names and the cities of the
pioneers and the droning
silence is witness to what
each has claimed, what each owned.
My father's grave is here some
where his tale lost like that jet
in clabber his children
scattered along the river
voices singing to the night.

Gerald Haslam

Few writers have done as much to bring the "other California" to readers than has Gerald Haslam (1937–). Born in Bakersfield, he was raised in the nearby working-class community of Oildale—where everyone "was called an Okie," even if their background, like Haslam's, didn't include a dustbowl pedigree. Even so, like many of the sons and daughters of migrant families, Haslam became familiar with hard work early. From the age of thirteen he worked in fields and packing sheds, "unwittingly acquiring," says critic Gerald Locklin, "what would prove a seemingly endless source of material." After flunking out of Bakersfield College, Haslam eventually earned degrees from San Franciso State University, Washington State University, and Union Graduate School. He teaches linguistics and Western literature at Sonoma State University.

Haslam's writing has earned him many awards and honors. He aims to touch the universal through the particular: "I use—or try to use—the valley to write about the world." His interest in the Central Valley is reflected in his stories—collected in Okies: Selected Stories, The Wages of Sin: Collected Stories, *and* That Constant Coyote: California Stories— *and his scholarly and nonfiction works. He has written a linguistic study,* The Language of the Oilfields, *and edited collections of California and Central Valley literature. Many of his essays, which have appeared in period-icals as diverse as* California English *and the* Nation, *take a sympathetic but never sentimental look at small-town residents of the Central Valley. In the essay, "The Lake That Will Not Die," that follows, Haslam describes the changes that human beings have wrought upon his native landscape.* 🍂

from The Other California

A brisk crosswind tugs at the car as it cruises through rain-cleansed air down Interstate 5 toward Oildale. To the east, the vast San Joaquin Plain is foreshortened all the way to muscular Sierras dusted with snow. Much closer, two long rows of palm trees stand as forlorn sentries along a soggy farm road. We are slipping down the Great Central Valley's western edge along the first rise of treeless western hills, emer-ald now and dotted with muddy cattle.

Hurrying south, past multicolored patches of vegetation flecked with standing water, the rich aroma of wet earth thickens the air; it is a smell, invasive and comforting, that city dwellers do not know. This country boy sucks it hungrily into his lungs.

"What smells so funny?" asks my son, Carlos. "Can I roll the window up?"

"No."

Roadside ditches are full, and occasional mallards and coots can be seen in them, but that does not prepare us for the vision that abruptly appears farther down the freeway: a vast and unexpected sheet of water extending as far as we can see, appearing to fill the entire southern end of the Great Valley.

I nose our car to a stop on the highway's shoulder, and Carlos, who has endured this trip many times, asks, "What's all that water, Dad? I don't remember it."

For a moment, I do not answer because we are seeing a ghost. Finally I reply, "Tulare Lake."

Tulare Lake was once the largest body of fresh water west of the Great Lakes. Formed by the entrapped drainage of four Sierra rivers—the Kings, Kaweah, White, and Tule—its highest level was recorded in 1862. That year it covered 486,400 acres to depths exceeding 40 feet, actually swallowing two other significant lakes, 8,300-acre Kern and 4,000-acre Buena Vista, which trapped drainage from the Sierra's longest stream, Kern River, in a subbasin to the south. In fact, the entire southern end of the Great Valley—120 miles by 50 miles—resembled a primordial sea, its broadened periphery dotted with displaced rabbits and foraging cattle, its shimmering surface darkened by uncountable waterfowl, for this was a linchpin in the Pacific Flyway.

Most wet years well into the late nineteenth century, Tulare Lake covered 200,000 acres and measured 75 miles by 25 during its high season, ebbing and flowing like a huge tidal pool in the midst of an otherwise desiccated landscape. Historian Frank Latta claims it virtually dried up during prolonged periods of drought. The annual pulsing of local wetlands was determined far less by its scant rainfall than by snowmelt in the southern Sierra Nevada, which fed all the streams that emptied into this basin.

As a result, the region was a land of startling contrasts: vast reed beds, marshes, and ponds surrounded by bleached grassland or land with no grass at all—even sand dunes on the lake's southern and southeastern shores—while mallards and coots and Canadian honkers fed in the proximity of horned toads and jackrabbits. To the east side, along the Kaweah River's alluvial fan, a dense oak forest extended to the water's edge, and alkali flats, like earth crusted with snow, could be found glaring along miles of marshes and sloughs.

Lakes and wetlands were the most unique features of a remarkable geomorphic amalgam known as Tulare Basin: Tulare Lake Basin to the north, Buena Vista Basin to the south. The northern basin was dominated by the large lake for which it was named. William Preston in *Vanishing Landscapes,* his benchmark study of the locale, describes it this way: "an area delimited on the north, west, and south by the boundaries of Tulare and Kings counties and on the east by vaguely determined but readily visible limits of cultivation...a topographic basin with interior drainage." Buena Vista Basin lay below the present Kern County line, enclosed roughly by the locations of present-day Delano, Wheeler Ridge, Taft and Buttonwillow. Southeast and southwest of Bakersfield, the aforementioned Kern and Buena Vista lakes collected the flow of Kern River, the Sierras' longest stream. Between and

---

Perhaps it may be well here to remark, that the San Joaquin River is divided into three branches, known, respectively, as the west, middle, and east channels—the latter named being not only the main stream, but the one used by the steamboats and sailing vessels bound to and from Stockton— or, at least, to within four miles of that city, from which point the Stockton Slough is used. The east, or main channel, is navigable for small, sternwheeled steamboats as high as Frezno City. Besides the three main channels of the San Joaquin, before mentioned, there are numerous tributaries, the principal of which are the Moquelumne, Calaveras, Stanislaus, Tuolumne, and Merced rivers.

An apparently interminable sea of tules extends nearly one hundred and fifty miles south, up the valley of the San Joaquin; and when these are on fire, as they not unfrequently are during the fall and early winter months, the broad sheet of licking and leaping flame and the vast volumes of smoke that rise and eddy and surge, hither and thither, present a scene of fearful grandeur at night that is suggestive of some earthly pandemonium.

The lumbering sound of the boat's machinery has suddenly ceased, and our high-pressure motive power, descended from a regular to an occasional snorting, gives us a reminder that we have reached Stockton. Time, half past two o'clock a.m.

—J. M. Hutchings, from *Scenes of Wonder and Curiosity in California* (1872)

among those two bodies of water existed many channels, marshes and swamps, while another good-sized, tule-lined pool called Goose Lake filled to the northwest near Buttonwillow.

During wet years, Buena Vista Slough linked the subbasins. As geographer Preston explains, despite the distinctness of those sections, "historically the word 'basin' was used to describe the entire southern end of the valley as a unified landscape." In years of extreme precipitation, such as 1862, the entire territory was a single vast lagoon.

The hub of it all was indeed vast Tulare Lake and its interconnected wetlands: a trough within a basin within a valley. Its volume swelled and shrank and swelled again in the west-center of the basin named for it, extending east from terraces near present-day Kettleman City toward gradually rising terrain adjacent to Corcoran. The site of Lemoore marks the lake's approximate northern boundary, while to the south the state historical monument at Allensworth stands on the edge of what was once shore.

In fact, attendant wetlands extended far south past Buttonwillow in Kern County, east toward Tulare and Visalia, and north along Fish Slough well into Fresno County; the west was sealed by the inner edge of the Coast Range, specifically Kettleman Hills. The Sierra Nevada and the Coast Range are nearly seventy-five miles apart here, deflecting rain clouds from the widened valley, so this is an arid to semiarid realm, a desert, absorbing only five to ten inches of rain annually. Nonetheless, in the past, standing water was its most signal characteristic.

Each spring Tulare Lake would swell with snowmelt, then recede dramatically by fall or early winter. Local pioneers played a kind of agricultural roulette by planting grain as water retreated on the drying lake bed, then harvesting before the next cycle's runoff once more filled the depression—they "plowed pollywogs in spring, and harvested frogs in winter," or so local folklore had it. It was usually a profitable strategy, but not always.

In 1906, for instance, a late date when most of the lake's tributaries had already been diverted for irrigation, William Hubbard found his equipment trapped when water rose faster and higher than expected. Hubbard, who farmed east of Delano and annually planted grain far to the northwest on the lake's rich floor, moved his threshing machines to an island locals had never seen covered with water, then escaped by boat. This was, however, a wet year and soon his gear was six feet below the lake's surface—an appropriate depth since all the machinery was ruined and so was the farmer.

Eventually the rusted equipment was dragged back to his yard where it stood for years, known as Hubbard's Junkpile.

The diversion of tributaries for irrigation had begun in the 1870s. That same surface water could no longer flow directly into Tulare Lake, which as a result suffered a steady decline not only in quantity but also in quality, because irrigation runoff leached salts from alkali soil. Streams continued to be diverted into this century and soon diminished runoff could no longer dilute intensified salinization; at the turn of the century the lake was too saline to support significant aquatic life and its once-thriving commercial fishery was finished.

Thirty years later, Kings River—the lake's most important source of water—was irrigating more land than any other stream in the world except the Nile and Indus rivers: over a million acres. Little wonder then that a only a piddling flow ever reached the old lake bed most years and, as Donald Worster points out, "that destroyed grower unity, and overloaded the courts" because ex-partners battled over limited resources. When dams such as Pine Flat and Isabella were finally built on major streams thirty-plus years ago, they served as coups de gras in a process of diminution that had begun nearly a century earlier.

Today, reclaimed and plowed and planted, the old lake bed is farmland. Cotton and safflowers are produced where fish were once netted. In fact, the very existence of that vast sheet of water is but a vague memory, which dramatically demonstrates how much humans have altered even this open terrain in California's core. Someone driving through the Central Valley today isn't apt to recognize that only four percent of the landscape is estimated to remain unaltered: nearly all of its natural wetlands are gone, nearly all of its native grasslands no longer exist, nearly all of its oak woodlands have been destroyed. In the nineteenth century, hogs were run on Atwell's Island southeast of Tulare, and no fences were needed because the settlement could be reached only by boat; today the island is a dry-land farming town called Alpaugh.

"Back in 1955, right after I finished high school," I tell Carlos, who thinks the fifties were neat, "a couple of buddies and I drove us to Alpaugh to do some duck hunting. I'd heard a pal of my dad's say there were lots of them at a place called Tulare Lake."

"Well, we crisscrossed dirt roads, drove along miles of ditches and sloughs, saw a million red-winged blackbirds and a billion tules, and one mud hen."

He laughs. "Only one mud hen."

"More than one. Anyway, we were half lost and felt like we were in the middle of nowhere, so when we finally ran into an old black man fishing in a canal, I stopped the car and went to talk with him. I started out by asking him if he'd caught any fish, and he smiled and showed me some small catfish he had in a bucket."

"Then I told him we were looking for ducks, and he smiled again: 'They's ducks all over here.'"

"That led me to ask him where Tulare Lake was, and he said, 'It ain't here no mo'."The finality of those words— 'no mo'—has stuck with me ever since. We never did see the lake."

Carlos gazes at me, then asks, "And then what happened?" He has seen many movies and expects action.

"Nothing," I admit. "We went home."

Tulare Lake Basin is now indistinguishable from the San Joaquin Plain that borders it to the north. Just above the alluvial fan that separates those two geomorphic regions, the San Joaquin River crosses the dominant prairie then winds north along the valley's western edge. Tributaries in that flat realm all drain into San Francisco Bay, and open grassland—not standing water—characterizes it. In 1861, William Henry Brewer described the San Joaquin as "a plain of absolute desolation." Today those two distinct environs—the barren plain and the boggy basin—have been rendered indistinguishable by development and reclamation, and they are lumped under a single name: the San Joaquin Valley.

Yet Tulare Lake Basin, also called Tulare Valley, once boasted its own distinct regional identity. An 1888 *Business Directory and Historical and Descriptive Hand-Book of Tulare County, California,* for instance, advised local residents, "All Tulareans should cooperate in giving the name of their great valley a wide and honorable notoriety, leaving the inhabitants of the San Joaquin to look out for the name and fortune of their portion of the state."

It is more than a little ironic that the same publication would complain about the lake itself, by then already diminished due to stream diversion and considered an impediment to agricultural development: "the one natural feature of the county that our conscience will not let us praise....It is a great unsightly mudhole."

Historically, although the huge lake was its nucleus, the basin housed those rich, complicated wetlands that included numerous freshwater aquatic communities. Marshes were defined by warm, shallow water clogged with dense masses of sedges, cattails, rushes, reeds, and other aquatic vegeta-tion—the generalized "tulares" for which the Spanish named this region. Small local swamps added trees and shrubs where riparian forests met marshes. Wildlife abounded in both. There were also many boggy ponds, convoluted sloughs or channels; everything was poorly drained and seasonal.

Floating "islands" of tules, many large enough to support the weight of several people, are reported to have drifted windblown across Tulare Lake's surface. Those bulrushes decomposed in the water, enriching it with their nutrients and triggering a complex and abundant food chain. Little won-der, since tules, some growing to a height of twenty feet, surrounded the water in unimaginable profligacy. In 1850, U.S. Army surveyor George Horatio Derby said he had to fight his way through a dense, two-mile-wide band of tules to reach open water on Tulare Lake. In *The Land of Little Rain* (1903), novelist Mary Austin described that ribbon of vegeta-tion this way:

> ...ghostly pale in winter, in summer deep, poisonous-looking green, the waters thick and brown, the reed beds breaking into dingy pools, clumps of rotting willows, narrow winding water lanes and sinking paths. The reeds grow inconceivably thick in places, standing man-high above water; cattle, no, not any fish nor fowl can penetrate them.

The region's long summers created a semitropical environment as cold snowmelt water sat among decaying vegetation in poorly drained, shallow beds where it warmed and evaporated, so diseases such as malaria were a menace. Zephryn Englehardt reports that malaria and cholera epidemics killed nearly three-quarters of the area's abundant Indian population in 1832–33.

Despite such pestilence, there was prescience in William Henry Brewer's observation: "The soil is fertile enough, but destitute of water, save the marshes near the river and near Tulare Lake." The dry land was indeed fer-tile, as development has proven, but Brewer added a caveat: "The marshy region is unhealthy and infested with mosquitoes in incredible numbers and of unparalleled ferocity. The dry plain on each side abounds in tarantulas."

During most years, the fluctuating water of Tulare Lake was plied by steamboats and various other vessels, since the lake sent waterfowl, fish, frogs' legs, and even turtles to faraway dining establishments. An 1883 his-tory of Kern County proudly states:

> From Tulare Lake come the turtles that make the rich turtle soups and stews in San Francisco hotels and restaurants....These turtles are sent in sacks to San Francisco. During the season more than a hundred and eighty dozen found a ready sale at the bay.

Local Indians, the Yokuts, had developed buoyant tule rafts with holes in their floors through which they could spear fish. After American settlement and control, professional fishermen during the 1870s and 1880s claimed to have caught up to eight tons of fish from the lake with only one haul of a horse-drawn seine.

In the old days, game was abundant here and the Yokuts had no tales of starvation in their repertoires. They were considered fortunate indeed by tribes dwelling in the surrounding hills. This area was also seen as a paradise by early American trappers and hunters. Beavers and otters were so common in the 1820s, for instance, that Jedediah Smith once took fifteen hundred pounds of pelts in a single tour. In 1844, John Charles Frémont was astounded by "multitudes of wild fowl, principally geese." Tule elk were still common then and pronghorn antelope also grazed the surrounding plain. Grizzly bears and coyotes abounded, and gray wolves were even reported. Wild horses—the progeny of escaped Spanish stock—had established themselves long before Frémont visited; "we found plenty of mustangs, wild horses, in 1807...," recounted Felipe Santiago Garcia, "and lots of mission cattle."

The entry of European livestock signaled a major, irreversible, but often unnoticed alteration of the basin's character. Today wild oats, European foxtail Bermuda grass, and bur clover are simply assumed to be common regional flora, but botanist Beecher Crampton points out that those weeds and grasses, among many others, were transported in packing material, in the soil surrounding cuttings, in ship ballast and, most importantly, in and on domestic animals, which were walking seed bags. As a result, even the Yokuts' usually benign practice of burning areas of dry prairie grasses to encourage earlier sprouting of the next crop actually helped hardy European annual weeds and grasses to replace natives.

By 1833, trapper Zenas Leonard observed that indigenous perennial bunchgrasses had been almost totally replaced. Consequences of that alteration were considerable, for this had been one of the world's great natural rangelands; both antelope and elk had depended upon bunchgrasses, so the natural web that included the ungulates was upset and their survival was threatened. By 1977, with antelope and elk long gone and most of the prairie gone too, another botanist, Harold Heady, suggested that "alien species should be considered as new and permanent members of the grassland rather than as aliens." This successful intrusion, of course, parallels the human dominance of one-time European immigrants over the few remaining Yokuts.

Another major change occurred when farmers began diverting the lake's feeder streams for irrigation. At that point the large but fragile pool began to shrink significantly. Twenty years later, the first of many reclamation districts was composed and initiated the process of opening to farming what had previously been lake bed: "as the waters vanished, speculators and settlers stampeded to Kings County," states a 1913 history of the region. Farmers no longer had to wait for the summer dry-up to plant there.

As geographer Preston points out, "reclamation abruptly terminated the lake's traditional role as habitat for migratory fowl." It also abruptly terminated the lake itself—even the idea of it in the minds of most people. Its fishery had been destroyed; its resident beavers and otters were gone; its grizzlies and elk decimated; its remaining water, impounded in a large evaporation pool, considered too salty to be of use. Ironically, the former lake bed would soon have to be irrigated.

Little of what was once natural in this basin has been saved. Great agricultural productivity has been gained, but there is deep irony that this once wildly diverse section of California strikes outsiders as homogeneous—fields and towns and roads that look too much alike. As novelist A. T. Bezzerides wrote in Long Haul (1938), one drives on, "passing through the small towns, Fowler and Kingsburg, Goshen and Pixley, town after town, Famosa and Bakersfield, mixing them up, thinking one was the other." The old lake bed now resembles nothing more than exactly what it has become, a grid of agribusiness.

Viewing the basin from an airplane, however, reveals the unerasable impress of sinuous, disorderly shores that were once edged by a miles-wide band of tules; the old lake's shadow is still distinctly there—however divided, however settled, however drained and irrigated—waiting for the next wet year. On it has been imposed the world's largest and most productive agricultural chessboard: what geographer Alvin Urquhart describes as geometry of ownership replacing geography of nature. But when nature provides more water than storage facilities can handle, the lake rises like a wet phoenix from the supine countryside—geography reasserts itself.

In 1969, for instance, the Kings River overflowed levees and suddenly Tulare Lake was again among the state's largest. Nine years later, following another generous spring runoff, the nonexistent lake covered some seventy square miles of land—a far cry from the seven hundred and eighty it once enveloped but enough to disturb farmers. Another of the levees keeping water out of the lake's old bed was breached in 1983 and thirty thousand acres of cropland were suddenly inundated.

That year the local irrigation district immediately sought permission to pump the offending water over the divide into the San Joaquin River, but there was a complication: white bass, an introduced, voracious predator of young of game fish, infested the lake's latest reincarnation. If allowed into the San Joaquin drainage, they might destroy its native fishery.

The following October, Tulare Lake's ghost was still there and the Corps of Engineers issued a permit for growers to pump their land dry, but required that fish screens be employed. Only twenty-four hours after the operation began, white bass were gillnetted downstream in the San Joaquin River, and pumping had to be halted. Then, reports Marc Reisner in *Cadillac Desert* (1986):

> Fish and Game—as if to underscore the catastrophic conse-
> quences of releasing white bass—poured a thousand gallons of
> rotenone, a virulent pesticide, into six miles of river around the
> fish screen.... A week later, Fish and Game performed a second
> mass poisoning.

Eventually, despite urgent legal efforts by sportsmen's groups and environmentalists to stop them, growers were again allowed to pump the nonexistent lake into the river, and even today no one is certain if that action may have doomed the Sacramento—San Joaquin Delta's rich fishery. Playing with nature is rarely without cost.

Meanwhile, their bottomland conveniently pumped dry, many local residents once more forgot the persistent lake, but some future wet winter it will be back to remind them. It will be back.

The special ecological and geographic distinctions that once defined Tulare Lake have been obscured by diversion of its major feeder streams, by the draining of its wetlands, and by the agricultural development of the basin; as a result many people who live in the area today are themselves unaware of its distinctiveness. They never saw that great sheet of water, those miles of tules, those uncountable waterfowl, and they cannot imagine them. In their experience, this has always been furrowed farmland, crossed by tractors and irrigated along shimmering rows. Lake? What lake?

"Tulare Lake," I repeat, not resisting the impulse to smile. "It doesn't exist."

This is just occult enough a statement to satisfy Carlos, so he says, "Far... out...," stretching the words.

After one more long look at history, I pull the car back onto the interstate and continue our journey, glancing more than a driver should at Tulare Lake's latest reincarnation.

We leave the freeway at Seventh Standard Road and drive east. On one side an oil pump bows to us as we pass an inundated cotton field while, on the other, an isolated storm cloud trails tendrils of rain like a dark jellyfish in the sky. Well ahead— our perspectives distorted by angle and distance and crisp air—we glimpse the roofs and dark tree clusters of Oildale, with steam plumes rising from the petroleum workings in the creased hills beyond. To the south, Bakersfield slopes on river bluffs.

Finally, as the road emerges from a stretch of orchards into open fields once more, I spy an irrigator, his legs encased in rubber boots that sag like a hippo's thick feet. He stands with hands cupping a smoke, leaning on a shovel, and he too surveys the distant glistening of a lake long dead. He waves as we pass and I give him thumbs up, then turn and smile at my son. Grandma and Grandpa's house is just ahead.

David Mas Masumoto

David Mas Masumoto(1954–) considers himself "a farmer first, and a writer a close second." His prose displays a seamless integration of each of these vocations. His eighty-acre Del Rey farm has provided inspiration for his writing, and he has repaid the debt by transplanting his peach orchards and vineyards into the fertile soil of his readers' imaginations.

A third-generation Japanese-American, Masumoto was born in Selma and attended the International Christian University, the University of California, Berkeley, and the University of California, Davis, where he earned an M.S. in 1982. Besides writing for many magazines, he has produced a collection of stories, Silent Strength; *an oral history,* Country Voices: The Oral History of a Japanese American Farm Community; *and the nonfiction* Harvest Son: Planting Roots in American Soil. *In* Epitaph for a Peach, *he describes the seasons on his family farm.* 🖍

from Epitaph for a Peach

WINTER'S FOG

On cold winter nights I step out onto our porch to check the thermometer. It has not changed much all day, ranging between a cold in the low thirties to a high in the mid-forties with a damp, biting fog blanketing the valley farmlands. From my porch I hear the *tap-tap-tap* of dewdrops trickling down the barren branches, falling and landing on the damp leaves below. I can feel the cold on my cheeks and the warmth of our home's wood stove still within my sweater.

Beyond me the vines and peach trees change seasons too. I think of the past year and the decisions I would have altered, modifications I can plan for in the coming season. Yet no matter what new course I may choose, a natural rhythm remains. I know the vines and trees will still be pruned soon, as they have been for generations.

The fog continues to roll in. Where it's heading I do not know. It passes in front of the porch like a shifting cloud. If I stare at it long enough, it seems that I start to move instead. I imagine our farmhouse cutting through the gray mist like a lost ship, my porch transformed into the bridge. I lean against the rail and peer into the drifting fog as my vessel heads into the night.

I sail on, the thermometer the only instrument on board. I like watching the gradual temperature changes, the measurement of a cold front moving in or the dramatic drop in readings with the loss of sunlight. Several years ago an arctic blast moved into the valley like a silent wolf. For days it hunted, freezing oranges and killing trees. I monitored its progress on my thermometer, recording historic low temperatures—dropping below twenty and never rising above freezing even in sunshine. Farmers could do little except watch. We only had our thermometers to help us verify what we already knew.

But a thermometer enables me to see the wild. The arctic wolf of that winter came alive in the dropping mercury. During the summer a different creature ventures into our valley—the searing heat that stays above 100 degrees into the evening hours. My senses feel the extremes and my thermometer enables me to process the impressions like a series of snapshots. The wild is seen.

A naturalist may disagree, claiming that agriculture tames the wild and farmers manipulate their world to disable the beast of nature. Judging by my last year trying to save a peach, though, I'd say that that gives us farmers too much credit. On a farm, much more is out of control than is in control. I fool myself when I call myself master of my farm. My thermometer reveals my impotence, for I cannot even consistently predict a day's highs or lows.

The fog carries a deep, penetrating cold with it. It doesn't take long before I'm chilled to the bone, especially when I'm in the fields, walking in the damp grass. Once my boots and pants get wet, I have only hours before my legs grow numb. At night while standing on my porch deck, I feel the fog invade my clothes, infiltrating the layers, announcing itself with my involuntary shiver.

I return inside, where I can watch the fog sail past our large windows. We have few curtains in our house, most of our windows are bare. From the inside I can see the panorama of the farm. I am exposed to the wild nature beyond the glass. I've spent hours in front of the windows, watching storms march in from the west and the wind blow rain and hail onto the porch. I can witness the sun rise and set on the mountains that ring the valley, study the ripples of August heat rising from the earth, and feel the glass warm against my skin.

The exchange is reciprocal, especially during the winter. The cold easily permeates the interiors, chilling the house and forcing me to wear sweaters even inside. The intrusion is welcomed, though, the seasons a natural cadence I feel within, a natural clock I respond to.

The change of season connects me with the surrounding wild, a wild I work within. I grow crops from the earth and have discovered that the best soil is also wild. This past year I have learned that productivity is little more than managed chaos, wildness the source of fertility.

In the fog I can hear the voices of farmers before me. Once I believed their old stubborn ways had no place in the progressive world of modern farming. But now they sing of traditions that have a place in my winter season more than ever.

Two wind socks flutter in the shifting fog. In Japanese, the wind is called kami, with an honorific sama often added. Wind is respected and revered, kamisama becomes a spirit that's alive. I can see that spirit in a wind sock, the energy captured for a moment in a dance of colors, then released as the tail flaps and waves.

Even in winter there is life on the farm. I feel something sacred, a meaning added to my work and my peaches and grapes. I feel connected with the universe. The world of nature and human nature are my teachers, showing and not telling me the secrets of the wild and sacred. From my porch deck I sail into a new world. Discoveries loom in the fog, opportunities inhabit this wilderness. It is a sacred place for myself and my family because I can call this farm home.

FARMING WITH GHOSTS

Silently I stand in the fog. The wet cloud envelops my farm, I cannot see more than a hundred feet. A dense billow rolls past and the barn disappears from view. I can barely distinguish the outline of the vines across my driveway, their stumps and arms like a band of tiny people marching in the mist. Marcy and the children pile into the car for work and school and, like a spaceship rocketing into the clouds, the car also disappears into the gray. I strain to hear the engine roar and fade in the distance.

The fog beguiles my senses, my vision is restricted and unreliable. Sounds seem to carry long distances. Do noises really echo differently in fog? Or is it that, without sight, I rely on my other senses and literally hear more? The grayness acts as a filter. I can hear individual noises distinctly: a dog yelps, a truck roars along the road, voices speaking Spanish carry through the mist. I listen to laughter and some Mexican music.

The fog shifts, yet I cannot decipher its direction. I'm used to monitoring clouds, especially threatening thunderstorms. Peering into the sky I can lock onto a faster-moving, usually lower and darker billow, freezing the pattern in order to detect motion. For a moment the higher strata seem to move in an opposite direction. A trained eye corrects the illusion and recognizes that both are in flight, the lower layer racing faster, speeding along in a passing wind lane. But the motion of fog seems random, swirling and spinning.

By midmorning the sun emerges as a light gray sphere suspended in the sky. Some of the haze runs away from the heat and an opening is created as the fog seems to part in reverence. Quickly the gesture is reconsidered and the fog returns to block the sunlight, teasing us earthlings. The game may continue for days. Marcy reports that people in town grow moody; being deprived of sunlight wears at their emotions. They too are gray.

I find the fog strangely comforting. I work my fields with the mist dancing around me, happy to be alone and hidden. I can literally feel the silence, an emotion others may find in freshly fallen snow.

The fog is rich with moisture and drips from the tips of shoots and branches. I can feel the mist licking my face. On cold mornings the dew freezes and then melts with the gray midday sun. I can hear the frozen water come to life and tap dance on fallen leaves. As I walk the fields, my boots are quickly soaked from the moisture trapped in the cover crops. My pants brush against the higher grasses and absorb water like a sponge. I'll use the same route through the lush undergrowth and break a trail that will last into spring. Even into the summer I can detect the paths I've traveled before.

In the middle of fog season, my shears cut through branches as I renew the ancient act of pruning. It has required ten years to hone my pruning skills. After a decade I've gained enough experience to know how to prune and to learn what I must accept. With different strategies I can amend errors of the past by cutting more wood or redirecting shapes. Opportunity is born with each new year. This is where life begins.

And continues. In the fog I feel alone but share work with the ghosts of farmers before me. The primitive ritual of pruning recalls a time when the first farmers began manipulating nature. A sacred act is performed and represented every winter, a moment on a cusp of nature's timeline where a single act connects the past, affects the present, and determines the future. In the veil of fog I can hide or be hidden, a wet blanket embraces and protects my farm, and the ghosts are easier to see.

Permissions

Anonymous. From *Island: Poetry and History of Chinese Immigrants on Angel Island, 1910-1040*. Seattle and London: University of Washington Press, 1980. Reprinted by permission of the publisher.

Arnold, Mary Ellicott and Mabel Reed. From *In the Land of the Grasshopper Song: Two Women in the Klamath River Indian Country in 1908–09*. Copyright © 1957 by Mary Ellicott Arnold. Reprinted by permission of the University of Nebraska Press.

Atherton, Gertrude. From *My San Francisco: A Wayward Biography*. Indianapolis & New York: The Bobbs-Merrill Company, 1946.

Austin, Mary. From *The Land of Little Rain*. Albuquerque: University of New Mexico Press, 1974.

Bixby-Smith, Sarah. From *Adobe Days*. Cedar Rapids, Iowa: The Torch Press, 1925.

Braudy, Leo. From *Roots and Branches: Contemporary Essays by West Coast Writers*, collected from *ZYZZYVA*. San Francisco: Mercury House, 1991.

Brautigan, Richard. From *Trout Fishing in America*. Copyright © 1968 by Richard Brautigan. Reprinted by permission of Houghton Mifflin Company/Seymour Lawrence. All rights reserved.

Brewer, William H. From *Up and Down California in 1860-1864*, ed. Francis Farquhar. Copyright © 1949 The Regents of the University of California. Berkeley: University of California Press.

Bukowski, Charles. From *The Last Night of the Earth Poems*. Santa Rosa, CA: Black Sparrow Press, 1992. Reprinted by permission of the publisher.

Cain, James M. From *Mildred Pierce* by James M. Cain. Copyright © 1941 and renewed 1969 by James M. Cain. Reprinted by permission of Alfred A. Knopf, a division of Random House, Inc.

Chase, J. Smeaton. From *Yosemite Trails*. Boston & New York: Houghton Mifflin Co., 1911.

Clappe, Louise. From *The Shirley Letters: From the California Mines, 1851–1852*. Berkeley: Heyday Books, 1998.

Clark, Walter Van Tilburg. From *The City of Trembling Leaves*. New York: Random House, 1945. Copyright © 1945 by Walter Van Tilburg Clark. Reprinted by permission of International Creative Management, Inc.

Coolbrith, Ina. From *Wings of Sunset*. Cambridge, MA: The Riverside Press, 1920.

Costanso, Miguel. From *The Discovery of San Francisco Bay: The Portolá Expedition of 1769–1770*. Lafayette, CA: Great West Books, 1992.

Dana, Richard Henry. From *Two Years Before the Mast*. New York: Signet Classics, 1964.

Didion, Joan. From *Slouching Towards Bethlehem*. Copyright © 1966, 1968, renewed 1996 by Joan Didion. Reprinted by permission of Farrar, Straus and Giroux, LLC.

Ehrlich, Gretel. From *A Match to the Heart* by Gretel Ehrlich. Copyright © 1994 by Gretel Ehrlich. Reprinted by permission of Pantheon Books, a division of Random House, Inc.

Everson, William. From *Single Source*. Berkeley: Oyez Press, 1966. Reprinted by permission of Jude Everson.

Farnham, Eliza W. From *California, In-doors and Out*. New York: Dix, Edwards, 1856.

Fisher, M. F. K. From *To Begin Again: Stories and Memoirs 1908–1929*. Copyright © 1990 by M. F. K. Fisher. Reprinted by permission of Pantheon Books, a division of Random House, Inc.

Font, Pedro. From *Font's Complete Diary: A Chronicle of the Founding of San Francisco*. Berkeley: University of California Press, 1933.

Foote, Mary Hallock. From *New Almaden or A California Mining Camp*. Reprinted from *Scribner's*, February 1878, by New Almaden Museum.

Fradkin, Philip L. From *The Seven States of California* by Philip L. Fradkin. Copyright ©1995 by Philip L. Fradkin. Reprinted by permission of Henry Holt and Company, LLC.

Frémont, John Charles. From *Geographical Memoir upon Upper California*. Washington, Wendell & Van Benthuysen printers, 1848.

Gioia, Dana. "California Hills in August," from *Daily Horoscope*. Copyright © 1986 by Dana Gioia. Reprinted by permission of Graywolf Press, Saint Paul, Minnesota.

Gioia, Dana. "Becoming a Redwood," from *The Gods of Winter*. Copyright © 1991 by Dana Gioia. Reprinted by permission of Graywolf Press, Saint Paul, Minnesota.

Haslam, Gerald W. From *The Other California: The Great Central Valley in Life and Letters*. Reno: University of Nevada Press, 1994. Reprinted by permission of the author.

Hearle, Kevin. From *Each Thing is Changed Because We Know It and Other Poems.* Boise, ID: Ahsahta Press, 1994.

Hill, Julia Butterfly. From *The Legacy of Luna.* San Francisco: Harper San Francisco, 2000.

Houston, James D. "Coast Range Sutra," 1997. Printed by permission of the author.

Hubbard, Harry D. From *Vallejo.* Boston: Meador Publishing Company, 1941.

Hutchings, J. M. From *Scenes of Wonder and Curiosity in California.* New York & San Francisco: A. Roman & Co., 1872.

Huxley, Aldous. From *Tomorrow and Tomorrow and Tomorrow.* New York: HarperCollins, 1956. Reprinted by permission of the Estate of Aldous Huxley.

Isherwood, Christopher. From *Exhumations.* Copyright © the Estate of Christopher Isherwood 1966. New York: Simon and Schuster. Reproduced with permission of Curtis Brown Ltd, London, on behalf of the Estate of Christopher Isherwood.

Jackson, Helen Hunt. From *Ramona.* New York: Signet Classics, 1988.

James, George Wharton. From *The Wonders of the Colorado Desert.* Boston: Little, Brown and Company, 1906.

Jeffers, Robinson. From *The Collected Poetry of Robinson Jeffers,* ed. Tim Hunt. Copyright © 1938, renewed 1966 by Donnan Jeffers and Garth Jeffers. Copyright transferred 1995 to the Board of Trustees of the Leland Stanford Junior University. Reprinted by permission of the publishers, Stanford University Press.

Jeffers, Una. From *Jeffers Country: The Seed Plots of Robinson Jeffers' Poetry* by Robinson Jeffers and Horace Lyons, Scrimshaw Press, 1971.

Jones, Idwal. From *The Pacific Coast Ranges,* ed. Roderick Peattie. New York: Vanguard, 1946.

Kerouac, Jack. From *The Dharma Bums* by Jack Kerouac. Copyright © 1958 by Jack Kerouac, copyright renewed 1986 by Stella Kerouac and Jan Kerouac. Used by permission of Viking Penguin, a division of Penguin Putnam Inc.

King, Clarence. From *Mountaineering in the Sierra Nevada.* Lincoln: University of Nebraska Press, 1970.

Kroeber, Theodora. From *Ishi in Two Worlds.* Berkeley: University of California Press, 1961. Reprinted by permission of Jed Riffe & Associates.

La Pérouse, Jean François. From *Life in a California Mission*. Berkeley: Heyday Books, 1989.

LeConte, Joseph. From *A Journal of Ramblings through the High Sierra of California*. San Francisco: Sierra Club Books, 1930.

Lewis, Janet. From *Against a Darkening Sky*. Copyright © 1943, 1985 by Janet Lewis Winters. Reprinted by permission of Ohio University Press/Swallow Press, Athens, Ohio.

London, Jack. From *The Valley of the Moon*. New York: Macmillan, 1913.

Mailer, Norman. From *The Deer Park*. New York: Putnam, 1955.

Manly, William Lewis. From *Death Valley in '49*. San Jose, CA: The Pacific Tree and Vine Co., 1891.

Markham, Edwin. From *California The Wonderful*. New York: Hearst's International Library Co., 1914.

Martien, Jerry. From *Shell Game: A True Account of Beads and Money in North America*. San Francisco: Mercury House, 1996.

Masumoto, David Mas. From *Epitaph for a Peach: Four Seasons on My Family Farm* by David Mas Masumoto. Copyright © 1995 by David Mas Masumoto. Reprinted by permission of HarperCollins Publishers, Inc.

Mayfield, Thomas Jefferson. From *Indian Summer: Life Among the Choinumne Indians of California's San Joaquin Valley*. Berkeley: Heyday Books, 1993.

McDaniel, Wilma Elizabeth. "Dustbowl Doxology," from *A Primer for Buford*. Copyright © 1990 by Wilma Elizabeth McDaniel. Reprinted by permission of Hanging Loose Press.

McDaniel, Wilma Elizabeth. "The Flower Lover" and "Viewing Kern County Desolation," from *I Killed a Bee for You. Blue Cloud Quarterly*, Vol. 34 No. 1, 1987. Reprinted by permission of the author.

McDaniel, Wilma Elizabeth. "First Spring in California, 1936," from *A Prince Albert Wind*. Albuquerque, NM: Mother Road Publications, 1994. Reprinted by permission of the author.

McWilliams, Carey. From *Southern California Country: An Island on the Land*. New York: Buell, Sloan & Pearce, 1946.

Miller, Henry. From *Big Sur and the Oranges of Hieronymus Bosch* by Henry Miller. Copyright © 1957 by New Directions Publishing Corp. Reprinted by permission of New Directions Publishing Corp.

Miller, Joaquin. From *Selected Writings of Joaquin Miller*. Urion Press, 1976.

Muir, John. From *The Mountains of California*. San Francisco: Sierra Club Books, 1988.

Noguchi, Yone. From *The Story of Yone Noguchi as told by himself.* Philadelphia: George W. Jacobs & Co., 1915.

Nordhoff, Charles. From *California for Health, Pleasure and Residence.* New York: Harper & Bros., 1872.

Norris, Frank. From *The Octopus.* New York: Sagamore Press, 1957.

Owens, Louis. From *Bone Game.* Copyright © 1994 by Louis Owens. Norman: University of Oklahoma Press, 1994. Reprinted by permission of the publisher.

Palmer, Tim. From *The Sierra Nevada: A Mountain Journey* by Tim Palmer. Copyright © 1988 by Tim Palmer. Published 1988 by Island Press. Reprinted by permission of Island Press.

Rexroth, Kenneth. From *Collected Shorter Poems.* Copyright © 1966 by Kenneth Rexroth. Reprinted by permission of New Directions Publishing Corp.

Rich, Adrienne. From *An Atlas of the Difficult World: Poems 1988–1991* by Adrienne Rich. Copyright © 1991 by Adrienne Rich. Used by permission of the author and W. W. Norton & Company, Inc.

Richardson, Steven. From *San Francisco Memoirs,* comp. Malcolm E. Barker. San Francisco: Londonborn Publications, 1994.

Ridge, John Rollin (Yellow Bird). From *The Life and Adventures of Joaquín Murieta: The Celebrated California Bandit.* Norman, OK: University of Oklahoma Press, 1955.

Royce, Sarah. From *A Frontier Lady: Recollections of the Gold Rush and Early California,* ed. Ralph Henry Gabriel. Copyright © 1932 by Yale University Press. New Haven, Yale University Press, 1932.

Saroyan, William. From *My Name is Aram.* New York: Harcourt, Brace and Company, 1937. Reprinted by permission of the Trustees of Leland Stanford Junior University.

Schultheis, Rob. From *Image,* May 4, 1986.

Snyder, Gary. "John Muir on Mt. Ritter," from *No Nature: New and Selected Poems.* Copyright © 1992 by Gary Snyder. Reprinted by permission of Pantheon Books, a division of Random House, Inc.

Snyder, Gary. "Burning the Small Dead," from *The Back Country.* Copyright © 1968 by Gary Snyder. Reprinted by permission of New Directions Publishing Corp.

Snyder, Gary. "The Canyon Wren," from *Axe Handles* by Gary Snyder. Copyright © 1983 by Gary Snyder. Reprinted by permission of North Point Press, a division of Farrar, Straus, and Giroux, LLC.

Soto, Gary. From *New and Selected Poems by Gary Soto,* copyright ©1995. Reprinted by permission of Chronicle Books, San Francisco.

Stegner, Wallace. From *All the Little Live Things.* Copyright © 1967 by Wallace Stegner. New York: Viking Press. Reprinted by permission of Brandt & Brandt Literary Agents, Inc.

Steinbeck, John. From *To a God Unknown.* Copyright © 1933, renewed 1961 by John Steinbeck. Used by permission of Viking Penguin, a division of Penguin Putnam Inc.

Stevenson, Robert Louis. "Monterey," from *An Inland Voyage, Travels with a Donkey, The Amateur Emigrant, together with The Old and New Pacific Capitals and The Silverado Squatters.* London: Collins, 1956.

Stevenson, Robert Louis. "The Sea Fogs," from *The Silverado Squatters.* London: Chatto & Windus, 1883.

Stoddard, Charles Warren. From *In the Footprints of the Padres.* San Francisco: A. M. Robertson, 1912.

Twain, Mark. From *Roughing It.* Copyright © 1972 by the Mark Twain Company. Berkeley & Los Angeles: University of California Press, 1972.

Wallace, David Rains. From *The Dark Range: A Naturalist's Night Notebook.* San Francisco: Sierra Club Books, 1978. Reprinted by permission of the author.

Wheelwright, Jane Hollister. From *The Ranch Papers: A California Memoir.* San Francisco: Lapis Press, 1988.

Williams, Sherley Anne. From *The Peacock Poems.* Copyright © 1975 by Sherley Williams, Wesleyan University Press by permission of University Press of New England. Reprinted by permission of the publisher.

Wilson, Darryl Babe. "Gedin Ch'lum'nu," originally published as "Let It Be This Way" in *The Sound of Rattles and Clappers,* ed. Greg Sarris. Tucson & London: University of Arizona Press, 1994. Reprinted by permission of the author.

Wright, Harold Bell. From *The Winning of Barbara Worth.* Chicago, IL: The Book Supply Company, 1911. Reprinted by Pelican Publishing Co., Gretna, LA.

Zamora, Bernice. From *Releasing Serpents* by Bernice Zamora. Copyright © 1994 by Bilingual Press/Editorial Bilingüe, Arizona State University, Tempe, AZ. Reprinted by permission of the publisher.

Bibliography

Besides standard reference works, the following sources have been especially helpful for preparing introductions for this book.

Baird, Newton D. and Robert Greenwood. *Annotated Bibliography of California Fiction 1664–1970.* Georgetown, CA: Talisman Literary Research, 1971.

Brewer, Gay. *Charles Bukowski.* New York: Twayne, 1997.

Clark, Donald Thomas. *Monterey County Place Names: A Geographical Dictionary.* Carmel Valley, CA: Kestral Press, 1991.

Clausen, Christopher. "Poetry Formal and Free." Review of *The Gods of Winter* by Dana Gioia. The Sewanee Review. 99.4 (1991).

Clendenning, John. *The Life and Thought of Josiah Royce.* Madison: University of Wisconsin Press, 1985.

Crow, Charles. *Janet Lewis.* Boise State University Western Writers Series, no. 41. Boise: Boise State University, 1980.

Davis, Mike. *City of Quartz: Excavating the Future in Los Angeles.* London: Verso, 1990.

Dean, Tim. *Gary Snyder and the American Unconscious: Inhabiting the Ground.* New York: St. Martin's Press, 1991.

Eiseley, Loren. Foreword to *Not Man Apart: Lines from Robinson Jeffers: Photographs of the Big Sur Coast,* ed. David Brower. San Francisco: Sierra Club Books, 1965.

Farquhar, Francis P. *History of the Sierra Nevada.* Berkeley: University of California Press, 1969.

Floan, Howard R. *William Saroyan.* New York: Twayne, 1966.

Gale, Robert L. *Charles Warren Stoddard.* Boise State University Western Writers Series, no. 30. Boise: Boise State University Press, 1977.

Gibson, Morgan. *Kenneth Rexroth.* New York: Twayne, 1972.

Gilliam, Ann, ed. *Voices for the Earth: A Treasury of the Sierra Club Bulletin.* San Francisco: Sierra Club Books, 1979.

Gioia, Dana. "Can Poetry Matter?" *The Atlantic Monthly,* May 1991.

Gudde, Erwin Gustav. *California Place Names: the Origin and Etymology of Current Geographical Names.* Berkeley: University of California Press, 1969.

Haft, James D. *A Companion to California*. rev. ed. New York: Oxford University Press, 1987.

Haslam, Gerald. Introduction to *A Primer for Buford,* by Wilma Elizabeth McDaniel. Brooklyn: Hanging Loose Press, 1990.

Haslam, Gerald, ed. *Many Californias: Literature from the Golden State.* Reno: University of Nevada Press, 1992.

Haslam, Gerald W. and James D. Houston, eds. *California Heartland: Writing from the Great Central Valley*. Santa Barbara: Capra Press, 1978.

Heizer, Robert F. ed. *The Costanoan Indians.* Local History Studies, vol. 18 Cupertino: California History Center, De Anza College, 1974.

Heizer, Robert F. and Albert B. Elsasser. *The Natural World of the California Indians.* Berkeley: University of California Press, 1980.

Hobbs, Fredric. *The Spirit of the Monterey Coast.* Palo Alto: Tioga Press, 1990.

Jackson, Joseph Henry. *Introduction to The Life and Adventures of Joaquin Murieta,* by John Rollin Ridge. 1854. Norman: University of Oklahoma Press, 1955.

Jarman, Mark. "Robinson Jeffers and the Female Archetype." In *Robinson Jeffers: Dimensions of a Poet,* ed. Robert Brophy. New York: Fordham University Press, 1995.

Jeffers, Robinson. Preface to *The Double Axe and Other Poems.* 1948. Reprint. New York: Liveright, 1977.

Labor, Earle, Robert C. Leitz, III, and I. Milo Shepard. Introduction to *The Letters of Jack London.* Stanford: Stafford University Press, 1988.

Lamar, Howard R. ed. *The New Encyclopedia of the American West.* New Haven: Yale University Press, 1998.

Lee, L. L. *Walter Van Tilburg Clark.* Boise State College Western Writers Series, no. 8. Boise: Boise State College, 1973.

Lewis, Merrill and Lorene. *Wallace Stegner.* Boise State College Western Writers Series, no. 4. Boise: Boise State College, 1972.

Locklin, Gerald. *Gerald Haslam.* Boise State University Western Writers Series, no. 77. Boise: Boise State University, 1987.

Margolin, Malcolm. *The Ohlone Way: Indian Life in the San Francisco-Monterey Bay Area.* Berkeley: Heyday Books, 1978.

Michaels, Leonard, David Reid, and Raquel Scherr, eds. *West of the West: Imagining California.* San Francisco: North Point Press, 1989.

Mitchell, Frederic. Publisher's foreword to *Jeffers Country: the Seed Plots of Robinson Jeffers' Poetry.* San Francisco: Scrimshaw Press, 1971.

Norris, Frank. "The Novel with a 'Purpose.'" *The Responsibilities of the Novelist and Other Literary Essays.* New York: Haskell House, 1969.

Parr, Barry. *San Francisco and the Bay Area.* Oakland: Compass American Guides, 1990.

Pearsall, Robert and Ursula Spier Erickson. *The Californians: Writings of Their Past and Present.* San Francisco: Hesperian House, 1961.

Peattie, Roderick. *Introduction to The Pacific Coast Range.* New York: The Vanguard Press, 1946.

Powell, Lawrence Clark. *California Classics: The Creative Literature of the Golden State.* Los Angeles: Ward Ritchie Press, 1971.

Rexroth, Kenneth. *An Autobiographical Novel,* edited by Linda Hamalian. rev. ed. New York: New Directions, 1991.

Rolle, Andrew F. *California: A History.* 2d ed. New York: Thomas Y. Crowell Company, 1969.

Schoenherr, Allan A. *A Natural History of California.* Berkeley: University of California Press, 1992.

Schoenherr, Allan A. et al. *Natural History of the Islands of California.* Berkeley: University of California Press, 1999.

Shebl, James. Introduction to *Mountaineering in the Sierra Nevada,* by Clarence King. Lincoln: University of Nebraska Press, 1970.

Smith-Baranzini, Marlene. Introduction to *The Shirley Letters: From the California Mines, 1851–1852,* by Louise Amelia Knapp Smith Clappe. Berkeley: Heyday Books, 1998.

Starr, Kevin. *Material Dreams.* New York: Oxford University Press, 1990.

Stegner, Wallace. *The Big Rock Candy Mountain.* 1938. Lincoln: University of Nebraska Press, 1983

Sterling, George. *Robinson Jeffers: the Man and the Artist.* New York: Boni and Liveright, 1926.

Steuding Bob. *Gary Snyder.* New York: Twayne, 1976.

Tagg, Lawrence V. *Harold Bell Wright.* Boise State University Western Writers Series, no. 115. Boise: Boise State University, 1994.

Taylor, J. Golden, et al., ed. *A Literary History of the American West.* Fort Worth: Texas Christian University Press, 1987.

Vogely, Nancy. "Bernice Zamora: Self and Community." In *Releasing Serpents,* by Bernice Zamora. Tempe, AZ: Bilingual Press, 1994.

Westbrook, Max. *Walter Van Tilburg Clark.* New York: Twayne, 1969.

Wilde, Alan. *Christopher Isherwood.* New York: Twayne, 1971.

Wilkins, Thurman. *John Muir: Apostle of Nature.* Norman: University of Oklahoma Press, 1995.

Yogi, Stan, ed. *Highway 99: A Literary Journey through California's Great Central Valley.* Berkeley: Heyday Books, 1996.

About the Editor

Terry Beers, associate professor of English at Santa Clara University, is past executive director of the Robinson Jeffers Association and the author of *A Thousand Graceful Subtleties: Rhetoric in the Poetry of Robinson Jeffers* (1995). Professor Beers is the general editor of the California Legacy series. He lives in north Monterey County.